# S U R V I V A L

# S U R V I V A L
## How to Prevail in Hostile Environments

XAVIER MANIGUET

Translated by Ivanka Roberts

Facts On File®

AN INFOBASE HOLDINGS COMPANY

**Survival: How to Prevail in Hostile Environments**

Original copyright © 1988 by Xavier Maniguet and Editions Albin Michel S.A.
Translation Copyright © 1994 by Facts On File, Inc.

Facts On File, Inc.
460 Park Avenue South
New York NY 10016

**Library of Congress Cataloging-in-Publication Data**
Maniguet, Xavier.
[Survivre. English]
Survival : how to prevail in hostile environments / Xavier
Maniguet ; translated by Ivanka Roberts.
    p.   cm.
Translation of: Survivre.
Includes bibliographical references (p. ) and index.
ISBN 0-8160-2518-5
1. Wilderness survival.   I. Title.
GV200.5.M3513   1993
613.6′9—dc20                                              93-16118

A British CIP catalogue record for this book is available from the
British Library.

Facts On File books are available at special discounts when purchased in bulk quantities for businesses, associations, institutions or sales promotions. Please call our Special Sales Department in New York at 212/683-2244 or 800/322-8755.

Text design by Robert Yaffe
Jacket design by Catherine Hyman
Composition and manufacturing by
The Maple-Vail Book Manufacturing Group
Printed in the United States of America

10 9 8 7 6 5 4 3 2 1

This book is printed on acid-free paper

# ACKNOWLEDGMENTS

I would like to thank all my friends who, at one time or another, allowed me to learn from their experiences, in particular:

Nano Chappel, ship's captain
Alain Heuzé, T.D.M. officer
Bob Maloubier, founder of the Frogmen Corps
Bernard Chavreau, test pilot
Rémy Julienne, the "Prince of Stuntmen"
Paul Barril, of the G.I.S.G.N.

and all those whose function prohibits me from naming them.

## BY THE SAME AUTHOR

*L'Aventure pour l'Aventure*, Carrère-Lafon, 1986.

# DISCLAIMER

This book is a guide to survival in difficult circumstances. Although the author recommends various medicines and procedures for specific situations, the book is not intended as a substitute for proper medical care or medical advice from your own doctor. None of the procedures or medicines suggested in this book should be used without first discussing your own medical condition and the book's procedures and medicines with your own doctor.

# CONTENTS

# PART I

# Major Threats

# COLD

- Facts

- Myths

- True Tales of Survival

- The Physiology of Adaptation to Cold

- A Clinical Summary of Adaptation to Cold

- Surviving Cold: Preventive Measures

# FACTS

○ New Year's Eve 1719: During a Swedish invasion of Norway, 3,500 of the recently deceased Swedish King Charles XII's 5,000 troops who crossed the border mountains into Norway died from the cold and the wind.

○ December 1914: In the Balkans, 10,000 Turkish soldiers (50 percent of the complement) died of cold during a single night.

○ 1914–1918: During World War I, 120,000 deaths in the French army and 300,000 in the Italian army were due to cold.

○ 1939–1945: During World War II, two million cold-related injuries were suffered by the Germans on the Russian front.

○ 1950–1951: During the Korean War, 85 percent of all injuries were attributable to the cold.

# MYTHS

○ *If you are shipwrecked, you should exercise in the water to warm up and stay warm:* In fact, all physical exercise burns energy, and thus reduces our threshold of tolerance, particularly in water.

○ *All liquids freeze at 32°F (0°C), including seawater:* In fact, the salinity of seawater considerably lowers its freezing point.

○ *There is no need to drink large quantities in cold weather:* On the contrary, a cold atmosphere is usually dry and therefore more fluids are required.

○ *There's nothing better than a shot of brandy to warm you in a blizzard:* In fact, alcohol provides "caloric stimulation," but this is quickly followed by a numbing of physiological responses.

○ *Eskimos are totally different from us, a fact that allows them to withstand the harsh polar climate:* In fact, there is no special gene to cope with the cold; what allows Eskimos to survive the rigors of the polar climate is adaptation acquired through experience.

○ *The way to treat frostbite is by vigorously rubbing, slapping, etc.:* In fact, this treatment is not only harsh, it is disastrous. Physical shocks, even small ones, never help to heal tissues that have become delicate because of the

4

edema (an excess of fluid) that occurs in frostbite.

Humans, unlike animals, are not good at protecting themselves from the cold. The military surgeon Baron Larrey left a shocking description of the effect of cold on Napoleon's troops during their retreat from Russia in 1812. More recently, two world wars and the Korean War have provided us with reliable observations of man's adjustment—or, unfortu-

nately more often, his maladjustment—to cold.

In earliest times, man suffered from his nudity, from his lack of a shell, which left him vulnerable to the claws of wild animals and the bite of the wind. He very quickly learned how to clothe himself, not because of modesty but because of necessity. Today we are constantly improving the quality of our artificial fibers, pushing back the limits of our tolerance to this age-old scourge: the cold.

---

# TRUE TALES OF SURVIVAL

## HYPOTHERMAL COMA

### June 1969, Cuba

At the age of 18, Armando Socarras Ramirez has had enough of Castro's regime. He knows that life could be different elsewhere. More important, he knows that the army will send him into the sugarcane fields in a few months. Between military service and civil service, he will not be free for nine years. During this time, he will not be allowed out after midnight, not to mention that he will be forbidden to meet girls his own age.

Therefore, without telling his parents or his six brothers and sisters, he decides to leave the country in any way he can. He has two accomplices: Jorge Perez Blanco, who is to go with him, and another friend who plans the means of escape.

At 6:30 P.M. on June 3, accompanied by his friend Blanco, Ramirez finds himself at Havana airport at the end of the runway where airliners test their engines before takeoff. The plane they are waiting for is an Iberia DC-8, which is to return to Madrid nonstop. Just as the four-engine jet comes to a stop, the two friends sprint toward the landing-gear hatches, carefully avoiding the hot exhaust of the jet engines. Ramirez takes up his position as best he can in the right main landing-gear compartment, while Blanco climbs into the left one.

The jet takes off immediately with a deafening roar, and the landing gear is retracted. Ramirez is astonished that he has not been crushed by the tremendous force of the hydraulic jacks. He has just begun to congratulate himself when the hatches abruptly reopen and the landing gear is lowered again. He catches a glimpse of the lights of Havana receding into the distance and then the landing gear is retracted again.

Ramirez is not particularly alarmed by this maneuver—but it marks the moment his friend Blanco is killed. Blanco's body, probably crushed by the left landing gear, has prevented the hatch from closing properly. The pilot notices a problem immediately as the three red indicators do not light up on his instrument panel. Lowering the landing gear undoubtedly allows Blanco's corpse to drop out and permits the landing gear to retract properly. From that point, nothing stands in the way of a normal transatlantic flight. Blanco's body will never officially be found.

## Madrid-Baragas Airport, June 4, 1969, 9:30 A.M.

Two Iberia ground crew members place the stops under the wheels of the DC-8 that has just taxied in to park after the passengers have disembarked.

Something tumbles heavily from the housing of the right landing gear. To the astonishment of the two employees, the stiff bundle turns out to be a human being.

The doctor "wouldn't bet a nickel on the survival" of this stowaway, who is frozen and in a coma. According to the administration of the hospital where he has been taken, his survival is considered to be "totally inexplicable" and, in any case, certainly temporary since "a human being cannot withstand $-40°F$ ($-40°C$) temperatures and hypoxia at an altitude of 30,000 feet for more than thirty minutes." The flight has taken eight hours!

In the emergency room, although they do not have much hope, Dr. Pojares' team treats the symptoms of hypothermal coma accompanied by anoxia of various organs: kidneys that have failed, a heart that has almost stopped beating, a brain in hibernation.

Twenty-four hours later, Ramirez is eating normally, he is urinating normally, and he is reading all about his sensational exploit in a newspaper.

---

Armando Socarras Ramirez was by no means the first to make such an attempt in an airplane; but all the others are dead, with one exception: a 17-year-old Colombian, Francisco Garcia, who crossed the cordillera of the Andes from Bogotá to Mexico in his shirtsleeves in 1966. He was a block of ice when he arrived, but he also "rose from the dead" in two days without any aftereffects.

Theoretically, no one who goes above 32,800 feet (10,000 meters) should have any chance of survival. The temperature becomes constant at the tropopause, i.e., $-61°F$ ($-52°C$) at 36,089–39,370 feet (11,000–12,000 meters) in temperate latitudes, and the degree of hypoxia at this altitude becomes a lethal factor in itself.

It is interesting to analyze the reasons for the young Cuban's survival within the general framework of knowledge anyone needs to survive in a cold environment.

■ Ramirez was young, just like Francisco Garcia.
■ He was in good physical condition (he played baseball regularly).
■ He was very motivated, and he had prepared for his attempt to escape as well as someone of his age could: He had taken cotton for his ears because he had been told the noise would deafen him, a rope and belt with which to attach himself, and a sketch of the compartment where he intended to hide. Apparently, though, he had not thought of warm clothing, since he had no knowledge of aeronautics or meteorology.
■ He had the carefree attitude of youth, and was not under any particular stress. He was fairly calm when he climbed into his hiding place. As he said later, once he realized what he had survived: "If I had known, I would never have dared." Had he known, and still dared, his anxiety would probably have been so great that he would have had no tolerance before he lost consciousness; his pulse rate, his arterial tension, and his consumption of oxygen would have increased considerably and his

body would already have been exhausted before being subjected to the low temperature.
■ As far as weather conditions are concerned, the temperature in the sun in June both in Cuba and Madrid is closer to 77°F (25°C) than to the so-called standard atmosphere, which is 59°F (15°C). Therefore the temperature probably bordered on −31°F (−35°C), rather than −49°F (−45°C) at an altitude of 29,527 feet (9,000 meters) (in a standard atmosphere, the rule of thumb is that the temperature drops by approximately 11°F [6°C] per 3,280 feet [1,000 meters] in the lower strata). On April 18, 1966 the body of a man who had died of cold was discovered in the landing gear compartment of a Moscow–Paris Caravelle. The Caravelle had not gone above 26,240 feet (8,000 meters), but the temperature in Moscow in April is much colder than that of Havana in June.
■ Ramirez was probably subjected to a dry cold, which is much less harmful than damp cold. With the exception of cloudy crossings—which are rare at or above 29,527 feet (9,000 meters)—the air at that altitude is dry; this explains why one gets thirsty in the mountains or even in a commercial plane, in which the interior atmosphere is maintained at a pressure equivalent to 5,900 feet (1,800 meters).
■ As to the flight itself, the rate of ascent to 32,800 feet (10,000

meters) had, by chance, provided ideal conditions for entering a state of hibernation rapidly enough to cause a sudden shutdown of the defense reflexes, yet slowly enough for the vital organs to enter a state of lethargy gradually: a decreased heart rate and a brain almost, but not quite, in hypoxia. (The brain is unquestionably dead within three minutes of cardiac arrest; if the heart is reactivated after a longer period the only possible outcome is a vegetative state.)

When the plane arrived at Madrid, the controller, waiting for traffic to clear, put it into a holding pattern at a much lower altitude. Since the pilot had received an estimate of a relatively long wait, he had descended very slowly to the prescribed holding pattern, which, in contrast to the takeoff, had allowed the "rewarming" to be gradual and thus compatible with survival. If it had taken half an hour longer, Ramirez may have climbed from his hiding place by himself.

This all happened in 1969, and the five doctors who treated him concluded: "He had zero chance of getting out alive—we will have to reevaluate our standards." In fact, there have been some major advances in the understanding and application of hibernation since then, particularly in infant heart surgery. To make it possible for doctors to perform this extremely delicate surgery, the internal temperature is lowered to 68°F (20°C), sometimes even 64°F (18°C), through external circulation, which permits the heart to be stopped for an hour without aftereffects.

---

## AQUATIC "PALEOMEMORY"
### January 15, 1984, Chicago

At the foot of some of the tallest buildings in the world, Lake Michigan begins to ice over. Four-year-old Jimmy Tontlewicz, impatient to try out his new sled, stands on the shore and faces the icy cold winds with his father.

Suddenly the sled slips down the bank and comes to rest below on the dark ice of the lake. The child jumps from the bank and breaks through the thin film across which his father is already walking. Both fall into the icy waters. The father manages to get to the bank, but his son sinks.

The rescue team arrives within five minutes, but it takes the divers 15 minutes to locate the boy's body.

After 20 minutes under water near 32°F (0°C), the child is clinically dead: his skin is cyanotic, there is no sign of respiration or heart beat, and he displays the clinical symptom that signals death: mydriasis of the pupils.

Nevertheless, the rescuers have incredible faith and do all they can: They administer artificial respiration and repeated cardiac shocks. The oscilloscope continues to register a discouragingly straight line, which is not surprising since all known limits of survival have been far exceeded. The child has been dead for one hour and 30 minutes with an internal temperature of 77°F (25°C), when suddenly a spike appears on the electrocardiograph. There is one isolated heartbeat, then nothing, then another a little later, and then another, and finally something that seems medically impossible: an irregular heartbeat, a heart that is beating after one and a half hours of clinical death.

Once the initial excitement has passed, the rescuers begin to wonder whether the recovery is permanent and especially what the quality of life will be: Since the brain was not irrigated for so long, even given the best circumstances, won't this mean that the child will be brain-dead? They consult Dr. Mac Lone, an internationally renowned neurologist. He encourages the team of rescuers to continue what they are doing, but to warm the child up very slowly.

---

The explanation for what the media called a "miracle" is due once again to the process of artificial hibernation, induced by the abrupt immersion in icy water. It is rare to survive such submersion even in cases where the victim is able to breathe. What saved the child, at least in part, was the abruptness of the accident. The sudden immersion prevented all defense reactions that could have exhausted his body and would have proved fatal. Instead, a primitive reflex was activated, one more easily evoked in the young. The existence of this reflex was only discovered a few years ago: Known as the "mammalian diving reflex," it is the reflex that enables seals, dolphins, and whales to remain under water for extended periods of time without breathing. When the animal dives, an inner survival instinct instantly cuts off respiration and drives the blood from the periphery of the body to the vital organs the heart and the brain—selectively supplying them with the oxygen still available through an interplay of vasoconstriction and vasodilation. At the same time, the heart rate and cerebral metabolism decrease considerably, thus reducing oxygen consumption. By this means, the heart rate of a diving whale can decrease to less than one beat per minute. Once the cooling starts, the body's metabolism spontaneously reinforces the decrease, following the general biological rule that all biochemical reactions decrease their rate by 50 percent with each 18°F (10°C) drop in temperature. This means that at 63°F (17°C) metabolism has slowed down by 75 percent compared to the rate at 98.6°F (37°C). This primitive reflex is a prime example of "paleomemory"—the primitive memory that we have inherited over the millennia from our distant aquatic ancestors and that, in certain cases, allows us to survive through instinct.

It is this primitive memory that comes into play in the "baby swimming reflex," discovered in the early 1970s by a Swiss swimmer who literally threw babies only a few weeks old into a swimming pool. At first the babies sank without swallowing water, and then they gradually turned onto their backs and, with a slow crawling movement, came back to the surface where they stayed with only their mouths above the water.

This reflex, paleomemory, played an essential role in the case of the child from Chicago, and it explains why his heart was able to tolerate 20 minutes of submersion and start beating again after one hour and 30 minutes.

But cerebral neurons are the body cells that consume the largest amount of oxygen, and the brain is an extremely complex organ, very sensitive to a lack of oxygen. The only hope of saving this organ is to make sure the body is not warmed up too quickly, as this would cause edema of the tissues, making the brain cells explode. The child was brought back to 98.6°F (37°C) over a period of a week and was kept in a barbiturate-induced semicoma in order to curb the cerebral metabolism, while his blood was oxygenated as much as possible through artificial hyperventilation.

The child recovered electroencephalographic impulses that could be stimulated, and after several months he returned to the mental level he had had before the accident. His brain had survived due to hypothermia. The same length of time submerged in water with a temperature of 68°F (20°C) would have been fatal, as in the case of a three-year-old boy who drowned in a swimming pool in Colombia. He was revived with an intracardiac injection of adrenaline after being clinically dead for twenty minutes, but he will forever remain in a deep coma and no treatment, however exceptional, will change this.

The accident in Lake Michigan is interesting in the context of survival techniques because the mechanisms that it set in motion were similar to those that saved Armando Socarras Ramirez and Francisco Garcia. They are the same mechanisms that we will see applied in practice when preparing for survival in a cold region. All these instances of survival have one thing in common: the absence of a phase of struggle, despite the extreme temperature, when the individual is first exposed to the cold.

This phase of struggle, which we all experience when we are cold, involves tachycardia (relatively rapid heart action), shivering that discharges adrenaline, an increase in muscle tension, and finally an active, voluntary reaction—such as swimming, if we are in cold water, or other types of physical exercise if we are on land. All these physiological reactions aim to keep our temperature constant, since man is meant to be homeothermal at 98.6°F (37°C).

But this group of defense mechanisms involves a considerable expenditure of energy, which weakens the body and ultimately makes it even more susceptible to harm. Glycogen, which is an essential energy factor, as we shall see later, is used up to maintain a constant body temperature, and it is no longer available, after one has lost consciousness, to ensure the minimum metabolic needs of the vital organs: the kidneys, the heart, and, above all, the brain. If these can no longer function, death inevitably follows.

Ramirez, Garcia, and Jimmy Tontlewicz did not experience this phase of struggle, since they quickly lost consciousness—the first two because of the combined action of hypoxia and cold, the third because of the unexpected contact with icy water, which set his primitive reflexes in motion.

Further evidence of this survival phenomenon has been furnished by alcoholics, who have been overcome by the cold while lying on sidewalks in winter in a deep alcoholic coma. Every year several of them are revived after being found in subfreezing conditions with an internal temperature that has dropped to 68°F (20°C). Their profound unconsciousness has prevented their bodies from struggling in vain against the cold; instead, their temperature has dropped gradually, preserving energy for their delicate organs.

Those who are accustomed or adapted to cold unconsciously make use of this capability. The Australian Aborigines' internal temperature drops during the night, and exceeds 98.6°F during the day. "Amas," the Japanese pearl divers, are able to dive all day in water that has a temperature of 46.4°F (8°C); their internal temperature drops to 91.4°F (33°C) but they do not experience any significant pathological manifestations. The tests that Arctic explorer J.-L. Étienne underwent after he returned from his solitary 70-day trip to the North Pole in 1986 show that his phase of struggle started at a temperature below 95°F (35°C), not 98.6°F as before his departure. This three-and-a-half-degree difference is very significant and demonstrates considerable economy in the use of energy.

The primary lesson to be learned from all these examples by anyone who may have to survive in a cold region is that he must train before his departure in order to rediscover his primitive reflexes.

# THE PHYSIOLOGY OF ADAPTATION TO COLD

Man is homeothermic: His body attempts to maintain an internal temperature of 98.6°F (37°C) at all times. This principle is equally valid in hot weather and cold, though the latter, as we already know, is more difficult to adjust to. Obviously, the mechanisms are different, but many simply follow an inverse logic, depending on whether we are dealing with heat or cold. This means that the concept of a "central nucleus" and an "external shell," which we shall elucidate in this chapter, also applies to the study of survival in a hot environment.

In simplified form and viewed exclusively from the aspect of calories, we can say that man consists of a central nucleus surrounded by a shell. The central nucleus encloses the vital organs—the heart, the kidneys, and the brain—and its temperature ideally should remain at 98.6°F, as any degree higher or lower marks the beginning of disequilibrium.

On the other hand, the temperature of the shell surrounding this nucleus has a very wide range of fluctuation. This shell, which serves as a buffer between the nucleus and the external environment, is composed of the limbs, with their large groups of muscles, and of the integuments, that

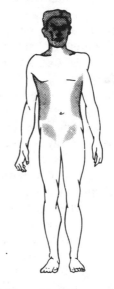

Maximum thermal loss zones of the body

is, the skin, from the epidermis to the deep layers that cover the muscles and the bones.

The communication route between the shell and the nucleus is the blood.

## FACTORS IN COOLING

The human organism, just like an inert body, follows the major principles of thermodynamics and loses its internal heat in four different ways:

1.  Convection: particularly when there is a wind;
2.  Radiation: man releases heat constantly like a radiator;

3. Evaporation: the evaporation of a bead of sweat is accompanied by a drop in temperature;
4. Conduction: particularly significant in water; at an equivalent temperature, cooling is 20 to 30 times more rapid in water than in dry air.

## In the Air

■ Air temperature can be very low. At Vostok, Antarctica, a temperature of −128.6°F was recorded in 1983.
■ At a temperature of −4°F (−20°C), a naked body will cool by 36°F (20°C) within one hour without wind, and within 80 seconds in a blizzard with 75 mile-per-hour (120 kilometer-per-hour) winds. Needless to say, to leave a tent naked under such conditions is to commit suicide. See chart on page 277.
■ Cooling can be moderated during the day if one can make use of the sun's rays, particularly in high mountains where there is less filtration of radiation due to the thinner atmosphere.

## In Water

■ Unlike air, water temperature is never very low. At the worst it is 32°F (0°C) in freshwater and 28.4°F (−2°C) in seawater.
■ On the other hand, water's ability to cool is very high because

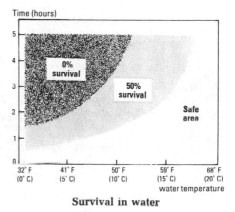

Survival in water

Chart from Molnar's work, indicating the probable length of time an individual can survive, depending on the temperature of the water (study of 160 clothed shipwrecked people).

water absorbs a lot of heat without changing its own temperature very much. Moreover, the specific heat of water is also very high, and this means that there is a great expenditure of calories to form a protective buffer of warmed water around the body—as is created by some diving suits and aquatic survival devices.

At an equivalent temperature, a body cools down much faster in water than in air. This explains, for example, the extremely high loss of life caused by the wreck of the *Titanic* in a totally calm sea (1912). In the more recent past, in 1963, the *Lakonia* sank in a calm sea. The water temperature was 62.6–64.4°F (17–18°C). Within three hours, 113 people had died in their life preservers. This lesson should be remembered well: The surface of half of all the oceans has a temperature below 68°F (20°C).

The length of time a person can survive in water at a temperature of 50°F is between an hour and an hour and a half; it is at most 30 minutes in water at a temperature of 32°F if the person is clothed. The length of survival may vary slightly with the individual: a higher percentage of body fat offers a slightly greater tolerance of the cold.

## MEANS OF DEFENSE

Man protects himself naturally against the onslaught of cold in two ways:

■ An increase in thermogenesis through metabolic factors; and
■ a decrease in peripheral thermolysis through insulation of the central nucleus.

These two terms, which describe phenomena that will be discussed again in the chapter on adaptation to heat, are essential: Thermogenesis is the generation of heat by the organism; thermolysis is the destruction of heat by the organism.

### Increase in Thermogenesis

This is accomplished in three ways, one voluntary and two involuntary.

■ Physical exercise: This is voluntary and conscious; it often enables prolonged survival in cold under two conditions:
—that a person is surrounded by air; and
—that a person has a sufficient amount of food.

This was why J.-L. Étienne was able to survive for 70 days on an ice floe in blizzards and a temperature of −61°F (−52°C): he had significant physical exercise every day because he pulled a 110-pound (50-kilogram) sled through a veritable labyrinth of ice, and he had a daily food ration of 4,000 calories per 143 pounds (65 kilograms).

Physical exercise produces four times more heat than it produces mechanical energy; the process, though very inefficient, does at least keep us warm in winter.

Exercise is not recommended if food provisions are insufficient. Physical exercise consumes a large part of the stored energy in the body, starting with glycogen, and this must be replaced by carbohydrates in foods such as concentrated milk, pasta and sugar. Physical exercise also increases calorie loss. The heat produced does not pass into the central nucleus in its entirety; instead, the majority escapes into the environment. This last point is especially true of exercise in water, which, as we shall see, should be strictly avoided in a survival situation.

■ Shivering. This is the body's involuntary physiological response to low temperature. Its effectiveness is limited:

—in intensity: The base metabolism can, at most, be multiplied by five to maintain a rectal temperature of 95°F (35°C).

—in time: Below 86°F (30°C) shivering can no longer compensate for heat loss and, in addition, the base metabolism decreases rapidly.

It is this last point in particular—the action limited in time that makes it important to be acclimated prior to an expedition into a cold region, so as to delay the onset of shivering. It is rather like having a large-caliber gun with a single cartridge, which would be wasted if used while the danger is still far away. The body must be trained to use its ammunition at the last possible moment.

■ An involuntary increase in the body's energy-burning processes caused by hormones, which are secreted under stress by the thyroid and the medullo-adrenal glands in the early phase of an assault.

### Decrease in Thermolysis

Thermolysis occurs primarily through the "outer shell," which enables greater or lesser cooling as it is open to circulation to a greater or lesser extent. If the environment is cold, the brain is notified of the drop in skin temperature by thermoreceptors distributed on the surface of the skin, and the brain then orders the vasoconstriction of the subcutaneous vessels. This vasoconstriction explains the paleness of the skin when it is cold, but its primary purpose is to maintain a safe internal temperature by keeping most of the blood in the central nucleus, since the blood flow that irrigates the skin drops from 3.7 quarts (3.5 liters) to .21 quarts (0.2 liters) per minute.

A fat person's adipose pannicle (fatty tissue in the hypodermis) is thick and will increase the efficiency of peripheral vasoconstriction in insulating the nucleus from the shell. This is why, for example, swimmers who cross the English Channel are generally well padded.

So the shell acts as a kind of thermal store of energy, allowing the body to incur a specific thermal debt without negative effects, just as one can incur an oxygen debt as a result of physical exertion.

# A CLINICAL SUMMARY OF ADAPTATION TO COLD

There are two types of response to extreme cold: maximum defense and minimum defense. Everyone—not just doctors—should know about both types in order to better understand the stage of survival he or she is in and, from the point of view of prevention, what must be avoided.

## THE MAXIMUM DEFENSE REACTION

This is how a person reacts when abruptly subjected to cold, unless he is injured or tired—a yachtsman who falls into water at a temperature of 59°F (15°C), for example, or a healthy and uninjured pilot after a forced landing. There is an initial stage of general shivering, and of metabolic, circulatory, and respiratory activity, up to the point when the body, exhausted by the intense shivering, begins to slow down. The temperature drops, the muscles become stiff, and mental problems appear: thinking becomes clouded, lethargy sets in, and then, once the body temperature has dropped to 87.8°F (31°C), the brain reaches unconsciousness.

Death most often occurs at a body temperature around 80.6–78.8°F (27–26°C). In medical experiments at Dachau concentration camp during World War II, the SS recorded a case of survival after the temperature had dropped to 77.4°F (25.2°C). Their criminal experiments on humans were carried out as follows: After arriving at the extermination camp, the most athletic Russian prisoners were thrown naked into a swimming pool of icy water, and the drop in temperature was recorded right to the extreme limits of survival. In at least seven known cases, the experiment was continued until death occurred. It was through these atrocious means that the Nazi doctors discovered that survival can be extended if the nape of the neck remains above water; this is because the bulbar centers of respiration and thermoregulation are located in this area. As a result of the experiments, the German air force's pilots were the first to benefit from an improved "Mae West" life jacket that kept the napes of their necks above water.

## THE MINIMUM DEFENSE REACTION

This is the reaction of a soldier who is tired or in bad physical shape and is subjected to an extended period of cold, even cold that is not terribly severe. This process was described perfectly by doctors in Napoleon's army, who saw it inevitably culminate in the "white" or "gentle" death, so called because it seemed to occur without any suffering, in a kind of sleep. In such a case there is no shivering; instead there is gradual cooling, and unconsciousness occurs quickly at a body temperature around 93°F (34°C).

As we have seen, this kind of cooling is compatible with survival despite extremely low internal temperatures, but only if the body is not totally exhausted. An example of this is a young woman from Chicago, whose temperature dropped to 64.4°F (18°C) during an alcoholic stupor but who was nevertheless successfully revived.

## SURVIVING COLD: PREVENTIVE MEASURES

During World War II, when circumstances forced the German general staff to transfer the units stationed in France to the Russian front in midwinter and without special training, 50 percent of the men died of exposure before reaching the front.

Contrary to common belief, Eskimos do not have any special physiological reaction to cold. Behavior, learned through experience, enables them to survive. They eat large quantities of walrus fat and they know how to dress for warmth. While furs in themselves do not warm the body, they effectively prevent cooling by creating an insulating layer of air between the skin and the clothing. Once heated through body contact, this layer of air remains thermally stable, the degree of stability depending on how tightly sealed the fur is.

### ACCLIMATIZATION

Eskimos have no special gene to make them bear the cold better than anyone else, but they are acclimatized to cold from earliest infancy, and this is what gives them their advantage. A baby born in an igloo and moved to a temperate region within the first few days of his life will react to cold exactly as his southern neighbors do. There is no evidence of any natural selection for tolerance to cold; we are all potential Eskimos as long as we are subjected to the same conditions. Acclimatization to cold is accomplished in the same way as physical training: through gradual intensification, regular exposure, willpower, and perseverance. Anyone incapable of such self-discipline—judging by the evidence—is psychologically unsuitable for expeditions to cold regions. Various methods, which need not be extreme, can be used. Before embarking on his trip in March 1986, J.-L. Étienne merely took a cold shower every morning starting in December; but he was already a mountain climber with many years of experience and had often confronted the cold of the Himalayas and the cordillera of the Andes. Each individual should proceed according to his own circumstances: he should hike through the snow wearing light clothing, swim in the sea in all kinds of weather, etc.

To prepare for survival in cold water, military doctors suggest a daily bath in cold water, lasting as long as one can tolerate. Within 15 days, the first signs of acclimatization become evident:

- the length of the bath increases as tolerance increases;
- the onset of shivering and pain in the extremities is delayed;
- manual dexterity improves, which is indispensable for survival in many cases.

Physical endurance exercises, such as swimming, cycling, or jogging, are also good training for cold. Vigorous exercise—undertaken in all kinds of weather—involves precisely the same vasoconstrictions and vasodilations that make survival in extreme cold possible.

Immersing one's hands and feet in icy water in order to adapt the body's extremities to cold provides excellent vasomotor training and is easily done at home. The fishermen of Gaspé at the mouth of the Saint Lawrence River in Canada fish with their bare hands all year round in glacial waters, and in effect are practicing adaptation on a daily basis: vasoconstriction changes to vasodilation in their hands and provides a strong flow of blood with a temperature of 98.6°F, thus protecting them against frostbite.

All tests and exertions we subject ourselves to must be voluntary. The body implements very complex biochemical adaptations that will enable us to survive: In the North Sea (average temperature 46.4°F [8°C]), divers working under oil drilling platforms find that their bodies develop a much thicker subcutaneous fatty tissue and an increased ability to catabolize, or to break down, these fats. A sedentary person, on the other hand, uses his reserves of carbohydrates for energy, and very little fat.

## FOOD IN A COLD REGION

Since cold is very costly in calories, consideration of food supply is essential. There has been much discussion about the relative caloric value of three kinds of foods and their faster or slower metabolism within the body:

- lipids, which in the past were recommended for cold weather, have a higher calorie content (9 calories per gram) but the body must be adapted to use them;

■ carbohydrates (4 calories per gram) are more immediately available, and can be digested more easily in cold conditions;

■ proteins (4 calories per gram) provide plenty of energy for the muscles, but only at the end of a long and complex metabolic chain.

A diet of 5,500 calories a day in severe cold used to be thought necessary, but now, based on military and civilian observations, and because of improvements in cold weather clothing, a more modest energy supply of about 4,000 calories per day is recommended, where carbohydrates make up at least 60 percent of the ration, lipids 25 to 30 percent, and proteins 10 to 15 percent. This ration proved satisfactory for an expedition to Greenland in which four men parachuted onto the glacial plateau and were isolated for 11 months at an altitude of 9,900 feet (3,000 meters), with temperatures ranging from 14°F (−10°C) to −65°F (−54°C); for French polar expeditions that stayed on the Adélie coast in eastern Antarctica; and, finally, for J.-L. Étienne's solo expedition to the Arctic in 1986.

Generally speaking, lipids should be consumed during the evening meal, in the shelter of the tent, and carbohydrates should preferably be consumed during exertion and exposure to the cold. Eating food rich in calories, such as lipids, stimulates the metabolism, speeds digestion, and increases body temperature, so eating them in the evening makes it easier to sleep.

We know that the three types of food have specific caloric values. But they also differ in the caloric supplement they provide when they are digested, i.e., the SDA (specific dynamic action). Proteins have an SDA that is far superior to that of fats and sugars, which explains the warm feeling one gets after eating a meal of meat. This must be kept in mind when considering a diet for a cold environment.

The reader should refer to the chapter on "The Survival Diet" for more details about foods that are appropriate for varying climates.

## THE NEED FOR WATER IN A COLD REGION

Usually, we wait until we feel thirsty before we drink—without realizing that this feeling is an alarm signal, a sign of the beginning of the body's disequilibrium. Though city life may forgive an occasional state of under-hydration, it is a very different matter in a survival situation, in which disequilibrium can set in very quickly. Here, drinking before thirst begins can be lifesaving.

Exposure to cold not only increases energy needs, it also increases the need for water, for the following reasons:

■ The capacity of cold air to become saturated with water vapor decreases as the temperature drops, which encourages evaporation and dries the mucous membranes.
■ Perspiration is taking place under clothing, which usually consists of several layers.
■ Rhinorrhea (nasal discharge) is relatively strong.
■ Urine output is increased by both physical exertion and stress.
■ Physical, aerobic exertion, which is much costlier in energy than muscular exertion, has a much lower yield at low temperatures, and this increases the need for water.
■ The respiration rate is increased by exertion (polypnea), and this increase is followed by loss of water through transpiration.

Dehydration causes exhaustion and hypothermia, so it is important to drink before one feels thirst. The best plan is to drink large quantities in cold weather: preferably hot liquids, in frequent small portions. At a higher altitude one should drink about 4.2 quarts (4 liters) per day and, if in doubt, it is better to drink too much than too little: no case of over-hydration in this context has ever been reported.

## What About Alcohol?

The image of a gentle Saint Bernard dog with his cask of brandy, saving the reckless mountaineer, should not be taken too literally. **Any significant amount of alcohol drunk in a cold region is definitely harmful.**
The calories it supplies are empty; instead, alcohol acts as a toxin that severely diminishes tolerance to cold. On the other hand, small doses of alcohol have their uses. Less than an ounce of brandy can have two temporarily positive effects:

■ it can cause peripheral vasodilation, which warms the extremities; and
■ it has an undeniable psychological effect, which can sometimes be useful for the final "big push," to enable one, for instance, to get to the nearest base.

Yet two negative effects preclude the repetition of these small doses:

■ the vasodilation mentioned above is, in fact, the shell's protection at the expense of the central organs, where hypothermia will be encouraged; and
■ even in moderate doses, alcohol can induce drowsiness as a side effect, and this is dangerous in a survival situation.

The ideal approach with alcohol is total abstinence, but small doses at the right moment can cause little harm.

## INDIVIDUAL FACTORS AND TOLERANCE OF COLD

Before leaving for a cold region, we must make certain that we are psychologically and physically equipped for the challenge, checking factors that have nothing to do with our desires or willpower.

### Metabolism

Obviously, some people feel the cold more than others, and there is no doubt that sensitivity to cold varies among individuals. In Himalayan expeditions one frequently comes across a climber who was subjected during the climb to the same hardships as his friends were, but who returns uninjured while the majority of the others are suffering from severe frostbite.

For a long time it was believed that these variations in individuals who had undergone the same training were due to differences in their vasomotor faculty—that is, the ability of the vessels in the skin, particularly capillaries, to increase or decrease their diameter.

But metabolism provides a better explanation: Not all people have the same basal metabolic rate—just as there are fat people and thin people, flabby people and well-toned people. Polymor-

phism can be found everywhere, including in the metabolism.

There are "exothermic individuals," who easily release a large amount of heat, and "endothermic individuals," who retain the heat produced in the central parts of the body. The former are said to be insensitive to cold: in winter they walk around in their shirtsleeves, their hands and feet always warm. The latter constantly complain that their extremities are cold. The connections between metabolism, sensitivity to cold, temperature, body fat, and muscle tone are well known in medicine in connection with thyroid disorders.

### Age

Fatty tissue atrophies with age, and this is one reason why older people are more sensitive to cold. Moreover, after age 65, it is more difficult to shiver—not because the individual is less sensitive to cold, but because there has been an "erosion" of the reflex circuits, which activate the secretion of adrenaline simultaneously with the shivering.

### Physical Strength

It is obvious that a healthy, athletic individual who does not drink, smoke, or take drugs will be much more tolerant to all forms of physical stress. But even with healthy people we must emphasize the necessity of checking for latent disorders before undertaking a potentially dangerous expedition. A benign disorder may not cause clinical problems in normal life, but it could cause a fatal disequilibrium in a survival situation. Simple decalcification (the loss of calcium from bones), for instance, can translate into a dangerous level of exhaustion in a life-threatening situation.

### Personality

It is a well-known fact that exposure to cold aggravates latent character flaws. In fact, psychological strength may be the first thing to deteriorate upon exposure to extreme cold. Moreover, the power of "morale," of strength of character, of the desire to hold out to the end, is primordial, and those who have this morale have the best chance of survival. This principle applies to all stress, but there is no doubt that it is the primary determinant in survival situations in cold regions, as has been demonstrated by numerous examples from the history of military operations on land and at sea, from mountain climbing, and from polar expediations.

The intense desire to survive the cold is in itself a precious incentive, and during winter campaigns military doctors have often recorded that the endurance of the volunteers was far superior to that of the conscripts, and that a much higher proportion of the latter fell

victim to accidents and injuries (particularly frostbite).

Therefore an individual should undergo the same degree of mental training as of physical acclimatization before departure. The potential survivor in a cold region must be aware of the terrible significance of apathy, of lethargy, and of drowsiness, which are the prelude to deep hypothermia. He has to know that he must resist at all costs the pressing need to stop and lie down to sleep, as it will lead to death. At the end of his preparations, his mental fitness should be equal to his physical fitness.

### Theoretical Training

Survival in a cold region, as elsewhere, does not require a special level of intelligence, but it does require a minimum of theoretical and practical knowledge, which will determine who survives in the field and who does not.

A knowledge of first aid is essential. For example, if we are aware how disastrous a frostbitten hand or foot can be in mountain climbing or in a polar region, it would be a great shame not to know that all one needs to do is to place a hand under one's armpit or a foot on the stomach of a friend to prevent severe frostbite; or that two people sleeping in the same sleeping bag can conserve enough heat to avoid deep hypothermia; or that survival may simply depend on how a lone individual chooses to build his shelter.

## SURVIVAL TACTICS

### In Water

At an equivalent temperature, cooling is 20 to 30 times faster in water than in dry air, due to the specific heat of water. It is widely believed that one should exercise to keep warm in the water if one is shipwrecked. However, a study has refuted this belief.

The basic parameter is an individual's body temperature. In the study, volunteers were immersed in calm water at a temperature of 77°F (25°C); some of them swam around and some stayed relatively still. In those who stayed relatively still, thermogenesis spread out the caloric losses, and their temperature remained at 98.6°F (37°C). On the other hand, in those who were active, thermogenesis was very quickly exceeded, and their internal temperature dropped. The results were even more dramatic in water at a temperature of 68°F (20°C), as the temperature of the individuals who were active dropped instantly.

The explanation is simple: Exercise burns up the calories that arrive at the surface of the body (the "shell") much faster than it causes peripheral vasodilation, and this sends a significant flow

The position that causes minimal thermal loss in water.

of blood from the nucleus to the epidermis, which is soaked in cold water. The calories escape into the water, and movement serves only to increase this loss. If the water around the body is agitated, the body does not have time to reheat as it would if the water stayed still. One can easily evoke this sensation of cooling: Hold your hand still in cool water, then move it. With motion, the water feels colder.

The farthest one can expect to travel in water with a temperature of 50°F (10°C) is 0.6 mile (one kilometer). Therefore, if one is wearing a life jacket, it is better to avoid all movement altogether: This will extend the time of survival by as much as 35 percent.

It is important to know that even if an individual dives into tropical waters with a temperature of 86°F (30°C), his body will cool quickly, especially if he is not wearing any clothes. At a water temperature of 34.8°F (5°C), death can occur within 30 minutes if the person is unclothed. If he is clothed and does not move, he can survive for one hour. A naked person in 59°F (15°C) water can die within one hour, but he can survive for five hours if he is clothed! Even wearing a simple T-shirt increases the thickness of the shell that protects the central organs of the body. All of this information demonstrates that hypothermia is a greater danger than drowning. In 1979 the majority of the shipwrecked people from the Fastnet regatta, victims of a storm in the North Sea, escaped drowning because their heads were kept above water by their life jackets. But their bodies froze: They died of cold.

To summarize, the optimum conditions for survival in water are as follows:

1. **Wear as much clothing as possible,** but not so much as to impede buoyancy.
2. **Keep the nape of your neck and your mouth above water** without exerting yourself. Any good life jacket should do this.
3. **Do not move** until help is available.

### In Air

Even in situations in which one must keep traveling, there are two main reasons why a shelter is indispensable, at least for sleeping:

■ A shelter, however temporary, always provides a temperature that is higher than the surrounding air.
■ A shelter provides protection against the wind, which is a determining factor if one recalls that, at an equivalent temperature, cooling can be 10 to 20 times more intense, depending on the speed of the wind.

One explorer who led expeditions on the Adélie coast of Antarctica, drew up his own table of the relationship between wind speed and temperature on the ice field:

■ with a wind speed of 11 miles per hour (18 kilometers per hour), a temperature of 32°F (0°C) is equivalent to 26.6°F (−3°C);
■ if the wind speed is over 22 miles per hour (36 kilometers per hour), the temperature is equivalent to 3.2°F (−16°C); and
■ if the wind speed is over 45 miles per hour (72 kilometers per hour), the temperature is equivalent to −5.8°F (−21°C).

Thus wind considerably increases the body's calorie loss, and a tightly sealed tent provides a double advantage by creating an atmosphere warmed by body heat and by affording protection against the wind. For accidental survival situations, constructing a shelter requires a degree of ingenuity in each type of environment.

If there is no reasonable protection, and if it is very cold, one must resist the temptation to sleep in order to avoid permanent lethargy. One author even suggested that one should sing to keep warm, and went so far as to quantify the amount of warming according to the nature of the song: "Aida: 27 calories; Cha-cha-cha: 8 calories; Jerk: 92 calories"!

## FROSTBITE

This subject deserves a section of its own. The consequences of frostbite are a real danger to survival in a cold region. Frostbite occurs under two sets of circumstances:

■ It accompanies final hypothermia in an exhausted individual who has already given up the struggle. It is painless, and it is only one of many signs of approaching death.
■ Or, as is very often the case, it occurs insidiously in an individual who is physically or mentally active, and suddenly deprives him of the use of a hand or a leg, immobilizing him, and leading to hypothermia and death. Examples of this are a mountain climber who is stuck in the middle of a rock wall because he can no longer feel his hand or foot, or a polar explorer who dies a few miles from the base because frostbite prevents him from walking any farther.

Therefore, even if one is unaware of the causes of frostbite, it is essential to learn the elementary techniques for avoiding it, especially since it occurs insidiously, gradually, and painlessly. At most, one feels a little numbness, a slight loss of sensitivity in the extremities. These simple symptoms should be treated as an alarm signal.

Starting around 1940, a traditional "vasomotric" explanation for frostbite was put forth. This explanation assumed that the cause was the differential between the time when cellular metabolism returns to normal and the time when circulation returns to normal. This differential involves two time spans: a period of exposure to cold, during which frostbite does not appear, and a second period during which frostbite does occur. This theory led to very unusual treatments, which have fortunately now been abandoned.

Currently, there is agreement on a different "thermal" explanation: The necrosis of frostbite is actually caused by the direct action of cold on the water of the cellular protoplasm. This water freezes in the heart of the cell, causing an excessive saline concentration and an osmotic and colloidal disequilibrium, which cannot sustain life beyond certain limits. We already know that anything that weakens the overall physical condition can encourage frostbite: alcoholism, inadequate athletic training, insufficient acclimatization to altitude in the case of mountain climbers, dehydration, insufficient food, and inappropriate equipment.

Various groups have tried to find forms of prevention, both topical and systemic. It is now clear that no general systemic treatment has been proven effective at "normal" altitudes (up to 6,500 feet [2,000 meters]). There is no preventive oral medication against frostbite. Prevention must be accomplished through localized, topical measures that protect thermogenesis.

### Clothing

Thorough studies of suitable clothing for the body's protection were made during polar and Himalayan expeditions, and have borne positive results. Fabrics are more effective as their thermal conductivity decreases, because this is what prevents calorie loss. Manufacturers, spurred by competition, have been forced to take this fact into account. For example, silk provides better thermal insulation than nylon; and several layers of clothing, separated by a layer of air, provide better thermal protection than a single-layered garment. One of the major advantages of synthetic garments is that they dry very quickly.

### Topical Prevention

As stated above, topical treatment is the only appropriate method for preventing frostbite. Topical applications of oily substances have long been known to be useful. Yet the medicinal substance in the cream or ointment is not the determining factor. Rather, it is the thermal conductivity coefficient of the base substance: lanolin, vaseline, or lard. Any oily ointment—anti-inflammatory pain-killing, counter-irritative, etc.—applied when the frostbite begins may result in improvement. However, the effect will not be due to the medicine in the ointment, but to the oily layer that insulated the skin from the surrounding air. For example, mechanics were able to repair trucks and tractors in the Antarctic with their bare hands during a blizzard, though they did not realize that it was the oil and grease that prevented them from suffering frostbite.

Such topical protection is certainly not foolproof, but it does considerably reduce the danger of getting frostbite. Experienced polar and Himalayan explorers have learned that they are less likely to suffer from frostbite if they do not wash the skin that would be exposed to the cold. After several days, this lack of hygiene forms a layer of well-blended dirt, boot grease, oil from sardines, and fat from sausages. Though this method may seem distasteful, survival is often bought at such cost, and scientific research has confirmed the validity of such observations made in the field.

## Treatment

If frostbite does occur, one must prevent it from spreading or causing complications. Some folk remedies must be avoided at all costs: for example, for a long time it was believed that beating the affected area could warm frostbite, because it would activate local circulation. As a result, during various mountain expeditions, several climbers who were suffering from frostbite were beaten with ropes with the laudable intention of "bringing back the circulation." This "therapy" must never be used.

Another method that is very popular in the mountains is rubbing frostbite with snow. This, too, is more dangerous than beneficial. Even a normal massage does more harm than good. A pilot who crash-landed in Alaska in 1954 recounted: "Both my feet were frostbitten. I proceeded to give them a brisk massage. For two hours I massaged them frantically, and I was in agony when the blood started to circulate again. At that point, I thought that the ordeal was over; but next morning

I had lumps of raw meat instead of feet, and all my toes had to be amputated."

The skin and all the underlying tissues become very delicate in severe cold and all vigorous physical treatments should definitely be rejected. So what is to be done?

One should attempt to find a way to heal frostbite by rewarming the affected tissue, in the same way as drinking cures thirst and resting relieves exhaustion. Once again, one should use common sense and realize that placing one's feet close to a fire or plunging one's hand into a basin of boiling water will do nothing but superimpose a burn over the frostbite.

In a survival situation, particularly if one is alone, it will be very difficult to implement the ideal method of rewarming: The tissue should be thawed in water baths at a temperature of 107.6°F (42°C)—no less, and no more. At 113°F (45°C), the water will scald. Below 107.6°F, studies have shown that the results are harmful. This demanding procedure means that one must have something with which to heat water and to maintain it at 107.6°F. Once the skin temperature has reached 98.6°F (37°C) the frostbite should be allowed to follow its natural course. The skin should be protected, and the affected limb should be moved normally to prevent the frostbite from spreading further.

At the same time, all compression dressings must be removed, since frostbite is accompanied by edema (an accumulation of excessive fluid in the tissues): the dressing would merely restrict the circulation even more. When lying down, if a lower limb is involved, the latter should be slightly raised to avoid stasis, which would aggravate frostbite.

Under no circumstances should any warming treatment be administered unless one is sure that the rewarming can be maintained until proper first aid can be given. The worst outcome is frostbite which has been rewarmed with a great amount of pain and which subsequently refreezes because the rewarming cannot be maintained. It would be better to do nothing at all than to risk being functionally even more handicapped than before: a rewarmed extremity cannot be saved if edema, pain, and its extreme fragility persist.

English doctors have proven that one can walk a considerable distance with frozen feet without risking complications. A specialist in frostbite in Alaska tells the story of 12 people who walked through the snow for three to four days with completely frozen feet. Some did not have to undergo any amputation at all while others lost a couple of toes.

Frostbite is sometimes terrifying because the victim believes that it is "the beginning of the end." His mind can be set at ease if he knows how frostbite develops:

■ It does not necessarily spread—even if it is not treated immediately and even if it looks very black.
■ It is always broader than it is deep, and therefore it looks a lot worse than it really is during the first weeks. For this reason, doctors in hospitals seldom perform amputations during the early stages of frostbite. Instead, they allow four to eight weeks to pass, in order to have a clearly defined area of necrosis.

These two points should reassure a cross-country skier or a hiker, suffering from frostbite, who must endure several more days of exposure to the cold. The fact that his toes or fingers turn black does not necessarily mean total amputation on his return to civilization. In contrast to a malignant tumor, where the surrounding tissues are always cut away, frostbite always involves very localized excision.

The only possible complications, apart from the frostbite spreading, are tetanus and infection. The problem of tetanus should not arise, since all adventurers should keep their vaccinations up to date—especially tetanus vaccinations, as the disease can be contracted at all latitudes. As far as other infections are concerned, the individual should take a broad-spectrum antibiotic every day (see "Medicine Without a Doctor" for information on the survival first aid kit).

## CHILBLAIN

Although not entirely similar to frostbite, chilblain most likely occurs in cold climates or upon prolonged exposure to moisture. Thus it is as much a danger to the shipwrecked passenger trapped in a lifeboat innundated with water as it is to a jungle explorer whose soaking feet are trapped in too-tight shoes (a condition known as trench foot, which was responsible for taking more GIs out of action during the Vietnam War than the most sophisticated mines and booby traps).

Redness, tingling sensation or pain, swelling and peeling skin are the main symptoms of chilblain. Treatment consists of rest, during which legs should be elevated and shoes and socks removed. Afflicted persons should not wear shoes again for at least 12 hours for fear of edema.

# HEAT

- Facts

- The Physiology of Adaptation to Heat

- Acclimating to Heat

- Fitness and Accidents

- Surviving the Heat: Preventive Measures

# FACTS

✿ A man can survive in an oven for two minutes at 392°F (200°C).

✿ The body functions best when its temperature is between 97.7°F (36.5°C) and 103.1°F (39.5°C). At 113°F (45°C) the cellular proteins congeal, causing rapid death. So many animals, including man, spend their entire lives a few degrees away from fatal overheating. The fact that man can withstand a temperature of 248°F (120°C) in dry air for 10 minutes gives some idea of the power and delicacy of the regulatory mechanisms that allow the body to maintain an internal temperature compatible with survival. If these regulators did not exist, the amount of heat generated by an athlete after one hour of intense exercise would be enough to raise his internal temperature from 98.6°F (37°C) to 140°F (60°C). Knowledge of these regulators is essential to anyone who confronts an inhospitably hot region, particularly a jungle or a desert.

✿ Man may be considered a tropical animal because when he is naked and unprotected, the temperature of his surroundings must be 82.4°F (28°C) for his metabolism to be maintained at a minimum base level, and for him to remain in thermal equilibrium. Temperatures on Earth range roughly between −58°F (−50°C) and 140°F (60°C). This means that the body must be able to maintain a temperature 156.6°F or 87°C higher than the surrounding environment in the coldest regions, and 41.4°F or 23°C cooler than the surrounding environment in the hottest regions. The energy diffused to maintain normal body temperature is quantitatively different in each case and is relatively economical for hot regions. The adaptation mechanisms for heat are based on evaporation of water from the body and on "vascular gymnastics"; the latter is a determining factor, just as it is in adaptation to cold. Therefore, once again, we are dealing with the concept of the central organs of the body and their protective shell.

# THE PHYSIOLOGY OF ADAPTATION TO HEAT

For a naked person in a normal atmosphere, the response to too much heat begins at an air temperature of 82.4°F (28°C). The body of a clothed individual begins to consume energy at 77°F (25°C) to prevent the body temperature from exceeding 98.6°F (37°C).

In July 1987, Greece suffered an unprecedented heat wave (up to 116.6°F [47°C] in the shade), which claimed 1,300 victims in two weeks. The majority were older or sick people, all of whom had one thing in common: a deficient or weak circulatory system that was incapable of adapting.

## VASODILATION IN THE SKIN

The first circulatory adaptation takes place in the peripheral vessels, and their diameter dilates as the heat increases. This dilation affects all vessels down to the smallest capillaries and causes the red color of skin that is exposed to heat. In normal temperatures, blood flow to the skin is at most 5 percent of the total cardiac output, but this proportion can exceed 25 percent in exceptional cases of exposure. The result of vasodilation is that a larger volume of blood is exposed to the surrounding air. Therefore there is a greater loss of calories to the external environment through conduction and radiation, assuming that the external temperature is lower than the skin temperature (if it is not, sweating plays the major role in adaptation).

The vasodilation in the shell is accompanied by vasoconstriction in the internal organs except for the brain and the cardiopulmonary system, which are the last to change. Below an air temperature of 71.6°F (22°C), 15.8 quarts (15 liters) of blood irrigate the muscles per minute while 11.6 quarts go to the skin. At 100.4°F (38°C), 13.7 quarts (13 liters) of blood are needed to act as a radiator to release internal heat, and the muscles receive only 10.6 quarts (10 liters).

This significant change in the distribution of the blood volume explains some problems that may occur, and one should know their cause in order to determine their severity.

■ Abdominal cramps or even digestive problems may arise because of the weak irrigation of the internal organs.
■ Difficulty in standing upright may arise because too much blood has gone to the lower limbs. This is why some people become dizzy when they stand up after taking a long, hot bath. In the desert, standing still is extremely unpleasant—in fact, it became the traditional punishment in some prison camps during World War II. It is better to walk, as the muscular contractions help to send the blood from the dilated veins toward the heart and then toward the brain.

These phenomena are harmless and should not be confused with "heat exhaustion" or "heat stroke." It should be noted that the heart adapts to the redistribution of the volume by increasing its rate in proportion to the increase in the body's temperature, an adjustment that is often sufficient to prevent dizziness.

## SWEATING

If circulatory adaptation proves inadequate to maintain body temperature, the sweat glands, controlled by the hypothalamus, come into play. At an ambient temperature of 59°F (15°C), sweating eliminates only 0.95 quarts (0.9 liters) of the total volume of 1.48 quarts (1.40 liters) of water eliminated in a day. At 89.6°F (32°C), sweat eliminates 2.59 quarts (2.45 liters) of the total 3.17 quarts (3 liters) of water that are lost. Above 91.4°F (33°C), body temperature is maintained exclusively through the evaporation of sweat.

Every drop of sweat that evaporates causes local cooling, which prevents the temperature of the skin surface from rising (0.60 kcal per evaporated drop). Therefore cooling will be proportional to the quantity of sweat eliminated through evaporation.

## WHAT IS SWEAT?

Ninety-nine percent of sweat is water. Therefore it must be compensated for by an equivalent intake of water. Although sweating eliminates some toxins, that function is negligible compared to its role as a thermal regulator.

Sweating is the result of the activity of 2 million to 5 million sweat glands, which are distributed over the entire surface of the body with the exception of the nails, the lips, and the genital organs. All essential elements of plasma are found in sweat and some of them are highly concentrated; in particular, these include urea, ammonia, pyruvic and lactic acids, and sodium chloride. The concentration of salt is the reason for the white patches that are left on other tissues by sweat, and confirms the necessity to compensate for sweat losses by an intake both of water and of minerals. The other elements cause a disagreeable odor and an acid pH (between 4 and 6.8).

A light sweat is rich in salt, but as sweating increases the salt content decreases. In other words, there is a maximum amount of salt, but not of water, that can be eliminated (there have been cases of individuals who lost up to 21 quarts [20 liters] in one day). Here, too, the hypothalamus controls the secretion by the sweat glands.

The hypothalamus is activated by one or several of the following stimuli:

■ *an increase in the internal temperature:* When an individual is abruptly exposed to heat, it takes some time before the internal temperature rises and before regulation through sweating begins.
■ *drinking something hot:* This activates sweating, even in cold

regions and even if the internal temperature has obviously not yet had time to rise. It is the same mechanism that causes sweating when one eats highly spiced exotic foods. But this has nothing to do with the thermal regulation we are discussing here.

■ *mental stress:* If an individual finds himself in a frightening situation, sweating is instantaneous, localized on the forehead, the palms, the soles, and under the armpits. This is the "cold sweat," which does not involve skin vasodilation; it, too, is a reflex reaction. Its functional significance is not known, but it is obvious that it will aggravate any dehydration due to heat. In this context, the conditions under which desert tank crews have to fight are especially arduous, partly because of the intense heat and partly because of the stress of battle.

Sweating starts in the lower limbs, then moves to the trunk, and finally occurs in the upper limbs and the head. Each sweat gland is activated in a cyclical manner, which provides time for the sweat to evaporate as well as providing periods of rest. Sweat begins to trickle across the skin once production has exceeded one-third of the maximum evaporative capacity. This capacity depends on the relative humidity. In stressful situations, 50 percent of the sweat is eliminated through the skin on the forehead, 25 percent by that on the head and upper limbs, and 25 percent by that on the lower limbs. The practical conclusion from this observation is that all these areas should be exposed to the air as much as possible to facilitate evaporation and cooling. This is easy in the desert but not in the jungle where insects, leeches, and vegetation make a minimum of clothing necessary for protection. It is especially important in respect to the head and forehead, since, as we have seen, the quantity of sweat eliminated from these areas can be as high as 75 percent. Therefore head coverings used as protection against the sun's radiation should be light colored, wide brimmed, and well ventilated.

## THE LIMITS OF COOLING THROUGH SWEATING

### Individual Factors

The average total number of sweat glands is around 2 million, but there are significant individual variations, and some people lack them altogether. In addition, an equal number of glands are more productive in an adapted individual than in one who is not. Therefore training, as we will see, is essential.

The critical amount of heat accumulation (from 90 to 110 kcal/$m^2$ depending on physical activity) also varies according to physical condition. Someone who has already been subjected to a survival situation for several days will be increasingly less tolerant to heat, and every movement will become more and more difficult and costly.

Experiments have shown that drinking a small dose of alcohol on the evening before exposure to heat decreases the individual's tolerance to heat almost by half.

## Climatic Factors

Sweat, like all liquids, evaporates more easily as the humidity of the ambient air drops. At 100 percent humidity, no evaporation is possible. Sweat no longer performs its cooling function, the body continues to heat up, the surface and the deep thermal receptors stimulate the hypothalamus even more, and the latter sends repeated impulses to the sweat glands, which secrete more than ever but to no avail. This vicious circle leads to acute dehydration within a few hours, and quickly causes death if the dehydration is not countered by the intake of an equivalent amount of liquid. Such conditions are not rare, and are found especially in hot and humid equatorial forests, where the dense vegetation prevents any breeze from reaching the ground.

Even at high ambient temperatures, if the humidity is at 50 to 60 percent, the body can maintain its temperature without any major problems, naturally assuming that there is an adequate intake of water. The relative humidity of some deserts, however (particularly the Arabian Desert), may be higher, especially if they are close to oceans.

Wind also affects the efficiency of sweating: evaporation is much greater if the drops of sweat are subjected to a current of air. A runner will take off his clothing not so much to remove a warm garment as to remove a "wind breaker," which inhibits evaporation and thus the cooling sensation on his skin.

## Transpiration

Calorie loss through the evaporation of water contained in the respiratory gases is accelerated by the increase of the respiration rate in a hot atmosphere, but it is negligible in comparison to sweating and cannot be accelerated voluntarily. Dogs, which do not have sweat glands, eliminate heat by panting, which increases transpiration.

Sleeping with a silk or cotton scarf over one's mouth in the desert will decrease water loss through transpiration, and will reduce morning thirstiness.

# ACCLIMATING TO HEAT

## PASSIVE ACCLIMATING

By passive acclimating we mean what the body does unconsciously in response to heat. After several days of exposure to heat, several adaptive phenomena come into play:

■ An increase in the intensity of sweating for the given conditions, resulting in an increased calorie loss and thus a lower skin temperature, which ensures better cooling of the circulating blood; this increase can be as much as 100 percent.
■ A simultaneous decrease in the mineral salt content: The fact that the deposits of mineral salts on surfaces tend to decrease over time is easily visible.
■ The redistribution of blood in different tissues returns to normal after several days, even if the exposure to heat remains the same. Therefore there will no longer be a danger of syncope (fainting) or abdominal cramps. At the same time, the cardiac output remains elevated, and the rate will gradually return to normal.

All these beneficial and spontaneous adaptations occur within four to seven days and spontaneous acclimating is complete by the end of 12 to 14 days. Exposure to a hot environment even for just one hour a day shows very positive results. Studies made in 1973 demonstrated that the minimum time necessary for acclimating, assuming a daily activity of six to eight hours in the hot environment, is four hours of exposure per day for eight to nine consecutive days. In other words, it takes about a week to reach peak fitness for a hot country; so there is a period of thermal adjustment, just as there is a period of adjustment to altitude or to jet lag. The acclimating lasts for several weeks, but one should not interrupt the period of exposure to heat, even briefly for rest periods.

## TRAINING

Those who have undergone training are more likely to be able to deal with heat than those who have not. Whether one runs in a race in high temperatures, makes an expedition through equatorial forests, or crosses a desert on foot, training will be a plus and could prove to be the only thing to guarantee success.

### Physical Endurance Exercises

These are effective in two ways:

■ they increase the internal temperature and thus activate the

same physiological mechanisms as exposure to a hot climate; and
■ muscular exercise causes "vascular gymnastics," which are a determining factor in adapting to cold as well as to heat.

Progressive endurance exercises in gradually increasing temperatures are best. A convenient way to accomplish this is to practice later and later in the day as temperatures rise. This will result in a beneficial adaptation of both the heart and the circulatory system.

### The Sauna

The exposure to hot, dry air in the sauna causes an increase in cardiac output, a decrease in the mean circulation time, and an increase in heart rate. This training method would not be my own choice, because it is static and does not involve the striated skeletal muscles. However, it can be a good adjunct to endurance exercises.

---

# FITNESS AND ACCIDENTS

It is obvious that those rare individuals who do not have sweat glands will be unfit to visit hot countries; but they should already be aware of this due to the extreme discomfort they feel in summer even in temperate latitudes. In this book I am addressing athletic adults in good health and therefore will not go into the numerous medical contraindications to heat (cardiopathy, varices, debilitating disorders, etc.). On the other hand, anyone can suffer an accident or injury due to heat, so elementary precautions should be taken.

### HEAT-INDUCED ASTHENIA

This condition is encountered primarily in hot and humid areas among the poorly acclimated. The symptoms include severe asthenia (loss of strength), headaches, nausea, anxiety often accompanied by insomnia, intense sweating, and an increased respiratory and heart rate. This can develop into depression and the inability to keep up with the expeditionary team.

Treatment is simple: The individual merely has to wear more suitable (light-colored and loose) clothing, sleep in a cooler environment, and stay in the same location for several days, giving himself enough time to adapt.

### DEHYDRATION

Dehydration can be insidious for people who only drink when they are very thirsty. Extreme thirst signals a point at which it may be too late to avoid the start of dehydration. Failing to compensate for loss of mineral salts due to sweating can have serious consequences.

Symptoms of dehydration are gradual and involve a loss of weight that becomes obvious through "skin folds": if dehydrated skin is pinched between two fingers, it retains the fold.

Tachycardia, or relatively rapid heartbeat, occurs, and there is a decrease in the volume of urine, which becomes concentrated and darker. The mucous membranes become dry, thirst is intense, muscular cramps begin in the legs and abdomen, and the muscles elsewhere tighten and twitch. When water loss reaches or exceeds 10 percent of the initial body weight, the signs become alarming: vision and hearing problems and difficulties in articulation. Without treatment, symptoms progress to delirium, convulsions, and coma.

These problems are caused by loss of salt and water, reduced plasma volume, insufficient renal function, acidosis, and an increase in blood viscosity by over 30 percent, leading to a decrease in blood flow and an increase in cardiac activity. The treatment is simple: Administer liquids and salt orally.

## HEAT EXHAUSTION

This normally occurs after extreme muscular exertion in a hot and humid region. The symptom is unconsciousness due to the heat, which is sometimes preceded by a cold sweat, nausea, and pallor, and is accompanied by accelerated perspiration, a drop in arterial pressure, a slow and weak pulse, a more or less normal temperature and damp skin. The damp skin indicates the persistence of the sweat function and is the distinguishing factor between heat exhaustion and heat stroke.

Heat exhaustion is caused by a sudden disequilibrium in the distribution of blood between the central organs and the shell: Excessive vasodilation in the skin and the muscles causes a significant drop in cardiac output and eventual unconsciousness. If the victim lies down, the results are excellent. The best treatment is to cease physical activity and, if possible, lie down in a cooler place.

## HEAT STROKE

This can be deadly, particularly in a survival situation where appropriate treatment is not available. Therefore heat stroke must be prevented so that it will never have to be treated.

For heat stroke to occur, several factors have to come together: intense temperature, high humidity, inadequate ventilation, and significant muscular exertion. The symptoms come on suddenly, sometimes preceded by prodomes (premonitory, or warning, symptoms). The temperature typically rises as high as 107.6°F (42°C). Therefore it is useful to have a thermometer available so as to distinguish heat stroke from other disorders. The individual suddenly suffers mental problems, including confusion, coma, and convulsions. Respiration is shallow. The skin is dry and very hot. This latter point is a determining factor to establish the diagnosis and the severity of the case. The condition of the skin demonstrates the absence of sweating caused by a total suspension of the thermal regulation centers. This results in an intense heating of the skin and an increase in the temperature of the central organs ("malignant hyperthermia"), accompanied by the destruction of cells, which rapidly becomes irreversible in the brain, kidneys, muscles, and liver. Death occurs within 24 hours.

The only treatment possible is immediate cooling in a bath at a temperature of 39°F (4°C). Such treatment is obviously impossible in an isolated location.

## SURVIVING THE HEAT: PREVENTIVE MEASURES

### GENERAL HEALTH

Alcohol merely augments the carbohydrate calorie ration and in no way helps thermoregulation. Tobacco causes artificial hypoxia, which counteracts respiratory adaptation (though to a lesser degree than during physical exercise at a high altitude).

### CLOTHING

This should be copied from the tested and proven customs of local populations. The higher the humidity, the looser the clothing should be, and it should allow air to pass through to increase calorie loss by convection. Cotton is ideal when it is dry, but it retains excess sweat and this moisture increases the weight of the fabric, inhibiting evaporation and keeping the body moist. If one is sheltered from insects and the sun, it would be best to wear nothing. Socks should be of natural yarn or cotton, as synthetic materials can cause water-soaked tissue to macerate and can encourage fungal infections.

Some form of head covering is indispensable in the sun, and it should be light in color.

### DRINKING

**It is essential to drink large quantities, and frequently.** Thirst is an alarm signal and evidence of a disequilibrium that has already begun. This is not a serious problem in a temperate climate, but it can be in intense heat. Therefore **one should drink before one feels thirsty,** several quarts per day if one is sweating. If in doubt, it is better to drink too much than too little. Drinking water even in large quantities is harmless, but chronic under-hydration can lead to excruciating attacks of renal colic because of an overconcentration of urine.

## WATCHING FOR SIGNS THAT INDICATE MALADJUSTMENT

At the smallest suspicious sign, drink water and rest in the shade for a few hours. It is usually easy to distinguish muscular cramps due to dehydration from abdominal cramps due to an inadequate distribution of blood, but, if in doubt, stop for a while and drink something. If a member of an expedition suffers behavioral problems, the team should stop immediately and suspect heat stroke.

## ADJUST THE INTENSITY OF PHYSICAL EXERTION TO THE TEMPERATURE

Be aware that base metabolism can be increased by a factor of 20 during strenuous exercise. If this exercise is performed in intense heat—in the desert, for example—there is a danger that adaptive fac-

ulties will quickly become overwhelmed.

If the supply of water is limited, but there is plenty of time, it is better to travel at night in the desert.

## SALT INTAKE

The occurrence of cramps in the muscles of the limbs and the abdominal wall seems to be as much due to the loss of salt as to dehydration. The two are closely linked, and it is often said that "salt drinks water."

Salt tablets distributed to South African miners have considerably decreased such "heat cramps." So should they be taken on a daily basis by anyone headed for the desert? Certainly not. Consumption depends totally on the intensity of sweating and on diet.

The maximum quantity of salt that can be lost is on the order of 0.5 to 0.7 ounce (15 to 20 grams) a day under particularly harsh conditions. Since a normal diet contains around 0.35 to 0.42 ounce (10 to 12 grams) of salt, a supplementary intake may be useful but should not be overdone. One salt tablet is normally sufficient; at most, two if the individual does not eat. These tablets should be taken with a large amount of water, to avoid the risk of stomach problems. Salt must not be taken, however, if water is not available (see chapter on "Thirst").

# THIRST

- Facts

- Questions

- Physiology of Thirst and Its Implications for Survival

- Water in Survival Situations

- Ways to Endure Thirst Better and Longer

# FACTS

☉ Sixty to 70 percent of the human body is made up of water.

☉ A loss in liquids equivalent to 2 percent of the body weight (i.e., 1.6 quarts [1.5 liters]) reduces the mental and muscular capacity by 20 percent; a loss of 4 percent reduces it by 40 percent.

☉ A diet that provides a daily ration of 3,500 calories necessitates an intake of 3.7 quarts (3.5 liters) of water; otherwise, water will be withdrawn from the body's reserves.

# QUESTIONS

☉ *If no water is available but there is plenty of food, should one eat?* No. The digestion of food consumes water.

☉ *Can one drink seawater, and in what amounts?* Yes, but very specific rules must be observed (see "The Sea and Shipwrecks").

☉ *Should one drink until satiated, or in smaller, more frequent amounts?* In smaller more frequent amounts, because the liquid can be utilized more efficiently that way.

☉ *Can one drink urine?* Yes.

The answers to these typical questions on survival are obvious once one understands what thirst is, and what physiological mechanisms activate it.

# PHYSIOLOGY OF THIRST AND ITS IMPLICATIONS FOR SURVIVAL

Life is born in water and water is indispensable to the maintenance of life. An organism can fast for several weeks but a lack of water can cause very severe problems after 48 hours.

Thirst is a specific state of alertness of the central nervous system. Stated more precisely, thirst is an alarm signal, sent by specific peripheral receptors to the hypothalamus, which controls all the reactions necessary for bodily equilibrium.

Thirst is the result of a deficiency of water and minerals caused by:

■ renal excretion, which is needed to eliminate waste and which cannot occur without also eliminating water
■ urea
■ pulmonary evaporation, its sig-

nificance increasing as the air becomes dryer and the respiratory rate greater
■ above all, sweating, which increases significantly in a hot climate or during intense physical exercise

Water is distributed between two sectors:

■ the extracellular sector, i.e., the blood that transports all the nutritive elements needed by cells; and
■ the intracellular sector

Both zones are present in every organ, and the passage from one to the other occurs through the interplay of the cellular membranes' differential permeabilities to sodium and potassium ions. The concentration of these ions on one side or the other determines osmotic pressure. This osmotic pressure, in its turn, controls the circulation of water between the two sectors, and the constant objective is to have a fixed distribution of water on both sides. For example, if a person who is normally in equilibrium is subjected to a water fast, there will be a gradual decrease of water in his blood and thus an increase in osmotic pressure due to the ions that are still there. The cells that still have a normal equilibrium between their ions and the intracellular water will let the water escape to the extracellular sector, always attempting to maintain

an equal amount of water on both sides. This results in intracellular dehydration, secondary to the blood dehydration. It is this dehydration mechanism that leads to the death of cells and then to the death of the organism.

On the other hand, if an individual only drinks water but does not eat, the osmotic pressure in the blood will decrease, followed by that in the cells, as the water in the blood passes to the interior of the cells. In an extreme case, cell destruction occurs (this is what happens to a freshwater drowning victim, because the red blood corpuscles, swollen by the water, burst).

Another example would be eating a meal of solid food, which necessarily contains mineral salts. If an individual does not drink, there will be increase in salt ions and thus an osmotic overload in the blood. This disequilibrium in distribution is temporary and not serious if it is compensated with water. In the opposite case, the disequilibrium will reach the cellular sector.

In a survival situation, **if an individual has nothing to drink, he must not eat,** since this will only aggravate thirst and, above all, dehydration.

There are two kinds of thirst:

■ Hypovolemic thirst, due to a decrease in the volume of water in the blood plasma. This is "extracellular thirst."

■ Osmotic thirst, due to an increase in osmotic pressure in the plasma. This disequilibrium leads to the dehydration of the cells: this is "intracellular thirst."

If there is no intake at all of food or water, the two types of thirst combine, and only when intake is irregular can one or the other can get the upper hand. In heat, since dehydration is accompanied by a loss of sodium chloride, thirst will not be relieved unless there is a simultaneous intake of water and electrolytes.

## THE LEVEL OF PERCEPTION OF THIRST

Thirst is experienced through a dry sensation in the mouth and a constriction of the pharynx, the glottis and the tongue.

The body makes use of volemic receptors and osmoreceptors, the latter located in the hypothalamus. The feeling of thirst comes from stimuli transmitted by specific receptors as soon as there is a

drop in blood volume. Thereupon the hypothalamus commands the pituitary gland to secrete an anti-diuretic hormone which halts all additional renal loss.

## HOW MUCH WATER TO DRINK

The amount of water an individual drank while water was still freely available will become ever more important as the length of privation increases. Does this mean that one should run the risk of drinking more than necessary and thus waste precious reserves? The answer is no, because everything is precisely controlled by the activity of the physiological regulators. Satiation occurs at the exact point of excess, beyond which the water is directly eliminated in the urine. Up to the point when an individual is completely rehydrated, water—even if drunk in large quantities and within a short time—will not cause a watery urine output. Beyond that point, water is eliminated with urine.

## LIMITS OF THE BODY'S TOLERANCE WITHOUT WATER

| AVERAGE TEMPERATURE OF AIR | AVERAGE LENGTH OF SURVIVAL |
|---|---|
| 89.6°F (32°C) | 3 days |
| 78.8°F (26°C) | 4 days |
| 69.8°F (21°C) | 6 days |
| 59°F (15°C) | 17 days |

As the table on p. 44 indicates, the length of survival is extended at a rate equal to the decrease in temperature. This justifies certain actions that are not necessarily obvious a priori. For example, in hot climates stay still in the shade during the day; only travel at night in the desert; and bathe in the sea frequently if you are shipwrecked in a hot region.

## THE APPROPRIATE USE OF SALT

After World War II, the use of salt tablets became widespread among oil workers in desert regions. As conditions improved, these men increasingly lived normal lives inside air-conditioned units. Proper, balanced nutrition was available to them, and therefore intake of additional salt became pointless. This supplement is not justified except when there is profuse sweating and the water intake is not accompanied by an adequate diet. An example of this would be a prospector who takes off for a day in the desert in an all-terrain, non-air-conditioned vehicle with a jerry-can of water but no special food.

Many people continue to cling to the idea that no one can live or travel in the desert, even in air-conditioning, without salt tablets. Every situation is unique, and an individual should be able to evaluate it according to his water losses, food intake, and needs; but he must remember that every gram of sodium chloride implies an additional intake of 70 ml of water (i.e., 1 liter per 14 g of salt, or 1 quart per 0.49 ounce). This is why some drinks rich in minerals will only quench thirst for a short while, and a larger quantity of them is necessary to provide the same benefit as smaller amounts of plain water. Salt should never be taken unless at least 1 liter (1 quart) of water per gram (0.03 ounce) of salt is available.

# WATER IN SURVIVAL SITUATIONS

We will not deal with methods of finding water here, since this problem is dealt with separately for each environment. We will only point out features that could be dangerous in some sources. The official standards of the World Health Organization specify that water is considered to be drinkable if it is fresh, limpid, clear, odorless, sufficiently aerated, slightly salted, and contains no toxic substances or microbes. Water with all these qualities is seldom found in a survival situation, and one has to make do with what one finds. However, certain elementary precautions must be taken.

## WATER FROM MELTED SNOW OR ICE

This can cause cramps and digestive problems because it is almost totally devoid of mineral salts. Therefore it should be accompanied by an intake of food or salt.

The ice or snow should be melted not in the mouth, but between the body and hands, into a container. Apart from significant local cooling, the presence of frozen water in the mouth can cause diarrhea, which could aggravate potential dehydration.

## SEAWATER

This is a very hypertonic fluid (its concentration of mineral salts is much higher than that of blood), which, by simple ingestion, would be enough to cause osmotic thirst in a normally hydrated individual. Therefore it should not be drunk except to "extend" significant, very hypotonic water reserves, and very specific rules must be followed (see "The Sea and Shipwrecks").

## URINE

As the intake of liquids decreases, urine becomes more concentrated and darker in color and acquires an ever greater osmotic pressure, which, however, remains lower than that of blood. This "recycling of waste" can therefore be used if no other source is available, with two qual-ifications: It must be drunk infrequently, because the approximately 0.7 ounce of urea per quart (20 grams per liter) of urine cannot be eliminated indefinitely without damage to the kidneys. And, urine must never be stored, because nitrites form quickly in it when exposed to air, and they are toxic if ingested.

## CLEANLINESS OF WATER

Any water of questionable cleanliness should be disinfected by filtration, boiling, or the addition of hypochlorite.

## COLD OR HOT?

Cool water is more thirst-quenching than hot, but it is not more effective from the point of view of hydration. Therefore, temperature makes no real difference. Naturally something very hot would be beneficial for a mountain climber stuck in a blizzard on the mountain: It would both rehydrate and warm him.

## QUALITY OF HYDRIC INTAKE

Water is the one and only drink that is truly indispensable. All others may be more agreeable or easier to absorb, but this is always to the detriment of the hydration-volume relation of the drink. For example, wine contains 80 percent water, which might seem like a significant hydric intake. But it also contains tannins, traces of sugars and salts, and, above all, alcohol, which gives it a caloric value of 560 per liter—calories which, in their turn, make an intake of 500 cm³ of water necessary. Therefore it is not a "neutral" drink and is particularly detrimental to hydration in a hot region.

There are two liquids of particular importance for survival because they are easy to transport and use, and also have certain bracing properties:

■ Coffee, the principal element of which is caffeine, is a stimulant. This can temporarily help to increase readiness for prompt physical action. But this action must not require precise movements, because caffeine also causes muscular trembling. This artificial hyperflexia does not affect ordinary muscular reflexes (the abuse of caffeine will do no harm during a forced march, for example, but it is incompatible with sharpshooting).

■ Tea basically has the same properties, but they are toned down and therefore tea can be consumed in greater quantities than coffee.

## STORING WATER

Check the color of the water every day, even if it is in a hermetically sealed container. There is always a chance of a proliferation of microscopic algae in water, and the higher the temperature gets, the more quickly this happens. If algae are discovered, the water should be drunk only after being filtered through the finest fabric possible (remember that the proliferation of algae, like that of other microorganisms, doubles every 18°F [10°C]).

# WAYS TO ENDURE THIRST BETTER AND LONGER

■ Before crossing a desert, flying across an ocean in a single-engine plane, or marching through a jungle without mapped water courses, drink as much water as possible—even beyond the point of satiation. Eat beforehand, but not to excess, so that the process of digestion will not increase the base metabolism too much during the subsequent hours. Refrain from eating fatty substances, which are badly tolerated in hot weather.

■ When suffering from thirst, avoid eating, especially sweet foods. One should, however, note that some fresh foods may contain a significant quantity of so-called endogenous water: For instance, mushrooms contain up to 90 percent. Consuming such foods is obviously better than eating dry biscuits. Still, **if one has nothing to drink, one should not eat.**

■ Decrease all water losses as much as possible, particularly those that are significant yet controllable, such as loss through sweating. In a hot sea, swimming and wearing wet clothes will help a person keep cool. (See chapters on "Heat," "The Sea and Shipwrecks" and "The Desert.")

## SHOULD WATER BE RATIONED?

If the supply of fresh water is limited, with no other source available, rationing will certainly prolong the length of survival; but discomfort will start on the first day, and the individual will continue to feel thirsty. In the case of shipwreck, the supply of fresh water should be made to last as long as possible by alternating it with sea water, or by drinking it following five to seven days of drinking only seawater. Refer to the diagrams in the chapter on "The Sea and Shipwrecks."

# PHYSICAL EXERTION

- Sources of Energy During Physical Exertion

- Physical Training

- Sports, Beneficial and Otherwise

- Sleep and Survival

Many survival situations require physical exertion at some point, and the ability to provide this exertion may make all the difference. Therefore it is imperative to stay in peak physical shape, especially if one intends to lead a life of adventure. Training—we emphasize its importance in almost every chapter—can be acquired through sports. Sports build up the muscles and the heart and they also induce the "vascular gymnastics" that are beneficial for thermal adaptation to both heat and cold.

Sports accelerate and develop the physiological mechanisms that all normal organisms need to maintain homeostasis. Keeping this in mind, we will define what can reasonably be considered true sports as opposed to all the activities that are called sports but are really only activities that require some conditioning.

## SOURCES OF ENERGY DURING PHYSICAL EXERTION

The fuel for all muscular contraction, as well as all cellular activity, is ATP (adenosine triphosphate). ATP is produced chiefly from carbohydrates and also from lipids and proteins. There are two methods of energy supply, distinguished by whether they require oxygen or not: Those that use oxygen are called aerobic and those that do not use oxygen are anaerobic. Direct use of oxygen is ideal, but the use of oxygen in any function requires a certain amount of time to set the energy in motion. Some kinds of immediate or sudden physical exertion are anaerobic: ducking a karate chop, sprinting a short distance, lifting a heavy load—any reflex action to save the organism from immediate physical danger. It is obvious that such physical actions are limited to a few seconds' duration.

On the other hand, muscular endurance activities—activities that last some time—are aerobic. They require oxygen intake by the cells in order to restore the supply of ATP necessary to continue the exertion: cross-country skiing, hiking through the jungle, climbing a high mountain, scuba diving.

The functions of these different energy-supply methods are summarized in the table below. They are linked to the two different types of muscle fiber.

■ *Type I fibers*, which contract slowly, give a red color to the muscles in which they predominate. The color comes from myoglobin, a red pigment that receives oxygen supplied by the blood. These fibers are used in prolonged exertion and need an abundant supply of oxygen. Therefore they

## SOURCES OF ENERGY IN DIFFERENT TYPES OF EXERTION

| FUNCTION | FUEL PROVIDING ATP | REPOSITORY | RESPONSE TIME | POSSIBLE DURATION | TYPES OF EXERTION | LIMITING FACTOR | TYPE OF MUSCLES |
|---|---|---|---|---|---|---|---|
| Anaerobic (without O₂) or during resistance | Phosphagen  Phosphocreatine | Muscle cell | Immediate | Maximum of 10 seconds | - Sprint (100 meters)  - Close combat | Exhaustion of immediately available reserves | Muscles rich in so-called rapid fibers (Type II) |
|  | Glycogen  Carbohydrate | Muscle cell | 15 seconds (maximum effect after 40 seconds) | 2 to 4 minutes | - 400 meters in 45 seconds  - A brawl  - Prolonged retention of breath under water | Accumulation of lactic acid |  |
| Aerobic (with O₂) or during endurance | Glycogen | Muscles Liver |  |  |  |  | Muscles rich in so-called slow fibers (Type I) that are highly vascularized |
|  | Fatty acids | Subcutaneous fat and blood lipids | Several minutes (maximum effect after 3 minutes) | Several hours | - Forced march  - Marathon  - Cross-country skiing | - Lack of oxygen  - Exhaustion of nutrients (glucose, fatty acids)  - Cardiac exhaustion |  |
|  | Amino acids | Blood proteins |  |  |  |  |  |

are richly vascularized and are abundant in enzyme systems (mitochondria), which permit the aerobic combustion of food.

■ *Type II fibers,* which contract rapidly, are, in contrast, not very vascularized (giving a paler color to the muscles), and are used for metabolism without oxygen. These fibers are for sudden and brief exertion.

Every muscle contains both types of fiber, but to a greater or lesser degree depending on its normal physiological function. Training can favor one of the two types: for example, a karate expert will be much faster and more effective if he builds up the Fiber II in his limbs and muscle attachments. Indeed, if there is any single area where one can say that the function creates the organ, it is that of muscle-oriented training: The muscles of the lower limbs of high-jumpers, for example, are rich in Fiber II, and the quadriceps of marathon runners are rich in Fiber I.

The two methods of energy supply often overlap in practice. This is how the organism finds its second wind during a long forced march: The exertion stops being laborious because there is perfect equilibrium between the oxygen demand and its supply to the muscles. There is no "oxygen debt"—unless one increases the speed of the march and thus exceeds what is called "VO$_2$ Max," i.e., the maximum consumption of oxygen (this naturally depends on the individual's lung, heart, and muscle capacity). If this increased exertion is sustained for too long, oxygen debt becomes significant, the heart and lungs become exhausted, and activity must stop.

On the other hand, if one suddenly has to climb over several obstacles during the march, one will utilize the muscle group with rapidly contracting Type II fibers, which are accustomed to functioning without oxygen for several seconds, and the overall rhythm of the march will not be affected, as long as it does not take too long to surmount the obstacles.

## PHYSICAL TRAINING

Sometimes survival depends on the effectiveness of the rapid muscles. This applies especially to stuntmen, who must have self-control and good reflexes and must be capable of extremely intense short-term exertion—for example, in order to escape from a burning car within a matter of seconds before the exit is blocked. Endurance training is always necessary for this type of "adventurer," but it must be combined with resistance training that involves rapid anaerobic fibers, such as combat sports and squash.

Endurance is the key to survival in many situations. This means that it will be easier to survive if one has regularly engaged in a sport. Jogging is particularly appropriate because it has the advantage that it can be done anywhere and in any weather, and it requires no special equipment other than a pair of suitable shoes. Endurance training provides many benefits:

- quick improvement of physical performance, easily and objectively measurable with a stopwatch
- significant slowing down of the heart rate, which generally drops from 70 to 50 beats per minute after a few months of normal training (for example, three or four jogging sessions per week, each 5 to 6 miles, or 8 to 10 kilometers, long); the enormous importance of decreasing the wear on the heart to such an extent cannot be overemphasized
- increase of self-control by decreasing the sympathetic tonus (partial muscle contraction) associated with stress in favor of parasympathetic tonus
- decrease in the tendency to get tired and in the amount of sleep required

It is never too late for a healthy person to start a physical training program. Even where improvement is quick, exercise should be performed regularly. For example, a person should jog for at least 90 minutes every week (divided into one, two, or three sessions) to maintain conditioning. When training stops, performance diminishes quickly. If training is totally cut off for three months, all improvement will be lost and one will have to start from scratch. Indeed, sometimes people leave on an expedition after neglecting physical training in order to organize the expedition. They rely on the peak condition they used to have—and this is a serious mistake.

## SPORTS, BENEFICIAL AND OTHERWISE

An activity is a sport if it builds up muscles, primarily those of the heart, the only muscle on which the life of the organism and the functioning of all the other muscles depends. By this definition, certain activities deserve to be called sports and others do not.

For example, there is no reason to call golf a sport for a 35-year-old adult. Like clay pigeon shooting and archery, it is an activity that, although it may require some physical conditioning, does not develop it. Relaxation, good respiration, and harmonious groups of muscles—all important in golf—have to be acquired by practicing another activity, one based on muscular endurance.

Other activities, such as hunting or fishing, are beneficial because of the relaxation they provide, but they are not sports for an adult under 50 years of age, even if they entail walking 9 to 12 miles (15 to 20 kilometers) every Sunday. One should not confuse games with sports, meditation in the fresh air with action, passive oxygenation with intense muscular exercise, or pleasant companionship with vigorous team sports.

Some activities make a greater claim to being called sports because they involve a certain amount of risk: deep-sea diving, sky-diving, aerobatics and automobile racing, for example. But these are not sports either, because participation does not require top physical conditioning.

In sum, any potential member of a dangerous expedition must ensure excellent physical fitness through endurance training that uses the largest number of muscles, such as rowing, swimming, cycling and jogging.

## SLEEP AND SURVIVAL

Sleep, necessary at all times, takes on even greater importance where survival depends on extreme physical demands. But many life-threatening situations inhibit or prohibit one from sleeping; due to discomfort, pain, anxiety, or the necessity to be wary or on guard. Experiments have been done with solo navigators who were required to keep a "sleep log." The results are important not only for sailors, but for everyone who is unable to sleep normally in a survival situation.

■ The best way to sleep is to break up the period of sleep. It is better to have three 20-minute naps than to sleep for one hour.
■ The minimum length of time needed in order to be refreshed by sleep is only 10 minutes. This very short period is necessary, but sufficient.
■ The length of time spent sleeping can be reduced to two hours per 24 hours without impairing one's vigilance, as long as the two hours are taken in short naps.

There is a reciprocal relationship between sleep and physical exertion: Minimal daily sleep is certainly necessary for sustained physical exertion or for skilled activities, which become impossible in the long term if the individual experiences insuperable drowsiness. At the same time, physical exertion affects sleep in two ways:

■ It eliminates residual sleepiness after one has had enough sleep (try running at dawn before taking your shower, and you will see the difference!).

■ It considerably reduces the amount of sleep necessary to recuperate.

# S H A R K S

- True Tales of Survival

- Facts

- Myths

- General Comments

- How the Shark Locates its Food

- Is There Any Protection Against Sharks?

- "Anti-Shark" Equipment

Why should a special chapter be dedicated to sharks when there are so many other species dangerous to man? Simply because—in contrast to terrestrial species that have all been exterminated or are in restricted areas—the population of Squalidae has never decreased, and they have a vast habitat, stretching from great ocean depths to the surface, from reefs to the open seas, from Greenland to Tasmania, and from estuaries to some lakes in America. In other words, this formidable predator is everywhere.

We will neither excessively dramatize the dangers nor accept the assurances of armchair adventures that sharks are not dangerous if one knows how to handle them. Claiming that one can sweet-talk such fearsome predators —which can grow to a length of 10 yards (9 meters) but have a brain that is hardly bigger than an orange—in a marine element that is not man's, is self-deception of a dangerous kind.

---

# TRUE TALES OF SURVIVAL

### Christian Troebst recounts:

"During the war, an American pilot crashed into the sea with two other airmen close to the coast of South America. After five hours, one of the two died of exhaustion; the pilot started to swim, pushing the corpse ahead of him. Suddenly, something jostled the corpse which disappeared permanently beneath the water. The survivor continued to swim through the night; but some hours later the second airman died. The pilot again started to push the corpse ahead of him. Meanwhile, the moon had risen and the light enabled him to distinguish the dorsal fins of a large number of sharks circling around him. Once again a jolt shook the corpse, which sank beneath the water for a moment, then bobbed to the surface again, without any feet. Horrified, the swimmer turned it around and grasped the shoulders. Immediately the corpse was pulled down for a second time, reappeared, and went under again. The sharks ate it bit by bit right to the shoulders. At dawn they began to attack the pilot, who was by this time very close to the shore. He started to shout and slap the water frantically and succeeded in climbing onto the shore unhurt."

An American sailor, whose destroyer sank in the open sea off Guadalcanal, testifies: "I had been drifting for 12 hours when suddenly my left foot began to itch. I lifted it above the water: blood was streaming from it. I put my head under water and saw the shark charging at me. I thrashed about wildly with my arms and legs; it came close, and brushed against me. Then it turned sharply on itself and came straight at me. I made a fist and struck it as hard as I could on its jaw. It drew back—but not before it tore a strip from my right hand. It attacked again, and I hammered away at its eyes and nose. When it moved away I discovered that it had slashed my left arm. My heel was also gone. At that moment a lifeboat approached. I began to signal it by waving my arms wildly, and forgot about the shark. It tore a strip from my hip, baring it to the bone. Then I was pulled into the boat."

These two impressive stories illustrate several important points: the serious danger encountered by shipwrecked people on the open sea; the sharks' attraction to injuries, and the precision of their attacks by night and day; the relative painlessness in the water of the torn-off flesh; and the effectiveness of some measures in making sharks beat a temporary retreat.

## FACTS

✪ Only about a dozen of the 250 varieties of sharks are officially included in the "man-eating" group.

✪ In August 1960, after a ship had capsized at the mouth of the Komati River on the Mozambique coast, a group of sharks mutilated 46 of the 49 survivors.

✪ All sharks can go for at least six weeks without eating; the record is 15 months.

## MYTHS

✪ *The most dangerous sharks are the largest:* Not true. The largest is the whale shark (up to 49 feet [15 meters] and 13 tons), which is absolutely harmless and feeds on plankton and small fishes. Yet a shark that is only 6 feet (1.8 meters) long—the tiger shark—can dismember a man in the blink of an eye.

✪ *Sharks are very tough:* Not so. They are dangerous, but they are very delicate and can be hurt with a direct hit.

# GENERAL COMMENTS

Sharks are fish that have not changed much since they first appeared about 400 million years ago. They have merely decreased in size, as is demonstrated by fossil teeth that are identical to those of the present white shark, but are 6 inches (15 centimeters) long. We can conclude from fossils that the ancestor of the most fearsome of the "man-eaters" must have been about 65.5 feet [20 meters] long.

Throughout history man has suffered from their attacks—the oldest known account of such an event is on a vase dating back to 725 B.C., found on the island of Ischia off Naples. Vasco de Gama, the 15th-century explorer, describes the teeth of "a terrible species" and the tendency of these sea monsters to devour a whole man at sea.

Some knowledge of the shark's anatomy and behavior is useful in understanding effective preventive measures.

There are about 20 families of sharks, the most important for our purposes being the "requiem sharks," which includes about 60 species. The name tells the story: This is the family of sharks that is known to attack humans.

Generally speaking, a shark is defined through five characteristics: a slender, very hydrodynamic shape; five to seven pairs of gills; a skin like sandpaper; a cartilaginous skeleton with jaws and teeth; and, finally, various numbers of pairs of fins. These points differentiate them from other fish with cartilaginous skeletons, such as skates, rays and lampreys.

Their internal anatomy is unique to their species as well: a very short intestine, a very large stomach and an enormous liver that enables the shark to regulate its buoyancy. The organs are not held in place with ligaments, as in most animals, but are loose in the abdominal cavity. This latter feature makes it a relatively fragile creature that is sensitive to impacts.

The arrangement of the shark's teeth is unique in the animal kingdom. Up to five sets of reserve teeth sit behind the set currently being used. Some are covered with a membrane in the mouth. If one or several of the teeth from the operational row are lost, broken, or torn out, the corresponding tooth or teeth of the next row rise up and become operational in their turn.

The teeth are attached to a very solid fibrous tissue, which allows them to stand erect when the shark opens its mouth. The movement turns them forward and outward, enabling the shark to bite hard and to hook what it bites. Each of these teeth is itself made up of smaller teeth, which make it resemble a saw, and the tooth's

## SHARKS REPUTED TO BE DANGEROUS

| SILHOUETTE | NAME | COLOR | SIZE, WEIGHT | HABITAT | CHARAC-TERISTICS | TEETH |
|---|---|---|---|---|---|---|
| | Great white shark | Gray-blue, white ventral surface | Up to 19.7 feet (6 meters) | All the oceans South Africa North and South America Australia New Zealand | The most dangerous of all marine predators | |
| | Common hammerhead shark | Olive-gray, white ventral surface | Up to 19.7 feet (6 meters) | All the oceans Tropical and subtropical waters | Head flattened, in the shape of a hammer | |
| | Mako shark | Dark blue, creamy white ventral surface | Up to 13 feet (4 meters) and 1,050 pounds | All the oceans, particularly the warm ones | Crescent-shaped tail. Very fast swimmer. Sometimes leaps out of the water | |
| | Tiger shark | Gray-blue with darker stripes, white ventral surface | Up to 19.7 feet (6 meters) and 1,550 pounds | The whole world Tropical and subtropical waters | Often close to the coastline | |

| | Name | Coloration | Size | Range | Characteristics | |
|---|---|---|---|---|---|---|
| | Bull shark, Zambesi shark, Lake Titicaca shark | Gray back, white ventral surface | Up to 9.8 feet (3 meters) | The most wide-ranging of all: everywhere, in all waters | Loves shallow waters, and often swims far up rivers | |
| | Blue shark | Characteristic bright blue back, white ventral surface | Up to 13 feet (4 meters), 500 pounds | All temperate and tropical seas Very wide-ranging on the high seas | Impervious to pain. Eats everything (boots, wood, swimmers) | |
| | Lemon shark (Thresher) | Generally yellow-brown back, white ventral surface | Up to 11 feet (3.3 meters) | West Atlantic South Pacific Indian Ocean Very common in the Caribbean | Very elongated caudal fin | |
| | Gray nurse shark | Gray-green, light ventral surface | Up to 13 feet (4 meters) | Atlantic East Pacific | Whiskers in front of the nostrils. Skin that is soft to the touch. Dorsal fins of equal length | |

backward slant when the mouth closes makes it work like a fish hook. This gives some idea why a shark is capable of inflicting severe or even fatal injuries.

Even after the creature is dead, there is still a potential danger, and one has to be very careful. Even when the jaw is cut and the muscles around it are severed, there is a danger that the jaw will abruptly snap shut when the fibrous joints contract—a significant problem for a man who does not remove his hand or arm fast enough. This kind of accident isn't uncommon.

For the same reason, it is best too wait until the following day before removing a hook from a shark's mouth. Apparent death in this primitive creature is often nothing but a sham; it may come to life even several hours after it has been taken out of the water.

Sharks do not have air bladders. This makes them heavier than water and forces them to swim constantly, both to avoid sinking and to ensure that a constant stream of oxygenated water passes through their gills. Some species have a vent behind each eye, which makes this method of oxygenation unnecessary. The latter can stay immobile on the sea bed, waiting for their prey to pass by, rather than constantly hunting. The carpet shark found in Australia and New Guinea is a good example: It remains nestled on the sea bed all day, blending in with its surroundings so well that one can step on its back in the shallows (in which case it sometimes reacts violently).

Compared to the very sedentary carpet shark, most sharks are true vagabonds. Some swim up to 35,000 miles (56,000 kilometers) a year. Some species change their color when they migrate—the bull shark, for example, which has the additional peculiarity of venturing into fresh water and swimming upstream to various lakes (Lake Zambezi in Africa, Lake Nicaragua in southern Nicaragua). Its color, usually light or dark gray with a white underside, turns a uniform light brown in fresh water, as if to enable it to move undetected through muddy waters. Some of these sharks spend the rest of their lives in the lakes they come to. If they do, they lose their "pilot fish" and sucking fish, which can only survive in salt water. But this does not prevent them from returning to the high seas, since the small companion fish are of no practical use to them, even though the sucking fish remove shrimp that live as parasites on their host's skin. Since these sharks, too, are aggressive toward man, they can spread mayhem even inland.

Sharks reproduce in three different ways, depending on the species: through a primitive oviparous tube; after letting their eggs mature inside the genital passages; or, like mammals, through placental gestation, which lasts about a year. At the end of the gestation period, the females withdraw far from the males into areas where they totally stop feeding. During this time, the males, who had done the same during the long period of fertilization, make up for lost time. This might be the reason for certain "periods of attack," such as the two weeks in 1916 on the New Jersey coast, during which time five victims were taken, one after another.

The enemies of these kings of the sea are killer whales, giant squid, and the saltwater crocodiles of Micronesia. Dolphins are also fearsome enemies who do not think twice about charging the sharks at top speed and puncturing their abdomen or gills with their sharp snouts. The two species do not get along well together, and sharks seldom stay in waters frequented by dolphins. The last enemy, which is much more modest in size but very effective, is the porcupine fish or moonfish, which suffocates any shark that tries to swallow it.

# HOW THE SHARK LOCATES ITS FOOD

Sharks are very effective in locating food, aided by sensory organs that are exceptionally sensitive. As a result, these creatures are perfectly adapted to their environment. As they approach their goal, an increasing number of sensory organs come into play to hone in on the location and nature of potential food.

## HEARING

The hearing of the sharks is acute, which is not surprising, since sound travels very quickly and very far in water before it loses its intensity. Sharks are especially attracted to low-frequency sound.

## SENSE OF SMELL

Second to hearing is the sense of smell, which extends to a distance of about 1,640 feet (500 meters). The nostrils do not open into the mouth, as in frogs, but are located behind the Schneider folds in such a way that the act of swimming creates a constant flow of water across the sensory cells inside the nasal cavity.

The shark's nostrils function independently (like our ears), and the animal orients itself toward the side where the sensory influx is strongest. This method of determining direction is reinforced by a horizontal balancing movement of the shark's head while

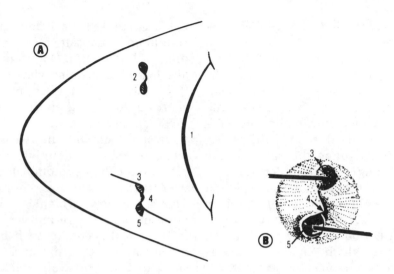

The special placement of a shark's nostrils,
enabling it to detect scent from a great distance

(A) 1. Mouth   2. Nostrils   3. Orifice for the entering current   4. Nose wings   5. Orifice
for the exiting current. The shark's forward movement causes the water to enter
through the entry orifice of the nostril; it then passes through the nasal pocket and
exits through the exit orifice. (B) Inside the nasal pocket there are numerous folds,
which appreciably increase the number of olfactory receptors exposed to the odors
transported by the water.

it is swimming; this enables the nostrils to test a broader scent stream. The sensitivity of this organ is impressive: A shark can detect one part of mammalian blood per 100 million parts of water.

When a shark is swimming, it is constantly picking up smells, some of which provoke it to hunt. Blood is not the only smell to do this; a shark is also attracted by the smell of secretions released by frightened fish. This was demonstrated in 1960 by Albert Tester in Hawaii. He placed uninjured fish of the same species into two containers. Then he caused panic in the second container by shouting and hitting the wall with a stick. He siphoned the water from the first container into a pool of sharks, but the sharks showed almost no reaction; on the other hand, the water from the second container with the panicked fish instantly caused intense hunting activity, and some of the sharks went so far as to bite the exit tube from the siphon.

One thing to remember from this experiment is that a shark will certainly "taste" any object that releases an interesting odor;

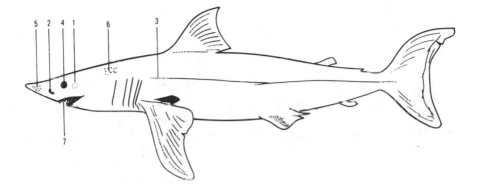

| SENSORY ORGANS | SENSITIVITY |
|---|---|
| 1 Placement of the ear | several miles |
| 2 Nostrils (Schneider folds) | several hundred yards |
| 3 Lateral line ("radar") | several hundred feet |
| 4 Eye | 66 feet (20 meters) |
| 5 The Lorenzini ampullae (pressure gauges) | about 1 foot |
| 6 Sensory crypts | "taste" the surrounding water |
| 7 Mouth | taste on contact |

for example, a dinghy that is leaking blood or vomit from a shipwrecked person.

## THE LATERAL LINE

As the shark closes in on its objective, the "lateral line" provides additional information. It acts as a motion detector, which picks up the slightest current in the water—for instance, a current caused by a panicked fish swimming quickly. It will naturally also detect a current caused by the beating of propellers or by a swimmer's hands on the surface of the water. The sensitive channels running along this line are, in a sense, the shark's radar, since they detect and amplify the vibrations of pressure waves.

## SENSORY CRYPTS

These are also called "pit organs," or neuromasts, and are distributed over the entire surface of the body, especially around the head. These cells are sensitive to variations in salinity, just as human skin contains thermoreceptors that are sensitive to variations in temperature. As an example, a sharp downpour of rain causes a drop in salinity along the coasts due to runoff. This drop attracts the sharks, which feed on the debris of animals washed down by the rivers. In the course of evolution, the shark's genetic code has been enriched by this detector, which has opened up new hunting grounds.

## VISION

A shark cannot see its prey until it is 50 to 65 feet (15 to 20 meters) away. Yet this is less a sensory defect than an adaptation to the environment: There are, in fact, very few regions in the world where visibility in water is greater than 65 feet. In addition, sharks cannot see colors; on the other hand, they can distinguish contrasts very well. The cells in the shark's retina are sensitive to shadow and light. This, too, is a matter of adaptation to the environment: All divers are well aware that red disappears below about 40 feet (12 meters), and that the sea bed becomes lighter and darker shades of a uniform greenish-gray. The shark is able to distinguish an object from its background quite efficiently, particularly if the object is moving.

## THE LORENZINI AMPULAE

A final sensory organ comes into action at close range. These are the "Lorenzini ampulae" and are located on the lower surface of the shark's nose. These small protuberances are sophisticated organs, sensitive to temperature, to differences in pressure, and—at distances of a few inches—to the electric potential of fish. Recent studies have shown that the Lorenzini ampulae also help the shark to find its bearings by detecting the Earth's magnetic field.

The shark does not use all the sensory organs all the time. The animal is unpredictable, often content merely with rough criteria to decide whether to taste or swallow an object that has aroused its curiosity. As a result, cans, rolls of toilet paper, other smaller sharks, a sea lion, turtles, and the carcass of a horse, a lamb, a pig, and even a dog harnessed to a sled have been found in the stomachs of sharks, particularly the great white sharks. When the number of these odds and ends becomes too great, the creature regurgitates them and sets off on its hunting patrols again.

# IS THERE ANY PROTECTION AGAINST SHARKS?

Too many authorities—not always scientific ones—have advanced theories, formulas, and statistics with great conviction, but the danger from sharks is in fact very difficult to guess in advance. Sharks are stupid and unpredictable and thus dangerous; there is no miracle procedure that will offer reliable protection. In fact, the only protection that can be said to be truly effective is a metal cage, but this has nothing to do with the type of survival we are talking about.

It was not until 1959 that the first systematic study of shark attacks was undertaken by the American Institute of Biological Sciences. Dr. Balbridge was a pioneer in the statistical data and collected evidence from all over the world, particularly from Australia and South Africa. The results were, to say the least, disappointing: Less than 50 percent of the sharks that had carried out attacks could be identified. This means that the list of sharks that we are sure are dangerous is radically incomplete. One of the statistics points to the conclusion that the majority of attacks occur less than 490 feet (150 meters) from the shore. Does this mean that "man-eaters" prefer to be close to shore? Certainly not. The simple fact is that the majority of people do not swim out farther than 490 feet.

In other words, this demonstrates the habits of man, not of sharks.

In the same way, Balbridge claimed that there were no attacks below 68°F (20°C). There are two possible reasons for this: The first is that few people like to swim at such a low temperature, and that this is all that the observation says; the second is that, since the shark is a cold-blooded creature, its temperature drops with that of its environment, slowing its metabolism and decreasing its need for food. Both conclusions may be valid, so we should remember that in regions frequented by sharks, even in cold temperatures, there is a dangerous season of the year:

■ from May to October in the northern hemisphere between latitudes 21°N and 42°N
■ from November to April in the southern hemisphere between latitudes 21°S and 42°S

The equatorial region between 21°N and 21°S is always dangerous.

From a purely geographical perspective, troublesome appearances have occurred in other temperate to cold regions, but there have been no known attacks. Therefore, we can assume that in both hemispheres latitudes above 45° are safe.

One theory used to assert that swimming after 1:00 P.M. is dangerous, following the observation that more attacks occur in the afternoon. This pseudo-observation should be rejected, since more people swim in the afternoon than in the morning. In fact, nighttime is most dangerous: 5.4 percent of attacks occurred after 7:00 P.M. although the number of people who swim at night is infinitesimal. Swimming at night in a shark-infested sea is plainly more dangerous. It seems that sharks prefer to hunt between dusk and dawn. This is logical, since a shark's eyesight, mediocre during the day, is even worse at night and if in doubt it will not hesitate to taste anything that moves. The introductory scene of the film *Jaws*, in which a beautiful midnight swimmer off Long Island is ripped apart by the protagonist's great teeth, is not at all unrealistic.

Certain factors can influence the behavior of sharks and these dictate the measures to be taken to avoid provoking them. For example, one should not wear a brightly colored swimsuit. Sharks are sensitive to contrasts of light and dark, and bright colors arouse their curiosity. Therefore the best swimwear is a one-piece, uniformly colored swimsuit that blends in with the surroundings. There is some reason to believe that black diving suits are the safest. Once again, there are exceptions to the rule, depending on the

region: Around California, sharks are in the habit of eating sea lions. A diver in a black suit bears a close resemblance to this creature in color, size, and even in the way he moves. Before diving, one should take care to find out about the habits of the sharks in the pertinent region.

Because of the shark's exceptional ability to detect certain odors, particularly blood, divers should avoid dragging wounded fish through the water, which would attract sharks because of the movement, the smell of blood, and the odor of the substance fish secrete when under stress. Avoid entering the water when injured, even if the injury is minor and is bandaged. Women should not swim in shark habitats while they have their menstrual period, even if they use tampons.

One should avoid swimming after heavy rain, particularly close to the mouth of a river. The danger there will be much greater, since the salinity will have dropped, and the water will be muddy. Murky water provides no protection; if anything it increases the danger, since the shark can use several sensory organs to locate its prey without resorting to vision. On board a boat, do not throw anything overboard, and do not trail your arms or legs in the water.

The world of sharks also has its "renegades," and occasionally one of them decides to live its life

| EXHIBITION | NORMAL |
|---|---|

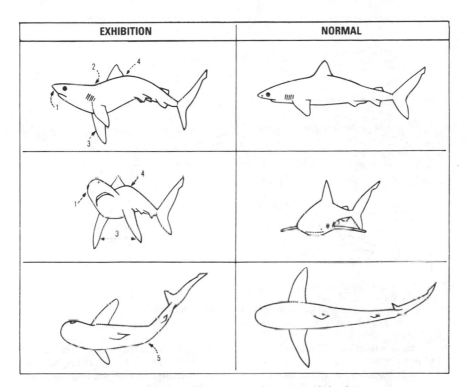

**Comparison of the posture of a gray reef shark's
normal way of swimming and its exhibition swimming**

Meaning of the arrows: 1. Raising of the nose   2. The resulting angle between the chondrocranium and the vertebral column   3. Lowering of the pectoral fins   4. Arching of the back, and   5. Lateral curve of the body.

in a different way than the others. Sometimes there are "old loners" patrolling certain parts of the coasts that they have adopted as their territory. Whether it is due to old age, sickness or some other mysterious motivation, the result is that one of these creatures, which are normally nomadic, may decide to become sedentary. It patrols regularly, inspecting anything that makes a noise, moves, sparkles in the sun or emits an odor. The loner has become a member of a "fringe population," one that does not conform to the normal habits of sharks. Such an isolated individual becomes a potential danger to all swimmers and divers in the area, and may be an explanation for some "attack frenzies."

All contacts with sharks are considered to be attacks in the statistical data if an injury has been sustained. In fact, it seems

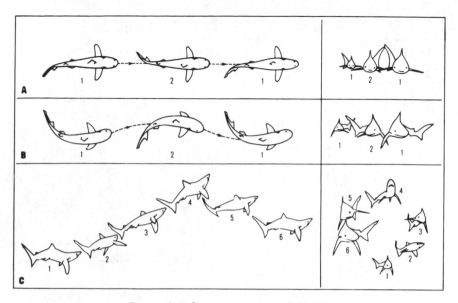

**Comparison between a gray reef shark's
normal swimming and exhibition swimming**

A. Normal swimming  B. Exhibition, with laterally exaggerated movements  C. Exhibition with rolls (1–2–1) and spiral loops (1–6). Although the tumbling is similar to the initial phases of the spiral loops, it can be distinguished by the fact that the shark returns to a horizontal exhibition posture, without following the up and down trajectory of the spiral loops.

The more marked the shark's reluctance to flee, the more exaggerated the exhibition becomes.

that the bites are not always due to hunger, but to curiosity and to the need to identify the object that attracted the shark's attention. Some victims have been seized in the jaws of a shark, shaken in all directions, very seriously injured, and then released. There is no doubt that, however tough a human body may be, it is still not tough enough to prevent a shark's teeth from cutting it in two. This is why Balbridge talks of "intimidation scratches," which a shark sometimes inflicts as if to defend its territory. A shark also may inflict "identification scratches." In fact, many victims have recounted that they were nuzzled before being bitten. It seems that in some cases, if the shark has difficult identifying an object, it can use its Lorenzini organs to help. Since these organs are located beneath the nose, it opens its mouth not to bite, but to get into a better position. As the mouth opens the teeth automatically emerge, and therefore there is a risk of injury even before the shark has decided to bite. The blood that spurts out of this unintended injury can then provoke the fatal attack.

Under water one can gauge the imminence of an attack in many sharks because they perform "exhibition swimming": They arch sharply in a lateral direction, bringing their heads very close to their tails first in one direction and then in the other. The swimming turns into a very characteristic "strut." Various species have even more complex movements, but all of them are very different from the normal fluid, supple and graceful motion of the animal, and a diver need only observe them to be on guard.

## "ANTI-SHARK" EQUIPMENT

Whatever the causes of shark attacks, all protective devices and procedures aim to avoid direct contact. At the outset, we should state that if there is such a thing as an absolutely effective weapon, it has not yet been discovered.

During World War II, the U.S. Army realized that too many pilots who crashed into the sea or people who were shipwrecked died as victims of sharks. Many poisons were tested, including arsenic and hydrocyanic acid. The trouble is that the shark's slow metabolism enables it to bite long before it succumbs to the poison, and the man himself is in danger of being the first to be killed by water contaminated by such strong poisons. High-frequency sound waves were tested, but were ineffective, as were dyes and inks. Then a biologist studied a phenomenon that had been noticed by fishermen in Florida long before: If a shark decayed in their nets, none of its fellow sharks could be found within a radius of several miles. Experiments yielded positive results: A piece of putrefying shark was enough to keep all the sharks from the area, even though sharks often cannibalize the first among them that is mortally wounded.

The miracle substance contained in the putrefying flesh was ammonium acetate, which emits acetic acid into the water. Experiments were successfully conducted off the coast of Florida using an analogous substance, copper acetate. Biologists threw a basket of small fish into the water and the sharks pounced on them greedily; then a second basket was thrown in, which contained copper acetate; during the next few seconds, the sharks beat a hasty retreat, and they circled the boat at a respectful distance but never touched it. These experiments were corroborated by others scientists in Australia, and from then on, Allied sailors and pilots were equipped with packets of "shark chasers" combining nigrosine dye with an acetate base. These packets allowed a mixture of ink and acetate to filter out very slowly, over several hours, around the floating potential victim.

Even though their effectiveness is not absolute, the packets should be included in all survival kits in civilian lifeboats. The original enthusiasm was, in fact, somewhat tempered during the 1950s when it was realized that especially aggressive species (for instance, the great white shark) were not particularly impressed by the shark chaser, and that the repellent was less effective in regions of the world where sharks are generally more aggressive than elsewhere. Two hundred different products have been tested, but none of them is effective for all species.

Still, shark repellent should be a part of marine survival equipment. It should be used intelligently, only if one is certain that there is imminent danger, because it can only be used once and lasts only for a few hours.

During the last 15 years or so, offensive methods against sharks have focused on equipment such as, for example, a mini-spear with an explosive head, which has a chamber for a .12-caliber cartridge at its tip. If the tip of the cylinder is pressed between the shark's eyes (for example, when pulling it aboard a boat), the primer is crushed by the hammer, and the projectile shoots straight into the brain of the shark, killing it instantly. The advantage is that there is no loss of force through the water, since it can only be fired in direct contact with the shark. This system has now been perfected with rapid-fire explosive heads for marine use and includes waterproof firing cartridges to eliminate firing problems. Unquestionably, this is the best individual means of defense ever devised, and is particularly useful in survival situations since it is not very bulky and is easy to carry.

Divers have several effective weapons, their use based on shark physiology. The first takes advantage of the fact that a shark's ability to swim depends on a direct relation between the power of its fins (proportional to its size), its weight, and the quantity of oil in its liver. Every species has its own characteristic proportions between these three factors, and if any one of them is disrupted, the shark can no longer maintain its depth.

The use of a little cylinder of carbon dioxide is the foundation for one of the most effective weapons against sharks. The cartridge of $CO_2$ is fixed to the tip of a spear and extended by a large needle. When the shark comes too close, the diver thrusts the needle firmly into any soft part of its body, if possible into its abdomen. Once it has been thrust in, it pushes another, finer, needle into the gas cartridge; the gas quickly enters the creature's body. This additional buoyancy propels the shark straight to the surface, in many cases killing it by causing a gas embolism. The advantage of this instrument is its simplicity and the absence of any mechanism that could jam in seawater. Still, attractive as the method is, it is more difficult to implement than it may appear. Floating anchors, which can be thrust into any part of the shark so as to inhibit its movements, have also been used. The results have been mixed, particularly with large sharks.

Another useful instrument is a 4-inch (10-centimeter)-long needle, connected to a very small battery which puts out 300 volts. This needle is fixed to the tip of a 3-yard (3-meter)-long spear, and detaches itself once it has been thrust into the body of the creature, thus forming a needle-shark-ocean circuit. Depending on the size of the shark, the shock causes either a quick death, or at least paralysis for the length of the life of the battery (10 minutes). In either case, it is long enough for the diver to get away.

There is one other defensive gadget that can be useful because it combines protection against sharks with protection against cold. It is a black plastic sack full of seawater, held at the surface by three inflatable buoys, into which the shipwrecked person can climb. Odors remain inside the sack, as do lost calories. The black color and the lack of obvious movement discourage attention from sharks. The advantage of this Johnson shark bag is its small size before it is used; the disadvantage is its fragility. However, considering its undeniable effectiveness and its light weight, it should be considered by anyone who may be exposed to the dangers of sharks.

Poisons with a strychnine base have been used, but they need at least 30 seconds to take effect and handling them is dangerous. Bulletproof vests are currently available made of Kevlar; they are completely effective against .357-caliber bullets yet are not bulky. Diving suits of the same material could transform injuries that are normally fatal into simple bruises.

Be aware that not every dorsal fin that breaks the surface is necessarily a reason to panic. The fin could belong to a dolphin or a porpoise (which generally leap out of the water, thus quickly removing any doubts), or to a whale, or even to a giant ray (in the latter case there would be two "wing tips" with an unusually synchronous movement). One should also know that—even though water is not our natural element—we can still move faster in it, at least over short distances, than can a large shark, which generally cannot stop suddenly or turn sharply.

**Sensitive areas on a shark that can be hit in order to repel an aggressive individual**

A. Areas that can be hit if one uses a blunt instrument, a knife or a hand (the latter should only be used as a last resort). In order of sensitivity:

1. The eye. In addition to the fact that the eye is very sensitive, one can blind the animal with a well-placed knife-thrust to the eye.

2. The nose. Its sensitivity is due to the concentration of various sensory organs, such as the lateral line, the Lorenzini ampullae, and the sensory crypts.

3. The gills. Their sensitivity is linked to their role in respiration, with a concentration of blood vessels and branchial nerves.

B. Areas that can be hit if one uses an underwater gun or an explosive-tipped weapon (listed in the order of areas one should aim at):

1. Directly downward between the eyes through the chondrocranium to reach the brain. A harpoon gun provides enough force for a harpoon to penetrate the shark's cartilaginous brainpan from 6½ feet (2 meters) away, if it is aimed well. This will immobilize or kill the animal.

2. Diagonally downward, toward the spinal column, the best location is in front: Avoid aiming directly through the thickest skin in the middle of the median dorsal line. A well-placed harpoon can instantly immobilize a shark from a distance of 6½ feet with a single shot, but the spine is much more difficult to reach than the brain.

3. Gills. If a shark is hit in this spot, it will not be immobilized instantly, even if fatally wounded. Remember that a harpoon entering from the front is better than from the side, since it handicaps the shark's ability to swim.

Note: Aiming at a shark is dangerous. It is a little like "catching a tiger by the tail." Unless the animal is instantly immobilized, it will turn against the harpoon, and if this happens, there is a strong probability that the diver will find himself in serious trouble.

(*Requins de Polynésie* ["Sharks of Polynesia"], R. H. Johnson, Editions du Pacifique.)

Sharks usually search for an easy meal, and several hard blows on the nose can make them go away. The danger caused by their lack of intelligence is moderated by their lack of self-confidence. Several punches aimed at its eyes or gills are often enough to make the aggressor flee, pursued by its fellow sharks, which are then attracted by its blood.

# SNAKES

- True Tales of Survival

- Facts

- Myths

- General Comments

- Geographic Distribution

- Identifying Poisonous Snakes

- Snakebite: Physiology and Motivation

- Venom and Its Effects

- Treatment of Snakebites in a Survival Situation

- Prevention of Snakebites

Men and snakes have never been able to live together amicably. Many adventure films feature an evil reptile that ends up decapitated, chopped to bits by a machete, or shot to pieces by a gun belonging to the courageous adventurer. These fictional portrayals of course have very little to do with reality. A snake's caution is matched by its fear, and it will not be aggressive unless it is forced to defend itself. At that point it can be very dangerous to the person who attacks it or even inadvertently surprises it.

The snake has been regarded as mythological, divine, mystical, an element of ritual, a symbol of sexual potency or authority, depending on the epoch and the people; the effect of its bite was first recorded on Egyptian papyrus scrolls in 1600 B.C.

○

# TRUE TALES OF SURVIVAL

## May 23, 1971

Nicole Viloteau is 25 years old. For a long time she has had an unusual passion which has provoked astonishment, sarcasm, and coarse jokes from those who have little patience with unconventional men, and even less with unconventional women. Yet Nicole remains unruffled. She serenely continues to indulge her love for snakes.

On this day, accompanied by two herpetologist colleagues, she is in a truck making an inventory of a delivery of non-native reptiles bundled in poorly labeled sacks. She unties them one by one and examines the animals, which seem half-stupefied by the rigors of the trip and the heat in the truck.

Suddenly, as she opens a sack she believes to contain a harmless snake, a head shoots out and strikes her a hard blow in the face. Before she can figure out what is happening, a snake with a rattle falls into her lap and slithers under the driver's seat.

Within seconds she realizes that it is a dangerous snake, since her lip, punctured by long, venomous fangs, is beginning to burn. She also realizes that she and her colleagues have no serum. She screams in terror, certain that she is going to die. Her two friends, powerless to help, are desperate.

Moments later, Nicole pulls herself together and squeezes her lip, which has already swollen to twice its normal size, as hard as she can. Her fingers slip in the saliva and cannot get a grip on the swollen flesh. She opens the glove compartment, takes out a hunting knife, and, after hesitating for a second, makes a deep incision in her lip. The blood spurts out. The driver, a former paratrooper used to difficult situations, regains his composure, contacts the emergency service by radio, and, with his horn blaring, drives at breakneck speed to the nearest emergency room.

The three friends are not in the tropics but in Burgundy, France. The hospital at Dijon is 25 miles (40 kilometers) away. Nicole vomits, shivers, sweats. She suffers hot flushes, she has problems with her vision, but she remains completely conscious. The driver brakes sharply and the rattlesnake rolls onto his feet; he does not flinch but continues to race through the red lights. A half hour has passed since Nicole was bitten. Suddenly they hear motorcycle sirens clearing the road to the hospital.

Nicole climbs out on her own, staggers, repeatedly dabs at her lip. She explains to the startled intern: "I was bitten by a rattlesnake. My blood will coagulate, my kidneys will shut down, we have no serum, I am going to die."

The bewildered doctor confirms the story with the two friends. A feeling of panic begins to spread. By the time the chief doctor arrives and takes over, the edema has reached Nicole's eyelids, and she can only see through narrow slits. She tells him her blood type before the edema in her lips prevents her from speaking. Fully conscious, she thinks about the fact that she should already be dead or at least in a coma.

She feels everything they do to her: intramuscular injections, perfusions, a nasal tube. Sounds fade into the distance.

They call the poison center at Lyons, but it only has antivenin serum for snakes that live in Europe. In desperation, Nicole's two friends suggest calling a Swiss herpetologist. He does have the serum, but how can he get it to her in time?

At the air base in Dijon, Colonel Archambaut, a fighter pilot, is about to leave on a military mission. He is contacted on Nicole's behalf. The target of his mission becomes Geneva airport, where a Swiss police helicopter has already delivered containers of the antivenin. The colonel's Mirage takes 56 minutes to make the round trip back to the Dijon base. A state police helicopter transports the two vials of serum to the hospital.

Nicole hears the helicopter land; she is clinging to life by a thread. An intramuscular injection of the serum is administered 2 hours and 40 minutes after she was bitten. This is already too late for it to be fully effective and in any case Nicole's body does not tolerate it well. An allergic reaction to the serum is added to the effects of the venom. She is still conscious, but her face is three times its size, and she can no longer see, speak, or breathe normally. She is in danger of suffocating. She feels the knife cutting her throat to reach the trachea beneath 2.75 inches (7 centimeters) of edema. The tracheotomy saves her from suffocating, but she is still in critical condition.

The doctors contact Dr. Raby, who discovered calcium heparinate, an anticoagulant that is indispensable in pathological coagulations. Large doses are injected into the dying woman, who by the following day seems to be bleeding from every pore. The hospital staff is helpless: they do not know what to do. By telephone, Dr. Raby instructs them to increase the doses of anticoagulant. At that time, such therapy seems to be contrary to common sense, since the patient is already hemorrhaging badly.

Considering they have nothing to lose, the doctors follow his advice and increase the heparin dose, despite their skepticism. To everyone's surprise, the hemorrhaging stops completely.

After two months in the hospital, Nicole Viloteau returns to her snakes. Had she been alone, without the medical and logistical facilities of a modern country, she would certainly have died.

---

As we will see at the end of the chapter, this woman's story is a model for what should—and should not—be done in the event of snakebite.

---

## August 1957, Colombia

Douglas Butler, accompanied by Manuel Vargas, has been living in the Colombian jungle for several months. Butler is an American engineer who has been commissioned to make a geodesic survey. Vargas is his guide and companion. After spending two months alone in this suffocating jungle, the two men hate each other, and they would use any pretext to get into a fight. Butler has already finished his coffee, and Vargas still has not come out of his tent. Ready to punch him out, Butler crawls on all fours into the flimsy shelter, but he freezes in his tracks, rooted to the spot by the intensity of his assistant's angry expression. Vargas's eyes look as if they are trying to speak. They angrily stare at the Butler, then look down at the ground several times. Why doesn't he say something? Why is he still in his sleeping bag, since he's awake? These thoughts flash through Butler's mind and then his blood turns to ice: He notices a round, coiled shape on his assistant's stomach under the sleeping bag; it must be a snake, and it is sure to be venomous, judging by his coworker's petrified expression.

How long has Vargas been keeping still? The reptile must have crawled in during the night, seeking warmth. Now it is sleeping; but the slightest movement will wake it, and the slightest vibration will make it bite. Vargas can neither talk nor move. If it is a fer-de-lance, a snake that can grow to 5 feet (1.5 meters), its bite would mean certain death. What should he do? How can he make the beast come out without touching it? Apparently Vargas's left hand is wedged against the snake. Only his right hand is lying motionless outside the sleeping bag.

Butler has an idea. He gets out of the tent as slowly as possible, then crawls back again a moment later armed with his rifle. If he aims at the lump from the side, he will blow away the snake without touching Vargas. But he will have to use a bullet; buckshot would be too dangerous. He takes up his position, then looks at Vargas, seeking approval. This time the angry eyes flash: No, no, not this way. Let's face it, he is in a better position to know where the snake's head is: Against his side? Between his legs? If he fires into the coil, and misses the head, the snake will bite instantly in a reflex reaction. He must try something else, but what?

Butler leaves the tent again. What else will he come up with? Vargas knows the only possible answer, but how can he make Butler understand?

If he speaks, his voice will reverberate in his chest, and even though snakes are deaf, they react to the slightest vibration.

Butler returns with his knife. He starts to cut a corner of the bag at Vargas's feet. Half an hour later, he has finally made a hole without attracting the attention of the snake, which has not moved. He goes out, then returns again with a plastic bag filled with smoke from the fire crackling outside. He places it against the hole in the sleeping bag and gently squeezes it. Vargas understands: Butler is trying to smoke out the snake. He'll never do it. Four times Butler returns, each time closing the hole so that the smoke cannot escape. It begins to come out at the other end of the bag. The last thing Vargas needs is to cough. He knows that it is the dangerous fer-de-lance and that his head is along his right thigh. The animal had slithered over his shoulder into his sleeping bag six hours ago—six hours during which Vargas had not dared to move or to sleep, and had been fighting cramps.

Suddenly, the snake moves. Vargas suppresses a terrible desire to leap up and put an end to this nightmare. But that would be a death sentence. And Butler is back again with his rifle, waiting for the snake to come out. The only problem is that the creature does not want to come out. As soon as the smoke has dissipated, it settles down again. The waiting resumes.

Butler exits the tent again and comes back with an insecticide spray. Vargas's eyes express intense anger at this new idea. Butler presses the spray button against the hole in the bag, and immediately a terrible hiss bursts from the can. He releases the button instantly, but an almost identical hiss issues from the other end of the bag, like an echo. The snake thinks that the hiss is coming from another angry snake, and its watchful head is now raised above Vargas's armpit. Vargas closes his eyes, waiting for the fatal bite. But the head settles down against him again.

Butler feels discouraged, he really does not know what else he can do. As for Vargas, he curses Butler's inability to find a solution. He indicates his right hand with his eyes. His fingers are moving, drawing shapes in the air, which Butler does not understand. And then, suddenly, he has a new idea. He crawls backward out of the tent and returns with the canister of coffee! What's he up to now? Vargas wonders. But this time the idea is good. Very cautiously, Butler spreads a layer of coffee under his assistant's hand. The latter starts to draw something that resembles a circle, moving only his fingers. And then little lines coming out of the circle. Butler takes out his notebook and writes: "The sun?" Vargas's eyes close several times. That's right. The sun .−.−. What is he trying to say?

Finally Butler understands. Why had he not thought of it sooner? He crawls out of the tent, which he proceeds to dismantle as carefully as possible. The operation takes more than half an hour. Luckily the tent has no attached ground sheet! The sleeping bag is now completely in the open, enclosing the petrified Vargas like a shroud. The sun, which is already high, now hits it directly. Douglas gently places his cap over Vargas's eyes. All one can do is wait. Why had he not remembered much earlier that a snake, whose blood temperature varies according to the surroundings, cannot stay motionless in the sun for any length of time? Its body would heat up like a branding iron, and therefore all snakes seek shelter from the heat. Vargas had been trying to make him understand this trick from the start.

Ten o'clock, ten-thirty, the sun beats down on them—it is lucky that their camp is in a clearing. Vargas still looks like a mummy. Ah, there it is, the bag starts to move; it undulates, a protuberance rises near Vargas's neck, and the head appears, triangular and bulbous. It is in fact the deadly fer-de-lance that Butler feared, with its mottled neck and pine-cone-shaped brown scales. There seems to be no end to it as it crawls out of the bag and slides past Vargas's cheek, as he lies there more rigidly than ever. It is well over a yard long. At last it is far enough away for Butler to empty two cartridges of buckshot into it. Vargas has been motionless for 12 hours. Some time later, after he has got rid of the stiffness, and after he has recovered with the help of some coffee, he asks Butler why he killed the snake. Was it to take revenge because he had been afraid?

Since snakes are most often active at night and spontaneously move toward infrared sources, this story ended well, due to the composure of the two men and, above all, to the knowledge that at least one of them had about the biology of reptiles. Composure and knowledge are the two crucial keys to survival.

## FACTS

❂ It is estimated that about 500,000 people are bitten by snakes each year throughout the world; 30,000 to 40,000 die, and more than 50 percent of these deaths are in India.

❂ The longest recorded snake is a 70-year-old reticulated python, which is 32.8 feet (10 meters) long and weighs 341 pounds (155 kilograms). The heaviest is an anaconda from Brazil, which weighed 506 pounds (230 kilograms) and had the diameter of a tree trunk: 43.25 inches (111 centimeters). Though their measurements are impressive, neither of these snakes is venomous.

❂ The longest venomous snake is the king cobra (*Ophiophagus hannah*); one of them, captured in Malaysia, grew to a length of 18.73 feet (5.71 meters) in captivity. The shortest is the dwarf speckled viper (*Bitis paucisquamata*) from southwestern Africa, which grows to 9 inches (23 centimeters) in its adult stage. The heaviest is the diamondback rattlesnake (*Crotalus adamanteus*)

# LIST OF THE MAJOR VENOMOUS SPECIES AND THEIR HABITATS

| ORDER | FAMILY | SPECIES: SCIENTIFIC NAME | COMMON NAME | HABITAT |
|---|---|---|---|---|
| Protero-glypha | Hydrophiidae (sea snakes) | Enhydrina schistosa | Beaked sea snake | Asia (India), Oceania |
| | | Hydrophis cyanocinctus | Blue-banded sea snake | Persian Gulf, New Guinea |
| | | Hydrophis belcheri[1] | — | Timor Sea (Australia) |
| | Elapidae | Bungarus caerulus[1] | Bungarus/Krait | Southeast Asia |
| | | Dendroaspis viridis[3] | Western green mamba | Africa south of the Sahara |
| | | Dendioaspis augusticeps[3] | Eastern green mamba | Eastern Africa |
| | | Hemachatus haemachatus | Ringhals, spitting snake | Southern Africa |
| | | Micrurus carallinus[6] | Coral snake or Harlequin | The Americas |
| | | Naja naja[5] | Asian cobra, Indian cobra, spectacled snake | Africa, India, Southeast Asia, Southern China, Malaysia |
| | | Naja nigricollis | Spitting snake, black-necked cobra | Australia, New Guinea |
| | | Acanthophis antarcticus[4] | Death adder | Australia |
| | | Oxyuranus scutellatus[2] | Taipan | Australia |
| | | Notechis | Tiger snake | Australia |
| | Viperinae (subfamily) | Bitis gabonica | Gaboon viper | Africa |
| | | Cerastes cerastes | Horned viper | Africa |
| | | Cerastes vipera | Sahara horned viper | Africa |
| | | Echis carinatus | Saw-scaled viper, Carpet viper | Chad, North Africa, India |
| | | Echis coloratus | Carpet viper, saw-scaled viper | Negev Desert |
| | | Vipera ammodytes | Sand viper | Europe, Asia |
| | | Vipera aspis[8] | Asp viper | Europe |
| | | Vipera berus | Adder | Europe |
| | | Bitis arietans | Puff adder | Africa |
| | | Vipera latastei | Lataste's viper | Europe, Africa |
| | | Vipera lebetina | Levant viper | Africa, Asia |

| | Scientific name | Common name | Distribution |
|---|---|---|---|
| Soleno-glypha | Vipera russelli[9]<br>Vipera ursinii<br><br>Vipera xanthina | Daboia or Russell's viper<br>Orsini viper, European meadow viper<br>— | Asia except Taiwan<br>Europe, Asia<br><br>Europe, Asia |
| Crotalinae (subfamily) | Agkistrodon contortrix<br>Agkistrodon rhodostoma<br>Eothrops alternatus<br>Eothrops sarabaca<br>Crotalus adamanteus<br><br>Trimeresurus flavoviridis<br>Bothrops atrox[7]<br><br>Crotalus viridis<br>Crotalus horridus[10]<br>Crotalus mutus (Lachesis mutas) | Copperhead<br>Malayan pit viper<br>Urutu<br>Wawaca<br>Eastern diamondback rattlesnake<br>Habu<br>Fer-de-lance viper<br><br>Prairie rattlesnake<br>Timber rattlesnake<br>Bushmaster | North America<br>Asia (Japan)<br>South America<br>South America<br>America<br><br>Asia<br>Mexico, Martinique, South America, Antilles<br>America<br>Eastern United States<br>South America |

1. The most toxic venom: 100 times more potent than that of the Taipan.
2. The most venomous terrestrial snake.
3. The fastest. Fatal in almost all untreated cases. Faster than a man if it is moving through the trees.
4. The death adder is not a viperid but an elapid. Its name is sometimes confused because the triangular shape of its head is characteristic of vipers. It is responsible for the largest number of deaths in Australia.
5. Naja is the scientific name for cobras. The term comes from the Indian word Naga which describes the seven-headed snake of Hindu mythology. The naja naja causes the majority of the deaths per year recorded in India due to ophidians. The pattern, shaped like spectacles on its hood, need not always be present.
6. Though it is lazy and not very aggressive, its venom, which is produced in very small quantities, is extremely toxic. Likes locations that offer a hiding place.
7. The most vicious and dangerous of the Crotalinae subfamily. Mostly nocturnal and it often floats on the surface of rivers and streams.
8. It is this viper, and only this one that has given rise to the erroneous belief that all vipers have snub noses.
9. Very toxic venom, always fatal if untreated, though it takes effect slowly.
10. This rattlesnake never misses its prey, and its terrifying attack is merciless. Rattlesnakes emit a sound from their caudal appendage, made of interlocking horny plaques that vibrate at 60 oscillations per second. There can be as many as 21 of these plaques, which are the remnants of skin lost during each molting period. It emits this sound if it is disturbed or attacked.

from the southeastern United States: 33 pounds (15 kilograms) and a length of 7.75 feet (2.36 meters).

☻ Snakes can survive very long periods of fasting provided they have water. The record in captivity is four years with a weight loss of only 50 percent. Their average life span is 20 years.

☻ One gram of cobra (also called naja) venom can kill 2,640 pounds (1,200 kilograms) of dogs, 17,600 pounds (8,000 kilograms) of mice and 22,000 pounds (10,000 kilograms) of humans.

## MYTHS

☻ *The longest and largest snakes are the most venomous:* In fact, the longest, the reticulated python, and the heaviest, the anaconda, are not venomous.

☻ *Snakes are exclusively terrestrial animals:* Not so. The most dangerous of all snakes, the *Hydrophis belcheri*, lives in the Timor Sea north of Australia and its venom is 100 times more potent than that of the Australian Taipan, a terrestrial snake, whose venom glands contain enough to kill 125,000 mice.

☻ *Small snakes have jaws that are too small to bite a human, except between his fingers or on his earlobe:* False. This naive belief is widespread and completely unjustified, since the smallest of the ophidians has the ability to open its jaws to a size much larger than its own body (see below, "Snakebite: Physiology and Motivation").

☻ *A snake can move as quick as a flash:* Not so. A karate chop, or even a normal blow with one's fist, is much faster than the movement of the fastest snakes, including the Crotalid called the fer-de-lance. The top speed of a *Crotalus viridis* is 7.9 feet per second (2.4 meters per second).

☻ *A snake can move very quickly, to the misfortune of the person it is chasing:* Untrue. Not only do the vast majority of snakes run away from men, but the black mamba, which is described as being "faster than a galloping horse," (close to 43.5 miles per hour [70 kilometers per hour]!) has never, in fact, exceeded 15 miles per hour (24 kilometers per hour). Admittedly, this is an impressive speed, but it is much slower than a sprinting man. Rattlesnakes do not exceed 2 miles per hour (3.5 kilometers per hour).

☻ *Green snakes are deadly:* This all-encompassing rule is too neat to have any truth to it. The green mamba is certainly deadly, but many harmless colubrids are also green. In fact, green is the most widespread color among ophidians, venomous or not.

⊙ *The caudal spine of burrowing snakes is dangerous:* No, this spine merely helps them bury themselves.

⊙ *Snakes have forked tongues with which they sting their victims:* False. All ophidians have forked tongues, but the tongue has nothing to do with injecting venom. Snakes only eject venom through their teeth: In the vast majority of cases they bite in order to inject it. "Spitting" najas eject the venom through the same teeth in a stream.

⊙ *As its name implies, the minute snake is one of the most dangerous and kills within seconds:* Untrue, and a great injustice toward these harmless burrowing snakes from Africa and Asia, commonly called "minute" snakes due to their small size.

⊙ *Snakes hypnotize their prey:* An attractive idea, but false. Animals become agitated when they are in the presence of a snake and never stay still, nor do they move directly toward a snake's mouth as some authors have described. Snakes do not hypnotize.

⊙ *Rattlesnakes get their name from the sound they always emit before they attack:* Not so. They are venomous snakes, characterized by their facial thermoreceptor pits, and with a tail that has a horny organ called a "crepticulum." This organ can emit a characteristic sound, a little like a rattle, through friction; but you can be close to such a snake and never hear a sound.

⊙ *Drinking alcohol is appropriate treatment if one is bitten:* Nothing could be farther from the truth, even though some inhabitants of India and southeastern Asia use this method as a last resort. In fact, it has been demonstrated that alcohol attracts the venom to the nervous system and makes the neurotoxins much more effective.

⊙ *The spectacled snake, or Indian cobra, can be charmed with music:* In fact, the animal is indifferent to music, and dangerous. The flute charms people rather than the snake. As to its training, there is nothing gentle about it: The charmers sometimes hit the cobra with a hard or hot object until it stops biting. Another alternative is to let it bite into a rag, which is then sharply pulled away and rips out the fangs. The latter grow back, but the method acts as a deterrent.

# GENERAL COMMENTS

Snakes, also called ophidians, are squamata like lizards; this means that they are covered with scales that are renewed periodically through shedding and regrowth. The scales have no similarity to fish scales, as they are interlinked, a bit like numerous flexible replicas of the same skin. When the snake sheds—about once a month during its active life—it uses stones and brush to pull off the skin, which turns inside-out like the finger of a glove. If one decides to eat a snake, its skin can be removed in one piece. Since the head is not covered with scales but with platelets (scutes), the incision should be made below the neck.

During the relatively long shedding period, the snake does not move around and does not eat. The membrane that covers its eyes becomes opaque and whitish, making it blind. All of this makes it highly irascible, and a poisonous snake in the process of shedding is certainly not less dangerous because it seems to be handicapped.

There are 2,700 species of snakes, 200 of which are dangerous to mammals, particularly to man. These primitive vertebrates first appeared 130 million years ago, at the time of the dinosaurs, and they have survived up to the present due to an ever increasing sophistication of their venom system and an ever greater ability for camouflage, which protects them from predators.

Snakes have a life span of about 20 years and are poikilothermic—that is, "cold-blooded," with a body temperature that varies depending on their surroundings. The normal range is between 95° and 104°F (35°–40°C) for most species and 86°F (30°C) for the nocturnal and burrowing species. They regulate their temperature by varying the amount of heat absorbed—by moving into the shade or into the sun, by using the earth's calorie absorption properties, or by changing their color (e.g., the mastigure). As the season gets colder, they become less active. Below 50°F (10°C) they become lethargic. This implies seasonal activity, which is more pronounced in specific regions. In the temperate regions of Europe there is no danger of being bitten by a viper in winter because it hibernates. In tropical regions, particularly in the grasslands, snakes undergo a similar phenomenon caused by the rise in temperature and the drop in humidity: This is called "estivation" and occurs during the dry season. During this period, African snakes hide in the earth, in hollow trees, and in termite mounds, and it is unlikely that a person will be bitten. On the other hand, when they reappear with the first rains, they are hyperactive and one should be wary of them. Activity can also vary as the day's temperature changes.

A snake has a large number of vertebrae (a python has 400, a cerastes has 138) and it uses them in locomotion. Each vertebra has a pair of ribs that can spread wide to allow the largest prey to pass since there is no sternum. The characteristic intimidation pose of the naja, which distends its neck and spreads its hood when it is agitated, is achieved by laterally straightening the cervical ribs, which are longer than the others.

## SENSE ORGANS AND METHODS OF DETECTING PREY

This is important in understanding how a snake detects its prey and approaches it, and how it perceives an aggressive presence and defends itself.

### Sense of Smell

The nasal cavities are relatively underdeveloped, but ophidians still have a sense of smell. In fact, they can differentiate the smell of a male from that of a female at some distance, and can detect their prey by the odor. The organ that enables them to smell is unique in the animal kingdom. It is called Jacobson's organ. The snake's tongue takes the place of a nose in gathering odor particles from the surrounding air. Once

charged with these particles, the two tips enter the two cavities of the Jacobson's organ, which analyzes the olfactory data. This is how the animal detects its prey, an enemy, a sexual partner or a rival. The organ is so sensitive that the snake is able to choose only fresh, unhatched eggs to eat because it detects them by smell.

If a snake sticks its tongue out at you, it is not necessarily the beginning of an attack but may be an attempt to identify you. Many people have been bitten because they have panicked and made an abrupt movement when faced with this inquiring pose.

### Hearing

It is useless to try to coax snakes with gentle words; they are deaf. They have no auricular orifice, external ear, tympanic cavity or eustachian tube. They have only a long columella, which enables them to sense low frequencies and to perceive the slightest vibration from the ground in their inner ear. While they are totally insensitive to the music of snake charmers, they can feel the vibrations of a foot tapping in time to the music; these vibrations are transmitted through the ventral scales and relayed directly to the skull bone.

### Vision

Eyesight is rather poor, in most snakes except for najas (which can hit your eyes if they decide to aim at them) and most of the arboreal species. The eyes have a peculiar feature in that the pupils can vary greatly even within the same species: They can be round or elliptical, vertical or horizontal. The fact that a snake's eyes are open does not mean it is awake: Since it has no eyelids, it sleeps with its eyes open. Some snakes are completely blind.

### Touch and Taste

In the absence of limbs, the forked, protractile tongue essentially fulfills the functions of touch and taste. The tongue can be extended through a small lower indentation even when the mouth is closed. The two tips can move easily in all directions and are able to vibrate very rapidly, gathering odor particles. The tongue plays no part in the injection of venom.

### Labial Pits

For a long time it was believed that the labial pits had an olfactory role. In fact, they are thermal detectors, through which the snakes can locate any warmblooded animal at a distance. It is a remarkable organ, which enables rattlesnakes or pit vipers to detect temperature variations of two-tenths of a degree elsius. The sensitivity of these infrared receptors means that darkness is no protection against ophidians; they will be able to find you in the darkest night, and, from a distance, they will consider you potential prey.

Venomous snakes can be found at all elevations from sea level to 15,100 feet (4,600 meters), and from the arctic circle (the adder) to latitude 44° South. Within these boundaries, there are very few regions where one is safe from them. In the vast majority of cases, these are islands. For example, there are no poisonous species in Madagascar, and therefore there would be no point in burdening oneself with serum for a trip exclusively to that island. The same applies to Guadeloupe, Cuba, Haiti, Jamaica, Puerto Rico, Corsica, Ireland, and, of course, the polar regions.

Some species are absent from certain regions. For example, Hydrophidae (sea snakes) are not found around the coasts of Africa but only in the Indian Ocean, the China Sea and in the Pacific (see the chapter on "The Sea and Shipwrecks"). There are no asps in Egypt, and therefore Cleopatra could not have committed suicide with one; she is more likely to have used a naja hadje, or Egyptian cobra. There are numerous Viperidae in Africa, but there are no rattlesnakes. Australia has no rattlesnakes or vipers but is infested with Elapidae and Hydrophidae.

Some species can be found only in specific areas. For example, the rattlesnake exclusively inhabits

## GEOGRAPHIC DISTRIBUTION

| CONTINENT | TYPES OF OPHIDIANS |
|---|---|
| Africa | No boas anywhere<br>No Hydrophidae along the coasts<br>No Crotalinae<br>Many Viperinae (horned vipers)<br>Many Elapidae (snake charmers' najas, mambas) |
| Australia | No Viperinae<br>No Crotalinae<br>Large numbers of Elapidae and Hydrophidae, including the most dangerous on earth (Taipan and *Hydrophis belcheri*). Also the tiger snake and death adder. |
| Guadeloupe, Cuba, Haiti, Jamaica, Puerto Rico, Madagascar, Corsica, Ireland, New Zealand, Iceland | No venomous species |
| Polynesia | No venomous terrestrial species |
| America | Many species of rattlesnakes, including the prairie rattlesnake (North America), the *Crotalus durissus* (South America, Mexico). Also coral snakes, moccasin snakes (particularly in the eastern United States). |
| Asia | Snake paradise: the only region where all families are represented. Numerous species of najas, kraits, coral snakes, vipers and rattlesnakes. |

the tropical regions of America and Asia. Africa has no region totally devoid of snakes, and 52 of the species found there are very dangerous to man.

Each environment has its own preferred species: Naturally there are no Hydrophidae in the desert, but there are small burrowing snakes that dig into the sand and vipers such as the cerastids (horned vipers). Cobras are found mainly in the grasslands, and mambas in the forest.

Several minutes of exposure to temperatures of 23°F (−5°C) or 122°F (50°C) will kill almost all species. Therefore one should

know that at a temperature of 122°F in the sun one will practically never come across a snake.

# IDENTIFYING POISONOUS SNAKES

Giving a precise scientific name to the ophidian that bit you will not be of much help, and even herpetologists often have to resort to their systematic catalogue to identify a specimen precisely. On the other hand it would be useful to know whether it was a naja or a member of the viper family, because the clinical symptoms, and thus the treatment, are different.

Morphological features, which differentiate a venomous species from a harmless related species are often minor and invisible at first glance. Most of the native ethnic groups in South America and Africa automatically assume that every snake is venomous. The native peoples kill them, slice up the largest (pythons, cobras, vipers) to roast or boil them, and throw the heads away, in order to ward off spells.

The key features that determine the species are always the same. They are the number of scales on the head, lips and temples; the color; and the type of dentition. But to allow the observer to put together this little jigsaw puzzle, the snake would have to cooperate by sitting still—an unlikely oc-

currence in a survival situation. Since it is impossible to provide pictures here of all the poisonous species, some general criteria for identification will suffice.

## IDENTIFICATION BY GENERAL DIMENSIONS

■ A snake that is very long—over 16½ feet (5 meters)—should be considered to belong to the Boidae, which are harmless from the aspect of venom but can bite if they are annoyed.
■ A snake with a very large diameter (anaconda) can also be considered harmless as far as venom is concerned but, here too, one should avoid being "caressed" by the creature. South American Indians are very familiar with this snake, and many carry a porcupine quill at the back of their loincloth, since the animal will release its grip by reflex action if it is pricked. Hikers can carry sharp needles.
■ Even a snake that is shorter than 8 inches (20 centimeters) may be dangerous if it is the young of a venomous species. Venom is present in its glands from birth.

■ The heaviest venomous snake is the *Crotalus adamanteus* variety of rattlesnake from the southeastern United States, which weighs 33 pounds (15 kilograms). A snake that is both long and weighs more than 33 pounds is never venomous.

## IDENTIFICATION BY MAJOR MORPHOLOGICAL CHARACTERISTICS

Refer to the Classification Table, below.

## IDENTIFICATION BY THE WAY THEY MOVE

Most Viperidae (and Boidae, which includes pythons, boas and wood snakes) move in a straight line. They do not undulate. Cerastes vipers move laterally and support themselves only on two separate points.

## IDENTIFICATION BY THE MANNER OF INTIMIDATION OR ATTACK

Some snakes adopt a characteristic pose when they are alarmed or excited.

■ Najas raise the anterior part of their bodies vertically, holding their heads back almost at a right angle, and inflate their necks to display their hoods.
■ Some vipers also expand their necks laterally, but to a lesser degree than najas. On the whole, Viperidae coil up and bend their necks into a "S" while raising the anterior portion of their bodies horizontally above the ground. This enables them to strike very hard and fast. As soon as the snake launches itself forward, it opens its jaws and seesaws its jawbone, projecting its fangs forward just before making contact with its prey or adversary.
■ Other snakes inflate their necks by inhaling a large amount of air, which they drive back into the trachea, while closing the glottis (*Disphollidus typus*). The fearsome *Thelotornis kirtlandii* does this in a vertical direction, and the inflation of the neck makes vibrant colors appear, which are invisible when it is at rest. This snake simultaneously shoots out its vermilion-colored tongue. Mambas also puff up their necks in a vertical direction.
■ Some species emit intimidating sounds: e.g., the *Bitis* (Viperinae), which hisses loudly when agitated; the Russel viper also hisses when it is angry. Others (echis and cerastids) hiss and emit a characteristic grating sound by rubbing their keeled scales against each other.

All these poses are the initial stages of an imminent attack, and therefore one should be able to recognize the threatening poses even if one cannot identify the species.

# SNAKEBITE: PHYSIOLOGY AND MOTIVATION

An understanding of the precise mechanism of a snake's bite, along with a general knowledge of its habits, is the key to intelligent protection and—in an emergency—the only way to estimate one's chances of surviving an attack. Herpetologists consider all snakes with one or more toxin-secreting glands to be venomous, irrespective of the type of dentition they have. This strict definition, however, is not necessarily relevant for considering the threat snakes pose to man.

## CLASSIFICATION ACCORDING TO TEETH

Classification by type of teeth is useful because the greater the sophistication of the dentition, the greater the danger the snake poses. If circumstances allow it, it is possible to get a rough idea of the potential toxicity from the type of teeth one can see. Normal teeth differ from teeth specialized to inject venom, which are called fangs.

■ Aglypha do not have fangs, but only have fine, sharp, teeth: They are harmless.
■ Opisthoglypha have fangs, but their location at the back of the jaw means that they are not particularly dangerous for an animal as large as a man.

■ Proteroglypha have firmly fixed fangs at the front of the jaw, and thus can easily plant them in their prey. They are very venomous and include two families: the Elapidae, which includes mambas, coral snakes, and cobras, sometimes called najas; and the Hydrophidae, or sea snakes. These animals normally do not release their prey after biting it.
■ Solenoglypha have movable fangs at the front of the jaw, which can be protracted (moved forward). This includes all members of the Viperidae. Their ability to camouflage themselves against their background makes them even more dangerous. In fact, they seem so sure of the effectiveness of their venom that they release their prey after biting it, returning to it only after it is motionless. The venom of tree snakes, which primarily eat birds, acts particularly quickly.

## THE MECHANISM OF THE BITE

Snakes never use their teeth to chew or grind, but only to hold on to something. Once the fangs have been plunged into the prey, Proteroglypha and Solenoglypha inject the venom through channels in the fangs by contracting the masseter muscles that partially cover the venom glands.

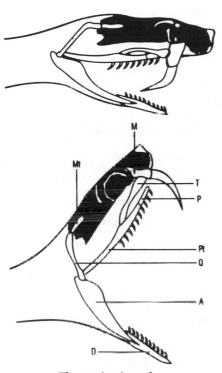

**The mechanism of a
viperidae bite (Solenoglypha)**

The bony arches move in such a way as
to project the part of the jaw with the fangs
forward. Their mobility, particularly the
mobility of the quadratum, enables the
mouth to open very wide, so that the
snake can swallow prey whose diameter
is much larger than that of the snake itself.

In addition, the lower jaw has two articulated symmetrical axes in front of the
quadratum, joined at the front by a fibrous
tissue that increases flexibility even more.
(A: Articular; D: Dental; M: Maxilla; P:
Palate; Q: Quadratum; Pt: False pteryg-
ium; T: Transverse; Mt: Mastoidean.)

The glands are thus squeezed in
proportion to the strength of the
contraction, and the quantity of
venom injected depends on the
length of the contraction: the

longer the contraction, the greater
the amount of poison. This mechanism explains why a bite is not
necessarily fatal, even if the species involved is especially dangerous. Snakes tend to be sparing of
their venom, preferring not to
waste it on animals they cannot
swallow. In fact, one should always remember that a snake swal-
lows its prey whole and cannot
tear it apart to make it smaller as
other carnivores do. Man is not
edible prey, and bites are only defensive attacks. A snake will often
be attracted by any warm-blooded
animal: A glance and a touch (if
the man doesn't move) will make
it abandon its hopes for a feast.

The Elapidae that have short
fangs, like the opisthoglyphic Colubridae, tend to hold on to their
prey and tighten their jaws repeatedly to ensure that their venom
penetrates farther. On the other
hand, Solenoglypha, which are
armed with fangs so efficient they
are practically venom syringes,
merely plunge the fangs in as far
as they will go, sharply contract
their temporal muscles and inject
their venom very deeply; finally
they release their prey and wait
for it to die quickly.

## SPECIAL FEATURES OF
## SPITTING ELAPIDAE

The *Naja nigricollis* and the
*Hemachatus haemachatus* can actually eject a mixture of saliva and
venom from a distance. When
faced with an enemy, the creature

# CLASSIFICATION TABLE

| INOCULATING DEVICE AND ORDER | SPECIAL FEATURES OF THE TEETH AND FANGS |
|---|---|
| AGLYPHA | No fangs<br>Small, fine, pointed teeth<br>Teeth solid—neither grooves nor channels |
| OPISTHOGLYPHA | Some fangs, but only at the back of the maxilla<br>No channel in the fangs, merely a groove on the outside at the front, which puts the venom into contact with prey that is in the process of being swallowed<br>Small teeth at the front, not venomous |
| PROTEROGLYPHA | Fixed fangs at the front of the upper maxilla<br>Small in size to allow the mouth to close<br>The base where the fangs are set is enlarged, forming a pedestal<br>Groove is more or less closed, channeling the trajectory of the venom |
| SOLENOGLYPHA | Mobile (protractable) fangs at the front of the maxilla<br>Very large in size; this is possible because they can be retracted against the palate when the mouth is closed<br>Inoculating channel at the center of the fang, enabling the venom to be injected deep and under pressure<br>If a fang is broken, it is immediately replaced by another from a series of reserve fangs<br>The fangs are automatically replaced every 6 to 10 weeks<br>When the snake bites, the angle between the maxilla and the fang can reach 120° |

| STRENGTH OF THE VENOM | FAMILIES | SPECIAL MORPHOLOGICAL FEATURES [1] |
|---|---|---|
| None | Most of the Colubridae, pythons, boas, anacondas | Round pupils<br>Long, pointed tail |
| Weak to none | Some of the Colubridae (only the *Thelotornis kirtlandii* and the *Dispholidus typus* that cause many incidents in Africa) | |
| Very strong | Two families:<br>Elapidae (terrestrial snakes), cobras, mambas, etc. | Oval-shaped head<br>No pits [2]<br><br>Very well developed frontal parietal and subocular scales<br>Cobras have a characteristic "hood" |
| | Hydrophidae (sea snakes) | Oval-shaped head<br>No pits<br>Flattened tail, shaped like a vertical fin |
| Strong | Viperidae, comprising two subfamilies:<br>Viperinae<br><br>Crotalinae | Spear-shaped head<br>No pits<br>The tail is usually short and rounded<br>Spear-shaped head<br>Have pits<br>Only some crotalids have a tail with a horny tip, the crepitacueum, that produces a characteristic rattling sound (rattlesnake) |

1. These external characteristics are not sufficient to safely distinguish a venomous snake from a harmless one.
2. The pits are located between the eye and the nose.

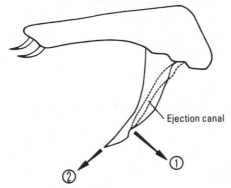

Ejection canal

**Direction of venom ejection: 1. In spitting snake; 2. In nonspitting snake**

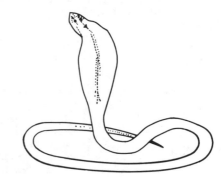

**Threatening posture of a naja**

draws itself up and, by sharply exhaling air, expels the fine droplets trickling from its fangs. This jet can cover a distance of 13 feet (4 meters) and can be repeated about a dozen times before the venom reserves are exhausted. The venom is absorbed quickly by osmosis around the eyes and the mucous membranes, or through open cuts and sores. Spitting snakes instinctively aim for the eyes and often hit them; this causes great pain, and the injuries can be severe enough to cause blindness.

A drop of poison from a *Hemachatus* in the eye of a rat will kill it in 30 minutes, whereas the venom from a viper has no effect. Therefore being able to recognize the characteristic silhouette of the naja is important, and it is essential that one automatically protect one's eyes, without waiting to find out whether it is a spitting snake or not.

## VENOM AND ITS EFFECTS

If a person is bitten, it is very useful to know how to identify the types of venom involved through the clinical symptoms it causes. The following will provide a guide to self-medication—assuming, of course, that a suitable first aid kit is available (see the First Aid Survival Kit table in the chapter on "Medicine Without a Doctor").

Venoms are colorless or yellowish, have an oily consistency, and are soluble in water (therefore the first response if venom from a spitting snake enters the eye is to rinse it with plenty of water—regardless of whether the water is clean or not). They are very complex, and the substances that constitute them vary from species to species. A snake is generally immune to large doses of venom from its own species but dies from the venom of a similar species. A cobra's venom provides a general idea of the toxicity of these poisons: though not the most potent snake poison, it is nevertheless 50 times more toxic than sodium cyanide and twice as toxic as strychnine. One gram of cobra venom can kill 165 men.

Since the venoms are viscous, they contain diffusion agents in order to penetrate the tissues of the prey more easily; the main agent is hyaluronidase, which is used in medicine to facilitate the intramuscular injection of viscous products. Venom is also used to counteract some types of hemorrhages, and cobra venom was used at one time against epilepsy and the pain of cancer, since its pain-killing properties are comparable to those of morphine. This partly explains the great difference between the intense pain felt after being bitten by a viper and the minor pain after being bitten by a cobra (or naja).

The primary toxic agents of the venoms are as follows:

■ paralyzing **neurotoxins,** the effect of which are comparable to curare, but which are not counteracted by curare antagonists such as eserine (therefore this product would be useless as an antidote)
■ **hemotoxins,** which are predominant among the Viperidae and cause hemorrhaging

■ **cytolysins,** which destroy cells and cause necrosis of the skin that sometimes spreads down to the bone (especially the myotoxins of the Hydrophidae)
■ **hemolysins,** which specifically attack the white blood cells and prevent phagocytosis; this explains why secondary infections often occur
■ **histaminic substances,** which involve vasomotor reactions and cause the shock that often follows the bite of a viper

There are many other substances with different enzymatic actions, and, since all venoms combine several of them, it is impossible to systematize them.

The following table shows a simplified schematic view of the primary actions and effects of the main types of venoms and the principal clinical symptoms they cause; the latter indicate the course of treatment that should be followed.

## AFTER BEING BITTEN BY A VIPERIDAE

Usually, you have several hours to inject the serum, unless the venom has directly entered a major vein—a rare event, but one that would lead to death within a few minutes.

## THE "COBRA SYNDROME" OF THE ELAPIDAE

The signs appear quickly— there is an insuperable desire to

## CLINICAL EFFECTS OF VARIOUS VENOMS

| | PREDOMINANT TOXIC EFFECT | LOCALIZED SYMPTOMS | GENERAL SYMPTOMS |
|---|---|---|---|
| Elapidae (Proteroglypha: cobras or najas, mambas, etc.) | Neurotoxic (paralyzing) No coagulating property | Few symptoms (a little muscular trembling) Little or no pain | Predominately due to the curare-like action General progressive paralysis, affecting the nerves, respiratory muscles, and central nervous system Rapid death within 6 to 12 hours, caused by respiratory paralysis and the effect of shock Lucidity is retained up until the final coma |
| Hydrophidae (sea snakes) | Neurotoxic Myotoxic | Symptoms similar to those caused by the Elapidae | |
| Viperidae (Solenoglypha: vipers, rattlesnakes) | General hypercoagulability Causes shock  Causes hemorrhage, particularly among the Crotalinae through exhausting the fibrinogen reserves | Appear very quickly (in a matter of minutes) Often very strong pain when bitten Steady edema, spreading along the whole limb, with a marbled appearance Significant local necroses are possible, spreading down to the bone | Delayed (several hours) Digestive problems (due to the contraction of the smooth muscles): vomiting and cramps State of shock: hypotension, tachycardia, anxiety, collapse, death |

sleep and the voice becomes almost inaudible due to paralysis of the cranial nerves. The tongue is paralyzed, and the head wobbles, giving the impression of a broken neck. The victim falls into a coma and collapses; death occurs within 6 to 12 hours, caused by respiratory paralysis. The person remains lucid until the coma begins. Elapidae poisoning kills more quickly than Viperidae bites, so there is a greater emergency with a cobra than with a viper. If untreated, a man dies on average within 2 to 7 hours after being bitten by a viper; and sometimes within just 10 minutes after being bitten by a green mamba. In the rare instances when the bite punctures a blood vessel or any part of the face, all these time periods will be considerably shorter.

## THE TOXIC ACTION OF HYDROPHIDAE VENOMS

The symptoms of a sea snake's bite are very similar to those of the Elapidae; the neurotoxins predominate and paralysis, to a greater or lesser degree, occurs. A sea snake's bite is painless, in contrast to that of a fish. If specific groups of muscles become painful to move within an hour of being bitten, the case is severe. The specific serum for this group of Proteroglypha is still effective eight hours after the incident, so there is plenty of time to administer it. If the poisoning proves mild, the serum should not be used, since it can itself sometimes be harmful.

The peculiarity of Hydrophidae venoms is that they poison the muscles as well as the nervous system. This assault on the muscles becomes apparent through myoglobinuria—that is, red urine appearing three to six hours after the bite. The appearance of this symptom several hours after being bitten by an unidentified creature in the sea can confirm the cause and severity of the case, and can indicate the appropriate treatment.

---

# TREATMENT OF SNAKEBITES IN A SURVIVAL SITUATION

Obviously, no one in a survival situation can reproduce the sophisticated hospital treatment that saved Nicole Viloteau in the account at the beginning of this chapter. But there are methods of first aid that every adventurer should know.

## A TOURNIQUET

This method is widespread, though unproven. Nevertheless, it is recommended, especially in combination with total immobility. Its purely mechanical action should slow down the diffusion of the venom and increase the bleeding around the bite. Properly used, a tourniquet should obstruct the venous and lymphatic flow, but not the arterial flow. Therefore it should not be too tight. It should be applied as quickly as possible and is useless after one hour. It should be as wide as possible (a piece of cloth makes a good one). Some people believe that a tourniquet encourages edema and necrosis—but it is better to lose a limb than one's life.

## SEROTHERAPY

This is always the best treatment in severe cases of envenomation and the only one that is sure to prevent death if administered in time. This assumes that a serum suitable for the region was included in the survival kit. The ideal situation would be to have a monovalent serum available, i.e., one that is effective specifically against the venom of the snake that inflicted the bite (there are now sera for all snakes with the exception of the Kirtland snake). However, this would mean that one would have to include as many sera as there are venomous species in the region—a cumbersome luxury in a survival situation. There is a polyvalent serum for every region—that is, one that counteracts the venom of most species found there. Generally speaking, this polyvalent serum is the one to carry, and it has the

additional advantage of eliminating the problem of choosing among various sera in the stressful moments after sustaining a bite from an unidentifiable snake. It is better to have several doses of a polyvalent serum than a single dose of several monovalent sera. In fact, in order for the serum to be effective, large doses are often required—larger than those contained in a single vial. There is no serum that counteracts all venoms.

Apart from sea snake bites, which can go untreated for up to eight hours, after any other bites the serum should be injected subcutaneously very quickly. The more dangerous the snake is, the faster clinical symptoms appear, the faster the serum should be injected. Though the serum can still neutralize venom after four hours, general problems and local damage may still occur.

The application of serotherapy presents several risks: The major danger is anaphylactic shock due to an allergy to the horse antigens in the serum. As in the case of antitetanus shots, there is no human-derived serum that would avoid the risk of an allergic reaction. Therefore, if your physical condition is good, and especially if you have a companion, you should use the "Beredka method" to inject the serum: Initially inject only 0.1 milliliter subcutaneously, then wait for 10 minutes. If there is no allergic reaction, inject the rest of the dose intravenously. The amount should be 0.09 milliliter per pound (0.2 milliliter per kilogram) if the injection is given within 20 minutes. If a long time has elapsed, the dosage may be as high as 0.45 milliliter per pound (1 milliliter per kilogram) depending on the severity of the symptoms.

Make a diagnosis based on the severity of the bite, and if the reaction is not brought to a halt, continue to administer additional doses of antivenin: minimal severity 5 to 8 vials; moderate severity 8 to 13 vials; severe, more than 13 vials.

As long as you have a polyvalent serum for the local snake population, even the stress of being alone in a dangerous situation will not prevent the immediate injection of the medicine. Most vials contain enough serum for a single dose as long as the injection is administered soon after the bite is sustained.

Remember, the injection should be administered intravenously. Serum degrades under unfavorable storage conditions. Although a serum can be preserved for five years if it is stored away from light at a temperature between 35.6 °F and 46.4 °F (2°C and 8°C), it is generally impossible to maintain these conditions during an expedition. Therefore, knowing the limits of tolerance is important: A serum can be kept at room temperature 59°F to 77°F (15°C to

25°C) for one to two months but its overall life span will be reduced to three years. The serum should also not be allowed to freeze.

Many of the venomous snakes inhabit very hot regions, and the serum's properties will weaken as the temperature of the vial rises. Therefore a survival kit should not be exposed to sunlight.

The effectiveness of a serum should not be overestimated if it is administered late, and there are considerable risks because of possible hyperallergic reactions. Therefore other therapeutic measures may prove indispensable in a survival situation.

## SUCTION

This eliminates a significant amount of the venom if it is done immediately, and therefore it slows down diffusion through the tissues; it also brings the venom, mixed with blood, back to the surface of the skin. Since venoms are destroyed in the stomach, the method poses no danger with one exception: the venom of spitting snakes, which is absorbed by osmosis through the mucous membranes. Ten minutes of suction will be enough.

Plastic suction gadgets are available in kits, which are relatively small and include a scalpel, a topical antiseptic, and a tourniquet cord. Other devices are also available, ranging from the cumbersome "milker" to the "aspivenin," and can be bought in some pharmacies.

## INCISION

There has been much debate as to the efficacy of an incision, since it does not slow the progress of the venom deeper in the body. If the incision is made immediately, it is obvious that the blood flowing from the wound will remove some of the venom; but the danger of infection and necrosis will increase, especially in a hot country. Some authors even believe that the wound increases the surface for absorption of the venom. But it is difficult to reject this method out of hand, since there is no scientific study either to establish or disprove its effectiveness.

If an incision is made, it should be parallel to the muscle fibers and shallow, so that it does not reach the connective tissue.

## MISCELLANEOUS MEASURES

Cooling the area of the bite along with the application of a tourniquet seems to slow down the spread of venom, which is logical because of the vasoconstriction and the slowing of metabolic reactions caused by cold. In a survival situation, any source of freshwater will be able to lower the temperature by several degrees. The anesthetizing effect of such a procedure is also important, as it is with any inflammation.

Topical disinfection is useful, as it is for any wound, but it is not vital, since the fangs cause deep punctures and surface application cannot reach them. A local population may have its own special topical products, but no miracle formula is known.

## IMMOBILIZATION

This simple method seems to have unanimous approval. Several experimenters have proven its efficacy, especially one Australian team that tested immobilization on macaques that had been injected with Elapidae venom. By tracing the circulation of the venom with radioactive tagging, the group demonstrated spectacular success in halting the spread through two simple measures: moderate compression of the limb above the bite (an elastic tape will do) and total immobilization of the affected limb with the use of splints.

The purpose is to eliminate or inhibit any acceleration of the circulation, which would diffuse the venom more rapidly. This involves general as well as local immobilization: It would be disastrous, for example, to run away after sustaining a bite. Apart from being pointless, the muscular exercise would significantly increase circulation and drain the poisoned limb more quickly.

Staying still is not enough; the effect of stress must also be decreased since stress can significantly increase the blood flow. Once again, prior psychological preparation and knowledge of the physiology of a snakebite will help (see below, "Prevention of Snakebites"). Avoid all exertion or intake of alcohol, since they will merely cause increased vasomotoric activity.

If you are alone, lie down immediately in a position that will facilitate breathing, and move only if it is absolutely necessary—for example, to inject the serum. If the bite was inflicted by a viper, which can cause intolerable pain, a pain-killing injection should be administered to decrease agitation. A tranquilizer that depresses the respiratory centers as little as possible (such as Valium) can also be useful.

If the bite was inflicted by an elapid, which has a paralyzing effect on the respiratory muscles, pain killers and depressant tranquilizers such as morphine must be avoided at all costs. Generally there is little or no pain, and a light tranquilizer is enough.

**Immediate immobilization is extremely important.** If transport to an emergency center is available, the limb can be immobilized in the same way as a fracture.

## EJECTION OF VENOM INTO THE EYES

The best treatment, as with any fluid that splashes into the eyes, is to rinse with plenty of water. The first thing to do would be to immerse the face in the water (even stagnant water) and then move it from side to side to ensure a current across the cornea. Then an antiseptic eyewash should be used.

Apart from its obvious effect against secondary infection, a topical antiseptic may partially destroy the venom on the surface of the wound (potassium permanganate in a 1 percent solution, chlorine at 1 to 60).

## USEFUL MEDICINES

All injectable products appropriate for snakebites, with the exception of specific sera or heparin, are the same as those recommended for the stings or bites of spiders, Hymenoptera, scorpions, and venomous marine animals. They are Adrenalin 1/1000 (which acts equally well on shock caused by the venom and potential shock caused by the serum), calcium gluconate, and the corticoids (100 mg of hydrocortisone administered immediately). It has been proven that antihistamines have no effect on snake bites. On the other hand, the effectiveness of heparin treatment has been universally accepted in dealing with the problem of coagulation caused by snake venom; it is also effective against pain if the injection is given early. The injection, which is easy to self-administer, should be subcutaneous and above the location of the bite.

It is very important to drink water to avoid a decrease in the circulation volume and to prevent renal failure.

Since the treatment of snakebites is one of the most important survival skills in dangerous re-gions, here is a summary of the information you should know. It may even be worthwhile to include a copy of this material in the first aid kit.

# PREVENTION OF SNAKEBITES

## BEFORE DEPARTURE

### Information

If one is planning an expedition to a dangerous area, one must find out about the species one is liable to encounter. Zoological societies and the public library are the best resources.

### The First Aid Kit

It is mandatory that the first aid kit take up as little space as possible. It should contain concentrated injectable products that can be packed into small containers, padded with styrofoam or other suitable packing material. A list of essential injectable products is provided in the table First Aid Survival Kit in the chapter on "Medicine Without a Doctor." Choose the products appropriate to the terrain in which you will be traveling.

### The Serum

The serum should be polyvalent for the various species one is likely to encounter. The date of manufacture should be as recent as possible, and the serum must be transported at a cool temperature between 32°F and 41°F (0°C and 5°C) for as long as possible. All airliners have refrigerated compartments, and it should be carried there.

Arrangements should be made to have fresh serum sent if you are headed for a hot region and intend to stay for more than three months (beyond three months at 95°F [35°C] the properties will have degraded to a considerable extent).

### Equipment

Most bites are on the lower limbs. Leather boots are therefore an absolute necessity. Rubber boots are unsuitable in hot environments because of the irritation they cause. Leather is very resistant and cannot easily be penetrated by fangs: It is not the thickness that is important (the longest recorded Viperidae fangs were 2 inches [5 centimeters]) but its resistance to being punctured. The boots should be knee-high and not too tight (riding boots may be attractive, but they are not as suitable as looser cowboy boots).

Protecting the upper limbs is less important and obviously is less practical in a jungle or desert environment. Very few bites occur on the face, but it may be advisable to wear glasses both as protection from the sun and, in regions where they are widespread (especially in Africa), to deflect the jet from a spitting naja.

### IN THE FIELD

#### Avoid Dangerous Sleeping Places

This is not always possible, and sleeping in a hammock is still the best way to avoid crawling creatures. This is an important point, as many snakes are nocturnal and move as well at night as during the day. Several species of snakes have the annoying tendency to enter tents at night, probably in search of warmth. Snakes are particularly susceptible to DDT and to organic chlorines. A minimal amount is enough to make a snake contract, suffocate, and die within a few seconds. This little-known vulnerability provides easy protection in a space as restricted as a tent or a sleeping bag: Take an insecticide spray along.

Some snakes—for example, the horned viper or cerastes that lives in the deserts and prairies of North Africa and Egypt—are attracted by campfires.

A river provides no protection because even terrestrial snakes not only climb, crawl, and jump, they can also swim, even if water is not their favorite element. Camping on an island in the middle of a wadi or river will not provide absolute protection.

### FACE TO FACE WITH A SNAKE

The most important thing is to detect the imminence of an attack; the attempt to identify the snake can come later.

Snakes are timid and will only bite if they are attacked, trampled on, threatened or cornered. They are sparing with their venom and generally reserve it for prey that is small enough for them to consume. Not even the largest of the Boidae has ever swallowed a man. This means that no snake, however poisonous or impressive in size, is reason for panic. The majority will run away, and the minority that do attack cannot chase a man running at normal speed.

The most aggressive of all snakes is the tree mamba, which is widespread in Africa. It is very active and will pursue anything that disturbs it, particularly during its reproductive period. Its speed on the ground is about 6.25 miles per hour (10 kilometers per hour), but in the trees it can move much faster than man. Anyone who encounters this snake, the venom of which is always fatal if untreated, should head away from trees and into a clearing. Mambas are the only snakes that give the lie to the rule: safety in flight. While they are found only in Africa, this still remains the golden rule on all other continents.

## Recognizing the Imminence of an Attack

The main principles are described above in the section on identifying poisonous snakes. Briefly, the attack postures that enable optimal penetration by the fangs are:

▪ A proteroglyph (naja) will raise the anterior part of its body vertically in an S-shape.
▪ A solenoglyph (viper, rattlesnake) will raise the anterior part of its body only slightly, forming a curve on a horizontal plane with its head slightly bent back.

As we have seen, classification according to teeth is best, since the teeth reveal the degree of danger and the manner of biting, as well as the method of intimidation that precedes the attack.

## If You Are Surprised at Close Range

It is possible to find yourself at close range with a snake—perhaps even as close as the inside of your sleeping bag. In such situations, **two things must be avoided: abrupt movement and talking.**

The creature will interpret movement as aggression, and it will bite. Talking causes vibrations, to which snakes are very sensitive. The solution is to wait for a change in temperature and to move, if at all, very carefully and slowly.

A deadly tradition provides a good illustration of how important it is not to make abrupt movements around a snake. The name of the ritual is "kiss of the virgin," and it kills many young women in Burma every year. The chosen women have to kiss the head of a cobra. In order to do so, they may begin by coaxing the snake and gently stroking the top of its head, and then they must place their lips on it. If they tremble, or make an abrupt movement, the snake often bites them, whether they are virgins or not. This ritual is one reason for the exceptionally high mortality rate due to snakes in Burma.

The distance between you and the snake is important. Snake charmers are well aware of this and always stay a little farther away than the distance between the snake's head and the ground. The snake strikes downward and forward, and the distance between its hood and the ground determines its range. Mongooses, a great predators of snakes, also use this basic principle and stay out of striking distance until they can surprise the snake from the rear.

You can move faster than a snake can react, so, provided you are initially out of striking distance, a quick blow with a machete can be effective—and can provide a meal in the bargain.

### IF A BITE IS INFLICTED

#### Do Not Run

It is absolutely essential to control the natural reflex to run away, especially in the case of Proteroglypha, which do not release their prey. Pulling one's hand away will only make the fangs sink deeper into one's flesh. The only solution is to squeeze the base of the animal's jaws with the thumb and index finger, which will force it to open its jaws and remove the fangs from the wound. This situation is rare in the field, since the snake usually bites to warn the man, and then runs away.

### START TREATMENT IMMEDIATELY

#### Identify the Snake

Sometimes a snake is seen and identified, sometimes it is not identified, and sometimes it is simply not seen, as happens so often when a bite is inflicted at night. However, there are two ways to identify the origin of the bite post facto:

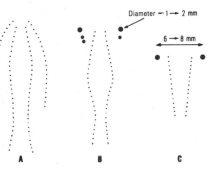

Imprints caused by snake bites

A.–Nonvenomous snake; no fang marks: Aglypha
B.–Venomous proteroglyph snakes: naja, elapids
C.–Venomous solenoglyph snakes: vipers, rattlesnakes
(After Frayrer and Calmette)

■ **The imprint left by teeth and/ or fangs:** Generally speaking, nonvenomous Colubridae leave four lines of small dots; Elapidae (najas) leave two lines of small dots and, outside them, several slightly larger dots; Viperidae leave two very short lines of small dots and two large dots outside them.

These imprints are clearly visible before swelling blurs or obliterates them (particularly in the case of Viperidae where edema is substantial and appears quickly). There may be several bite marks if the animal repeatedly plunged its fangs into the flesh. The fang marks are encircled by a purplish-red ring, several millimeters in diameter, which persists for eight to ten days.

■ **The first clinical symptoms:** Re-

## SUMMARY OF ACTIONS TO BE TAKEN AFTER POISONING BY A SNAKE OR ANY OTHER VENOMOUS CREATURE

| THERAPEUTIC ACTION IN CHRONOLOGICAL ORDER (IDEAL) | INTENDED EFFECT | METHOD |
|---|---|---|
| IMMOBILIZATION | Slow down circulation and thus the diffusion of the venom. | Immobilization should be done in two ways:<br>1. total immobilization of the affected limb<br>2. immobilization of the whole body |
| TOURNIQUET | Prevent or slow down the diffusion of the venom. | The tourniquet should be as wide as possible; it is useless 1 hour after bite was inflicted.<br>■ Length of time it should be applied: 1 hour.<br>■ Move it toward the base of the limb every 5 minutes. |
| POLYVALENT SERUM | Neutralize the venom around the bite and elsewhere. | Administer as quickly as possible if it is available:<br>1. 0.1 ml subcutaneously<br>If there is no allergic reaction after 10 minutes:<br>2. .09 ml/lb (0.2 ml/kg) intravenously |
| SUCTION | Suck out as much of the venom around the wound as possible. | Length of time to be applied: 10 minutes |
| INCISION | Eliminate some of the venom with the blood. | Shallow incision, parallel to the muscle fibers |
| COOLING | Curb local enzymatic reactions. Anesthetize. | If no ice is available, soak the bitten limb in water. |

| THERAPEUTIC ACTION IN CHRONOLOGICAL ORDER (IDEAL) | INTENDED EFFECT | METHOD |
| --- | --- | --- |
| CORTICOIDS | Antiallergic and antishock effect of corticoids. | Self-injecting vials, intramuscularly, to be repeated depending on the individual's condition |
| ADRENALIN 1/1000 | Counteract cardiac problems due to the state of shock. | Slowly, intravenously or subcutaneously |
| CALCIUM GLUCONATE | Counteract allergic shock. | Slowly, intravenously, (very difficult if one is alone), 10 to 20 ml |
| HEPARIN | Counteract coagulation problems. | Subcutaneously into the abdomen, 0.1 ml per 10 kg (22 lbs) (the vials contain 1 ml) |
| VITAMIN C (1,000 mg) | Detoxifying role. | Pills, according to personal choice |
| VITAMIN B$_1$ (250 mg) | Counteract nerves being affected if envenomation was by an elapid. | Pills, according to personal choice (6 to begin with) |
| HYDRATION | Avoid aggravation of shock through hypovolemia. | Drink as much as possible while conscious |
| TOPICAL ANTISEPTIC | Avoid superinfection, and possibly to partially destroy the venom remaining on the surface of the wound. | Generous application. |
| LOCAL CURES | The action of some plants or barks, which has not yet been explained but is sometimes very effective. | In a situation where there is nothing more to lose, let the local medicine man or witch doctor administer the treatment. |

member the general features: very strong local pain with secondary shock in the case of the Viperidae (vipers, rattlesnakes); no strong pain at the location of the bite, but progressive paralysis in the case of the Elapidae and Hydrophidae (cobras and najas, mambas, sea snakes).

In most cases, these two methods can be used to determine the order to which the snake belongs, and this will enable the administration of the appropriate treatment.

## Do Not Panic

■—Frequently a bite is a simple defensive reflex, and only some of the venom is injected, or none at all.
■ A bite does not necessarily mean poisoning: Studies have shown that poisoning occurs in only 50 percent of bites. Bites can be ineffectual because of bad aim, broken fangs, the ineffective functioning of the injecting mechanism or the small amount of venom injected.
■ In addition, if venom is injected, the amount injected is not always enough to cause death or even serious poisoning.

Therefore, if a bite is inflicted, survival is likely even if appropriate treatment is not available.

There are no vaccines against snakebite. The complexity and toxicity of venoms is such that testing them is difficult and time-consuming. Although animals that feed on snakes (mongooses, hedgehogs) are immune, they are only immune to their favorite species, and so far nothing has demonstrated that this method of immunization can be applied to man.

# OTHER VENOMOUS AND POISONOUS CREATURES

- Myths

- Venomous Terrestrial Arthropods

- Venomous Toads

- Venomous Aquatic Animals

- A Special Environment: The Seashore

Although the two words are informally used interchangeably (as in the previous chapter), there is an important distinction to be made between poisonous and venomous. Poisonous creatures are those that cause poisoning when eaten; venomous animals are armed with glands that secrete venom through a sting or bite. A venomous creature is not necessarily poisonous, and can safely be eaten (for example, snakes and several venomous fishes). One creature may be both venomous and poisonous, while another may be poisonous only on occasion. The fine line between the two can sometimes be moot, as in the case with creatures that are "passively venomous" and do not have a specialized injection mechanism, such as some toads. In any case, both groups present dangers to a person in a survival situation.

## MYTHS

✪ *A scorpion that is about to die commits suicide by stinging itself with its fearsome stinger:* False. A scorpion surrounded by flames, for instance, will curl up to avoid the heat and thus look as if it were stinging itself. This gives the appearance of "suicide," which would be impossible anyway, since—like most venomous creatures—the scorpion is immune to its own venom.

✪ *A scorpion can sting several times, because its stinger is made up of segments:* Though this notion is widespread, it is both wrong and simplistic.

✪ *Yellow and green scorpions are the most dangerous:* Not so. Color has nothing to do with toxicity.

✪ *The largest spiders (tarantulas, trap-door spiders) are the most dangerous:* Wrong. The most venomous spider is *Lactrodectus* which is 0.39–0.58 inches (1–1.5 centimeters) long. Ctenizidae, which can also kill a man within hours after a sting, are very small.

✪ *Spiders have a stinger beneath the abdomen:* No. They have articulated pincers on the thorax.

✪ *A venomous creature is inedible:* False. What is venomous is not necessarily poisonous.

# VENOMOUS TERRESTRIAL ARTHROPODS

## ARACHNIDS

### Scorpions

There are 1,000 different varieties of scorpions; only about a dozen of those found in North Africa and America are dangerous, and only five have a deadly sting: *Androctonus australis hector* (Southern Algeria and Tunisia), *Leiurus quinquestriatus* (Egypt and Israel), *Centruroides noxious* (Mexico), *Centruroides sculpturatus* (Arizona) and *Tityus serrulatus* (Brazil). All of those belong to the same family of Buthidae.

The little black scorpions with flat pincers (*Auscorpus*) or the yellow ones with elongated pincers (*Buthus*), among others, cause stings that are painful but not dangerous. There are very few countries where one is liable to encounter a deadly scorpion, and, like snakes, they only sting if they are threatened or taken by surprise. Many Bedouins on the Arabian Peninsula, for example, are stung by desert scorpions when they step on them with their bare feet, but suffer no adverse reaction.

The poison gland is located not at the base of the tail, but in the last segment in the form of an enlarged pouch armed with a tapered stinger. The venoms are almost exclusively neurotoxic, and death is caused through respiratory paralysis.

For treatment information, refer to the table above on the treatment of snakebites. The principles are the same. Both monovalent and polyvalent sera exist.

### Spiders

Only about 100 of the 20,000 known species of spiders are considered dangerous, and of these only about a dozen are deadly.

*Latrodectus mactans* is the most venomous. This is a small spider with thin legs; it is never longer than 0.6 inch (1.5 centimeters), and it is always black with or without red, white, or yellow markings. Its name differs according to country: "black widow" in North America, "arana brava" in Chile, "iucacha" in Peru, "ménavoude" in Madagascar and "katipo " in New Zealand. It can be found everywhere in the tropics and lives in fields, under stones, under shrubs and on the bare earth, as well as in buildings and particularly in toilets. It is not aggressive, and its bite is often a defensive reaction. The sting causes muscle contractions, sweating, bronchial congestion, and severe weakness; it seldom leads to death.

Trap-door spiders are hairy, large and very aggressive even when they are not threatened. They are equipped with two strong chelicerae (anterior ap-

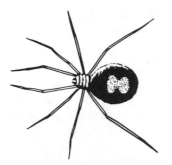

**Black widow** (*Lactrodectus*)

pendages), which enable them to eat small vertebrates (for example, young mice). They only live in hot regions, usually in trees or in holes in the ground. The *atrax* variety, found in Australia, is extremely venomous. It is hairy, brownish in color, and nocturnal. Its bite can be fatal.

Ctenizidae or phonentria are small and very aggressive. They live in South America and their venom is capable of killing within a matter of hours.

Tarantulas, which belong to the family Lycosidae, are more impressive in their size and hairiness than in their toxicity. They are found in tropical America. Their bite is painful and can cause significant necrosis of the tissues but it is not fatal.

Loxosceli cause serious injuries in North and South America and also in Europe. Their venom causes necroses that are sometimes very harmful. All of the Loxosceli spiders (except for those in one nonvenomous family) have a pair of poison glands

at the tip of a mobile digit on the anterior appendages or chelicerae. This location permits them to bite (or, to be more precise, to pinch) and simultaneously to inject venom, paralyzing their prey.

A spider does not sting, since it has no stinger with which to inject the venom. This fact is very important in determining the origin of a bite or sting sustained at night: All spider stings leave two very distinct marks, corresponding to the points of penetration of the chelicerae. It is impossible to confuse this with the marks left by an insect, a scorpion, or a snake: Insects and scorpions leave a puncture-like scar; a snake leaves an imprint characteristic of its family (see chapter on " Snakes").

The symptoms can be explained by the nature of the venom, which is always neurotoxic to a greater or lesser extent: the clinical picture may include peritonitis, due to the contraction of the abdominal muscles; chest pain; pain in the limbs; and mental problems such as agitation or stupor. These symptoms appear

**Tarantula**

one to two hours after envenomation. If Lycosidae or Loxosceli are involved, the venom also contains a substantial amount of hyaluronidase, which is the reason for the necroses that often spread around the bite.

Treatment follows the same principles as that for snakebites, but intravenous and intramuscular calcium seems to be more effective—the victim shows signs of improvement within 30 minutes (20 ml of calcium gluconate intravenously, plus an additional 10 ml intramuscularly)—while morphine is ineffective. Specific sera are available, but if only one is to be packed, snake serum is the better choice.

## Ticks

Only one species is potentially deadly, and it is only found in the jungles of eastern Australia (*Ixodes holocyclus*). It can transmit tropical fevers, which can only be diagnosed by a specialist; therefore all one can do is administer aspirin and antibiotics or sulphamides to treat the symptoms. A tick should never be pulled out, since this can cause infection; instead, it should be burned or covered with tincture of iodine.

## MYRIAPODS

Better know as "centipedes," these arthropods are made up of segments, each with one or two pairs of legs. The Scolopendridae have 21 segments and 42 legs. Some tropical centipedes, such as the *Scolopendre gigentea* in the Philippines, are believed to be deadly. They can grow to 11.7 inches (30 cms) in length and have sharp claws and a nasty sting. The only way to get rid of them is to wait until they leave of their own accord, or to help them do so by pushing them in the right direction—in other words in the direction they are already moving.

I remember one of these Scolopendridae centipedes falling on my sleeping mat when I was with the Dayaks of Borneo, and the reaction of the people who saw it: they quickly removed themselves to a respectful distance. The village chief, who chopped up the intruder with a machete, seemed to have a personal score to settle with the creature.

## INSECTS

There are large numbers of insects in the tropics and they can make life miserable in many ways. While some are truly life-threatening—blood-sucking mosquitoes can transmit malaria, yellow fever and arboviruses among other things—they are more often a source of unbearable itching and seemingly permanent discomfort. Mosquitoes are of course widespread in jungles and swamps, and they can also swarm during certain seasons in areas where one would not necessarily expect them. It is best to assume that they will be present wherever one intends to go, particularly the Russian taiga or northern Canada during the summer. A man who has never been subjected to myriad mosquitoes, gnats or other microscopic creatures cannot appreciate the bliss of a tent or a mosquito net that is truly insect-proof.

European Hymenoptera are well known: bees with a sting that they can use only once; and wasps, bumble bees and hornets with a sting that has no hook and that remains an integral part of the insect, ready to sting again. In the tropics there are multitudes of Hymenoptera, both in variety and number, and they are considerably larger than the familiar European and North American species. Stings should be disinfected, the stinger removed if necessary, and the general symptoms treated with antihistamines, corticoids and calcium gluconate. Serious injuries are rare.

Anthills are very numerous in the tropics, and since the ants are usually 0.75–1.2 inches (2–3 centimeters) long, one should avoid camping in their path: No tent fabric or sleeping bag will offer much protection.

## PROTECTION AGAINST ARTHROPODS

### Before Departure

■ Learn as much as possible about the species of Hymenoptera you are likely to encounter in the pertinent region, and arm yourself with injectable medicine, pills, lotions and necessary repellents.

■ There is a desensitization treatment for those people who are allergic to Hymenoptera, i.e., those who have an abnormally strong reaction to wasp, bee and hornet stings in Europe and North America. This treatment could be described as a "vaccination," and its results can be spectacular: it is, in fact, possible to get the individual to have a "normal" reaction to stings by injecting him with increasing doses every day.

The desensitization can be achieved within seven days under hospital supervision. Anyone who habitually develops widespread edema from Hymenoptera stings should undergo such preventive treatment, since such a reaction can cause fatal asphyxia. This preventive treatment is obviously important if you are planning a trip to any of a number of countries where the Hymenoptera are virulent all year round and where the smallest of them is the size of hornets. It is relatively safe to assume that the effect of this treatment may, at least partially, extend to the venoms of arachnids and scorpions, since some of their allergenic molecules are common to all insects. The elimination of the allergy, however, does not mean the elimination of the normal toxic reaction, and therefore precautions against stings are still in order.

### In the Field

Keep covered as much as possible, depending on the local climate. A cotton shirt will not prevent a sting from penetrating, but it will prevent direct contact between the insect and the skin and thus considerably decrease the risk: it eliminates the involuntary, sharp reflex reaction that causes "defense stings." Proper, solid, fine-meshed mosquito netting is essential equipment in the camp.

Avoid the favorite haunts of the arthropods that are likely to inhabit the region: swamps in the jungle, stony and sunken regions in the desert and isolated thickets. When moving about at night, shine a light on the path ahead, since many arthropods, especially scorpions, are particularly active at night. Examine your shoes and clothing in the morning, since scorpions and some spiders like to hide there.

## VENOMOUS TOADS

These animals have no specialized organs to inject their venom. Nevertheless, contact with them can be very toxic. The Dendrobatac of the Amazon, for example, a tiny, red, arboreal frog, has skin and some glands that secrete an extremely virulent poison (batrachotoxin), as potent as curare, which is used by the Indians to coat their arrows. Some toads have warts or sacs on their skin that are, in fact, poison glands, capable of killing any animal if administered in sufficient quantity. Therefore, do not touch any small toads in the jungle, and eat only the large ones after removing the skin. If in doubt, avoid contact with all toads that have bumps on their skin.

## VENOMOUS AQUATIC ANIMALS

### MEDUSAS AND PORTUGUESE MEN-OF-WAR

These lower aquatic animals, also called Coelenterata, have specialized stinging cells called nematocysts, with which they paralyze their prey. Anyone who swims or dives regularly has a good chance of coming into contact with them, and such contact can have very disagreeable consequences. Since they are made up of 95 to 98 percent water, these creatures have no nutritional value. In a tropical region they should be handled only with gloves.

Medusas have a gelatinous, translucent appearance and a bell-like shape, with the mouth and tentacles on the underside. Some species are very dangerous. The *Chironex fleckerii*, or box jelly-fish, found on the northern and eastern shores of Australia, has a cube-shaped body, and the trans-lucent tentacles can attain a length of 26 to 33 feet (8 to 10 meters). A diver who encounters it may die within minutes, de-pending on how many points of contact were made with the nema-tocysts. One must always wear a lightweight diving suit when div-ing in the tropics, since a suit of-fers the only possible protection against venomous creatures and corals.

Portuguese men-of-war are very numerous in warm waters and very dangerous because of their transparency, which makes them almost invisible. They have air bladders, so they can float on the surface, and they frequently move in large groups. During some sea-sons, they literally cover the sur-face with a compact net of pink and blue threads that is some-times several yards deep. In such cases, going into the water is im-possible—every square inch of uncovered skin will come into contact with the nematocysts. The contact feels like a whiplash fol-lowed by a sharp burning sensa-tion. A naked swimmer who finds himself in a group of Portuguese men-of-war may lose conscious-ness from the pain as much as from shock. His body will be cov-ered with stinging welts wherever the nematocysts touched him. De-pending on individual sensitivity and the expanse of the contact surface, he may collapse and suf-fer respiratory problems, which is especially dangerous if he is alone. Any subsequent contact with a Portuguese man-of-war is always more serious than the first.

The only truly effective preven-tive measure is never to enter tropical waters without gloves or clothing, or at least to cover as much of one's body as possible. Once again, if one is poisoned, the treatment is based on calcium gluconate, corticoids and antihis-tamines. If you have nothing else, rubbing the lesions with a fine sand mixed with sea water can give some relief.

## CONE SHELLS

Among the dangers of tropical seas, cone shells, a type of venom-ous snail, rank high. Their shells have vibrant colors, which make them attractive to collectors.

Several species are very danger-ous, since they have harpoon-like teeth, which they project forward and which inject a very toxic venom that has both local and sys-temic effects. Death can occur within several hours due to respiratory paralysis, cardiac arrest, or asphyxia as a result of edema of the glottis. Some cone shells, which must be avoided at all costs, are *Conus textilis, Conus anticus* and *Conus geographus.*

On an island, never explore the beaches or atolls in bare feet. Lacking footwear, you should carefully examine the ground be fore taking each step, particularly on Indian Ocean beaches and throughout the Pacific. Cones are easy to spot among the edible shellfish and are the only ones that are venomous. Shellfish may prove poisonous for other reasons, but they contain no natural toxins. Shellfish filter dozens, if not hundreds, of quarts of water per day, and thus can concentrate toxic substances or microorganisms. In a survival situation, there is no way of determining whether a shellfish is toxic or not, and therefore it is better to be cautious and taste only a small amount. Then increase the quantity, preferably after boiling the shellfish (many toxins break down in heat). The only shellfish that should categorically be rejected is the terebridae or augers, which has a very elongated, conical shape.

## OCTOPI

Octopi, sometimes nicknamed "devilfish," are molluscs without shells and are armed with long arms with suckers. They are edible and not venomous, with the exception of the blue ring octopus with luminescent blue markings that is dangerous to the touch and that inhabits the Great Barrier Reef of Australia.

## FISH

There are 250 species of fish that are venomous either through their saliva if they bite, or, more often, through venomous spines on their fins. Some species, such as stingfish, rays, and stonefish, hide under the sand, and stepping on them with bare feet or brushing them with a hand can cause poisoning. Others, like the morays and the porcupine fish, bite if they are disturbed or attacked. These fish are primarily found in the Pacific and the Indian oceans.

Here are the four categories of venomous fish, in descending order of toxicity:

### Synanceja, or "Stonefish"

The name "stonefish" is extremely appropriate, and the creature has a remarkable gift for camouflage. Not only do stonefish remain immobile and blend their colors with their background, but they also have an extraordinary irregularity of contours, which truly makes them look like stones. A diver may inadvertently take hold of one for support. There are several species of this fish and they are called "toads of the sea" in the Antilles and "nohus" in Polynesia. They have dorsal spines that inject venom from glands located at their base. These glands are squeezed by ligaments to circulate the venom through lateral grooves along the spines. There are up to 13 spines. The severity of the poisoning of course depends on the amount of venom injected, and this is proportional to the number of spines that puncture the skin, the depth of the penetration and the size of the fish. Poisoning is always accompanied by severe pain, which may cause unconsciousness and is especially dangerous for a diver at a great depth. It can lead to cardio-respiratory complications and in tegumentary necroses around the wound. Death is rare and depends on each individual's past history: asthma, chronic eczema and prior envenomation are all danger signs. Treatment consists of soaking the area in water at a temperature of 131°F (55°C) because the venom is thermolabile; the best treatment is to administer an "anti-stonefish" or Melbourne serum subcutaneously around the wound.

### Scorpaenidae, or Scorpion Fish

These are very beautiful and very toxic; they have vibrant colors, lovely stripes, and numerous, long, venomous spines. Their venom is toxic, but seldom fatal.

### Rockfish

These look more like fish than stonefish do; they are more rounded and have scales. They are less venomous and very numerous—fishermen often catch them in their nets. The injuries they cause can become necrotic.

### Rays

There are 300 species of rays, most of which do not have a venomous sting. Those that do are called stingrays and their caudal fin is replaced by a fearsome whip, which is longer than their body. At the base of this appendage there are one, two or three stingers with sharp teeth permanently coated with venom. The stingers point upward and their sole purpose is to repulse aggressors; rays never attack man, but accidental contact is possible, especially since they often hide under the sand.

Most accidents in tropical waters are caused by the leopard ray. In rare cases, its very painful sting can be fatal. Many injuries are sustained by fishermen who handle rays believing them to be dead. Treatment is the same as for all venom poisonings.

### Porcupine Fish—Poisonous, but Not Venomous

These are seldom longer than 19.5 inches (50 centimeters), and they have a very distinctive appearance: The puff up like a stiff balloon if attacked. They can be found in all shallower tropical waters. They are not venomous, but they are very poisonous. Eating them causes 200 deaths a year in Japan, in spite of cooks who specialize in preparing them by removing the poisonous parts. Porcupine fish should categorically be rejected, as should all other similar fish that have a hard shell or that puff themselves up (for example, tetraodontiformes). Porcupine fish suffocate sharks that swallow them and are therefore one of the Squalidae's few enemies.

Most venomous fish are unusual looking, so be suspicious of all shapes or colors that are out of the ordinary. Evolution has found two seemingly contradictory methods of achieving the same end: On the one hand, stonefish, rockfish and rays camouflage themselves perfectly; on the other, the vibrant colors of scorpion and surgeon fish advertise themselves—and their dangerousness—with vibrant colors.

## Ciguatera, or Ichthyosarcotoxism

Ciguatera is fish poisoning, which results when fish eat microscopic algae that parasitize some corals (Dinoflagellida). The toxins in the algae contaminate the fish but cause them no harm. In their turn, these fish are eaten by larger carnivorous fish. Man is contaminated by ingesting the meat of these carnivorous fish and can develop serious clinical symptoms: vomiting, diarrhea, a drop in blood pressure or even collapse, neurological problems and joint and muscle pains. Fatalities are rare, and the symptoms usually abate in 8 to 10 days, but they often leave allergic aftereffects. All people who eat fish in tropical areas should be aware of this sickness. For example, this applies to shipwrecked people who land on a coral island, or to people from the interior who must survive on a lagoon for some time. In the Antilles and Polynesia entire sections of the population are contaminated to a greater or lesser degree, depending on whether fish constitute their total diet or only a part of it.

Some simple principles will make it possible for a person to survive in a contaminated area where fish are the sole source of food.

■ Large carnivorous fish should be avoided, since they are likely to become increasingly contaminated as they get older.
■ No species can be guaranteed to be harmless, but a person shipwrecked on the high seas has little chance of catching a toxic fish, since no coral reefs form at great depths. Fish caught out at sea (tuna, bonitos) are safer than the large predators of the coral reef (barracudas, scads, bass).
■ If possible, one should only eat

fish that have been caught on the leeward shores of the island.

- One should eat only filleted fish, after all internal and genital organs have been removed.

# A SPECIAL ENVIRONMENT: THE SEASHORE

All the venomous or poisonous creatures we have mentioned have their own very specific ecosystems: atolls, lagoons, coral reefs, tidal lagoons—broadly speaking, the ecosystems of tropical seashores. Most of these dangers do not exist on the high seas, where the flora and fauna are very different. Corals only grow on sea beds to which the sun's rays penetrate; they attract small vegetarian fish, which, in turn, attract larger carnivorous fish, and so the food chain proceeds up to the sharks, which can frequently be seen even in enclosed lagoons.

## MISCELLANEOUS DANGERS

Apart from the harmless sleeping sharks, which are indigenous to calm waters, the most dangerous sharks also regularly visit the seashore, attracted by the varied fauna. Other predatory fish can be found there, particularly barracudas, which look like a pike and can grow to a length of 6½ feet (2 meters). People often encounter them during skindiving expeditions, but barracudas never attack first. However, one should be careful not to carry any wounded fish, since the blood is sure to attract barracudas (as it does most carnivorous fish, whether piranhas, Pacific bass or sharks). The severity of the injury caused by a barracuda's bite is due to its large number of firmly implanted, very sharp teeth.

The green and spotted morays are also regular visitors to coastal caves and rocks, and it is easy to disturb them inadvertently, particularly when diving. The green moray rarely attacks—in spite of its ferocious appearance and its 6½ to 10 feet (2 to 3 meters) of solid muscle—except to defend itself. If it does attack, its bite is debilitating and there is always a danger of secondary infection since its mouth is a haven for all kinds of bacteria. It lives in the darkness of its hiding place and is seldom encountered during the day. The spotted moray grows to a maximum length of 3 feet (1 meter) and is less sedentary.

Monitor lizards, large 6½- to 10-feet-long carnivorous reptiles, should be mentioned among the curious, aggressive creatures that may frequent the seashores. Some have survived in Africa and Asia, especially on the island of Komodo in Indonesia.

Among creatures found along the seashore are the marine crocodiles (the names "alligator" and "caiman" describe only the American crocodilian that can grow to 16½ feet [5 meters]). These crocodiles like the sea as much as they do swamps and can be found in some tidal lagoons, especially in Australia where they are reputed to be man-eaters. They can grow 20 to 23 feet (6 to 7 meters), and they habitually seize their prey and pull it to the bottom to drown it before devouring it.

## FISH OR SNAKE?

A person might climb out of the water after being bitten or stung, feel alarming general symptoms, and wonder what animal caused them. The answer is simple: a fish sting is followed by strong localized pain, while a sea snake's bite is painless. Moreover, stings by fish occur much more frequently than snakebites, although the latter are very serious if total envenomation occurs, as it does in about a quarter of all cases. The venom of sea snakes is very toxic (twice as potent as a cobra) and death often occurs if the bite is left untreated. Many pearl fishers have lost their lives this way in the Persian Gulf.

Sea snakes usually move along the surface, but they have been found at depths of 131 to 197 feet (40 to 60 meters). They are also frequently found close to the shore. Their habit of moving around in groups or shoals adds to the danger. They are at most 5 feet (1.5 meters) long, and the tip of their tail is shaped like a vertical fin. They are most common in the Indian Ocean, the Persian Gulf, the China Sea, to the north of Australia, and around all the Asian islands. Sea snake antivenin is manufactured in Australia. It should only be included in the survival kit if you intend to walk, swim or dive regularly in coastal waters that harbor this dangerous species.

# SURVIVAL IN
# A GROUP

- True Stories of Panic

- Disastrous Group Behavior

- The Makeup of a Team

- Selection and Training of Team Members

- The Selection of a Leader

- Isolation

# TRUE STORIES OF PANIC

## July 2, 1816

The French frigate La Méduse runs aground on a sandbank about 62 miles (100 kilometers) from the African coast. The six lifeboats on board can only hold 250 of the 400 passengers and a huge raft is constructed to carry the remaining passengers as well as some food. The lifeboats are to tow the raft toward the shore. They have traveled two leagues from the Méduse when the tow-line breaks or is cut, and the boats abandon the raft and its passengers to their fate. One hundred forty-six people remain on board, including one woman; they have only a few casks of wine, several barrels of water and 22 pounds (10 kilograms) of biscuits. They have no sail, no rope, no anchor and no map.

During the first night several men drown, carried away by the waves or crushed between the broken timbers. During the second night, after drinking a cask of wine, the men mutiny against the few officers present in a general fit of madness. Sixty survivors die during this night, either run through by the sword or held under water until they drown. By dawn of the third day, there are only 67 survivors. The water and food are gone, and one of the men starts to dismember a corpse. Instantly dozens throw themselves on the "prey" like a pack of wolves. After a mere three days it could only be the fear of starvation and not starvation itself, that could push them to do something so drastic. The following night hysteria continues, causing 12 more deaths. By the morning of the fifth day, after more sailors and passengers have killed each other, there are only 30 survivors—and all of them are wounded.

On the sixth day, after a short discussion, the dying are simply thrown to the sharks that have been following the raft from the outset. Six days later, the remaining passengers are found and saved after 13 days of senseless atrocities.

## Summer 1983

A French and American team is searching for the wreck of the Titanic, which, 70 years after its sinking has lost none of its attraction. The search is a long shot: Many people believe it will be impossible to find a wreck at a depth of 13,120 feet (4,000 meters), particularly since only an approximate location of the disaster is known. Moreover, while the liner was sinking into the abyss, it could have continued to move along a relatively horizontal trajectory and thus could be several miles farther on.

But suddenly the sensational news flashes round the world: The Titanic has been found! A few unremarkable

125

photos of the wreck are brought back, but the divers do not venture too deep for fear of snagging a propeller in the cables. *National Geographic* publishes the first photos of a wreck that has become very fragile. A second exploratory expedition undertakes a more thorough search of the two parts of the wreck, which are separated by more than 2,624 feet (800 meters). The ship is split one-third of the way between the bow and the stern and displays its entrails to the fascinated aquanauts. What they discover is both extraordinary and appalling. They will never talk about it and, above all, no picture will ever be published in conformance with a well-established tradition. The site is classified as a "memorial" by the Americans, although the wreck is outside America's territorial waters.

Around the wreck, and particularly inside of it, hundreds of corpses are frozen in place, transfixed by the enormous pressure and the total absence of currents at this depth. The ghastly flesh is slightly withered and the clothing has disappeared, but it is possible to distinguish between the young and the old, between women with long hair and women with short hair. The exceptional state of preservation is unexpected, even in these waters where the temperature is below 32°F (0°C). It also proves that no carnivore ever troubles these glacial depths.

But this is not the most shocking discovery. It is natural that there would be at least skeletons in the wreck that caused 1,513 deaths. What is shocking is that the vast majority of the corpses are found on the lower decks and practically none are found on the upper decks. Seventy years later, the most outrageous allegations become reality, the most questionable witnesses become credible. Apparently, during the hours when the ship was sinking, the exits from the lower decks to the upper decks had been sealed. In a fit of panic, mothers, respectable gentlemen and responsible crew members grabbed for themselves the only chance to survive—the few lifeboats available.

---

✪

## February 1984

Toward the end of the afternoon the weather turns nasty in the Mediterranean, and a fierce, cold wind rises. The heavy helicopter is midway between the coast and an island where it is to drop 12 marine commandos, when its two engines ice up and die. The two experienced pilots succeed in restarting the propeller just above the waves and the helicopter comes to rest on the water, sustaining little damage despite the angry sea. The machine has been built to float for a while, long enough to enable the crew to evacuate into boats. The helicopter is equipped with two boats, each with room for about 15 people, that can be inflated automatically by breaking a gas cartridge.

Once the fear caused by the sudden fall subsides, the passengers start to congratulate each other. Not only is the machine afloat, but the radio is still working, and the pilots succeed in sending a mayday signal with their approximate location. Relief gives way to group euphoria. The passengers admire the construction of a helicopter that is so large, yet is able to float following such a crash. They compliment the skill of the pilots and are happy that help is on the way. They forget that the lifeboats have to be made ready, that it is winter, that the sea is stormy, that they are not in a boat but in a helicopter, and that the rescue team will certainly not arrive before the helicopter sinks.

Suddenly they realize that the floor is sinking and the water is rising. They seize the first boat and throw it out of the rear doors, forgetting to pull the cord to release the gas. Still encased in its container, the boat disappears beneath the waves and sinks within a matter of seconds while the water continues to enter the passenger compartment. They now realize that they should have deployed the boats much earlier. They rush to the other container, falling over each other in an effort to do everything at once; there is total panic. Finally they break the cartridge to inflate the dinghy but forget to push it out of the door first. Within three seconds the enormous tube fills the passenger compartment. The passengers throw themselves into

the water in total chaos. One hour later the rescue team arrives and finds the victims dispersed, floating in their life jackets. Thirteen of them are dead. The only survivor is saved in extremis with internal temperature of 95°F (35°C).

All of them died within an hour—of cold, to be sure, but above all because they panicked, because of lack of foresight and the absence of a leader.

The captain of the aircraft should have remained the sole master on board, even after it had landed on the water; it was his duty to delegate his authority if he felt unequal to the task or if the leader of the commandos seemed to have more experience than he had himself in dealing with such situations. He was not injured and therefore had no valid reason not to assume his responsibilities.

Group euphoria, which causes a lack of concern and a carefree feeling, is contagious, as is panic. All 14 men suffered from these contradictory emotions, which have equally disastrous consequences. The excess of optimism that engulfed them during the first minutes was not moderated by anyone. Used to following orders, the copilot was right in relying on the captain, and the commandos on their leader. But neither of the two men, whose titles made them responsible, did anything—and they led the men to their deaths.

---

This is the account of the sole survivor, a marine whose identity and nationality we will not further specify. We will confine ourselves to discussing the specific

aberrations in the behavior of the group:

■ the contagiousness of specific states of mind, which were totally inappropriate for the situation: euphoria followed by panic. The panic was more pronounced because it followed the opposite emotional state.

■ the inexplicable failure of the leader's authority.

■ the lack of initiative on the part of the victims of the crash, possibly because they were afraid of being accused of cowardice or, more probably, of a lack of respect for the hierarchy. The lack of a leader is even more disastrous among military servicemen, who are trained to follow orders absolutely.

■ the failure to implement elementary rescue practices. The behavior of the pilots is especially incomprehensible since they had repeatedly practiced this kind of accident.

# DISASTROUS GROUP BEHAVIOR

The behaviors best adapted to difficult situations appear particularly in military disasters. The professionalism and training of soldiers, who are prepared especially for such situations, prevents surprise or paralysis in dangerous situations. Discipline, the command structure and team spirit form a protective shield that enables the preservation of self-control and the implementation of appropriate measures.

On the other hand, when disasters affect groups of individuals who are used to acting and reacting on their own, there is often a confusion–inhibition–stupor reaction, which leaves the victims dazed and lacking in initiative.

Some authors estimate that in most disasters 15 percent of the individuals manifest pathological reactions, 70 percent apparently remain calm but are, in fact, in a state of emotional shock and loss of initiative, and only 15 percent retain their self-control.

Under the influence of strong emotion, a normal individual may flee, display uncoordinated agitation and aggression, or go into a state of numbed shock. Frequently these reactions are transitory and are followed by senseless self-criticism. Mass fear is generally released by "panic germs," i.e., weak individuals, whose panic is contagious, inducing in others impaired judgment and a propensity to go along with the most senseless acts. In this way, a mob becomes impulsive, aggressive and lacking in foresight. Every individual feels he is anonymous and participates in violence without accountability. As a part of a cohesive group, on the other hand, individual reactions are easier to channel—as long as the individuals can rely on well-learned instructions and a real leader. An attempt to identify the latter must be made when selecting a group; this is, however, not always easy.

The group should form an entity that reacts to external aggressions as one man. From this perspective, each member of the team should feel that he shares motivations or goals in common with the rest of the team.

Obviously one cannot expect hundreds of passengers, traveling together by chance on an ocean liner, to adopt a common interest, let alone similar motivations. In a shipwreck, everyone experiences his own personal self-preservation reflex. The purpose of a cruise is not to create a common bond between people, who often have nothing to say to each other in any case—except concerning preparations for an improbable potential shipwreck.

The criteria are very different for the composition of a group of people who intend to go on an expedition. These people will be pursuing the same purposes and using the same means to get there. However, their motivations may be very different, depending on the personality of each individual, since the success of the expedition depends not on the uniformity of the members but on their unity.

This cohesive capacity of the group arises from a state of mind that cannot be acquired within a couple of months. Either a person is suited for survival in a group or he is not. The problem is that no medical examination can categorically reveal this suitability. Some psychological tests may give a rough idea, but they are fallible. It would be worthwhile for the leader of the group to arrange some preliminary exercises in the field: a short cruise on a small boat; a long, hard hike; and possibly even a pleasant social evening by the fireside. But it is not possible to change the deeper nature of an adult within a few days and instill in him ideas of civic duty, altruism or group values that he never before possessed.

## THE MAKEUP OF A TEAM

Recruiting in an elite corps such as France's GISGN (the Specialized Intervention Group of the National Gendarmerie—the French equivalent of an American SWAT team), follows standard criteria in relation to physical condition, but the people in command insist that there is no typical psychological profile. The variety of the missions they must perform enables the leader of the corps to choose individuals who seem best suited to the needs of the moment on a case-by-case basis. Moreover, and this may be the most important point, the multiplicity of personalities makes it possible to maintain an adaptability to all environments and all situations in each member through competition and team spirit. The flexibility obtained through this variety of abilities provides a good foundation for confronting difficult and unforeseen situations in a group. The complementary qualities of the members within a team will unite them more tightly. The U.S. Marines are very uniform on all levels, but the missions for which they are trained are equally uniform. When these well-trained troops found themselves in Vietnam facing an elusive enemy that lived in underground passages, they were unable to adapt, and it was the individualists among them who became the specialists in a war that was both unpredictable and merciless.

The ideal situation in an expedition comprising several people is to choose multitalented members. The multiplicity of their abilities will give them a broader mindset, which is more propitious for life in a group—in addition to the fact that they will be useful in as many ways as possible. For instance, a doctor who is nothing but a doctor will prove to be dead weight on an expedition. The explorer Jacques Cousteau was well aware of this, and his crew on the *Calypso* was always made up of members who could not only maneuver the ship, but could also dive, film, weld, cook, clean, navigate and more. Multifaceted individuals are more useful to an expedition than superspecialists.

## SELECTION AND TRAINING OF TEAM MEMBERS

Selection in the field can be done in a variety of ways, not necessarily in direct relation to the planned activity. An underwater environment, without question, is the most demanding and the most likely to expose certain latent defects quickly: claustrophobia, excitability, the inability to deal with danger, inability to concentrate, an intolerance for shortness of breath, the lack of quick reflexes, sensitivity to the cold, etc.

Whatever the discipline, only time will turn an amateur into a professional. During the Battle of Britain in World War II, young British pilots were, by necessity, sent up in fighter planes after only 30 hours of flying. The death rate was very high and many were shot down by German raiders on their first flights, while veteran pilots survived through their acquired mastery over themselves and their planes.

When assembling a group, one must choose team members that are both multifaceted and experienced—and the very young rarely meet this requirement.

# THE SELECTION OF A LEADER

One of the leader's tasks is to provide objective and calming information to his team. He must know how to delegate some of his authority in predetermined areas. He must have the necessary humility to transfer command if he feels unsuited to dealing with the events and one of his teammates seems to be better qualified. If such a teammate does not exist, he must remain the leader, and outwardly he must remain calm and retain his self-control.

In the army, each officer passes through the hierarchical ranks according to his seniority and according to his ability to command. This is particularly true of elite units, in which one will seldom find an officer who has "risen to his level of incompetence." It is less true in other hierarchies.

In civilian life, the choice is more difficult, especially if the initiator of the expedition believes that he should legitimately be the leader. The ability to organize an expedition does not necessarily correlate with the ability to lead it. Thus many expeditions that were well prepared to begin with foundered because the initiator was not suited to lead in the field. The unity of the team is determined by each of its members, but it is the leader who sets the tone.

# ISOLATION

Isolation is the usual fate of a man in a survival situation, both personally and geographically. It may be a refuge for an individual for whom survival in a group has become impossible. There may even be a kind of collective isolation for a group lost in inhospitable terrain.

It is interesting to examine some examples of ordinary people who were able to survive for years, cut off from their families, their civilized activities, their friends, their culture and their emotional and material environment, while subjected to extreme deprivation, abysmal physical conditions and threats and dangers of every kind.

Does isolation, of itself, cause stress that is sufficiently severe mentally and physically to prevent survival in a hostile environment? The answer is no. Michel Sifre's many experiments during the 1960s confirm that man can endure isolation well. He pushed himself to the limit when he isolated himself for 60 days at the bottom of a pit. The only contact he had with the outside world was a telephone, but he forbade all assistance for the first 30 days, which made his chances of getting out alive, had there been any physical problems, minimal. Despite his total break with society and the suppression of the normal rhythm of days and nights, Sifre preserved a more or less normal sleep-wake cycle and suffered no mental disturbances or psychological problems. Solitude, silence, darkness and cold did not affect his physical health in the long term, and the only thing he had to do when the experiment was over was spend several days readjusting to sunlight. Moreover, it proves that speleological encampments deep underground do not pose any special problems. Admittedly, Michel Sifre was not just anyone, but a passionate scientist, so determined that he became physically involved with his own experiments.

In the context of morale, isolation is endured more easily if internal resources can act as a substitute for a physical companion. During his ordeal at the North Pole in 1986, J.-L. Étienne invented people to talk to, so that he would feel less alone. He used familiar objects to act as witnesses to his difficulties and pleasures, he talked to his pots, encouraged his sled and scolded his recalcitrant hot plate.

Group isolation also occurs, and its nature may affect the survival of the whole group: The chief danger is that panic will arise within groups in which each individual has been more or less left to his own devices. It seems that save for the presence of a strong leader, total isolation can make all personal initiative useless. Witness the German World

War II submarine fleet, a branch of service that paid a high price: 32,000 deaths out of 40,000 men, and 780 U-boats sunk out of 1,100. The testimony of survivors indicates that there was intense fear when a submarine was trapped by a vessel on the surface. Forced to stop the engines for hours on end to eliminate all sound, the crew had to wait for the end of the torpedoing that threatened to tear apart the hull at any moment. The absence of mass panic was due not only to the presence of a commander and to respect for the hierarchy, but also to the fact that there was no alternative: Since they were stuck at a depth of 394 feet (120 meters), the limit at which the hull could be ruptured by the pressure, it is unlikely that any one plan would work better than any other. The group was an entity that would either die or escape—there was no room for individual initiative.

Panic, in fact, only occurs when there is a range of options, and when individuals desperately grasp at one rather than another. On a raft or on a sinking ocean liner, each person may have his own ideas and want to impose his own will, and he will panic when no one follows him since he is sure that he is right. Only the authority of a leader accepted and recognized by the majority can bring everyone into harmony and calm the fears of those who need it.

# PART II

## Hostile Environments

# THE SEA AND SHIPWRECKS

- Facts

- Myths

- Location by Ocean-Going Ships

- Drinking Seawater

- Fish as a Source of Water

- Other Sources of Hypotonic Fluid

- Storage Containers and Receptacles

- Fighting Dehydration at Sea

- Fishing: Targets and Methods

- Sharks

- Whales

- Physical Confinement: Effects and Remedies

- Mandatory Equipment for Lifeboats

- Procedures in Case of Shipwreck

- Special Medical Problems of the Shipwrecked

- Mental Stress

- Conclusion

# FACTS

⚙ Seas and oceans cover 65 percent of the planet's surface.

⚙ Ninety percent of shipwrecked people die during the three days following a shipwreck, yet it takes much longer to die of hunger or thirst.

⚙ The blue whale can grow to a length of 98 feet (30 meters) and weigh 150 tons. It eats up to 8 tons of krill per day.

# MYTHS

⚙ *Birds are a sign that land is close by; the species may even indicate the maximum distance from shore:* Absolutely untrue.

⚙ *Under no circumstances should you drink seawater or urine, which will merely hasten death:* Properly used, both seawater and urine can be lifesaving. But knowledge of how to use them is essential.

The picture of a man alone in the vastness of the ocean, lost on a flimsy boat without food or water, is many a person's nightmare, the very image of impending torment and death. But in reality, it need not be so.

Unquestionably, shipwreck is a representative model of all life-threatening circumstances. Shipwrecks occur frequently, and they involve large numbers of people, even those who have no intention of becoming adventurers.

Some extraordinary survival stories will allow us to examine the techniques of surviving in such circumstances. A study of these situations will help us to refute false beliefs, learn new techniques, and finally accept the possibility of shipwreck with a calmness justified by a firm knowledge of what to do to survive.

Every sea is different. In the cold seas people may die of hunger and cold; in warm waters of thirst; in temperate waters one is at the mercy of variable meteorological conditions and one may die of cold or heat, thirst or hunger. In all cases people suffer from isolation, stiffness, avitaminosis, skin lesions, exhaustion and moments of despair.

Nevertheless, survival is always possible—it depends on common sense, organization, moral strength, aggressiveness against adverse elements, and, above all, on acquired knowledge. Understanding the mechanism of hunger, thirst, and anxiety; the habits of fishes; various ways of obtaining potable liquids; practical tricks and formulas for fishing; how to find one's bearings, calculate the drift, or seal a leak in a dinghy can make the difference between a survivor and a casualty.

Even the smallest sea has tides, breezes, dominant winds, storms, hot currents, cold currents and surface currents. So many displacement vectors make for many reasons never to despair, never to believe that you will remain becalmed indefinitely in an area without food and water, without ships, and without reaching land. In tropical seas, the flora and fauna are different, and the climatic conditions very variable; but in all seas there is one constant that makes survival at least in part a matter of patience: There is no such thing as a static sea.

Just as there has never been a plane that did not come back to earth in one way or another, there has never been a floating device that has not, sooner or later, reached terra firma. The only question is how long it will take—**a shipwrecked person must survive long enough to reach a shore or to be picked up.**

Take, for example, Poon Lim, a Chinese sailor on the British cargo ship *Ben Lomona,* who was the sole survivor after his ship was torpedoed on November 23, 1942 in the middle of the Atlantic Ocean close to the equator. He drifted for 130 days, alone on a raft, fighting sharks and despair, before he was picked up in sight of the Brazilian coast on April 1, 1943. He still holds the record for the longest survival at sea, which is particularly remarkable since he had very few provisions to begin with. When he was picked up, he looked like a skeleton, but within three months he had recovered completely.

## LOCATION BY OCEAN-GOING SHIPS

A raft or a dinghy, even if it is bright orange, is very difficult to see, especially from the bridge of a ship, where the horizon is often obstructed by the surrounding waves. Many shipwrecked people have used flares, but have not been seen by anyone even at night. The difficulty of spotting a victim is even greater today because, due to automation, there is often only one man on watch, and he is more interested in what he sees on the radar screen than what he sees on the open sea. The only ships that keep a constant 360-degree visual watch are naval ships, and therefore they may see a flare; but there are relatively few naval ships at sea. Many shipwrecked people have given up after spotting a ship but failing to attract its attention.

The Baileys, a couple who drifted for 117 days north of the Galápagos Islands in 1973, saw seven ships before the eighth finally spotted them. Lucien

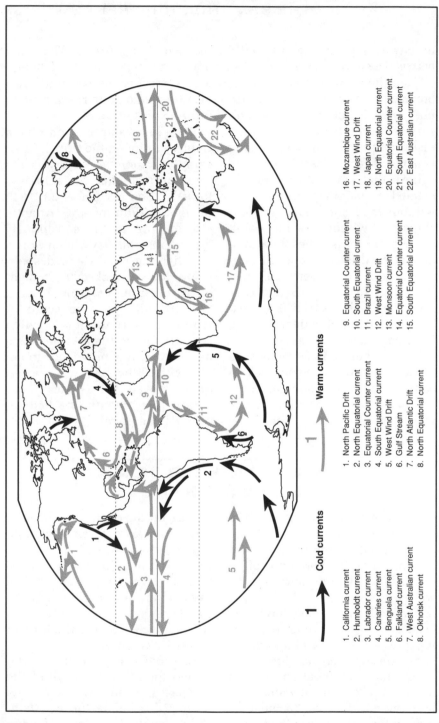

Cold currents

1. California current
2. Humboldt current
3. Labrador current
4. Canaries current
5. Benguela current
6. Falkland current
7. West Australian current
8. Okhotsk current

Warm currents

1. North Pacific Drift
2. North Equatorial current
3. Equatorial Counter current
4. South Equatorial current
5. West Wind Drift
6. Gulf Stream
7. North Atlantic Drift
8. North Equatorial current

9. Equatorial Counter current
10. South Equatorial current
11. Brazil current
12. West Wind Drift
13. Monsoon current
14. Equatorial Counter current
15. South Equatorial current

16. Mozambique current
17. West Wind Drift
18. Japan current
19. North Equatorial current
20. Equatorial Counter current
21. South Equatorial current
22. East Australian current

Schiltz and Catherine Plessz saw a dozen ships when they were lost in a dinghy, 6.5 feet (2 meters) in diameter, in the Mediterranean in 1972. During the two weeks they were adrift, some ships passed within hailing distance, some even splashed them with their wake. Not one heard them. One night, lights appeared less than a mile away. Lucien lit one of the three phosphorous flares he had and waved it desperately, burning his hand badly in the process. The ship changed course and searched intensely with a spotlight. Lucien lit the last two phosphorous flares, in vain. At dawn, the ship sailed off having given up the search.

In 1955 Arne Nicolaysen fell into the water between Cuba and Florida on Christmas night. He had no raft, not even a life jacket. Normally, this would be tantamount to a death sentence. In the majority of cases, a man in the sea is a dead man, since he is exposed to cold and exhaustion and, in addition, is almost invisible from a ship's bridge. A head and a wav-ing arm are minute dots, lost in the vastness of the waves. During the 29 hours that Nicolaysen survived in the water, he saw between 15 and 20 ships, some of them very close by. Surly and aggressive, he swore at them every time. Had he been passive and resigned, he would have drowned very quickly. In the middle of the night he saw the lights of a ship coming straight toward him. He swam desperately to get as close to it as possible, and shouted as loudly as he could. His heart almost stopped when he heard the engines slow down. A life belt landed close to him: He had been saved.

Poon Lim, who holds the record for survival at sea, saw ships at the beginning of his ordeal in the equatorial seas in 1942; though he stood on his raft and waved his arms like a madman, no one saw him, and he was forced to suffer months of agony.

Every tale of shipwreck and survival is unique. The following account is proof that no situation is truly as hopeless as it seems.

---

## Early 1980s

A Greek cargo ship is several hundred miles from the Panama coast, its destination. For a reason known only to himself, one of the crew members falls overboard and finds himself alone in the middle of the ocean in a desperate predicament. Without a life jacket, his prospects for survival are near zero. Some hours after his ship disappears, he sees a huge fin, followed by an immense wake, rushing toward him.

His disappearance is not noticed until the following day. The captain orders the ship to turn about in a very precise maneuver that will enable it to retrace its exact route in the opposite direction. The entire crew is on lookout for hours, but they see nothing. No one on board has the slightest illusion that they will find the man, but his family must be told that the crew did at least try.

The man is listed as missing, and several days later the company informs his family of the sad news. One week later the crew receives a notice from the U.S. Navy that a Greek sailor was found floating in the middle of the Caribbean—or, to be more precise, he was found clinging to an American warship! The fin had been the periscope of a submarine and the man had grabbed onto it as it passed.

# DRINKING SEAWATER

The question of whether or not seawater can safely be drunk has long been debated, and for centuries the debate was dominated by stories of the agonizing deaths suffered by those who had tried to drink it. These stories have been picked up by some navies, which feel obliged to publish regulations categorically prohibiting the intake of seawater. The French navy, for example, declared in 1966: "Do not drink seawater, even if it has been diluted with freshwater." This is bad advice. Even at its most salty, seawater contains 3.5 ounces of salt per quart (100 grams per liter), and adding a glass of seawater to a liter of fresh water will produce a liquid with the same osmotic pressure as beer, for example!

The intake of seawater can be beneficial under certain circumstances. Experience and experiment have shown that:

■ Seawater should be drunk before you start to feel thirsty. Once conditions have deteriorated so far that drinking it is necessary (lack of reserves of freshwater and no prospects of rain in the near future), the intake should correspond with the maximum daily need for sodium chloride, i.e., about half a liter (1 pint) of seawater containing 35 grams of sodium chloride per liter per day.

■ Intake should be divided up into about 10 portions, of two to three mouthfuls each per day.

■ It should be limited to no more than five to seven days if drunk constantly, to avoid the danger of exceeding the limits of renal function. If, after this length of time, you succeed in obtaining freshwater from fish, turtles, algae, or rain, you can again drink seawater in small doses for another cycle of five to seven days.

Two shipwrecked men survived for 14 days in the Mediterranean adhering to this method; they drank nothing but seawater for 10 of the days and used water from fish for the other 4 days. Neither of the men suffered from thirst, diarrhea or vomiting.

If a little freshwater is available

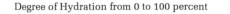

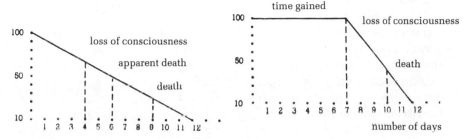

**Without any water, dehydration is steady and irreversible. Death occurs between the seventh and ninth day.**

Using seawater, hydration remains regular for about seven days (deterioration increases beyond seven days; death also occurs between the eighth and ninth day). But during the seven normal days, one can look for alternative sources of liquids (fish juices, rainwater) or rescue. (Extract from *Naufragé volontaire*, A. Bombard)

to begin with, there are several ways to make it last, but the fundamental principles remain the same:

■ Consume the freshwater—carefully—while it is available, so that you do not start drinking seawater in a state of dehydration.
■ At the beginning, either drink freshwater exclusively, or alternate one day of freshwater with one day of seawater.
■ Dilute the freshwater with seawater. In 1947 Thor Heyerdahl and his crew made a transoceanic expedition aboard the raft *Kon-Tiki*. Heyerdahl added 30 to 40 percent seawater to the fresh water he had available and successfully extended his supply.

These procedures enable survival for several days giving time to collect rainwater or catch fish.

Recent experiments justify the intake of seawater according to the above-mentioned procedures. They demonstrate that although seawater does not increase the total time of survival, it does extend the time during which the shipwrecked person remains conscious and capable of action.

**Without water of any kind, dehydration is steady and relentless; it leads to loss of consciousness around the third day and to death between the seventh and eighth days.**

If seawater is drunk, hydration remains normal for about seven days, though death still occurs around the eighth or ninth day. However, the main point is that the individual remains perfectly conscious for seven days. This time span is a determining factor: It enables a person to get organized, allows an ecosystem to develop under the boat, as we shall see later, and enables the individual to study his surroundings. After the seventh day decompensation (lack of adequate circulation by the heart) will set in rapidly, but seven days of relative comfort will have been gained. Obviously, these time limits may be shortened considerably if the heat is intense, but the general outlines of the two scenarios remain the same. In 1954, 61-year-old William Willis left Callao in Peru on a raft made of six trunks of balsa wood. He landed in the Samoan Islands 117 days later, having traveled 6,700 miles. In the middle of the Pacific he was horrified to find that his water containers had been punctured, and the water had leaked out. He spent half his journey drinking a bowl of freshwater per day, which he alternated with 16.5 ounces (500 ml) of seawater. He experienced no discomfort, despite the tropical latitudes, and arrived in excellent condition. There are many examples of shipwrecked people who would be dead if they had not used similar methods.

## ENEMAS OF BRACKISH WATER

This is a method of fluid absorption that Lynn Robertson, who was shipwrecked with her husband, Dougal, and four children, focused on with very interesting results. Its effectiveness is not surprising, since the mucous membranes of the colon reabsorb water contained in the feces.

Several quarts of seawater should be injected (Lynn Robertson used the tube from an air pump with a plastic bag that acted as a funnel) to enable sufficient absorption. This is an intriguing method, because the mucous membrane of the colon has a filtering ability that the mucous membrane in the mouth lacks. Some birds have such a filter, which enables them to rehydrate their bodies in the middle of an ocean (putting to rest the false belief that the presence of a bird indicates the proximity of land). This method of absorbing seawater through the colon merits research to determine whether it is as effective as it appears to be.

## FISH AS A SOURCE OF WATER

Many people who succeed in catching fish, sometimes in large numbers, do not eat them because they have no water. Adapting diet to water reserves is a good principle, but fish are a food source that contains a large quantity of endogenous water (60 to 80 percent, depending on the species). During his voyage, Alain Bombard survived for 24 days drinking exclusively seawater and fish juices (see Bibliography). Since he foresaw this, he had taken a fruit press

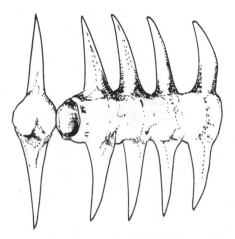

It is possible to suck the fluid from the cavities in a fish's vertebrae.

squeeze out the juice (it is better to use a shirt than an absorbent towel!). Another method, which can be used for larger fish, is to make successive incisions lengthwise along its back, deep enough to reach the muscle mass. The fish is then held horizontally until the incisions turn into channels full of fluid. This fluid should be collected in a container so it will not be lost. This cannot be done along the ventral surface, as there are no muscles there and the internal organs are directly beneath the skin.

Fish also have two other sources of hypotonic fluid:

along with him. In fact, up to 15 ounces (450 ml) of water per 2.2 pounds (1 kilogram) of fish can be extracted in the following manner:

■ the eyes, the fluids of which contain 90 percent water,
■ the cephalo-spinal fluid, which is easy to collect from large fish by cutting the vertebral column close to the tail and pouring out the liquid. As it is in all vertebrates, this fluid is pure and clear.

■ The internal organs of the fish must first be removed, and then the muscle masses must be cut into cubes.
■ After this, the cubes should be wrapped in a piece of linen or a garment, which is twisted to

In large fish the individual vertebrae can be crushed between the fingers and the fluid sucked out.

# OTHER SOURCES OF HYPOTONIC FLUID

## RAINWATER

The sea is almost as much a "kingdom of thirst" as is the desert, except that clouds form more frequently above the oceans and

therefore it is more likely to rain. If you can influence the direction of drift, steer toward those regions where there is a better likelihood of finding rain clouds. Do no simply wait for the first rain with your mouth open—prepare as many containers as possible and as large a surface as possible to catch the water: sails, clothing, canvas, etc. The bottom of the boat should always be kept clean and should regularly be rinsed down with seawater so that the water that collects there will not contain too many impurities.

The biggest problem is to make sure that all collection surfaces are usable, particularly the raft's canopy, which is normally covered with spray and salt. A daily rinsing with plenty of seawater will remove most of the salt, since it will dissolve in the seawater, which is far from saturated with sodium chloride. The remaining salt will be quickly washed away by the first heavy rain shower and there should not be enough left to make the water brackish.

Daily preventive rinsing, beginning on the first day, will also cut down on the strong rubbery taste in the collected water. The surfaces of all rubber boats impart this strong taste when the boats are first removed from their containers. Few people can stomach the taste, and it often causes nausea and vomiting.

In addition, shipwrecked people should completely expose themselves to the rain, using it to wash themselves in order to slow down or inhibit the development of skin sores, which, as we shall see, are caused both by lack of exercise and by irritation from the salt. The expediency of these showers naturally depends on the temperature and on the shipwrecked person's state of health.

## WATER FROM CONDENSATION

Some shipwrecked people lick the "dew" from the linings of their boats as soon as they wake up. This means that the temperature difference between night and day must be large enough for the water vapor contained in the hot air of the day to condense during the night and be deposited on cold objects. On some mornings Bombard collected as much as a quart of water from dew with the help of a sponge. This is another reason to rinse the walls of the boat with seawater every evening.

## URINE

In the discussion of thirst, above, we justified drinking urine. At sea, as in the desert, it is advisable to recycle hypotonic fluids if you have nothing else. In relation to osmotic concentration, it has been demonstrated that urine has a higher salt concentration than seawater.

## ICE FROM THE SEA

Shipwrecked people in cold seas should know that salt tends to separate from water when it freezes. The salt becomes concentrated in pockets of water that remain liquid for the very reason that the concentration of salt is so great. In other words, there is a spontaneous separation of salt and frozen water. People who are shipwrecked in the higher latitudes should also be aware that icebergs are made of freshwater, since they come from glaciers that plunge into the sea.

## TURTLE'S BLOOD

It is a major mistake not to quench your thirst with this precious fluid. It should be drunk immediately after the turtle has been killed (see below for methods of catching turtles), because it starts to coagulate within a few minutes. Therefore the jugular arteries and veins in the neck should be cut after a large container has been placed beneath them. It is useful to remember that sea turtles, unlike land tortoises, cannot retract their heads, and therefore their neck's are always accessible. In 1882 an adventurer named Gilbey traveled 7,000 miles (11,200 kilometers) from San Francisco to Australia. He caught a large number of turtles but threw the blood overboard instead of drinking it. This negligence not only made it more difficult for him to survive, but also attracted an enormous hammerhead shark, which he could not scare off even when he shot at it.

## WATER FROM ALGAE

Floating algae, like all plants, contain a considerable amount of hypotonic fluid.

## DESALINIZED WATER

One of the greatest lessons learned from Steven Callahan's experiences during his odyssey in 1983 is the decisive importance of the presence of solar distilling condensers on board (see Bibliography). It is astonishing that this equipment, which is light and takes up little space, is almost never included in a lifeboat's kit. But it is of primary importance— as important as having a multifunctional knife. It is about as large as an 8 × 11-inch note pad and is flexible enough to be bent for storage. It should be mandatory in the boat. The principle is very simple and must be understood before one can use the machine efficiently and repair it if necessary. The distilling condenser uses the greenhouse effect, then evaporation, and then the condensation of water against a colder surface to produce freshwater. Water placed in this device, like water in a greenhouse, heats up very quickly due to the transparent frame that protects it from the external atmosphere, particularly if the water is placed in a black base. Vapor rises until it reaches the transparent cover that is much colder. The vapor

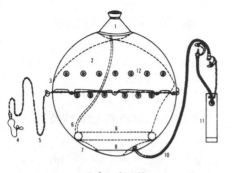

**Solar distiller**

1.–Receptacle for seawater 2.–Internal covering of the evaporator, made of dark material 3.–Transparent plastic covering 4.–Hothouse wires 5.–Assembly cord 6.–Tube for filling the ballast 7.–Siphon for freshwater 8.–Fabric drain for saline water 9. Ballast tube 10. Tube to inflate the distiller and its connection with the container 11. Container for freshwater 12. Tenons separating the covers

thus cools and condenses against the internal wall. The drops trickle down along the interior wall, which is more or less spherical, and are collected in a gutter below. Using this method, one can obtain 33 to 49.5 fluid ounces (1,000 to 1,500 ml) of pure water per day at the equator and 16.5 fluid ounces (500 ml) per day in temperate latitudes, even during the winter (the system functions, if less efficiently, even if the sun is hidden behind a light cloud cover). Its advantage is that it produces a significant amount of freshwater, enough for one ship-wrecked person (if extended by a little seawater), and that it can be used for several weeks. The disadvantage is that it is relatively fragile, which means that the distilling condenser must be taken down or sheltered during storms. In order to use this process, the device must be suspended in some way, but this should not pose a problem nowadays, since all lifeboats must now have tops and inflated rubber arches.

Another method is a miniaturized version of a device used in industrial desalinization plants, which is based on ion exchanger membranes. It is a specially treated rubber sheath containing a membrane based on silver zeolite and barium. The silver and barium react with the sodium chloride and magnesium salts contained in seawater to form silver chloride and magnesium chloride, which are deposited and leave a liquid very close to freshwater floating on the surface. The main disadvantage of the system is that it can only be used a few times since the salts gradually become exhausted. The advantage is that it is less breakable in comparison to the distilling condenser and can also be used at night. In conclusion, every lifeboat should have at least two distilling condensers on board.

# STORAGE CONTAINERS AND RECEPTACLES

It is not only important but in fact vital to have adequate storage containers, since any source of water is necessarily irregular and depends on the weather, on the state of the equipment and on the ability of the shipwrecked person to exploit it. The best containers are plastic cans, and as many of them as possible should be collected before the ship sinks. They should be carefully attached to the lifeboat so they will not be lost if the boat capsizes. Make sure that all the cans are bouyant, i.e., that they have a pocket of air in them, which will keep them afloat.

Plastic receptacles and containers cannot be corroded by salt and are truly impervious without being rigid. Tupperware-type containers and plastic bags are suitable and should be on board. These bags can be folded, closed with a knot and piled in a corner of the boat. Bombard kept his freshwater in an inflatable cushion, and Dougal Robertson used a tube from his damaged boat as a container. Others have used the intestines of large fish or turtles, which they have turned inside out and then tied at both ends.

In the latter case, in particular, watch for possible contamination every day. As soon as algae appear, the contents of the receptacle must be drunk immediately or the supply will go to waste.

# FIGHTING DEHYDRATION AT SEA

Survival depends not only on finding sources of freshwater, but also on economizing water losses. Most shipwrecked people find themselves exposed to the sun, which means losses through sweat. This is yet another reason to have a boat with a top in warm climates, and to keep wet with plenty of water. The ideal situation is to take a swim, and the enormous importance of this will be shown in a later section. A way to keep wet is to wear water-soaked clothing for as long as possible, preferably preserving another set of dry clothing. Tropical waters are generally quite a lot cooler than the surrounding air, and thus in themselves ensure cooling. With the additional effect of evaporation, substantial local cooling is assured. If there is a light breeze, there will be optimum cooling. One can decrease one's thirst by covering one's face with a cloth soaked in seawater, and turning it toward the sun.

# FISHING: TARGETS AND METHODS

Despite the occasional birds and the usually inadequate survival rations of lifeboats, the only way to deal with hunger on board on a long-term basis is by fishing. We have already seen how important fish are as sources of water. Fishing means catching fish, turtles, sharks, flying fish, plankton, and algae, and learning how to profit from these surrounding riches.

Aquatic fauna is present everywhere from the North Pole to the South Pole, and the only problem is knowing how to adapt to the habits of the local biotope in order to survive. We will consider fishing in its widest sense, which means the sum of all the means that can bring on board anything that lives in the oceans: traditional fishing and plankton nets, a sail to catch flying fish, a rope to snare turtles.

Many shipwrecked people who have fishing equipment but do not succeed in catching anything during the first few days give up altogether on this extremely valuable means of obtaining food, erroneously believing that they are in a region without fauna. Had they persisted for a week, they would have been pleasantly surprised by their success. How many shipwrecked people are aware of the fact that there is nothing less attractive to a fish (with the exception of a shark) than a rubbery fabric, smooth as silk, with a repulsive synthetic odor? Yet after several days, or sooner in warmer waters, plant and animal organisms attach themselves to the bottom of a boat and gradually cover its surface with an ever thicker layer.

Such a food base on the high seas very quickly attracts small fish that are in turn eaten by larger fish. This creates an artificial biotope beneath the boat, which moves along with it as it drifts at the mercy of the currents and the winds. Since the relative speed in relation to the water is very low or zero, a colony of various species can stabilize literally within reach of the shipwrecked person: attached to the boat, you will find limpets, small crustaceans with an edible stem, and barnacles, crustaceans that look like mollusks because of their chalky shells.

## In the Seychelles

On February 1, 1953 the *Marie-Jeanne*, a 32-foot (10-meter)-long old tub, leaves the small island of Praslin to sail to Mahé, 20 miles away in the Seychelles archipelago. There are 10 passengers on board, including two women in their sixties and eight men of various ages.

Ten miles from Mahé the crude engine breaks down, and they start to drift. The scant supplies are soon exhausted, but they wait until the 13th day before they make their first timid attempt to catch a fish with a piece of wire. Since they come up empty-handed, they conclude that fishing is not possible. For 18 days, the passengers have nothing to eat and they avoid dehydration by taking refuge under some canvas that is regularly washed down with seawater and rain.

On the 33rd day a captured bird provides each of them with a mouthful of food. From that point on, they survive exclusively on gifts from heaven: some flying fish that commit suicide on the deck and two gulls that land there. They make no more attempts to catch fish; in fact the idea never even crosses their minds. The gulls announce the proximity of Agalela Island, and its shores are sighted with great euphoria on the 36th day. Skillfully, the captain hoists a makeshift sail and steers toward the island. The younger passengers desperately try to help, using little oars without thole pins. They see the houses and the coconut palms. Suddenly the wind drops and an adverse current prevents them from getting any closer. At the end of their strength, the men

collapse at their oars, and the boat drifts away again. No one has seen them. One can easily imagine the terrible disappointment that floods through the 10 passengers, still alive after 36 days. The first woman dies on the 40th day. Three days later, the other woman dies. On the 50th day the first man dies, and he is followed by two more on the 52nd day. Sharks immediately start to trail the boat. No one thinks of catching them, although they are biting at everything in sight and aggressively bunging against the hull. The smallest piece of meat attached to the crudest of hooks would be enough to provide several pounds of food and fresh blood; in the terrible predicament they are in, it would even be conceivable to use one of the corpses of their companions, since they have to throw them overboard anyway—and once in the water the corpses are promptly devoured by the sharks following the boat.

On the 70th day one of the three survivors dies of a sudden hemorrhage. Too weak to throw him overboard, the two young survivors cover his face with a sack. Since the stench quickly become unbearable, they spray his corpse with foam from the extinguisher. They are finally picked up by an Italian tanker on the 74th day in abominable condition.

---

The important lesson to be learned from this tragedy is that none of the passengers had organized a long-term attempt to catch fish. They had numerous ropes of various thicknesses at their disposal, as well as various utensils that could have been fashioned into grapnels or hooks (for example, the bolt from the extinguisher). The presence of the sharks was not merely due to the macabre anticipation of corpses, but primarily to the existence of a true biotope beneath the hull of the boat. It is incredible that they only made a single attempt to catch fish, and it can only be explained by paradoxical group behavior: occasional euphoria, more often panic, which in this specific case caused an irrational collective mental block, a fatal inability to do anything. Thus they died of hunger even though, in a tropical sea, only dehydration—once an individual has reached the limits of his strength—should lead to death. The length of the time they survived confirms the real cause of this tragedy: they starved when food was readily available.

Sometimes, right from the beginning, shipwrecked people feel the noses of fish bumping against the soft bottom of the boat. Steven Callahan slept very badly, largely due to the dolphin fish that bumped their prominent foreheads against all the bulges on the boat. He slept badly—but he had enough to eat.

The mandatory fishing equipment in all lifeboats is almost always insufficient or inappropriate. If the hooks are not corroded by rust, there are not enough of them and they are much too small. Even medium-sized hooks only weigh a few ounces, so why be so miserly with them? Why take hooks that rust when there are hooks made of rust-proof materials? Why take unmounted hooks without eyes? Why take only two or three different sizes of wire?

Saving space and restricting the weight in this way is especially ridiculous, considering the fact that some of the gadgets included are totally useless; for example, the Robertsons found themselves with a reel and two hooks. It is impossible to catch large fish with such flimsy gear; harpoons and gaffs, such as those fashioned by Dougal Robertson, are what is needed. Marilyn and Maurice Bailey had no fishing gear at all when they survived for 117 days in the Pacific. However, their wealth of ingenuity and patience enabled them to catch so much that they later wrote what is practically a treatise on fishing at sea! They started with safety pins that they cut and reshaped. Others have fashioned hooks from the tops of cans. Poon Lim caught fish with the same rusty bent nail for almost his entire voyage. Bombard used a bone that is located just behind a dolphin's shoulder.

A line can be made of any nylon string, rope or cable. The ease with which one finds the first successful lure is in direct relation to the naiveté and curiosity of fish. Fish are not especially intelligent, making little distinction between living prey and a piece of metal twisting in the water and even less between organic debris and a piece of cloth. The only problem is to know how to vary the lures so as to catch the fish either because of their curiosity or because of their hunger.

Experts suggest taking along a

can of mussels, which are excellent bait and can easily be preserved for long periods of time. Barnacles can be used after removing them from their shells—and they are easily available because they quickly colonize the bottom of the boat.

The best position for catching fish also happens to be the most accessible: leaning over the side of the boat. The advantages are obvious: You can fish by sight and choose your target, and the fish are most plentiful near the boat, since they seek its shade and feed on the organisms that colonize its fabric. These fish, which live symbiotically with the boat, would be inaccessible with a trolling line.

A harpoon is a very good tool for catching fish by sight, and the only difficulty is to get used to the refraction that distorts the angle of the view (this disadvantage can be eliminated by throwing straight down). Obviously, the ideal would be to have an underwater gun and a mask, but these are relatively bulky.

Judging from the experience of shipwrecked people, a gaff, or spear, seems to be the best means to catch fish. The method is forbidden in sports fishing because it is so effective. Any size of hook attached to the tip of a pole or to an oar makes an ideal gaff.

Bombard used a bent knife on an oar, and another shipwrecked person used the sharp point of a bent compass needle. Many others, unfortunately, did not think of this tool, although they had all the materials necessary to make one. Using the tool is easy, since you just have to harpoon a fish swimming close to the boat. Catches as large as 22 pounds (10 kilograms) are easy to hook in this way.

Visibility beneath the boat does not pose a problem on the high seas, particularly in calm weather. In bad weather, fish tend to head for calmer, and thus deeper, waters; as for the shipwrecked person, he will be too preoccupied protecting himself from the waves or collecting water from the rain that often accompanies bad weather. There is a hierarchy of priorities, and keeping in rhythm with them is an integral part of surviving at sea.

A common problem with all methods of fishing is that one must avoid tearing the inflated rubber tube of the boat if the fish is fighting hard. The only effective way is to paralyze the catch by jabbing the thumb and middle finger into its eyes. This is enough to allow cutting the caudal fin, which can cause havoc if the fish is struggling.

An original and efficient method of fishing was used by Marilyn Bailey, who captured and dismembered a gannet and then immersed its bleeding wing in the water. The voracious fish attacked this lure and abruptly found themselves on the bottom of the boat. She caught an enormous number of fish using this unlikely bait, repeating the method with equal success using small pieces of turtle, sharkskin, and pieces of cloth soaked in blood. Everyone knows about a shark's attraction to the smallest drop of blood, but all carnivorous fish are attracted to the same thing, even if their sense organs are much less acute than those of a shark.

## MAIN SPECIES OF FISH ENCOUNTERED BY SHIPWRECKED PEOPLE

Apart from sharks, primarily the following species of fish are caught:

■ **Dolphin:** a tropical or subtropical fish that can weigh as much as 66 pounds (30 kilograms) and attains a length of 5 feet (1.5 meters); it often takes shelter in the shadow of the boat and bumps it with its projecting forehead. It

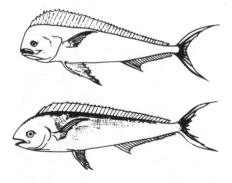

Dolphin: male (with the prominent forehead) and female

likes to hunt flying fish and, in fact, is in many cases the reason why they fly.

■ **Triggerfish:** the variety that lives on reefs is not edible, but the pelagic kind, which likes to shelter under boats, is edible and often constitutes the main diet of a shipwrecked person. It is a small fish, seldom longer than 7.8 inches (20 cms), and is found everywhere, even in the Mediterranean.

■ **Flying fish or exocoetus:** about 40 species, some of them in the Mediterranean. They are at most 17.5 inches (45 centimeters) long. They are often found in the digestive tract of dolphins as they constitute the latter's favorite food (when found there, they can be eaten, since the predigestion is not harmful in any way).

■ **Sucking fish:** characterized by its dorsal sucker, which enables it to attach itself to any large mobile support: Cetacea, sharks, turtles, as well as boats. It can be found in tropical and temperate waters. It can reach a length of 3 feet (1 meter). Thor Heyerdahl rediscovered a very old method of fishing using this fish: It should not be killed when found on a large fish but should be put back in the water with a line tied around its caudal stem. It will attach itself first to the boat and then to any opportune host, and all one has to do is pull on the line to recover the sucking fish as well as the fish to which it is attached!

## EATING FISH

There is much talk about the toxicity of tropical fish. This should not worry a shipwrecked person, since he is trying to survive on the high seas far from the coral reefs, which cause the toxicity of some fish (see "Major Threats: Other Venomous and Poisonous Creatures"). **There are no poisonous fish on the high seas.** The only things to be avoided are jellyfish and Portuguese men-of-war, which invade certain seas seasonally. These have long stinging filaments, and little if any nutritional value.

A real danger is insidious anorexia brought on by a progressive distaste for a monotonous diet and a radical reduction in food intake, even where food is plentiful. This situation could become a serious problem for a shipwrecked person who has to survive for a considerable length of time. The answer is to alternate the kind of fish; to mix them with turtle's blood, liver, or eggs; and to add fish roe to the diet. The Baileys attained a kind of expertise in this area, and future shipwrecked gourmets should consult their book, *Staying Alive*.

To preserve fish, the internal organs must be removed as soon as the fish is brought on board. Under a tropical sun the whole fish goes bad within a matter of hours. Short-term preservation (several days) can be achieved by placing the fillets in the shade, wrapped in a piece of cloth that is regularly moistened with seawater: the ensuing evaporation will cool the fish. Long-term preservation can only be assured by drying: the fillets are hung directly in the sun. They will turn spontaneously, exposing all sides to the sun's rays. Callahan became a master at this, and he even called the part of his boat where he dried the fillets of dolphin the "fish market." Luckily he had a boat with an inflated arch, which enabled him to hang his supplies. One should always have a covered boat, but for those people who find themselves on a raft with no way to hang anything, the secret of drying is to avoid all contact with damp surfaces (place the fillets on a dry, warm cloth, moving them to a dry section two or three times per hour).

Drying will take several hours to several days, depending on the thickness of the fillets and the intensity of the sun's rays. Therefore the fillets should be squeezed to protect them from the air as much as possible, and they should be examined regularly to check for any trace of mold.

## SHARK FISHING

Sharks are relatively easy to catch, and they are plentiful everywhere (some species even live in the English Channel). Naturally, one should only tackle the

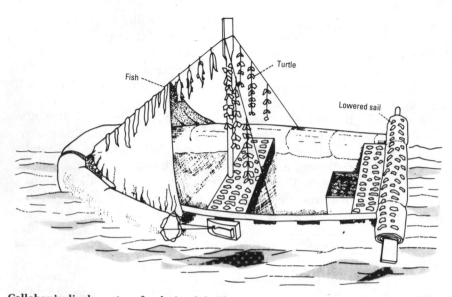

**Callahan's dinghy, set up for drying fish fillets (Drawing by Callahan)**

smaller ones, i.e., those under 5 feet (1.5 meters). This choice eliminates trolling, which, as we have seen, is not the best method anyway. Once again, the best position is from the side of the boat, and the best method is by hand. Though this may be surprising, considering how dreaded the species is, it is the most effective method and the one used most by shipwrecked people. It consists of seizing the shark's caudal fin as it moves slowly beneath the boat. This fin has a twofold advantage: it is easy to hold, and it immobilizes the shark, which uses the caudal fin as its main means of propulsion. The shark's rough skin prevents one's hand from slipping. As one pulls the shark upward, it is wise to push some

object into its mouth for it to bite on.

The final step is to kill the shark before bringing it on board. The quickest method is to give it a hard blow on the tapering tip of its nose. This area is not well protected—the bones covering the brain are very delicate. An air pump or cylinder can be used as a club. Once stunned, the shark will stop moving, and a knife can be plunged as deep as possible into its eye. The gills should also be cut. Make sure that the shark is really dead before hauling it on board. It will provide a significant amount of meat, although it is acrid and pungent. Do not ignore the liver, which is very rich in lipids and vitamins (it should be eaten first, since it cannot be preserved by drying). Keep the jaw, which can be made into any number of tools (a saw, chopper, gaff).

## FLYING FISH OR EXOCOETUS

This species can "fly" for a distance of more than 300 feet at a height of about 3 feet. They often land in boats, but even more frequently they fly over them. Therefore vertical traps should be set for them, using whatever is available: sails, shirts and nets stretched across the widest possible area. When he was in the Atlantic, Alain Bombard collected 5 to 15 flying fish every morning this way, as they got caught in his sail during the night. A large number of shipwrecked people have survived thanks to this kind of passive fishing.

## TURTLES

Theoretically, turtles can be found anywhere between 40°N and 40°S, but in practice they are found regularly only in certain regions of the Pacific Ocean, the Indian Ocean and the Caribbean. There are five species; the one that is of greatest interest to a shipwrecked person is the green turtle because it migrates over great distances, traveling on the surface where it is easy to catch. Since its reproductive period varies according to the geographic region, it can be found at all times of the year.

The Baileys caught 22 green turtles and even went so far as to keep some in reserve, tying them to the boat by a hind leg. The Robertsons caught 10, but they neglected to drink the blood of the first ones and did not eat the liver since they believed it to be toxic. Over time, they learned to use every part of the reptile, especially the grease covering the shell; they extracted an oil from it, which they used to lubricate their tools, protect their sores, massage their children's stiff legs, and even calm the waves that were threatening to engulf their boat! (This use of oil is an old tradition, often employed by large ships to calm the rough waters around a light craft they are trying to help.)

Concentrate on young turtles, since the adults, particularly the enormous leatherback turtles, can weigh as much as 1,320 pounds (600 kilograms). If the turtle is sleeping on the surface, just approach it quietly; if it is swimming, it will often come to the raft on its own, believing it to be a fellow turtle, or because it is curious.

A turtle can be caught by hand by the base of one of its legs. The aim is to slide the turtle into the boat on its back to prevent the claws from tearing the boat, so it must be turned over with both hands. If you need time to think, attach the turtle to the boat by one of its legs. It must never be killed in the water. It is almost impossible to drown a turtle (a turtle can survive under water for at least 20 minutes), and cutting its throat would be very dangerous because of the sharks that would certainly come for the spoils.

Once the turtle is on its back on the bottom of the boat, it should be immobilized to eliminate danger from the claws. To do this, kneel on its front legs, and then cut its throat with a knife. The ventral plastron should be cut off around the edge and all the internal adhesions must be severed. The intestines should be removed in one piece, taking care to avoid fecal contamination. The large muscle masses are concentrated at the base of the legs and adhere to the shell. A young turtle that weighs about 60–88 pounds (30–40 kilograms) will provide 22–33 pounds (10–15 kilograms) of meat. The liver should be eaten quickly, and the gall bladder should be removed very carefully, making sure not to break it. Eggs are nutritious but impossible to preserve, and if they are found, they should be eaten immediately after the liver.

## CRUSTACEANS

Apart from the delicious "squillfish," which can be found floating on the surface in some parts of the world during their reproductive period, crustaceans are rare on the high seas. At best, small crabs and barnacles attach themselves below the water line, but they are not very appetizing. Poon Lim and Gilbey were among the few shipwrecked people who resorted to this food source, but only when their other food sources were scarce.

## PLANKTON

Even if he has no fish hook, gaff, harpoon or knife, a shipwrecked person can survive, as far as food is concerned, by making use of the veritable "raw fish soup" in which he is drifting. Consider this: The largest animals in the world, Cetacea with baleens, survive entirely by eating the smallest organisms suspended in the water. The blue whale, which can weigh as much as 100 tons, eats nothing but krill and filters up to 8 tons of these miniature organisms per day. It should certainly be possible to keep a 165-pound (75-kilogram) human mammal alive indefinitely using the same food source that enables a sea mammal to grow to 100 tons.

The only problem is to find an artificial filter to replace the natural filter of the baleens and to obtain a sufficient flow. It is obvious that a rorqual moving at 30 knots will filter hundreds of tons of water every day through its several square feet of baleen.

Thor Heyerdahl took along a plankton net made by a biologist, Baikov, on the *Kon-Tiki* in 1947. This net had almost 3,000 meshes per square inch, forming a kind of silk funnel with a diameter of 19.5 inches (50 centimeters) that was dragged behind the raft. The catch varied, as with all fishing, depending on the location and the time. An interesting detail is that the catch was greater by night than by day, as if the microorganisms were avoiding the sun's rays that penetrate the water.

Heyerdahl described this mixture, horrible-looking and foul-smelling, yet displaying a wonderful variety of shapes and colors: "miniature crustaceans shaped like shrimp, fish eggs, various larvae, multicolored mini-crabs, jellyfish, and a thousand kinds of small creatures." In the Humboldt current he collected several pounds of this glutinous mass per hour. "When placed in a heap, the plankton looked like a cake with colored layers, brown, red, gray, and green, depending on the plankton fields one crossed. They were luminescent by night, and it looked as if we were pulling a sack of sparkling jewels from the water. . . . They tasted delicious—once one plucked up enough courage to place a spoonful of the luminescent mixture into one's mouth. . . . It was almost like eating shrimp, lobster, or crab paté. When the mass contained eggs, it tasted like caviar or oysters. On the other hand, plant plankton was revolting."

Alain Bombard emphasized the nutritional value of plankton be-cause of its high vitamin C content. He only used his net for half an hour each day, just to get his ration of vitamin C, since he had plenty of fish to supply everything else.

If nothing else is available, a silk or nylon stocking can do the job, but a special net should be obligatory as part of the equipment on a lifeboat, just as a solar distilling condenser should be. Apart from its specific use, the condenser can also be used as a stabilizer, or as a supplement to, or replacement for, a deep-sea anchor.

## ALGAE

Though algae are mainly a coastal resource, they can be present in some areas of the high seas. The Sargasso Sea is a prime example. Algae provide both calories and hypotonic fluids. Bernard Robin, in his book Survivre à la dérive ("Survival Adrift"), 1977, recounts the story of Wiktors Zvejnieks, who survived for 46 days exclusively eating floating algae.

## OCTOPI

Octopi are sometimes found on the surface. Téchu Makimare, a Polynesian, drifted around the Pacific for 64 days in 1963 eating birds, coconuts he found floating on the surface of the sea, flying fish and about 15 octopi, which latched onto his hand one day as he was trailing it in the water. These octopi are the base diet of enormous sperm whales and can be found on the surface of the seas where these Cetacea live, even though their habitat is normally at greater depths.

## BIRDS

Birds have always been important to shipwrecked people for two reasons: first as a source of food, and second—though wrongly—as an indicator of proximity to a shore. To be practical and accurate, we should emphasize that birds are only important as a source of food. Most shipwrecked people succeed in catching birds in their hands or with the help of a piece of clothing. All sea birds should be considered to be edible: blue-headed Pacific boobies, brown boobies, petrels, frigate birds, albatrosses, common terns—all these birds have, time and again, helped shipwrecked people to survive, even though their meat is not particularly tasty.

## CONCLUSION

All these observations demonstrate that the shipwrecked person should constantly keep his eyes open in the environment surrounding him. How otherwise would he notice the coconuts that sometimes drift thousands of miles from the island they came

from, or the algae, octopi, turtles, Cetacea that surface, flying fish trying to escape from dolphins—all of them direct or indirect signs of potential food?

There is no need to demonstrate how important lifeboats are, but they have been made so waterproof that they restrict a shipwrecked person's vision too much. Steven Callahan's exceptional survival in such a boat seems to prove the point: except for those times when he was fishing and knelt close to the only opening, he stayed inside the boat as if in a tent and could see only a few degrees of the horizon through the single plastic porthole. As a result, although he was shipwrecked in the same region as the Robertson family, he caught only fish—he did not catch any birds, turtles, or any other sources of food, as the Robertsons did on a regular basis from their frail little boat, which was open to the winds. The tent covering the boat should have portholes placed low enough for a shipwrecked person to see all around him even when lying down.

Another equally useful modification which must not damage the rigidity of the bottom of the boat, would be to put a flexible porthole in the bottom of the boat. This would be useful for examining the evolution of the biotope, seeing any large predators, and getting an idea of the speed of the boat in relation to suspended matter moving past.

# SHARKS

Sharks almost always appear in the stories of people shipwrecked in tropical waters. The sharks' presence is episodic but regular, always disquieting, preventing the people from going into the water and hindering their fishing. The sharks involved are not always the same species, but their threat is a constant.

Some sharks swim around the boat in concentric circles, coming closer and closer before they attack; others rub against the bottom of the boat, and some even tear at the boat. Some can be chased away by a simple blow from an oar, a knife or a flashlight.

Without repeating the information contained in the chapter on sharks, we will emphasize here how important it is for sailors to be aware of sharks' habits.

❂

In January 1942, a U.S. Navy torpedo bomber, caught in a storm, landed in the middle of the Pacific Ocean. The three crew members took refuge in a 8- by 4-foot (2.5- by 1.25-meter) dinghy; the only equipment they had was a pocket knife, a gun and a pair of pliers. By the fifth day, the restricted space began to be a problem, but the sharks prevented them from stretching their muscles by swimming and they were forced to broil in the tropical furnace. The radio operator, named Aldrick, proved to be exceptionally good at catching fish, which he speared with his knife.

Because of him, the men survived for 34 days. Then one night, Aldrick put his hand into the water to verify the direction of the current. Unfortunately, a shark was prowling around and immediately snapped at his fingers, slashing them down to the bone. The injury quickly became infected, but one of his companions incised the wound, allowing the pus to run out and enabling Aldrick to resume his highly effective fishing exploits. The first sharks were small, but a few days later they crossed a region infested with leopard sharks that were "so aggressive they threatened to overturn our raft. At one point, we had to repel one of the sharks by hammering its snout with our fists, and we succeeded in killing another with our gun before the weapon became so rusty that it was unusable."

For a long time, sharks prowled around Bombard's *Hérétique*; they violently bumped the hull of the *Marie-Jeanne* off the Seychelles; they threatened the Robertson family; and they repeatedly jostled Callahan's flimsy raft. Sharks are aggressive toward anything that moves, and therefore they pose a grave danger to a shipwrecked person who decides to swim near them. Their curiosity in respect to an inflatable boat is tempered only because the boat usually makes no noise, and has a regular shape with no floating appendages, no mobile organs, no organic odor and a uniform color.

On the other hand, sharks are attracted by the fish that follow the boat, themselves attracted by the boat's shadow and by the biotope that forms within a matter of days. If, in addition to this, the shipwrecked people throw scraps from fish, blood, and other kinds of garbage overboard, the sharks will very quickly become permanent companions.

# WHALES

These marine mammals are large enough to cause real trouble for any pleasure craft.

---

In the middle of the South Pacific, at latitude 47°S, on November 13, 1820, the *Essex*, a whaling ship from Nantucket, comes across a "school of sperm whales." The whaleboats are launched. Chace recounts the story: "As soon as one of the animals in the group was 'speared,' the strongest of the whales detached itself from the others and charged the ship. The furious Cetacean shattered the false keel with the first blow of its head. The sailors saw it open its mouth and try to break pieces from the hull with its jaws. Since it was unable to destroy the boat in this way, the large sperm whale swam to a distance of about two cable lengths and charged for a second time. The jolt shook the *Essex*. Water flooded in through the portholes at the stern of the vessel, which, no longer balanced, capsized and drowned the captain and all other crew members who were not participating in the hunt on the whaleboats."

Only two boats are found: one after several days, the other after three months. The latter contained six men at the start, but there are only three by the end of the odyssey; the survivors ate their companions.

. . . In the same year, to the east of the Marquesas Islands, the *Albatross* is rammed by a large Cetacean, which the whalers had harpooned. The breach in the hull caused by the animal is large enough to sink the vessel. In 1870 a rorqual charges the three-master *Sorensen* and sends it to the bottom of the North Atlantic. In 1894, in a Norwegian fjord, a blue whale rams the whaling ship *Garcia* and sinks it, despite its reinforced hull.

On June 15, 1972, the *Lucette* has just left the Galápagos Islands. It is a 43-foot- (13-meter-) long schooner and weighs 19 tons. On board are Dougal and Lynn Robertson, accompanied by two children and two teenagers. Two hundred miles out to sea, the schooner is attacked by a school of killer whales. The planking bursts into pieces, and the *Lucette* sinks in four minutes. Suddenly, six people go from a happy, carefree existence to that of shipwrecked survivors, trying to cling to life on board a ludicrously small dinghy. It is the start of an agonizing ordeal that lasts 38 days.

On March 4, 1973, the *Auralyn* is 300 miles north of the Galápagos Islands. The well-built sailing ship is suddenly struck by a sperm whale that has been driven insane by a wound inflicted by a whaler several hours earlier. The leak below the water line cannot be repaired and 40 minutes later Marilyn and Maurice Bailey find themselves on a 9-foot- (2.75-meter-) long Avon lifeboat. It is the beginning of an extraordinary odyssey in the middle of the Pacific that lasts 117 days.

January 29, 1982, 11:00 P.M. In the Atlantic. Steven Callahan is dozing on board the *Solo*, a small sailing vessel, which he has built himself and which is now sailing toward the Caribbean. A deafening explosion suddenly throws him from his berth while water floods into the ship. Callahan does not have time to see whether the monster shattered the bow or the stern of his ship. The water is already up to his waist by the time he tries to unstrap his survival kit. It is too late; the *Solo* is already sinking, bow first, and Callahan merely has time to get out of the cabin, cut the straps that secure the life raft, and throw himself on board; the only thing he has with him is his knife. Within 30 seconds the man has gone from comfort to having absolutely nothing. Callahan survives for 76 days before he sights Guadeloupe, where he is picked up by a fisherman.

Whales are a major cause of unexplained disappearances of experienced sailors. The large marine mammals sometimes approach a boat out of curiosity, or to scratch their backs against the keel so as to get rid of some of their parasites, or sometimes to attack it because they object to a stranger's intrusion into their territory. Since they breathe air, they surface regularly—and this is when the danger occurs. Their intrusion into the world of air is turbulent, and many species literally leap out of the water. I had the good fortune to be able to watch from close at hand as a whole group of sperm whales came completely out of the waves off Senegal; elsewhere in the Pacific, humpback whales burst forth from the depths, and return to the water several dozen feet farther on after performing arabesques in the air. It is not difficult to imagine these creatures falling back into sailboats that are in the wrong place at the wrong time. Even if the crew is not killed by the blow, the boat can be shattered, lifeboats destroyed, with disaster instantaneous. So it is useful to know the major distinctive features of Cetacea, as well as their favorite habitats.

There are two large groups of whales: those with teeth, the Odontoceti, and those with baleens, the Mysteceti. In addition to their mass, the former have impressively large jaws that can crush a boat several yards long (a killer whale's teeth grow to an average length of 7 inches (18 centimeters).

## TOOTHED WHALES (ODONTOCETI)

**Sperm Whales:** The males grow to a maximum of 59 feet (18 meters). They are pelagic (that is, they live in the open sea). The males have a worldwide range, but the females are found only between 40°N and 40°S where reproduction takes place. They dive to 3,280 feet (1,000 meters) for up to 90 minutes. They feed on cephalopods (squid and octopi).

**Killer Whales or Orcas:** The males grow to 29 feet (9 meters). They have a dorsal fin that can grow to 6 feet (1.8 meters, far larger than that of a shark). They roam the Arctic and Antarctic, living in groups of ten to several hundred. They are fearsome predators that hunt in coordinated groups. Their prey varies: other marine mammals, lone whales, fish and birds. Human remains have been found in the stomach of at least one of them.

**Narwhals:** The males grow to 20 feet (6 meters). They have a long, spiral tusk that can grow to 10 feet (3 meters). They always live in groups numbering from one hundred to several hundred individuals. They feed on cephalopods and crustacea.

**Belugas:** They grow to 20 feet (6 meters). They are called "white whales" because of their characteristic color. They are found in the Arctic living in gregarious groups of up to 1,000 individuals. They are found particularly along coasts and around estuaries and are not normally encountered on the high seas. They feed on fish (particularly Arctic cod, herring and halibut) and sometimes crustacea (shrimp).

**Porpoises:** The maximum length is 6½ feet (2 meters). They are found only in the northern hemisphere: the Atlantic, the Baltic, the White Sea and the Barents Sea. They are frequently found near shore and around estuaries, and they often swim up rivers. They do not normally approach boats. They feed on fish.

**Common Dolphins:** They grow to 8 feet (2.5 meters). They are found in warm and temperate waters, always in groups of ten to several hundred. They often play with the stem posts of ships. They feed on fish (sardines and anchovies).

## BALEEN WHALES (MYSTECETI)

This group includes true whales and rorquals, or Balae-

**Toothed whales**

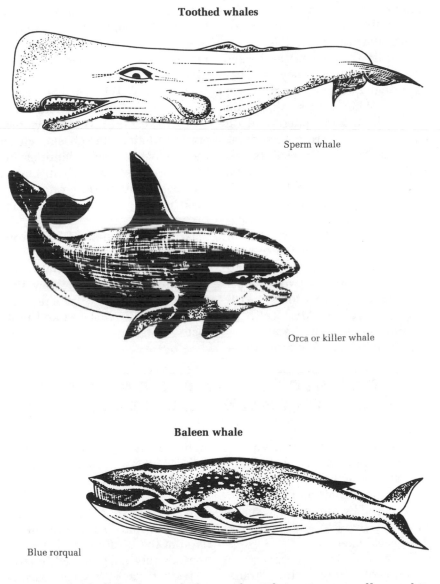

Sperm whale

Orca or killer whale

**Baleen whale**

Blue rorqual

noptera, which differ from whales in their striated ventral surface and dorsal fin.

The baleen whale's jaws have bristles that filter and retain plankton with their ragged inside edge. They cannot swallow or bite larger prey. They attain their tremendous size eating only plankton, which can be an important source of food for humans at sea as well. There is plankton in all the seas, and baleen whales range all over the globe.

**Common Rorquals:** They grow to 79 feet (24 meters) and have worldwide range. They are pelagic, living in groups in the open sea and feeding on small fish in the northern hemisphere and on krill in the southern hemisphere.

**Blue Rorquals, Great Rorquals or Blue Whales:** They grow to 98 feet (30 meters), weigh a maximum of 150 tons and are the largest animals that have ever existed. They prefer cold waters, but they are found in all the oceans. These pelagic animals are found alone or in groups of two or three. They eat up to eight tons of krill a day. As with all Mysteceti, the female is larger than the male.

**Gray Whales:** They grow to 49 feet (15 meters). Found only in the north Pacific, they migrate over vast distances—up to 5,590 miles (9,000 kilometers) along the coasts.

**Humpback Whales:** They grow to 53 feet (16 meters) and have worldwide range. Generally they are found along the coasts, where they have become familiar to whale watchers for their spectacular leaps out of the water. The head is covered with characteristic nodules.

**Greenland Whales:** They grow to 66 feet (20 meters) and have an enormous head, which takes up one-third of the body. They live only in the Arctic, where they feed on small crustacea and molluscs.

# PHYSICAL CONFINEMENT: EFFECTS AND REMEDIES

Shipwrecked people who are picked up are usually in an advanced state of physical distress, even if they have had water and food. Some of their problems have been caused by the confined space they have lived in and their lack of physical exercise.

The record, in this respect, is undoubtedly held by Franz Romer, before Alain Bombard's time, who crossed the Atlantic in 1928 in a long fabric kayak filled with 630 quarts (600 liters) of supplies and who was forced to remain in the same sitting position—unable to move and steeped in a veritable sweat bath—for 88 days. The lower part of his body was totally immobilized and the upper half was exposed to the elements, to flying fish, and, worst of all, to the harsh summer tropical sun. When he arrived at the Virgin Islands he was immediately hospitalized, unable to walk because his leg muscles had completely atrophied.

## MUSCLE AND JOINT PROBLEMS

The extremely confined space of a lifeboat forces the occupants into a permanent state of quasi-immobility, which very quickly leads to a general atrophying of muscles, particularly of the lower limbs. His plight exacerbated by malnutrition, the shipwrecked person quickly finds himself in the same situation as a bedridden person suffering from a broken leg, and then, in the final stages, an old person confined to bed.

To begin, there is rapid muscle loss; for example, if the thighs are inactive, the loss of the quadriceps can decrease the circumference of the thighs by 2 inches (5 centimeters) within a week. The emaciation gradually starts to affect the adipose tissue between the muscles and the prominent bones; the skin presses against these bones, and persistent dampness can cause skin ulcerations and ultimately bed sores in the advanced stages.

Immobilization also causes gradual loss of bone calcium. Loss of calcium, stiffness, rheumatism and skin lesions are the direct consequences of immobility. The cautions and remedies described below are designed to combat these phenomena.

■ Avoid soaking in excessively damp surroundings, exacerbated by moist clothing or the wet bottom of a boat.
■ Change position regularly in order to make sure that the same body parts are not always resting on the uncomfortable surface.
■ When preparing for the trip, include an inflatable mattress, which can be used for many other things (a container, a life buoy, shelter against the wind or protection against the sun).
■ Keep moving. Aerobics or stretching exercises may be impossible, but a few push-ups or abdominal exercises can be done several times a day on any boat. Limbering-up exercises can also prevent stiffness without consuming too many calories. All exercises should be done at night so as to avoid water loss through sweating. Massaging the muscles can also be very beneficial.

The best exercise, where it is possible, is swimming.

## THE USEFULNESS OF SWIMMING

In the Bay of Bengal in 1795, after spending 22 days in the mast house of his ship, which was still floating just beneath the surface because of its cargo of teak, John Rackay and a few exhausted survivors throw themselves into the water when they sight land. He recounts: "A moment earlier, I could hardly move my joints, but the moment I entered the water, my limbs recovered their suppleness."

In 1940 the cargo ship *Anglo-Saxon* is torpedoed by a U-boat south of the Azores. Only seven men survive on board an 18-foot (5.5-meter)-long rowboat. Among them are the radio operator, whose leg has been blown off; the gunner, whose hip is badly lacerated; and the cook, whose ankle is cut in half. The ship's first officer takes command, and they set sail for the Antilles, 3,000 miles away. After the first day, they remain becalmed under the oppressively hot sun, and the fetid odor of gangrene emanates from the wounds of the injured men. Malnutrition and dehydration start to take their toll. The four men who are not injured swim and feel strengthened. The radio operator asks for his ration of water to be given to his friend, and he dies the following day. By the 14th day all the water is gone. The first officer, who has behaved admirably up to this point, collapses at the tiller. Despite his injury, the gunner replaces him, but he is washed overboard by a wave and disappears. On the 16th day the first officer comes out of his stupor, says he is going to throw himself overboard, and invites his companions to do the same. The engineer accepts. The two men drink a glass of seawater and laboriously straddle the gunwale. They disappear. Only three survivors remain. One morning a sailor named Morgan announces that he is going out on the town, and he throws himself overboard, sinking without a word.

Widdicombe and Tapscott remain on board. After a few more days without water, Tapscott suggests to his companion that they put an end to it all. The latter agrees and immediately jumps into the water, but he quickly grabs the lifeline. Tapscott jumps in his turn, but he does not sink either. Since Widdicombe has refused to let

himself drown, Tapscott joins him on the lifeline. Tapscott is surprised that he is able to swim the crawl, but he continues to exhort his companion to put an end to it all. Widdicombe feels invigorated after his swim and states that all his pains and aches have gone. He convinces Tapscott that if he is able to swim, he is not finished yet. Finally the two men reach an agreement and succeed in hauling themselves back on board with a strange feeling of euphoria, as if they have had a stay of execution.

The following morning, after eight days without water, they are awakened by a long-awaited rain shower.

On the 49th day, which they only live to see thanks to infrequent rain showers and a few flying fish that land in their rowboat, they finally see a ship a mile away. Though they hoist their sail and wave their arms wildly, the ship does not see them. But this time, despite the terrible disappointment, they do not consider suicide.

On the 53rd day a storm provides them with water, but they also have to bail out the boat frantically for two days to prevent it from sinking. After the storm passes, constantly hungry, they are reduced to eating the skin peeling from their bodies in strips because of the sun. They also chew on the radio operator's tobacco pouch.

They have no memory of the last two weeks. After 70 days of agony, they land at Eleuthera, an island in the Bahamas. They receive treatment, and they survive.

---

Without their abortive suicide swim, there is no doubt that the two men would never have survived, would never have endured the ordeal still awaiting them, and would never have become aware of something they thought they had lost: the will to live.

Swimming plays a major role in preserving proper hydration because it allows the internal temperature to drop. Regular swimming can considerably slow down wasting of the muscles and prevent stiffening of the joints. Many shipwrecked people have refused to swim, because they were afraid of sharks, or because they were afraid they would not be able to get back into the boat. If nothing is thrown overboard for several hours, however, it is unlikely that there will be any sharks around. A shark, unless it finds food near the boat, never follows a boat that is drifting slowly for more than a few hours. To be sure, swimming under such conditions is not relaxing. This is one good reason to wear a mask and a snorkel: not only will this help avoid unpleasant encounters with sharks, but it will also help one to see the fauna around the boat and make fishing easier. If a mask is too bulky, goggles made of flexible rubber will do the job just as well.

Always attach a rope to the boat when swimming: the lightest breeze can push a boat along at a speed faster than even the best swimmer can match. Even if it does not have a sail, the inflated rubber tube offers a surface of up to 3.6 square yards (3 square meters) and provides an extremely efficient thrust, especially since these light, keelless boats have no inertia. Alain Bombard almost lost his boat this way at the beginning of his adventure, and it was only due to his physical fitness and outstanding swimming ability that he was able to catch up with it. Others have committed the same error with deadly results, and this is why empty dinghies, which have obviously been used, are found every year.

Trapeze artists and stuntmen do not leap into a void without a double life belt with special shoulder straps and clasps that release quickly. Responsible divers never dive with oxygen tanks beyond certain depths without compression tables attached to their belts, a snorkel and proper knife strapped to their legs, and a life buoy around their chests. It is a serious oversight for a skipper not to know what is contained in the survival kit, and it is an unpardonable mistake if the kit is not adequately equipped.

## MANDATORY EQUIPMENT FOR LIFEBOATS

The table below lists essential equipment, in addition to the basics. Legal regulations differ from country to country, and possible additions are left to the choice of the individual. You might add hand-held red lights, in addition to the regular parachute flares,

## LIST OF EQUIPMENT THAT MUST BE ABOARD A LIFEBOAT
(apart from the equipment required by international regulations)

| TOOL | NUMBER | COMMENTS |
|---|---|---|
| DISTILLER | 2 | Bring material to repair it with. |
| MULTIFUNCTIONAL POCKETKNIFE | 1 | Such as Swiss Army knife. |
| "SURVIVAL KNIFE," STRONG AND SOLID | 1 | Many uses: to kill large catches, cutting up and dismembering the catch, can be used as a harpoon. |
| PLANKTON NET | 1 | Can serve as a floating anchor. Can be improvised using silk or parachute fabric or a woman's stocking. |
| PLASTIC WHISTLE | 1 | |
| SIGNALING MIRROR | 1 | Should be perforated. |
| PEN SIGNAL FLARES | 1 | Very small and light, can be slipped into an oilcloth sack. |
| RED FLARES | 10 | Do not be stingy with the number, as one is seldom seen by the first boat that comes along. |
| COMPASS | 1 | Not a compass set into a knife handle. Must be capable of taking bearings. |
| FISHING TACKLE BOX | 1 | Must include mounted noncorrodible hooks of all sizes. |
| BOX OF MUSSELS | 1 | Excellent bait, and keep for a long time. |
| LARGE HOOKS | 3 or 4 | In order to make some gaffs. |
| AIR PUMP | 1 | |
| SPONGES | 2 to 4 | The only way to dry the deck of the boat completely. |
| PLASTIC GARBAGE BAGS | 2 packets | Many uses. |
| WATERPROOF LAMPS | 2 | Also take replacement bulbs and waterproof batteries. |

| TOOL | NUMBER | COMMENTS |
|---|---|---|
| AIR MATTRESS | 1 | For comfort, as well as a possible replacement tube if one should tear, or as a "wave-breaker," receptacle, etc. |
| FIRST AID KIT | 1 | Should be complete. The safety pins can be used as hooks, the scissors as a knife, the adhesive bandages as waterproof patches, the cloth bandages as ropes, the iodine to color lures, the scalpel blades to cut up the catch, etc. |
| NONCORRODIBLE METAL WIRE | 16 feet (5 meters) | Many uses |
| UP-TO-DATE REPAIR KIT | 1 | By "up-to-date" we mean made of plastic with adhesive that can be used in water (used in the production of laminated plastic swimming pools). |
| SWIMMING GOGGLES | 1 | Made of plastic, very light, waterproof, and can be used as a mask, as sun glasses and as a blindfold if one gets solar uveitis. |
| PROTRACTOR | 1 | Made of flexible plastic; it will enable one to make comparative calculations of latitude. |

rubber balloons covered with metallic paint that can serve as radar reflectors, a water pump, etc. Material for makeshift rigging might also be included.

We had the opportunity to test a lifeboat intended for eight people. The boat was built in 1983 and sold for about $4,000. During our inspection in March 1987 we threw the folded lifeboat into the sea, attached to the back of the ship by a nylon rope that also released the carbon gas for inflating the boat. The latter worked perfectly and inflated the lifeboat within a matter of seconds. However, we immediately heard disquieting hisses and discovered leaks coming from several places:

■ On the upper "tire," the piece of fabric with the maker's name and the standards of the boat had come loose, pulling away the rubber to which it was attached and making the fabric porous.
■ On the upper and lower "tires," the fabric surrounding the manual inflation plugs had come loose.
■ Only the arch over the lifeboat had remained airtight.

Two minutes later, the lifeboat looked like a giant sock immersed in the water, kept on the surface only by the arch. Seeing all this, we carried out a thorough check of everything on board, and made the following discoveries:

■ Five of the 14 water bottles were empty, corroded by rust. The 12.6 quarts (12 liters) of water provided for eight people were stored in ferrous containers, like in the good old days before plastic was invented! The expiration date on these containers was November 1987.
■ The biscuits provided were floating in water that had leaked out of the containers.

■ The battery that was designed to be immersed in seawater in order to provide auxiliary power for the light capping the arch had burst.
■ The two cylindrical 1.5-volt batteries were rusted through.
■ The two paddles were eaten away by oxidation.
■ The hooks were stuck together with rust.
■ The first aid kit, inadequate to begin with, was soaked, making the adhesive bandages and most of the pills unusable. A cheap Tupperware container would at least have been waterproof.

Two findings could possibly have made us feel better:

■ The two sponges were undamaged by the water.
■ The manufacturer explained that the rubber had been attacked by a "kind of cancer," and therefore we could exchange the lifeboat for another. Since these lifeboats were meant to last for 12 years, the manufacturer suggested that we buy a new lifeboat—for only 75 percent of the normal purchase price!

The advice in the table is provided merely as a guideline and is based on the inadequacies that

# PROCEDURES IN CASE OF SHIPWRECK

Surviving a shipwreck begins with planning in port before departure. At the time of the shipwreck, it depends on quick reflexes and on calmness and common sense. Finally, it depends on moral strength and acquired knowledge.

## BEFORE DEPARTURE

Far too few skippers check the contents of the survival kit on the bridge of their sailing vessel. There is the engine on board, of course—part of the furniture—and there's a backup engine too, which is all we'll need in case of an emergency. That will do the trick—so what more do we need?

Countless people have disappeared and died due to just such an attitude. It takes very little time to open the container, check what is inside, and add whatever is necessary to complete the equipment, which is always inadequate, often deplorably so. When a skipper takes time to check the kit, he not only fulfills his responsibilities, he also gains mental reassurance, which will prove its worth in an emergency.

Preventive measures should be learned and repeated to a point where they are no longer a burden, but an unconscious reflex. The measures should be as automatic as putting on the seat belt in a plane or a car, or a helmet when riding a motorbike or climbing a mountain or skydiving—these things are done so automatically that they become an integral part of our physical and mental comfort.

## DURING THE SHIPWRECK

"STOP, LOOK, THINK AND CHOOSE"

This general principle, which applies to all dangerous situations that persist for a period of time, comes into full force during a shipwreck. Unfasten the self-inflating container, attach the lifeboat securely to the sinking vessel, and stay on the latter as long as possible in order to save as much equipment as possible. There is no danger of being pulled down into the depths by a sinking vessel, since the suction is not strong enough. Moreover, windjammers can sink right down to their bridge, and then float like that for months. if this happens, do not leave the wreck. Cut the ropes and recover as many containers as possible, gather anything that can float, anything that can help you determine position and bearings and that is not already provided in the lifeboat (charts, compass, sextant). All these materials should be thrown into the lifeboat.

Life jackets should always be worn on a lifeboat. Apart from the fact that they prevent one from going under in soaked woolen garments or in boots, they often contain several useful instruments, such as a whistle or a mirror, and they can make bathing safe, pad the bottom of the boat, substitute for a defective flotation device, etc. Special vests may be used instead of the cumbersome life jackets: these are waterproof and lined with asbestos. They are buoyant, but not bulky, and they allow freedom of movement on board while providing maximum safety in case of an accident.

Naturally the backup dinghy should be attached to the lifeboat. This saved the Robertsons' lives, since their lifeboat sank after a few weeks of drifting, and they were able to take refuge on the second dinghy for several additional weeks.

---

❂

---

Lucien Schiltz and Catherine Plessz were caught in a storm in September 1972—the type of storm that the sea reserves especially for those who disdain it. Their steel sailboat, the *Njord*, keeled over under a wave and was partially flooded, but it did not sink for a while. Lucien checked the lifeboat, but he was afraid that it would not inflate when they needed it. So he pulled the cord, and the boat inflated perfectly. It could not stay where it was, tossed by the wind between the shroud lines: so Lucien secured it firmly to the stern of the *Njord*.

Catherine was 19 years old and Lucien 25. At this point, their attitude became totally paradoxical. Though the large cutter was floating well and contained enough food for months, since they were outward bound for a long cruise to the tropics, they took refuge in the dinghy, as if this frail, small "life" boat were the solution to all the problems that could arise at sea. At 8:00 P.M. the rope securing the lifeboat to the *Njord* broke. Their problems had started at 5:30 P.M During these two and a half hours the only things they had thrown into the lifeboat were a few cans, some distress flares, two 21-quart (20-liter) drums of water, a compass and their papers. They did not tie anything down. After their line broke, the shadow of the cutter disappeared into the night, not into the depths of the sea! During the next eight hours, they capsized three times, losing all their food and provisions, as they had not secured them to the boat. Their lack of experience, their panic—their abandoning ship and failure to provision the lifeboat—would cost them 12 days of indescribable suffering that even led to ideas of cannibalism.

---

The important feature in their adventure is the total lack of any clear analysis of the situation. Their plight was not desperate, since the *Njord* had not sunk. They suffered a kind of "mental block" for more than two hours, and seemed to be irresistibly drawn toward the lifeboat, as though they expected it to solve everything—forgetting that it can never be more than a last resort. In fact the *Njord* was found, still afloat, long before they themselves were seen by a cargo ship.

**Never leave a wreck while it is still afloat.** Bernard Robin, in *Survivre à la dérive* ("Survival Adrift") (1977), tells the story of two other shipwrecked people who posed for a last photo on the bridge as their ship was sinking instead of busying themselves gathering as much material as they could. At least these people did not panic, but their negligence made their survival much more difficult.

After an unexpected storm overtook the competitors of the Fastnet yacht race in the Irish Sea, in 1979, many victims, ironically, were found dead of cold, floating in their life jackets, while their yachts were still afloat. They had put on the life jackets when the storm blew in, but they had not chosen to or been able to stay with their boats.

## AFTER THE SHIPWRECK

One of the ordeals that most shipwrecked people face is capsizing. Buffeted by the waves and the wind, a keelless boat overturns very easily. Many people have exhausted themselves trying to turn a boat right side up, and have lost everything that was not firmly tied down. Capsizing can be avoided by throwing bodyweight against the windward inflated tube, thus providing a counterweight to the wave that is lifting it. This technique should be used in all rough weather and, though it may be tiring, it is much less exhausting than capsizing. If the capsized boat is very heavy, patience is essential. Attach a rope to one side of the boat, wait for the wind and a wave to combine to lift it, and pull on the rope, bracing yourself against the opposite side of the boat. Some boats have pockets hanging below them, positioned at 180° to each other, which prevent capsizing by using the weight of the seawater in them as ballast. The pockets can be pulled up to allow the boat to drift with the wind.

# SPECIAL MEDICAL PROBLEMS OF THE SHIPWRECKED

In addition to stresses such as hunger and thirst, cold and heat, isolation and anxiety, there are other dangers specific to the marine environment that cause unique medical problems.

## HUMIDITY AND SALT

Dampness and salt cause skin problems: superficial lesions, light sores that ulcerate due to the action of the salt and that do not heal unless they are protected with some cream or the grease, for example, from the fat of a turtle. The sores should be exposed to air whenever the weather is not rough and there is little danger that they will get spray on them. Sores that are wet will not heal. They should be exposed to rain as often as possible, but must be dried immediately.

## THE SUN

Inflammation from the sun occurs quickly at sea. It makes the skin more delicate and opens the way to ulceration. It is possible to adapt to this, but gradual exposure is essential to give the skin time to produce the melanin that protects it. Eye inflammation is just as common, because of the spray and the wind, and it should be treated in the same way as snow blindness. Makeshift glasses should be fashioned if necessary (using a piece of cardboard, for example). Let an affected eye rest beneath a gauze pad, to prevent being handicapped in both eyes some days later.

## IMMOBILITY

This is a great source of discomfort, causing problems in the mus-cles and joints, as mentioned above, and in many cases producing insomnia. The insomnia can be dealt with artificially with a sleeping pill—a treatment that aims to improve the chances of survival by eliminating an additional cause of physical exhaustion.

## SEASICKNESS

The movement of a lifeboat is very different from that of a 5- or 10-ton ship, making it necessary to reacclimatize. If this is not done quickly, during the first couple of days, vomiting can cause debilitating exhaustion, because of dehydration and electrolytic losses. A little seawater will compensate for the electrolytic losses (sodium and chloride are, in fact, the electrolytes lost in the largest amounts when vomiting gastric juices or bile). Drink fresh water to compensate for the hydric losses and, at the very least, lie down.

## INTAKE OF SEAWATER

Old stories give horrifying descriptions of the symptoms preceding the death of those who dared to drink seawater. None of the symptoms occurs if the water is drunk in the manner described previously, particularly if it is drunk at the start, before dehydration has set in. The kidneys can tolerate it for a limited time, but after seven days the danger of irreversible nephritis becomes serious, and the kidneys must be allowed to recover before starting again.

## UNDERNOURISHMENT

One of the consequences of undernourishment among all shipwrecked people is almost constant constipation, which often lasts for weeks but should not be a reason for alarm. In fact, it is due to dehydration, inactivity, and the infrequency of food intake, particularly the absence of vegetable fibers. It has nothing to do with an intestinal obstruction and should not be an additional source of anxiety.

Diarrhea is rare, but it is obviously very serious, since it is an aggravating factor for dehydration, which is a constant danger. Maurice Bailey suffered from diarrhea, probably because he ate some spoiled fish or turtle.

Usually the biggest nutritional problem is the lack of carbohydrates, because the only source of food is fish, which, of course, contain none. For example, Alain Bombard lost 55 pounds (25 kilograms) in 65 days, Dougal Robertson 33 pounds (15 kilograms) in 38 days, and each of the Baileys 44 pounds (20 kilograms) in 117 days. This is a large loss, and yet each of these shipwrecked people ate the fruits of his catch very regularly.

The final problem that a shipwrecked person must overcome is eating a normal diet again. In 1558 a boat from the future port of Rio de Janeiro arrived in Brittany with 30 survivors who had suffered 38 days of scarcity; shortly after their arrival, 20 of them died "because they gorged themselves too fast." After being deprived of food, normal eating should be undertaken gradually. One cannot go from the state of being a "living corpse" to that of a normal man in a matter of hours. Start with a purely liquid diet for the first few days (based on sweetened milk, or example), and then gradually change over to solid food.

## MENTAL STRESS

Apart from the extreme physical conditions, a shipwrecked person is also subjected to intense mental stress, which will be tolerated in very different ways according to the personality and past experiences of the individual. The state of mind of the shipwreck survivor may well determine the fate of his weakened body.

The mental stress that a shipwrecked person must face can be summarized in one word: monotony. Monotony of geography, occupation, relations—the entire physical surroundings combine to numb the responses of a shipwrecked person. Even if he is drifting at the mercy of the winds and the currents, the shipwrecked person survives in an unchanging "landscape." The living space is certainly not that of a normal human being, not even that of a prisoner, whose mattress is as large as the whole raft. The survivor must try to enlarge it artificially by going for swims, and through autosuggestion by deciding that the whole sea is his own. If he can set up some makeshift rigging and steer the boat at least a little, the survivor can feel more in control of his fate, using his own powers to concentrate on finding an escape from his plight.

Unfortunately, the shipwrecked person very often senses that he is at the mercy of the waves, powerless and seeking a free will that no longer really exists. He must protect himself against this impotence by action. If he has the will, he can quickly discover many things to do, even when confined to a pathetic little lifeboat. Activities that would seem petty or futile in normal life acquire vital importance for a shipwrecked person and renew his sense of control over his life.

The monotony caused by isolation and lack of living space can also be overcome through willpower. Space and time should be organized, by setting goals and adhering to strict self-imposed rules. Sleep as long as possible, because thirst and insomnia are the two

most loyal companions of shipwrecked people. When you wake up, after collecting the water from condensation that was deposited during the night, do some limbering up exercises. Make your meals from the meager supplies into a ritual by keeping to the same schedule one would in normal life.

Catch fish in the morning and then, after a siesta, again in the afternoon. Try to keep a journal before dinner, and end the day with an exercise session after nightfall. Make a notch for every day that passes, remembering that hundreds of shipwrecked people have survived in total destitution for many weeks, indeed for two to three months, before returning to a normal life. Creating habits, even if they are artificial, is the only way to make the days pass more quickly.

Getting along with fellow victims—or surviving without companionship—can also be stressful. If the shipwrecked person is not alone, he will have to deal with the behavioral problems of a group in a life-threatening situation. If he is alone, he will be thrown back on his own intellectual resources. The richer one's internal life is, the easier it is to survive alone.

Some people, though they are rare, ascribe a mystical significance to their adventure. Others assign very precise functions to their immediate surroundings:

For example, as mentioned above, Steven Callahan designated the part of his tiny boat that he used to dry the fillets of dolphin fish he caught daily the "fish market." He also kept a journal and made the first sketches of what would become his future boat. This ability to transcend the reality of the situation is certainly not within the grasp of all shipwrecked people, and therefore the situation must be made into a physical challenge, a matter of honor, an act of defiance, a determination that one will prevail at all costs.

## CONCLUSION

Survival often begins before departure through a minimum amount of foresight, and there is no doubt that the elements water and air are the least forgiving.

From the skipper who hides his lifeboat at the bottom of an inaccessible compartment, to the man who does not take a sextant because he owns the latest satellite navigational equipment, there are plenty of examples of apparently innocuous precautions not being taken and ultimately costing the lives of excellent sailors. What can one say about the five yachtsmen who, wishing to take advantage of a beautifully calm sea, jumped into the water from the bridge of their luxury yacht, forgetting that no one was left on board, that no rope was trailing in the water, and that no ladder had been dropped into the water? There was not even a breath of wind, and everything went well until they decided to get back on board: how can you catch hold of a smooth vertical hull, towering 6 feet (2 meters) above you, when you are in your birthday suit? You cannot. Their yacht was discovered much later, just as they had left it, but only a couple of the bodies were ever found.

Even if they had remembered to provide a means to get back on board, they would still have run the risk that the slightest breeze could have pushed their sailboat away, and they would not have been able to catch up with it. One must never leave a vessel that is not lying at anchor, unless one is tied to it in some way.

The next chapter deals with technical features of diving, with which one should be familiar. This is not merely because diving is so alluring, but because all ocean-going vessels should automatically have diving equipment on board. How otherwise can one untangle an anchor wedged under a chain in 98 feet (30 meters) of water in a harbor, or against the bottom of a coral reef in the middle of the Pacific? How can one quickly change a propeller that has been lost, broken or twisted? How can one free it from the cable that has jammed it? How can one stop a water leak, release a jammed log reel, or loosen a rudder blade? Often one cannot hold one's breath long enough for the work, and it is certainly not feasible at depths greater than 49 feet (15 meters). One of my friends could have lost a brand-new boat in this way. His wife drew his attention to a strange noise that prevented her from sleeping, and he found that more than a ton of water had flooded the bottom of his boat. Since he had taken his diving equipment along, however, it took only 10 minutes for him to locate the origin of the leak and to replace the screw clamp, which had disappeared from the packing that was meant to secure the seal around the propeller shaft.

Some skippers use weight and volume as an excuse to leave such equipment behind, but what are 77 extra pounds (35 kilograms) on a boat that weighs 10 tons? On the other hand, one can economize on the compressor and simply refill the bottle or bottles in the ports that have the necessary material available (Bauer manufactures small 200-bar three-stage compressors that weigh no more than 66 pounds).

On a ship, survival starts before departure.

# UNDER THE WATER

- A True Tale of Survival

- A Very Special Physical Environment

- Facts for Underwater Survival

- Free Diving or Skin Diving

- Scuba Diving

- Proper Tactics to Avoid Diving Accidents

# A TRUE TALE OF SURVIVAL

## 1977, Cozumel Island, Mexico

For the last two hours two men, each equipped with a pair of aqualungs, have been exploring the edge of one of the most beautiful underwater faults in the Caribbean. As they emerge from the long channel through an enormous rock balanced on the edge of the trench, X suddenly feels an irrepressible urge to dive "into the great blue yonder," as if he were standing at the door of a plane, just before skydiving.

Always one to go where others will not, X does not stop to think about it but instinctively does a kind of underwater swan dive and rapidly descends, head first, with a couple of strokes of his flippers. He reaches 148 feet (45 meters), 164 feet (50 meters); the needle of his depth meter now seems to be turning of its own accord. X glances at the instrument and thinks to himself that the needle is moving much more slowly than when he is parachuting through air. Yet the dive is just as exhilarating; he would like to go even faster and descend into this great black hole at 124 miles per hour (200 kilometers per hour).

He now glides, still descending, keeping his arms and legs still. It is a strange feeling; the steep rock wall passes by a few inches from his mask and becomes grayer and grayer. How fascinating it is to know that this "wall" continues on for 1,148 feet (350 meters) and disappears in the shadows below. X experiences a wonderful dizzy sensation when he sees the blue night of the chasm; he no longer knows whether it is above or below him. Diving is certainly fantastic, and anyone who says that depth has nothing to do with the thrill of it is an idiot. What X does not realize is that it is a dive toward death, a euphoric death in the dizziness of the depths, and that the sense of recklessness is caused by nitrogen narcosis.

At 197 feet (60 meters) his neoprene suit is crushed by the pressure and loses its buoyancy. At the same time, his lead belt becomes heavier and heavier, literally sucking the diver into the depths.

Mario has not seen X for more than a minute but he is not worried. It does not cross his mind for a second that his companion has made an excursion into the dangerous depths.

X passes the 197-feet mark still in a state of euphoria; then he sees an enormous branch of precious black coral on the rock face. Such a treasure cannot be left there. X stretches out his hand, turns right side up, and paddles his flippers, trying to swim upward.

To his great disappointment, the branch of coral disappears above him, and he continues to descend. He paddles furiously with his flippers and succeeds in stabilizing his position. He absolutely must find the branch. For about 20 seconds he examines the wall, hanging on with his hands to stay at the same level.

Suddenly he has a pang of fear: Why is it so difficult to breathe? Why does he have to exert so much effort to suck in air that now seems so heavy? Has the aqualung run out of

180

oxygen? It is impossible to get back to the surface from a depth of 197 feet while holding your breath. X now has the irresistible urge to get back to the surface quickly, but the surface is so far away. He paddles harder and harder with his flippers but only succeeds in ascending a few yards. His heart is beating wildly and he has terrible difficulty breathing. He feels like tearing off the pressure reducer so that he can call to Mario, who must be above him. Why can't he move upward? Why has he suddenly become so heavy?

X has the urge to dump all these things that are suffocating him, these enormous aqualungs that are pulling him down, this damned pressure reducer that he has to fight to get a few mouthfuls of air. That's it! Why had he not thought of the pressure reducer before? All he has to do is press its center to get a greater flow of air. X hastily puts his thought into action and anxiously presses the button, naively expecting immediate comfort from a flood of air. He is so absorbed in trying to find relief from his breathlessness that he forgets to use his flippers for a few seconds, and he descends several yards.

At 213 feet (65 meters) it is almost night. The euphoria has given way to deadly fear. Stress increases his breathlessness. X thinks of death, this implacable mistress with which he has flirted so many times. He has to think, think and extricate himself from this situation. He clings to the wall and tries not to move. He keeps pressing the pressure reducer, but his ears are buzzing and his head is aching. He is unable to analyze what is happening. He looks for the valve of the Fenzy buoy with which he dives

almost every day. Unfortunately, on the island, he never brings it along because it is so bulky.

How can he get back to the surface? How can he become as light as the bubbles that are escaping toward the surface? Why does he have this leaden weight on him, trapping him on the wall like a beginning diver suffering from dizziness?

The word "lead" echoes through his mind. Of course, that's it: lead. He has 4.4 pounds (2 kilograms) of lead around his belt; it is insane to weigh oneself down with lead! He lets go of the pressure reducer and the rock he is clinging to. Using the automatic release, he unfastens the belt within a matter of seconds. X drops it into the depths, and instantly grabs hold of the wall, helping himself with his flippers. This time he feels he is slowly moving upward. One yard, two yards; this is impossible, he cannot succeed in ascending from a depth of more than 200 feet when it is so difficult! He feels an ever greater urge to tear off his mask, but he continues to move upward imperceptibly, pulling himself along by his arms, pushing with his flippers, trying futilely to flood his lungs with air. He reaches 180 feet (55 meters)—he has ascended 32 feet, but at what price? He is on the verge of asphyxiation. However, a small glimmer at the back of his mind forces him to continue. His sight is now becoming cloudy; his heartbeats echo in his ears, drowning out the roar of the bubbles, which he is breathing out faster and faster.

As the sun penetrates the surface above him, X recovers from his lethargy. At last Mario has joined him, forcing him to stop below 33 feet (10 meters) and to breathe more deeply.

His breathing is still very laborious, but suddenly everything becomes clear. X realizes the stroke of luck he had when he passed the branch of black coral: If he had not, he would not have suffered from the breathlessness, and he would probably already be dead—he would have run out of air and disappeared into the shadows. The breathlessness cut short his euphoria and made him decide to try to return to the surface no matter

what. Once he succeeded in reaching about 131 feet (40 meters), he ascended faster and faster, almost without effort, until he reached Mario.

Since X has a tendency to "float," Mario gives him his own lead belt, so that X will not have to use the flippers too much and thus exacerbate his breathlessness. Thirty minutes later, they reach the surface, a surface that X thought he would never see again.

---

This experience serves as a good example in several ways:

■ Diving is always dangerous, even for experienced divers, and should always be done with a companion. Keep your companion in sight at all times. In a survival situation this rule might have to be broken, but be well informed about the risks.
■ Great depth is not a part of the attraction of diving. Apart from the fact that the colors disappear, the consumption of air grows increasingly, and the danger of nitrogen narcosis is very great below 164 feet (50 meters).
■ Whenever possible, dive with a Fenzy or another comparable buoy. It enables stabilization at any depth and eliminates unnecessary exertion to stay in place. Moreover, by discharging its small bottle, you can "blow up" to the surface if there is an accident.
■ Be aware of the physical and mental phenomena caused by

pressure. Why does a neoprene suit stop being buoyant at 164 feet? Why does one consume six times more air at that depth than at the surface?
■ Remain very humble in this environment, which is not that of man, and remember that, even if he is in excellent physical shape, any diver may, one day, fall victim to "the rapture of the deep."

A book dealing with hostile environments cannot ignore the underwater world. If it did, it would ignore 65 percent of the planet's surface, which is becoming increasingly accessible to man with each day that passes. It is a world in most ways alien to man.

Yet we can understand why men find this world so fascinating: The underwater world conceals almost half the gold on earth, thousands of wrecks rest a few dozen yards below the surface, and it is an area unspoiled by tour guides.

Diving is an activity that all adventurers may have to participate in at one time or another, from a boat, a ship or a shore. Whether one is skin-diving or scuba-diving, the least negligence can prove fatal, and ignoring the fundamental concepts of physiology will sooner or later lead to a fatal accident.

# A VERY SPECIAL PHYSICAL ENVIRONMENT

## PRESSURE

The weight of the atmosphere on the earth's crust is equal to 30 inches (760 millimeters) of mercury or 1,013 millibars. This is the standard atmospheric pressure, which can be rounded off to 1 bar. In addition, a depth of 33 feet (10 meters) of water also weighs 1 bar per square centimeter, i.e., approximately 1 kilogram per square centimeter.

■ At a depth of 33 feet (10 meters) the pressure will therefore be equal to 1 bar of atmospheric pressure plus 1 bar of hydrostatic pressure, for an absolute value of 2 bars.
■ At 66 feet (20 meters) the pressure will be 3 bars.
■ At 98 feet (30 meters) the pressure will be 4 bars.

The pressure increases 100 percent between the surface and a depth of 33 feet. For it to increase another 100 percent, one has to descend not to 66 feet, but to 98. Between 130 feet and 164 feet (40 and 50 meters), the pressure only increases by another 20 percent. This significant difference for an equal depth of water explains the frequency of accidents between 66 feet and the surface during ascent.

Moreover, Mariotte's law states that:

$$Pressure \times Volume = Constant$$

This means that, in contrast to liquids, which are incompressible, the volume of a gas at a constant temperature will decrease in proportion to the pressure applied to it, and vice versa. Thus a volume of 5.25 quarts (5 liters) at a depth of 33 feet (10 meters) will be 10.5 quarts (10 liters) at the surface and 2.6 quarts (2.5 liters) at 98 feet. All divers must remember this one law, even if they know no other.

The second law concerns the partial pressure of a gas, i.e., the pressure that it exerts on its own account in a gaseous mixture. Thus, at ground level, given that air contains 21 percent oxygen and 79 percent nitrogen, the partial pressure of oxygen is 0.21 bars and that of nitrogen is 0.79 bars.

$$\text{Partial pressure} = \text{Concentration} \times \text{Total pressure}$$

At 130 feet (40 meters), nitrogen will have a partial pressure of:

$$\text{Partial pressure} = 0.79 \times 5 \text{ bars} = \text{approximately 4 bars.}$$

The equivalent for oxygen will be:

$$\text{Partial pressure} = 0.21 \times 5 \text{ bars} = \text{approximately 1 bar.}$$

This is important because the diffusion of a gas in a liquid is proportional to its partial pressure at the surface of the liquid. Thus the diffusion of oxygen and nitrogen in the blood will be five times faster at 131 feet (40 meters) than at the surface. Diffusion increases with the depth and the length of time spent there. As a result, the decompression stops that are necessary when ascending will be much longer, in order to allow the gas dissolved in the blood to find its way out through the pulmonary alveoli.

These two laws of physics explain almost all diving accidents, and no responsible diver would think of ignoring them.

## BUOYANCY

Buoyancy varies according to the size of the diver and to how much neoprene he is wearing.

The ideal situation for a diver would be to have zero buoyancy, which would allow effortless ascending and descending. Buoyancy varies according to depth: Suppose that a diver, weighted with 4.4 pounds (2 kilograms) of lead, has zero buoyancy at 33 feet (10 meters) and that he decides to make a short excursion to a depth of 164 feet (50 meters). The pressure will go from 2 bars to 6 bars, which means that all gaseous volumes will be compressed, and their volume will be divided by three; the volume of the neoprene in the suit will thus be reduced by 66 percent, as will the abdominal gas, which aids buoyancy. There are two ways the diver can compensate for this:

■ He can use his flippers to stop himself from descending, but he will not be able to work comfortably, and his consumption of air will increase.
■ He can counterbalance the negative buoyancy by orally inflating a buoy, which he has around his chest (such as a Fenzy or a Submarex).

Lacking such a buoy, the only solution to breathlessness is to take off the lead belt. An experienced diver uses weights to achieve zero buoyancy at the specific depth to which he intends to go. He will take short, small breaths during the descent in order to reach this level more easily.

## SOUNDS IN THE WATER

■ The speed of sound is five times greater in water than in air, because liquids are incompressible and sound energy is transmitted faster and over greater distances.
■ Water promotes acoustic resonance as long as it originates in the liquid environment. Underwater, you can hear a propeller a half mile away, but not the background noise, however loud, of a seashore in summer.
■ The absorption of sound increases by the square of the sound frequency, and high-pitched sounds are muffled more quickly than low-pitched sounds. The farther you are from a source of sound, the lower the portion of the sound spectrum you hear.
■ The direction from which the sound comes is very difficult, if not impossible, to determine in water and you should not rely on your judgment if you hear a propeller approaching and you are close to the surface. Always dive down a few yards—this is the only way to be absolutely sure you will not be struck.
■ The reflection of sound waves against the seabed or against any obstacle submerged in water has been used since World War II to

detect submarines and to calculate how far away they are (telemetry). This is the principle of sonar, or echo sounding, and the equipment is now widely available to sailors.

One can use these principles of underwater sound transmission to communicate with teammates even if they are at some distance. The edge of a knife tapped against an aqualung is, in fact, a well-known and very effective means of communication under water.

## VISIBILITY IN WATER

■ Light: Some tropical waters are still transparent at 164 feet (50 meters), while many ponds are murky below the first few inches. This difference is due to the concentration of suspended particles. Calm waters above a rocky bed have few suspended particles, whereas turbulent waters above a deep sandy bed are, so to speak, "saturated." All seas have plankton or other mineral particles in suspension, and total murkiness occurs within a matter of feet, depending on the level of turbidity. The order of magnitude of residual light relative to the surface is 50 percent at 10 feet, 25 percent at 20 feet, 13 percent at 40 feet, 7 percent at 80 feet, and 1 percent at 230 feet. These numbers assume maximum light at the surface, i.e., at midday; these are the average values that, for instance, apply to

the Mediterranean, falling between the extreme values of the murky English Channel and the crystal clear Great Barrier Reef.
- The loss of the light spectrum with increasing depth also depends on the wave length. Infrared rays stop completely around 13 feet (4 meters), and ultraviolet rays around 40 feet (12 meters). This is why water is always colder a few yards below the surface, a fact that is important for a shipwrecked person who would like to cool himself off in tropical waters. In a different context, the gradual extinguishing of the light spectrum accounts for the extraordinary variability of coral reefs between the surface and the depths. The red disappears at 30 feet (9 meters), orange at 66 feet (20 meters), violet at 98 feet (30 meters), yellow at 130 feet (40 meters), green at 164 feet (50 meters) and blue at a much greater depth, since it is the last color visible before total darkness descends. These physical facts account for the visual phenomena that all divers notice regularly.

Between the wonder of the first few meters amid multicolored flora, and the dizziness of the great blue depths, the palette of colors becomes considerably poorer until all shapes and all flora are covered with a monotonous greenish tinge. Dreamers will be disappointed if they believe that visual beauty is synonymous with depth, and they would be better off snorkeling (studying the seabed from the surface through a mask with an air tube). A waterproof lamp, which restores a complete light spectrum for a short distance, can bring out the true colors. It is enough to drive out morays, ready to pounce from their hiding places, or to detect "red coral," which is very poisonous to the touch.

Light rays penetrating the water are close to vertical, since they penetrate an environment with an elevated index of refraction. On the other hand, the eye fixed on the sun will follow a trajectory that is not a straight line, but diverges from the vertical once it reaches the surface. The trajectory of the straight line through water reaches an image of the sun that is closer to the vertical than the true sun. Therefore, if you aim a bow or spear at a fish, you must aim between the fish and yourself in as vertical a line as possible so as to decrease the angular error. In other words, a person who intends to harpoon a fish next to his boat must aim at an invisible fish located between himself and the fish he actually sees.

Why can a diver see better with a mask than without one? Because the human eye is constructed to have clear vision in air, not in water. The difference of the indices of refraction between the cornea and the air is 0.3, which is equivalent to a convergency of 60 diopters and which allows images arriving on the cornea to be projected onto the retina and thus to provide physiologically perfect vision. In water the difference of the indices of refraction is no more than 0.04 (since the cornea is very rich in water, its index is close to that of water), and this is equivalent to a convergency power of only 18 diopters. Therefore the images will form behind the retina, and vision will be blurred. This is equivalent to very significant, artificial hypermetropia (long-sightedness). This is what happens when an individual swims underwater with his eyes open: He can make out the shapes and colors but finds it difficult to see the contours.

The mask eliminates this problem totally from the point of view of clarity, but the objects look 25 percent larger and seem to be 25 percent closer. A fish never looks as impressive on the surface as in the water.

The refraction also restricts the visual field under water to 97° (48.5 × 2), whereas the visual field in air is 200° horizontally and 130° vertically. It is pointless to enlarge the size of the glass in the mask—doing so it will not improve the field of vision.

## COOLING WHEN DIVING

We have already mentioned how cold water affects the internal temperature of a shipwrecked person or of a pilot who lands in the water, and what should and should not be done under such circumstances. Divers must take preventive measures. These measures mainly involve equipment. Professional divers wear suits that are supplied with warm water from the surface through a hose. The amateur diver, however, will truly be on his own and will have to use his own methods to conserve calories.

■ Loss through conductibility in contact with water is less significant than loss through convection because a boundary layer is formed, especially if the body is covered with some sort of garment. Conductibility will become a determining factor if the water is rough, because it is much greater than the conductibility of air.

■ Convection, on the other hand, is very costly in calories and is linked to the circulation of the surrounding fluid. Convection increases as movements become more vigorous. This naturally affects the diver moving through the water. His motion is costly both in the amount of oxygen it consumes (the reason for recourse to hyperventilation) and in calorie loss that, in its turn, sets thermal regulation in motion, which also requires oxygen. This is why the same diver at the same depth will consume up to two times as much oxygen if he is moving around

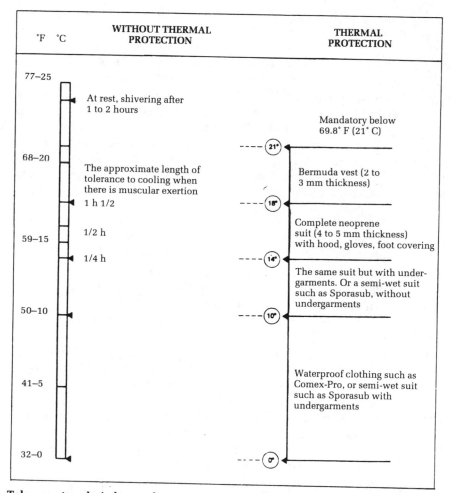

| °F   °C | WITHOUT THERMAL PROTECTION | THERMAL PROTECTION |
|---|---|---|
| 77–25 | | |
| | At rest, shivering after 1 to 2 hours | |
| | | Mandatory below 69.8° F (21°C) |
| 68–20 | | 21° |
| | The approximate length of tolerance to cooling when there is muscular exertion | Bermuda vest (2 to 3 mm thickness) |
| | 1 h 1/2 | 18° |
| 59–15 | 1/2 h | Complete neoprene suit (4 to 5 mm thickness) with hood, gloves, foot covering |
| | 1/4 h | 14° |
| | | The same suit but with under-garments. Or a semi-wet suit such as Sporasub, without undergarments |
| 50–10 | | 10° |
| 41–5 | | Waterproof clothing such as Comex-Pro, or semi-wet suit such as Sporasub with undergarments |
| 32–0 | | 0° |

Tolerance to calorie loss under water. Means of protection according to temperature and time limits set by Comex-Pro tables (According to R. Sciarli and X. Fructus, Marseille)

than if he stays motionless on the bottom.

■ Losses through evaporation occur in the lungs of a diver where the cold dry air from the aqualung becomes saturated with water vapor at 98.6°F (37°C) in the alveoli. (Since the air expands, it is cooled at the exit from the valve, just before it is breathed in.)

■ Losses through radiation are negligible (radiation is the direct exchange of heat between two separate bodies with different temperatures, for example the sun and the earth).

Thermal comfort is achieved at an internal temperature of 98.6°F (37°C) and a skin temperature of 91.4–93.2°F (33–34°C). These conditions are met when air temperature is 77°F (25°C), as long as there is no wind, the humidity is normal and the person performs no strenuous activity.

Calm waters would have to have a temperature of 91–93°F to reach thermal comfort for a naked man. The difference between air and water is due to very different thermal conductibility: This means that if a person is wearing only a swimsuit, he will cool off in any water with a temperature below 91°F. The number of enclosed seas that reach this temperature can be counted on the fingers of one hand, and they do so only at certain times of the year.

■ At 75.2°F (24°C) in still air, a man only loses 2 watts per 11 square feet (per 1 square meter), i.e., 3.6 watts for an average surface of 19 square feet (1.8 square meters).

■ At 89.6°F (32°C) in water, a man in a swimsuit will lose 100 watts per 11 square feet (1 square meter), i.e., 180 watts! [360 at 87.8°F (31°C), 540 at 86°F (30°C), etc.].

All movement in water aggravates losses, just like wind aggravates losses in air at the same temperature. This is because the "boundary layer" is swept away by movement. The diver must thus retain and expand this boundary layer. A woolen sweater is better than nothing, but the best layer would be an isothermal garment of neoprene. There are many brands, but those with a smooth surface should be avoided. Uneven surfaces are more efficient in retaining a boundary layer.

## THERMAL PROTECTION

Above 70°F (21°C) protective clothing is unnecessary, but remember that you will lose about 2,000 watts at 70°F and that the aqualung will empty much faster. Below 69.8°F, Sciarli and Fructus advise systematic protection through clothing, in accordance with the following principles:

# FACTS FOR UNDERWATER SURVIVAL

■ Arterial pressure, with a maximum value of 13 to 14 and minimum value of 8 to 9 for a young adult, varies according to weight. In a person standing upright, this pressure increases by 0.39 inches (10 millimeters) of mercury for every 4.7 inches (12 centimeters) below the heart and decreases by the same amount above the heart. Thus the pressure is 210 mm Hg at the feet compared to 90 at the brain. If the same individual is lying on water, he will have an equal pressure of 120 mm Hg from his head to his feet. When he dives, the pressures are reversed, and thus the pressure is greater in his brain. These differences play a significant role in some accidents, especially toward the end of an ascent following the last in a succession of free dives when the body is tired and suffering from oxygen debt.

■ A man's arm and leg muscles are well adapted to physical exertion in air; but the muscles that control breathing (diaphragm and intercostals) are designed exclusively for an air environment of about 760 mm Hg and are unable to deal with high pressures compressing the thoracic cavity. For every descent of 33 feet, pressure increases by 1 atmosphere (760 mm Hg). It would be impossible for an individual under water to breathe through a 16-inch-long (40-centimeter-long) tube, since his muscles could not deal with the pressure of 16 inches of water. This shows the lack of realism of films in which the hero escapes his pursuers by hiding under water and using a bamboo cane to breathe air from the surface. This is not a technique that would be recommended in a commando training camp!

■ Breathing under water is only possible with the help of a pressure reducer, which equalizes the hydrostatic pressure exerted on the thoracic cavity with the pressure of the mixture coming from the aqualung to the upper air passages. It is a simple device that provides the appropriate air pressure at all depths. This is a device that should be treated with great care—the diver's life depends on it. It should never be dragged through the sand, it should be exposed to the sun as little as possible, and it should frequently be rinsed in freshwater.

■ The term "dead space" describes the volume of air that remains in the upper air passages after a normal intake of breath and is ejected without ever reaching the lungs. This dead space starts at the bronchi, followed by the trachea, the pharynx, the mouth and the nasal cavities. If all these cavities and natural passages were extended in a hermetic fashion by artificial passages, the dead space would increase to a point where it was larger than the volume of the air intake. This is what happens to the unrealistic movie hero we mentioned above. The mouthpiece and the pressure reducer also increase the dead space but to a much more limited extent.

Moreover, when an individual exhales, roughly 3 quarts (3 liters) of air remain in the lungs and the concentration of oxygen is, at most, 15 percent. This demonstrates the importance of voluntarily taking deep breaths before any type of exertion so as to benefit from maximum oxygenation.

This technique is especially valuable to use before getting into the water to free dive.

It also demonstrates the value of relaxation exercises that include breathing control. Learning to control breathing can radically improve a diver's self-sufficiency. It is better to breathe slowly and deeply, rather than increasing the rate without changing the amount of air taken in on each breath. The latter procedure increases the dead space and aggravates breathlessness. Any diver who has not sufficiently prolonged his exhalation will be affected by breathlessness, and this will get worse the deeper he goes: for example, at 164 feet (50 meters) the air will be six times as heavy as at the surface, thus increasing the exertion demanded from the respiratory muscles. This exertion will be made even worse by the struggle against the mechanical resistance of the pressure reducer, which can be significant.

# FREE DIVING OR SKIN DIVING

Anyone in a survival situation on an island or at sea may have to dive and remain below water for a certain length of time, in order to hunt, to repair a leak or to free a propeller or an anchor. Therefore it is appropriate to include some brief advice on the best way to proceed.

In 1983 a Frenchman named Jacques Mayol, at the age of 56, attained the extraordinary depth of 344 feet (105 meters) without prior intake of pure oxygen. That record was broken in 1989 by Angela Bandini, an Italian woman who dove to 351 feet (107 meters). But the depths that interest us are between 33 and 66 feet (10 and 20 meters).

The ability to hold one's breath depends on very specific training and special mental preparation, rather than on an exceptional athletic condition. The difficulty is in continuing to hang on when you feel the irresistible urge to breathe in before reaching the surface.

## INCREASING BREATH-HOLDING ABILITY

Leaving theoretical explanations to the experts, we offer here a few practical suggestions.

### Mental State

**Motivation** will extend the length of time you can hold your breath: A starving individual pursuing a fish within the range of his harpoon will unconsciously improve his performance.

**Mental stress,** whether caused by a pleasant surprise or impending danger, can extend, or abruptly interrupt, the ability of an individual to hold his breath. The differences depend on personality and past experience. This means that before you begin a dive, you should try to foresee all the types of encounters you may face. The appearance of a shark, for example, is less stressful if you are prepared for it.

**The psychological profile** should be considered. A member of a crew who suffers from claustrophobia or has a strong aversion to certain underwater predators should obviously not be sent to disengage an anchor 46 feet (14 meters) below the surface.

## The Rhythm of Holding One's Breath

Breathing between periods of holding your breath is of primary importance. If the period of normal breathing is insufficient, the individual will suffer from oxygen debt, which will become worse with every dive, finally leading to unconsciousness. If a person starts a long-distance race too fast, he can compensate the debt by temporarily slowing the rhythm and breathing deeply. This is obviously not possible under water, and therefore he must have a sufficiently long break before diving again.

## Hyperventilation

This consists of breathing deeper and faster than normal in order to eliminate carbon dioxide from the blood and store as much oxygen as possible. This technique is very effective in extending the time an individual can hold his breath, but it is dangerous if not practiced according to very strict rules.

With a stopwatch in hand, a person should experimentally hyperventilate until he feels slightly dizzy. This dizziness is caused by alkalosis, i.e., the blood becomes alkaline, since the carboxylic gas is eliminated by the deep, rapid breathing. It is this phenomenon that causes dizziness when a person blows up an air mattress too quickly by mouth.

The appearance of discomfort should be timed (generally between one and two minutes). Never allow hyperventilation to last longer than one-third of the time it takes to become dizzy.

When hyperventilating, a person should keep his chest above the water or lie on the water (because of the pressure mentioned previously), otherwise he will lose 50 percent of his expiratory reserve and 10 percent of his lung capacity, which are enormous amounts.

## Muscular Activity Under Water

Since all muscular activity consumes oxygen, such activity will decrease the time an individual can hold his breath in proportion to the intensity of the activity. However, for physiological reasons that are not entirely clear, moderate muscular activity while holding one's breath paradoxically delays rupture. Therefore paddling gently with the flippers will not have a negative effect on holding one's breath.

### Cardiopulmonary Training

According to resent research, the average lengths of time a man on the surface can hold his breath are:

following forced exhalation: 15 seconds
following normal exhalation: 20 seconds
following normal inhalation: 30 seconds
following forced inhalation: 50 to 60 seconds
following pulmonary hyperventilation: 90 to 150 seconds

It is useful to know that physical conditioning makes little difference in the ability to hold one's breath. This supports the logical theory that localized cardiopulmonary training should be practiced, totally independent of muscular training. A look at free divers confirms that the best are not necessarily the most athletic.

Lung capacity is a direct factor, and it can be developed both by long-distance sports activities (running, cycling, swimming) and by specific training, i.e., regular sessions in which an individual holds his breath, but that do not include any specific muscle exercises.

The preceding observations naturally lead to two comments:

■ Free diving is a sport, as is any activity that develops the pulmonary capacity and the resulting volume of the heart muscle.
■ Scuba diving is not truly a sport, as we see it, because it calls on mental, rather than heart or pulmonary, qualities.

### Breathing Exercises

Breathing exercises ensure an increase in oxygen reserves through improved alveolar action.

### Relaxation

There are various relaxation techniques that aim to eliminate all unnecessary muscular exertion; using such techniques can preserve oxygen in two ways: by reducing muscular consumption on the one hand, and by suppressing emotional stress on the other.

### During the Free Dive

In addition to relaxation and the elimination of all extraneous action, exhaling slowly and more shallowly two or three times at the end of the free dive will delay the rupture point by decreasing expiratory stimuli.

## Additional Methods

The ideal diet for free diving is food rich in sugars, which will make the brain better able to deal with apnea and which supply ideal muscular energy. Alcohol has a very negative effect, because it causes skin vasodilation, which results in a pure loss in the dispersion of oxygen reserves. (These dietary problems will naturally not apply to an individual in a survival situation.)

A free diver should know the effect of water temperature on the length of time he remains below the surface: The lower the water temperature, the greater his consumption of oxygen and his loss of body heat. Therefore one should be clothed at least to some extent in order to last under water.

## ACCIDENTS DURING FREE DIVING

### Loss of Consciousness and/or Death Due to Immersion in Cold Water

This can happen to a person who jumps naked into water that is much colder than his body. The difference between the two temperatures is of primary importance, as is the speed with which the person plunges in. In order to prevent unconsciousness and/or death due to cold water one must enter the water gradually if there is a large difference in tempera-

ture. Fainting, and even death, caused by a sudden drop in blood pressure can occur even in temperate waters if one has been exposed to the sun for a long time, since the latter increases the difference between the temperatures by raising that of the body. A hood protecting the head and nape of the neck is very useful when one enters the water or swims at greater depths where the water becomes colder. The medulla oblongata is that part of the brain that is located at the nape of the neck and contains numerous vital centers, including those that control breathing; it is assumed that the abrupt cooling of this bulb is the cause of fainting, which can of course be fatal if one is diving alone.

### Other Diving Accidents

The vast majority of diving accidents happen at a depth of 33 to 50 feet (between 10 and 15 meters). Without making a scientific analysis, various objective factors combine to present a fascinating preliminary outline for explaining all these accidents:

■ During the descent, the brain is well irrigated because the head is down, the partial pressure of the oxygen in the lungs increases as one goes down, and one "feels better and better."
■ During the ascent, the brain loses its preferential irrigation,

and the alveolar partial pressure of oxygen suddenly decreases in a ratio of approximately 1 to 6 (due to a decrease in hydrostatic pressure on the one hand and to the body's consumption on the other).

Other factors have been put forward, such as the stretching of the carotid sinus when the face is held up toward the surface, the stimuli resulting from the stretching of the intercostal muscles, or inadequate venous cardiac supply. What one absolutely must remember is the unpredictability of accidents, even with a diver in perfect physical condition and with the feeling of security that comes from it. Free diving alone is a dangerous activity.

## SCUBA DIVING

There are many situations in which scuba diving is essential. Diving with aqualungs may be an integral part of an expedition to explore the seabed, find shipwrecks, explore underwater passages in speleology. It may also be the only means available on board to repair a leak, free an anchor stuck at a great depth, or hunt some underwater creatures. It is particularly dangerous if undertaken without a knowledge of the fundamental safety rules that follow directly from the physical properties of gases and some basic facts of physiology.

### THE FIXATION OF BUBBLES

Gases can be dangerous in two ways:

■ Nitrogen or helium, inert gases that the body does not normally consume, cause problems during decompression when they are dissolved in various body tissues. Accidents related to this are called *biophysical* accidents.

■ Accidents related to a gas that can be metabolized, such as oxygen or carbon dioxide, or even nitrogen under pressure are called *biochemical* accidents.

The dissolution of inhaled gases in the blood is proportional to their partial pressure and to time. The deeper a diver goes and the longer it takes, the larger the amount of nitrogen in solution in the blood. Beyond a specific depth and length of time, this translates into the "rapture of the deep" (biochemical nitrogen toxicity). When the diver ascends, the length of time at each stop should be consistent with the amount of nitrogen in the blood. The transfer of nitrogen from the blood to the air exhaled must be gradual in order to avoid accidents. If the ascent is too quick, the "bends" may result—bubbles of air under the skin or in the joints. In the worst case, this can cause instant death due to large bubbles of nitrogen that are set loose in the blood.

Gases dissolve in the blood to a greater or lesser degree depending on their solubility; for example, nitrogen has a solubility that is five times higher in fats than in water, which explains the much greater frequency of decompression accidents among fat people. Vascularization differs depending on the organs, which explains why a working muscle becomes saturated more quickly than a muscle at rest, and why bone marrow, which is fatty and badly vascularized, becomes saturated (or desaturated) very slowly. Nitrogen dissipates from different organs at different rates.

A diver must always be sure to maintain a speed of ascent that provides all tissues enough time to get rid of all their dissolved gases. This means that the diving tables must be compiled according to the "slowest" tissues. As an example, blood is the fastest tissue (with a semi-saturation time of 2 to 3 minutes), muscle is a medium tissue (2 to 4 minutes), and bone marrow is the slowest tissue (120 to 240 minutes). The fastest tissues set the times for the deeper stops and the slowest set the time for the last stop at 10 feet (3 meters). Some inexperienced divers believe that the entire decompression procedure can be done at 10 feet, as long as the individual stays there long enough. This is a serious error because the fast tissues will "degas" very quickly, almost twice as fast as at 20 feet (6 meters), and therefore they may form macroscopic bubbles instead of microscopic ones.

A simplified way of understanding what happens to a man after scuba diving to a depth greater than 66 feet (20 meters) for longer than half an hour is to consider him as a bottle of carbonated water that you are trying to open without allowing bubbles to form. These bubbles form around preexisting gaseous nuclei. If there were no such nuclei, there would not be a problem with decompression, and no bubbles would form. These nuclei cannot be avoided but can only be kept to a minimum. Very active movement of the joints will encourage the "bends" when an individual emerges from the water. Therefore, at the end of a dive the joints should be moved as little as possible.

Carbon dioxide also seems to encourage the formation of gaseous nuclei on the interior of microvessels. This theory was confirmed by the observation that the most frequent types of accidents during the dive, especially during the ascent, were accompanied by intense exertion or by breathlessness. There should be no intense muscular activity when diving, especially during the ascent.

## OXYGEN: NEGATIVE EFFECTS AND ADVANTAGES

Although oxygen is of course essential to life, there is no reason to believe that hyperoxygenation (pressure that is higher than normal at sea level, i.e., 0.21 atmosphere) is beneficial.

Oxygen under increased pressure has neurotoxic effects that cause convulsions similar to an epileptic attack. If this occurs under water, and the diver is alone, he will drown. The neurotoxicity can only occur with excessively oxygenated mixtures or with pure oxygen. The only people who use aqualungs containing 100 percent oxygen are military frogmen. Such aqualungs have three advantages:

■ They are very compact.
■ They provide optimal oxygenation for the body, which permits significant self-sufficiency.
■ Ascension stops are not necessary, since there are no inert gases.

These three advantages allow the equipment to be "closed-circuit" rigs, i.e., the exhaled gases are recovered in a special circuit where they are recycled after the carbon dioxide has been removed through special pellets. With this equipment, the diver produces no bubbles, so he cannot be located by their presence.

The toxicity of pure oxygen is such that it causes a convulsive attack within a matter of minutes below a depth of 79 feet (24 meters). The attack occurs so suddenly that during tests in a hyperbaric chamber, frogmen are equipped with helmets. If there is no physical exertion, one can remain at 33 feet (10 meters) for 3 hours. If there is physical exertion, cold and stress, the curve changes completely, and one can last for:

30 minutes at 33 feet (10 meters)
60 minutes at 26 feet (8 meters)
120 minutes at 10 feet (3 meters)

Due to this curve, frogmen never move around below 23 feet (7 meters), except for short periods, and this provides them with at least one hour for work with no danger of convulsive attacks.

Civilian divers may occasionally use pure oxygen, since in many countries diving boats have oxygen available for "therapeutic stops" in the water. Oxygen is, in fact, the chosen treatment for decompression accidents if no decompression chamber is available. It is unnecessary to go into greater detail here, but remember that pure oxygen must not be used below the 20-feet (6-meter) stop.

## CARBON DIOXIDE

Carbon dioxide ($CO_2$) is a product of cellular metabolism. It is eliminated through the lungs and should not cause any problems for a diver, except under two circumstances when exhaling can no longer eliminate a major concentration of carbon dioxide in the blood:

■ Excessive muscular activity can result in not only a major consumption of air but at the same time a considerable production of carbon dioxide. Man is designed for exertion in an air environment, and performing equivalent work under water is always a drain on energy (there is no foothold for support, one must keep at the same level, the temperature is often cold, there is greater or lesser latent physical stress). Unless the diver takes great care, the result is a feeling of breathlessness, which can degenerate into a serious accident.

■ Excessive concentration of carbon dioxide in the compressed air is not unusual and can cause true poisoning during the dive. It can happen when an aqualung is filled in a badly ventilated place, or when the intake of air comes from a badly placed compressor—placed too close to the exhaust from an engine, perhaps, or in a location where the air is polluted with exhaust fumes. In the latter case the air will contain not only carbon dioxide but also carbon monoxide (CO), which is very toxic. There are small 200-atmosphere compressors with three settings that are not very bulky, are easy to manipulate on a boat and can fill a bottle within half an

hour. The filling should be done on the bridge, upwind from the exhaust. This point is especially important if there is no extension for the air intake. In the same way as a skydiver prefers to pack his own parachute, the diver should fill his own tank: This will provide the self-assurance he needs.

## NITROGEN NARCOSIS: PREVENTION

Beyond a specific depth, which differs for each individual, the partial pressure of nitrogen causes problems in the brain. The danger of this narcosis comes from its apparent harmlessness, which is why it is called "the rapture of the deep": The diver experiences euphoria that can lead to irrational action, such as pulling off the mask or the desire to go as far down as possible. By the time anxiety replaces the euphoria, it is often too late for a diver who is alone.

■ Down to 98 feet (30 meters), no normal diver experiences such problems.
■ Between 98 and 131 feet (30 and 40 meters), many divers experience a feeling of well-being that enchants them, but that does not go quite as far as euphoria. Therefore, there is no danger of narcosis yet.
■ Below 131 feet, any neophyte diver may become "enraptured." Some divers retain total mental

acuity down to 164 or 197 feet (50 or 60 meters), but until one has been there, it is impossible to know how one will behave at these depths. Therefore diving alone to a depth greater than 131 feet for the first time is reckless.

The only prevention is gradual training and testing at increasing depths: a couple of minutes at 148 feet (45 meters) the first day, 10 minutes the second day, down to 164 feet (50 meters) the third day. One should never dive below 115 feet (35 meters) alone.

At the slightest unusual symptom below 131 feet, go back up 30 to 35 feet, exhaling calmly and deeply: If the symptom was one of prenarcosis, it will disappear immediately. This symptom may be euphoria, but it may also be anxiety, or auditory or visual hallucinations.

## BREATHLESSNESS: PREVENTION

Breathlessness need not necessarily be linked to muscular exertion: it may occur after one or several of the following factors:

■ maladjusted respiration: holding one's breath or breathing rapidly and shallowly or otherwise irregularly
■ emotional stress (sharks, using the reserve, anxiety in a tunnel, etc.)
■ excessive cooling

■ struggling against a counter-current

Once it has started, breathlessness must be controlled, because it may lead to acute respiratory deficiency and unconsciousness.

The air is heavier, and thus more difficult to breathe, below the surface. One quart (1 liter) of dry air weighs 0.04 ounces (1.13 gram) at 98.6°F (37°C) at the surface and 0.28 ounces (8 grams) at 197 feet (60 meters). The dead space in the air passages increases and even a high-quality pressure reducer always presents some resistance.

All these factors become worse as the depth increases. Prevention depends wholly on willpower and self-control: The diver must learn to control both the rhythm of his respiration and the pauses. Relaxation techniques that concentrate on respiration are very important in this respect, and they can be practiced at any time in a normal air environment.

1. Exhaling air is the control factor in the respiratory cycle.
2. A relatively long pause should be made at the end of an inhalation so that the total amount of inhaled air can be used. In addition, this pause slows down consumption and provides time to become aware of respiratory rhythm.
3. In each respiratory cycle the

lungs must be emptied as far as possible through forced exhalation. It is the only way to eliminate the carbon dioxide, which is the major cause of breathlessness under water (in air, lack of oxygen is the primary cause of breathlessness).

## EAR PROBLEMS WHEN DIVING: PREVENTION

In contrast to a fish, which only has to control an air bladder, the human body is made up of numerous cavities of all kinds, which can cause various problems unless the pressure on either side of the cell walls is equalized. The middle and inner ear suffer most because of these pressure problems. The two portions of the ear are separated from the external environment by the very fragile tympanic membrane. The equalization of pressure is accomplished through the Eustachian tube, which goes from the floor of the middle ear and emerges in the nasopharynx. If this tube is obstructed for any reason, the hytatic pressure presses the tympanic membrane toward the inside and quickly causes a rupture, even at a depth of only 16 feet (5 meters). The pain and the surge of water into the middle ear are accompanied by a buzzing sound and may cause unconsciousness or dizziness. Therefore the descent should be slow and controlled at the so-called tubal permeability level, i.e., the level at which free passage of air can take place from the nasal cavity into the middle ear through the Eustachian tube. The simple act of swallowing is usually enough to open the tube in most circumstances, but swallowing is not always enough when diving. Here, pressure must be equalized using the Valsalva maneuver (named for the anatomist Antonio Maria Valsalva, 1666–1723): The diver holds his nose, and with his mouth closed gently forces himself to exhale. The air that is under excessive pressure will force its way to the middle ear and thus reestablish the pressure. When this maneuver is successful a slight whistle is heard in both ears. The maneuver must be gradual, not abrupt. In most cases it has to be used down to 49 feet (15 meters); beyond that it is unnecessary because the pressure gradient becomes less severe.

The maneuver can be slightly risky but should not be rejected out of hand, because most divers could not descend at all without it. Sometimes it does not work the first time, and the diver must go back up for several yards, then redescend more slowly and try the maneuver at a lesser depth than the first time. He can also take off his mask before going back down, which often proves to be enough. Or he can descend on his back at a sharper or lesser angle. He should make only a couple of attempts because if he tries too often, he runs the risk of getting barotraumatic otitis (inflammation of the tympanic membrane due to excess pressure) or a tubal inflammation, which will make subsequent dives more difficult.

Obviously the Valsalva maneuver cannot be used when ascending. Accidents with pressure equalization are very rare when ascending, and all a diver has to do is go back down again and then reascend more slowly (as long as there is enough air in the reserve!).

## THE SINUSES

Sinus cavities are not flexible, and therefore there is no voluntary equalization maneuver for them. Barotraumatisms affect primarily the frontal sinuses, which are connected to the nasal cavity by a long, straight bone duct. Accidents are rare and occur during the descent or if the person has chronic rhinopharyngitis or acute coryza. Diving should probably not be undertaken by those so affected.

## TEETH

There are never any problems with healthy teeth and gums. But problems do occur if one has badly made fillings, i.e., ones that have a small cavity in the radicular canals. If the opening through

which the air enters is obstructed during the ascent, it can cause intolerable pain because the dental pulp is compressed. The only thing to do is to pop out the filling if it does not come out on its own.

## THE LUNGS AND EXCESSIVE PULMONARY PRESSURE

Excessive pressure on the lungs is often fatal. Lungs are cavities that can expand and are elastic, but only within certain limits. Every beginning diver learns that he must ascend slowly (56 feet [17 meters] per minutes, slower than the bubbles), in order to have time to exhale the surplus air in his lungs. During the last 33 feet (10 meters) one should expel half the air in the lungs, since the pressure decreases by 50 percent.

What happens if the diver forgets?

Let us assume that he inhales only 4 quarts (4 liters) at 33 feet, whereas he has a pulmonary capacity of 5 quarts. Once he arrives at the surface, these 4 quarts will become 8 quarts. This volume is obviously too great for the lungs. The extra 3 quarts of air will force a passage to wherever they can, and unfortunately this will never be through the throat.

The air passes through the pulmonary alveoli, causing a painful cough and bloodstained sputum when the diver emerges from the water. The air may then spill out between the bronchi, the heart, and the trachea and in many cases rises up to the throat, which becomes swollen with a skin rash that is very easy to recognize, and crackles under one's fingers like snow. Death may be caused by respiratory deficiency and/or by heart problems due to compression.

The air also moves toward the pleura, the space between the lung and the thoracic cavity. This can cause the lung to collapse completely, preventing all respiration on that side. This causes acute respiratory problems that quickly become fatal unless there is a doctor present first to diagnose it and then to implement the only action that can save the person: puncturing the thorax in order to empty the pocket of air

About 10 years ago a professional diver suffered a hemopneumothorax (i.e., pneumothorax with an effusion of blood) on a large boat with 120 people. He described precisely what he had, and asked to be evacuated by helicopter because there was not even a medical orderly on board. But he could not be evacuated due to a storm. Two hours after the accident, his breathing became so labored that the others started to doubt that he could survive. Four hours later he died with dozens of helpless people looking on— though an action that could have been executed in 30 seconds would have saved his life.

The last and most frequent path taken by air under pressure is the vascular passage, and this results in a cerebral air embolism. The air passes through the arteries to the brain, where it causes gaseous embolisms. On getting out of the water, the individual suffers from various neurological problems: loss of consciousness, convulsions, speech and vision problems or paralysis. The only treatment is recompression in a chamber, which, unfortunately, is impossible in isolated environments—in such a case, all one can do is hope. If the individual is not dead after 30 to 60 minutes, there is a good chance that he will recover without aftereffects.

Prevention of this fatal excess pressure is based on two principles:

■ Ascend slowly.
■ Never obstruct respiration during the ascent.

## DECOMPRESSION ACCIDENTS

### Skin Injuries: "Fleas and Sheep"

"Fleas" are irritating itches that can be both localized or general and are caused by the releases of nitrogen in the skin. They resemble hives. "Sheep" stand out more, since they are small swellings of the skin, and they are less painful than "fleas."

These injuries are very rare among nonprofessionals, since they dive in "wet suits" in contrast to the "dry suits" that professionals wear. Without a doubt, the explanation for the infrequency of these skin ailments among sport divers is the constant hydrostatic pressure of their integuments.

These accidents result from an ascent that is too fast and does not have enough stops. Dissolved nitrogen turns into numerous bubbles of various sizes. The severity of the symptoms depends on where the bubbles are, their number and their size. If the error in decompression was moderate, more moderate symptoms follow, with skin and joint problems usually occurring.

If the error was serious, for example ascending without stops after a dive that lasted 50 minutes at a depth of 115 feet (35 meters), the injury may be a cerebral gaseous embolism (often fatal), or paraplegia, which may be irreversible.

### Injuries of the Joints: The "Bends"

This disorder is common among sport divers, affecting in particular the joints that were subjected to the greatest exertion during the dive. The term was coined at the beginning of the century because of the bent position that many divers adopted after working in water. This posture decreases the pain caused by intra-articular air bubbles.

The symptom of this injury is,

in fact, pain that occurs soon after the dive, generally only in one joint (in order of decreasing frequency: shoulder, knee, elbow, hip, wrist and ankle). This pain is exacerbated by movements and resists all traditional painkillers. The only treatment is recompression with oxygen, which is impossible in an isolated situation. Therefore one would have to redescend, accompanied by a partner, and make a stop for as long as possible around 10 or 20 feet (3 or 6 meters), depending on the depth at which the pain disappears. Recompression in an aquatic environment is merely a last resort and should never be done if there are any neurological symptoms. Ideally, the boat should be equipped with a hose on board that will enable a victim of the bends to breathe at the depth of the stop, and with a ring connected to the boat by a rope, so that he can relax completely during the stop.

### Neurological Injuries

This type of injury can begin insidiously several hours after the ascent, or it can be masked by the bends or by respiratory problems. In very serious cases, one may lose consciousness immediately following the dive. The longer it takes for the injury to appear, the less serious its consequences will be in the long run (after six hours, aftereffects are rare).

The most frequent injury is paraplegia: tingling in the legs, the inability to stand upright, general discomfort and then gradual paralysis of the lower limbs with urination problems and urine retention. This paraplegia has a mechanical origin, as do all symptoms that occur in the pathology of diving: An air bubble compresses the spine and causes paralysis of all lower neural controls. Recompression in a chamber will make this bubble disappear (the amount of pressure required is in proportion to the size of the bubble) and the symptoms stop immediately. A long period of decompression is necessary to allow for the gradual removal of the gas. It is thought that the frequency of paraplegia is due to the significant fatty membrane that surrounds the lumbar spinal cord.

# PROPER TACTICS TO AVOID DIVING ACCIDENTS

Treatment necessitates two things that are rarely available to divers in an isolated region: a hyperbaric chamber, and a doctor who is a specialist or at least a diver himself. If these are not available, there are other therapeutic methods available to any team member.

## PREVENTION

Most important, however, the following errors must be avoided to *prevent* accidents:

■ Never dive in poor physical condition: It unquestionably encourages decompression accidents.
■ Never dive without a hood, in order to protect the nape of the neck and the internal ear from water that is too cold. (See "Appendix: Technical Equipment.")
■ Never dive alone.

## TECHNIQUE

■ Adhere strictly to the dive tables. There are minor differences between the American or English tables and, for example, the Comex tables. All are the result of experience, and they should be observed scrupulously in respect to both the depth of the stops and the length of time one should stay there.
■ Rest for three minutes before ascending (unless the reserve bottle is already being used) and breathe in such a way as to eliminate as much carbon dioxide as possible. Hypercapnia due to muscular exertion encourages the formation of bubbles.
■ Follow the dive tables, rounding off the depths to the next higher number: If you stay at a depth of 105 feet (32 meters) for 22 minutes, look up 25 minutes

at 108 feet (33 meters) in the table, which would require a 1-minute stop at 20 feet and 8 minutes at 10 feet.

■ If considerable effort has been exerted, professional tables or the English tables should be used as they assume physical effort as their basis. If the diver does not have such tables, he should automatically increase the stops by 5 minutes whenever physical effort is involved. If he dives in such a way that his depth and time do not require any obligatory stop (for example 25 minutes at 79 feet [24 meters]), it is advisable to make a stop of 3 to 5 minutes at 10 feet.

■ Avoid all physical effort during the hour following the ascent, since this encourages the occurrence of the bends in the joints. For example, if you haul up the anchor chain as soon as you get out of the water, it will encourage the formation of bubbles in the shoulders.

■ If the diver decides to "blow up" (see below, "Running Out of Air in the Deep") for any reason, he should consider the incident to be an accident, particularly if it was below 66 feet (20 meters), and he should immediately dive down again within three minutes (this is time enough to change the aqualung if necessary).

Obviously, this assumes that excess pulmonary pressure does not occur instantly, in which case diving again would be impossible.

The diver should go down to about 39 feet (12 meters) and stay there for one-quarter of the time of the 10-foot stop indicated in the table for the dive that was interrupted by the "blow up." One must remain at 30 feet (9 meters) for a third of the time of the 10-foot stop indicated by the table. At 20 feet (6 meters) one should stay for half the time of the 10-foot stop indicated by the table. At 10 feet one should stay for one and a half times longer than indicated for the 10-foot stop in the table.

The diver should take at least one minute to ascend from one stop to the next. If logistics allow it, the last two stops should be done with oxygen.

■ Never execute the "Valsalva" maneuver when ascending. It will not help, and it could cause dizziness, a decompression accident or excess pulmonary pressure.

■ Between the last dive and a flight in an airplane, adhere to the following delays: 12 hours for any dive below 131 feet (40 meters) and 6 hours if one spent 40 minutes at a depth between 33 and 50 feet (10 and 15 meters).

This problem is often ignored. Be aware that decompression rules are based on returning to sea level, not to an altitude of 8,200 feet (2,500 meters), which is the usual pressurization in airlines. The pressure at 8,200 feet decreases by about 25 percent, and at that pressure, a clinically latent bubble can grow and cause a decompression accident.

## EQUIPMENT AND SUPPLIES

The following equipment is essential to have on board:

■ At least one bottle of oxygen: This will enable you to make stops with oxygen if there is an accident, and it is the primary treatment that should be given for all diving accidents if a decompression chamber is not available. The Comex-Pro inhaler is an ideal portable model.

■ A Trendelenburg board: a simple board that is $74 \times 23 \times 0.75$ inches ($190 \times 60 \times 2$ centimeters) and enables a person to lie with his head down, at an angle of 30° from the horizontal plane. There are blocks for the shoulders and a hinged frame at the other end, with which the board can be inclined. This time-honored device enables an accident victim to remain in an ideal position while waiting, as well as allowing water to drain out of his respiratory passages if that becomes necessary.

■ Very large doses of aspirin and of corticoids are additional medical treatment for therapeutic recompression. Their action breaks up bubbles. There are other medicines that can be administered only by doctors.

Most divers will dive without easy access to a doctor or a hyperbaric chamber. There is nothing wrong with this, provided you understand the dangers and absolutely never ignore any of the preventive measures.

## HELPFUL HINTS

### Vacuum Suction by the Mask

This can happen to an inexperienced diver who forgets to blow into his mask through his nose when he begins his descent. The mask changes into a vacuum device, sucking at the organs that it covers, causing edema of the face, hemorrhages of the conjunctiva and nose bleeds. The accident is not serious and often the diver is surprised when he finds blood on his mask when he resurfaces. Remember to blow through the nose into the mask when beginning a descent.

### Running Out of Air in the Deep

If the reserve air has been exhausted and you are alone (two mistakes), the only hope is a buoy around your neck that can be inflated using a small bottle (not having one constitutes a third mistake). You may decide to "blow up" by discharging the bottle into the buoy. This involves two things: the ability to hold your breath until you reach the surface, and not forgetting (yet another mistake!) to blow out the air in your lungs and in the buoy while ascending. If a stop is required, you must quickly find another bottle on board the boat so as to descend again as quickly as possible to make the required stop (the stop should then be much longer, and you should be accompanied by a partner). An experienced and very cool-headed diver can trade the nozzle of the pressure reducer for the one that arrives with the buoy. He then fills the latter gradually using his bottle and gently inhales the contents when starting the ascent.

# THE DESERT

- Facts

- Myths

- Geography

- Weather

- Phenomena Unique to Deserts

- Finding Water

- Diet and Desert Conditions

- Finding Food

- Surviving in the Desert

- The Vital Importance of Thermal Layers in an Arid Region

# FACTS

○ Deserts cover 20 percent of the earth. The surface of the Sahara is 2.9 million square miles (7.5 million square kilometers). Deserts occupy more than half of the Australian continent.

○ The highest recorded temperature in the shade is 136.4°F (58°C), at Al-Aziziyah, Libya.

○ Solar radiation is almost three times greater in North Africa than in temperate Europe (200 to 220 kcal per square centimeter [0.39 square inch] versus 80 kcal per square centimeter).

# MYTHS

○ In the desert you should economize on water from the outset, and only drink when you cannot stand the thirst any longer: Not so. Economizing on water does not mean drinking at the last moment when the body can no longer function with optimal efficiency.

○ The desert is the realm of death, where the temperature is always like an inferno and there are no sources of water: Untrue. The nights are often cool and water is available if you know how to find it.

○ In order to tolerate the heat longer, take off clothes, stripping to the waist: Not so. You should be protected against the sun's rays and wear a light-colored, loose garment.

○ If you are lost in the desert, all you have to do is walk long enough, and you will find an oasis: False. Oases are extremely rare.

○

### April 1943, The Mediterranean

The American B-24 *Lady Be Good* is returning to its base in Libya after bombing Naples. At midnight the pilot requests bearings from his base. A strong wind impedes the progress of the plane, but the coast should be visible within the next hour. The crew vainly search the shadows for some lights: They see nothing as they lose altitude. Their radio is no longer working, and from that point on they can get no bearings from the base. The pilot descends slowly, hoping to see the sea or the sand; then, although the gas tank is almost empty, he climbs again just as one of the engines misfires. The pressure indicators light up, and the pilot gives the command to bail out of the plane after he throws the life buoys into the sea. He is the last to jump, and the men hear the sound of the plane crash even before they hit the water. An American rescue team searches for several days, then declares the plane and crew missing in action.

## November 9, 1958

15 years and 7 months later, an oil prospector crosses the Libyan desert in a plane and notices something glittering in the vastness of the sand. His pilot descends toward what seems to be a large, dark mound. There is no doubt about it: It is a four-engine airplane, intact, with American markings on the fuselage. It must have landed recently, since the paint is in good condition and the sun's rays reflect from the cockpit windows, which are intact. Except for one thing—these airplanes have not been seen in Libya for a long time, and the two men feel somewhat bewildered as they return to the Kufrah oasis, 140 miles (230 kilometers) away. During the next few months they make inquiries and learn that a B-24 bomber with the registration number 4124301 had been reported as missing on April 4, 1943 and that none of the nine-member crew has ever been found. A great deal of guessing has gone on about their fate and some farfetched theories have been proposed: They were prisoners of the Italians, hostages of the nomads, Robinson Crusoes lost in an oasis.

On July 16, 1959, three trucks set off in the direction of the wreck, headed by Captain Fuller and accompanied by Karadzic, an expert on the desert. After traveling for two days, the men reach the wreck and stop at a respectful distance, fascinated by the idea that they are only the second in 16 years to see the B-24. The plane is still intact despite the fact that it had allegedly disappeared in the sea or crashed in the desert.

Are there any corpses behind the windows, which have almost no dust on them? The plane is incredibly well preserved, as if it had been there only a few days. The two men approach slowly, and since the plane had landed on its belly, they can easily see into the cockpit. It seems to be deserted. Fuller slides one of the windows open and they enter the cockpit: the high-altitude flying suits are in their proper places, and sticks of chewing gum and packets of cigarettes are strewn around the floor. They find a thermos flask in the cockpit. Karadzic opens it and tests the liquid with his finger: coffee! For several hours they make an inventory of the wreck. The only things missing are the log book, the parachutes, the life jackets, and . . . the corpses. The crew must have parachuted out, thinking that they were over the sea. They must have regrouped and headed northward, for the coast. The men climb back into their trucks and begin to drive in large concentric circles to the north of the wreck. They stop at some large tire tracks. Karadzic is sure that they have been made by an Italian truck—a type of truck that has not been in Libya since the Italians had given up this part of the desert 17 years earlier. The tracks are 17 years old, almost intact, and hardly blurred by the sands and the winds. During all these years it may have rained once or twice, or maybe not at all, and the region is so flat that there is nothing for the wind to pick up— which explains why these imprints from another age are still here. The men think that the crew may have discovered and followed the tracks, and therefore they do the same, keeping an eye out for the smallest traces.

Half an hour later, they discover two boots, burned by the sun. There is no doubt about it: they are American, and they must have belonged to one of the men from the *Lady Be Good*. They were set in a V, as if to indicate the direction the men had taken. They drive all day but find nothing else. On the following day they leave very early, still following the same tracks. Very soon they discover other signs: another arrow made from the straps of a parachute and weighted down with pebbles, pointing in the same direction as the Italian truck tracks. They cross other tracks, which Karadzic identifies as those from British trucks from the same era. During the day they discover five additional arrows, made from strips from a parachute. They are now 37 miles (60 kilometers) from the B-24 and Karadzic estimates that the crew could not have gone much farther. "We will either find them tomorrow, or they were picked up."

At dawn the next morning, they find an eighth arrow, this time in the direction of the British trucks, as if the men had split up. And then, on February 11, 1960, they discover the tragic ending. Fuller finds the log book that had been kept by Lieutenant Turner, the copilot. The plane had lost its way because of a navigational error. The men had regrouped, and since one was missing, they had left the arrows for him.

By the third day, the pilot was distributing only one spoonful of water to each man, which is as good as nothing at all. One part of the group had followed the tracks made by the British trucks and then had returned. On April 10, the sixth day, five of them could go no farther, and they had stayed where they were while the other three had gone on.

Turner writes: "We pray that help will come. Nothing new, except for a couple of birds in the sky. Everyone is very weak. We can neither walk nor sleep. We want to die." On April 12: "No help. Very cold night . . ." These are the last words; the writing is almost illegible.

Next to the logbook were found five skeletons in flying suits bearing their names: Hatton, the pilot; Turner, the copilot; Hays, the navigator; Adams, the machine-gunner; and Smith, the bombadier. Nineteen miles (30 kilometers) farther on they find the other three. Only one, Sergeant Roore, has never been found.

---

In reading this story, we wonder why the pilot had not decided to try to find the wreck of the plane. He could not have known that it was intact but, even had it been smashed to pieces and burned, it would have attracted the attention of military convoys or air traffic. They would not have lost much time, since they had jumped from a low altitude and had heard the plane crash. They probably still thought that they were close to the coast, at most about 10 miles inland.

## December 1984, The Sahara

Mr. and Mrs. Barrot decide to spend Christmas in the desert, accompanied by their daughters Marie-Pierre and Colette. They have lived in Algeria for six years, and they know the desert well, especially the In-Salah–Tamanrasset route on which they are traveling. What they do not know is that the desert heat has made the road they are on impassable. No matter, they have a Lada 4×4 vehicle, and Mr. Barrot decides to follow a track parallel to the route but a little farther to the west. He loses sight of the normal route, but the track seems to be traveled regularly and it seems to be going in the right direction. It should be possible to rejoin the regular road farther on. The only problem is fuel consumption, but they have a reserve tank. What the Barrot family is not aware of is that vehicle tracks can stay imprinted in the sand for a very long time. Every time another track crosses their own, they choose the one they think goes in the most southerly direction. After they cover a few hundred miles, they realize that they must be several degrees off the route they should be following.

By dawn on the second day the Barrots realize that they are lost, but they continue to travel south. This is where they make an error in judgment: Realizing that they were lost, Mr. Barrot should have driven east. This would certainly have taken them back to a road that ran north–south.

During the second night, they use up the last of their 13-gallon (50-liter) gas reserve. When they left they had taken 10.5 quarts (10 liters) of water and 2 quarts (2 liters) of milk with them. That was all for four people.

Christmas Day is marked by growing fear: They have not seen a living soul for three days. They decide not to leave their car, and they are right—this is a fundamental principle in the desert. They believe that its orange-red color will make it easier to locate them. This, however, is a mistake because the whole desert looks orange from a plane, and in any case a car is no more than a pinhead amid the dunes. They trace large S.O.S.'s over several miles. One week goes by. It is winter and the temperature is mild during the day, only 72°F (22°C). But it is cold at night. They see three planes, which certainly do not see their emergency signals. The only chance they would have of being located is to set fire to the car. Colette hoists a flag above the car, a pathetically inadequate signal. They sleep in sleeping bags lined with metal foil, which helps them fight dehydration. By the beginning of the third week they are almost out of water. Dehydration hollows their cheeks and they suffer from cramps and headaches. They force themselves to eat. At this point, their son, who had stayed in France, begins to worry because his sister fails to arrive on January 4 as planned. He notifies the authorities and takes a plane to Tamanrasset on the January 6.

Mr. Barrot stays riveted to the car seat, suffering from rheumatism, which he has had for a long time. Little by little Colette watches her parents and her sister sink into a coma.

Colette's condition worsens more slowly, but she no longer feels thirst or pain, and sometimes she wonders whether she is dead or still alive. When rescue finally arrives after 21 days, her father and her sister are dead. Her mother dies the following night. She herself has fallen into a coma. Colette has lost 44 of the 132 pounds (20 of the 60 kilos) she had weighed and 40 percent of her water; her kidneys are no longer functioning, her blood will not clot and she is suffering from pulmonary lesions. She comes out of her coma on January 22 after eight days of intensive care in Paris.

---

Such tragedies should serve as a lesson to anyone preparing to make a similar trip. The desert is like the sea or the mountains: It does not forgive lack of preparation. An accumulation of small accidents and minor oversights can turn a harmless expedition into a tragedy.

■ Always get background information from the local people about the conditions that can be expected: the weather, the state of the roads, supplies, etc.
■ Never set off on a 720-mile (1,200-kilometer) trip in the desert with only 13 gallons (50 liters) of gas in reserve.
■ Never set off with only 12.5 quarts (12 liters) of fluids for four people.
■ Never set off without a decent compass.
■ If you go off course, analyze the possible reasons for the deviation. The Barrot family followed a track that was approximately parallel to the route they were looking for, and they were found only 24.6 miles (40 kilometers) from the Timissao–Tamanrasset road.

## GEOGRAPHY

Deserts are not always the oceans of sand depicted in the movies. The largest sand desert is not the Sahara but the Taklimakan, which stretches north of Tibet and is 745 miles (1,200 kilometers) long and 310.5 miles (500 kilometers) wide. But deserts take many geological forms, often more than one in the same desert. Knowing the nature of the terrain is essential to determining the best route and proper equipment.

■ Seventy percent of the Sahara and the Kalahari are made up of *hammadas,* huge rocky plateaus formed from silicates, iron pyrites and manganese. Under the action of the heat, the rocks crack and gradually turn into small-sized rock fragments that crumble at the bottom of steep slopes.
■ *Takyrs* are large wastelands devoid of vegetation, formed from hard clay that splits into polygonal slabs. This configuration is caused by pools of stagnant rain on impermeable clay. The water quickly evaporates and the softened clay cracks again. Such takyrs can be found in (former)

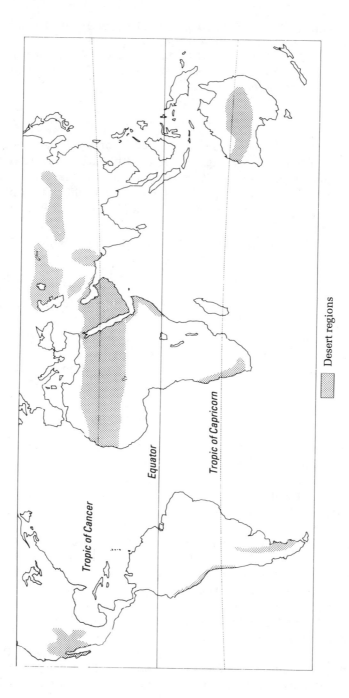

Desert regions

Soviet Asia and on the Arabian Peninsula.

■ The *serir* is a flat sand desert covered with fine stones, and its visual uniformity is astonishing.

■ Most deserts have a succession of these different landscapes. In some, walking is easy; in others, one simply sinks into the sand.

Some types of terrain are so firm and flat that one can drive a car at 125 miles per hour (200 kilometers per hour), while on others one cannot go faster than 62 miles per hour because the rough ground will shake loose every bolt in the car.

---

# WEATHER

The temperature of the air is very high—over 77°F (25°C) in the shade in summer, and it can reach 131°F (55°C). The normal clarity of the air and lack of haze has two effects: very strong solar radiation during the day on the one hand, and a dramatic drop in temperature during the night on the other. The heat of the ground exposed to the sun's rays can reach 158°F to 176°F (70°C to 80°C) during the day, and in some desert topographies it can (though rarely) sink to 6.8°F (−14°C) during the night in winter.

Precipitation is extremely rare. In some regions of Libya and Nubia the annual amount of rain is often zero. When it does rain, the precipitation often comes in the form of cloud bursts that drop torrents of water on the caked earth, which has become impermeable due to the long period of drought. As a result, if one happens to be in a thalweg, the natural water course of a valley, in the Sinai Desert, for example, one can be carried away by a flash flood.

Old wadis (season watercourses) may become temporarily flooded, but this is rare, and one cannot rely on them to supply water in the desert. These flash floods cause the astonishing branchlike networks visible from the air over some desert regions, the tracks of these one-day rivers.

The humidity during the day ranges between 5 and 20 percent in most deserts and reaches 20 to 60 percent during the night. There are two deserts that are an exception to this rule: the Atlantic portion of the Sahara, and the desert that borders on the Persian Gulf. In these regions the humidity can rise as high as 95 percent and sometimes even causes fog.

The wind is often considered the great master of the desert. "In the Sahara the wind rises and drops with the sun": This Arabic proverb refers to the sirocco, but it could just as well be applied to the Arabian *khamsin*, or the Australian brickfielder. Deserts are always enormous expanses and their topography has very few rocks that jut out; therefore the winds acquire a steady speed and direction. Under their force, the landscape metamorphoses, the hills grow or diminish and the dunes move regularly, covering and uncovering the same places.

The winds are generally hot and dry and usually reach a temperature of 118°F to 122°F (48°C to 50°C). Therefore they encourage sweat to evaporate; but the extremely high temperature makes this phenomenon useless and increases the internal body temperature even more, rather like a convection heater. The winds may cause fogs, sand storms and "walls of sand," and the traveler should always stop where he is and wait them out. Such phenomena interfere with radio communications or make them totally impossible. Do not waste your radio's batteries during a sandstorm.

Some arid deserts, such as the Gobi in Central Asia and the Kyzyl Kum in Kazakhstan and Uzbekistan, may have a temperature of around −40°F (−40°C) during the winter. They are intensely inhospitable, since they receive no more snow in winter than rain in summer—a total of just 0.2 inch (5 millimeters) per year!

The wind and the thermals caused by solar radiation serve to reinforce the dryness of the atmosphere, which makes it impossible for clouds to form. The rare instances of precipitation are caused by the advection, or horizontal movement, of large masses of water-laden air from the oceans (see chapter on "Weather and Survival").

# PHENOMENA UNIQUE TO DESERTS

## SAND WINDS

Ranging from a light breeze to a gale, all these phenomena are caused by the suspension of sand or dust in the air.

### Sand Swirls

These are columns of sand that form in regions that are extremely hot. They only form during the day, usually in the afternoon, during the hot season. They have a vertical major axis and they can rotate either clockwise or counterclockwise. Their diameter varies from 6.5 feet (2 meters) to several dozen yards. These spiral thermal currents are visible because of the sand they carry and are not dangerous. Moreover, they are not precursors of more dangerous meteorological phenomena, since their formation is exclusively due to very localized shear winds and

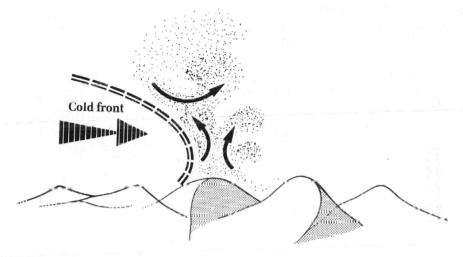

**A sand storm**

thermal convection. Some sand swirls with a horizontal axis sometimes form behind dunes, which appear to "smoke."

## Sand Drifts

These are made up of sand that has been raised by a strong wind. They often precede a warm front and form a true sand altostratus; they are dust storms rather than sand storms and at ground level they are not dangerous.

## Sand Storms

**These are dangerous, and it is imperative to seek shelter.** A sand storm is not a localized phenomenon but marks the arrival of a strong cold front, the mass of which thrusts the previous hot air up to altitudes of 6,560 to 13,120 feet (2,000 to 4,000 meters) and

forms a "wall of sand." This brown, opaque mass advances at 25 to 30 knots and is accompanied by turbulence and electrical disturbances that cause major interference in radio transmissions. It is followed by a storm that is 37 to 93 miles (60 to 150 kilometers) in depth. Therefore it passes relatively quickly, and usually a person only has to wait one to three hours with his back to the wind and his face carefully protected. These storms often move across 620 miles (1,000 kilometers), and they must be avoided by all aircraft, large and small.

## Sand Fog

Following a sand drift or a sand storm, the atmosphere often remains loaded with fine, suspended sand, known as sand fog. This sand can be carried very high and far. When south winds blow during the spring, it is not unusual to find the snow of the Alps turn a reddish brown color from windborne Sahara sands. This fog reduces visibility, but it is not dangerous.

### Sand Winds

Caused by the uniting of small thermal currents, these winds carry sand that rises for several feet into the air and impairs visibility. This is the simoon or simoon wind that is often encountered in the Sahara. The phenomenon is a nuisance rather than dangerous and stops as soon as the wind dies down.

## SOUNDS

In calm weather, the desert is even more silent than the mountain. This cloak of silence, which is a part of the magic of the desert, does, however, change. Apart from the deafening storms with their metallic vibrations caused by the friction of the grains of sand, there are sounds that can take the neophyte by surprise. In stony deserts (hammadas), outright detonations can sometimes be heard. These are rocks bursting, broken down by the action of the temperature variations, their splinters augmenting the scree cones at the base of the slopes.

In a more poetic vein, Marco Polo talked about the "singing sands" of the dune deserts. It is true that all sand deserts emit sounds, but they actually sound more like rumbling than singing. The shape, particularly the slope, of the dunes varies considerably due to the action of the winds. The angle of this slope is very sharp on the leeward side of the wind and can temporarily exceed the angle of stability, which is 34 degrees for dry sand. The slightest turbulence can make a small portion of the ridge collapse, causing a growing avalanche across the surface, and the friction of sand on sand gives rise to the rumble. The pitch of the sound depends on the nature of the sand (calcareous or quartziferous), its moisture content and its shape. The important point is that a man alone, seeking rest, should not be distressed if he hears some noise.

## MIRAGES

These are optical illusions brought on by the extreme heat of the earth when the sun reaches its zenith. Layers of air of unequal density are superimposed in the lower strata of the atmosphere, and the refraction of the light rays makes anything appear on the horizon that a suggestible person wants to see: oases, lakes, mountains, dunes floating on the water and even cities. Mirages can also appear just before sunrise if there is a sand fog. These mirages can be so convincing that even experienced travelers have sometimes changed their route to chase them.

## DANGEROUS ANIMALS

Dangerous creatures are everywhere in the desert. The reader should refer to the appropriate chapters for more details on snakes, scorpions and spiders. In order to minimize the risk, wear relatively high boots and choose a shelter at night that is some distance from stones, grasses and other potential hiding places; do not lie down directly on the sand; and carefully check clothing and boots before putting them on.

### Snakes

In the deserts of central Asia: *Naja naja oxiana* (a type of cobra), *Echis carinata* and *Vipera leventina*.

In the African deserts: *Vipera arietans* (Cape viper), *Cerastes cornutus* (Egyptian horned viper).

All these snakes are potentially deadly.

### Scorpions

See the chapter "Other Venomous and Poisonous Creatures."

### Spiders

In particular, *Lathrodectus tredecimguttatus*: This is a small black spider and the female of the species has red or white markings. It is unimpressive in appearance—only a centimeter long—but extremely dangerous. It is one of the few deadly spiders and it usually hides at the base of grass stems.

### Solifugae

These arachnids are common in deserts. They are large (almost 3 inches [7 cms] long) and have a yellowish color; they are covered with long, fine bristles and look very frightening. Their bite is very painful, but harmless.

---

# FINDING WATER

There are only two major sources of water in the desert: condensation and subsurface water. Rain is rare and cannot be relied on, but water often makes its way to the surface. It is sometimes only a few yards underground: between 10 and 98 feet (3 and 30 meters) in the Sahara and in the Arabian and Iranian deserts, and between 5 and 13 feet (1.5 and 4 meters) in the deserts of central Asia.

## WATER FROM CONDENSATION

### Dew

The temperature difference between night and day is very large, and the change happens quickly in low latitudes when the sun drops below the horizon. All objects that change temperature slowly tend to be covered with dew in the morning as the humidity in the air condenses on their cold surfaces. This obviously includes metal objects; it also includes stones, rocks and small plants. Desert people have always made use of this condensation, particularly in the rocky deserts (for example, the Kalahari in the middle of Africa).

A large pile of stones, cleaned of dust, will collect water by morning. The amount can be large if the night is cold, i.e., especially in winter in those deserts that have a significant seasonal variation in temperature. The amount of condensation will also increase as the nocturnal humidity rises (especially in deserts bordering on the sea). The best way to collect the condensation is to pile some stones in a hollowed-out crater in the sand and to line the crater with a plastic sheet onto which the dew can drip.

## Subsurface Moisture

Subsurface condensation does not occur without human intervention, but it is not difficult to gather the moisture it produces. The illustration below demonstrates the technique of digging a hole in the sand to allow moisture to condense on a plastic sheet. The sheet acts as a funnel and

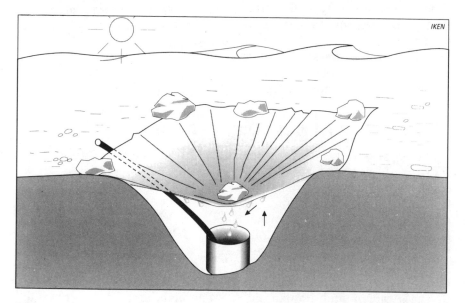

**Solar condenser**

the water is gathered in a bucket under the plastic.

One to 1.5 quarts (1 to 1.5 liters) of water can be collected per day using this method. The result can be improved by placing vegetable matter, which always contains abundant water, inside the hole. The darker the terrain, the more it will absorb heat, and the greater the amount of water it will produce. A flexible tube can be used to draw the water from the container without dismantling the device. This is similar to the device used to collect dew, but in this case the bottom of the container must be perforated.

## WATER CONTAINED IN THE SOIL

Water in the soil is difficult to find, but the task is not as hopeless as it seems at first sight. Deserts are inhabited, and the people who live in them know how to find water.

Because of the scarce vegetation, there are very few outward signs to indicate where water may be found. Topography is the guide to where to look.

### Dry Wadis

Even if a wadi is completely dry, there is often water to be found underground in the hollows of the bends. At a depth of 3 to 6 feet (1 to 2 meters) the color of the sand will become darker, indicating the presence of mois-ture. The water will slowly ooze out and fill the bottom of the hole.

### The Foot of the Dunes

Nomads often set up their tents at the foot of the dunes, on the leeward side and on stony ground. It seems that there is a better chance of finding water if the dune is high and the stony base is low, so choose the lowest point in the region. Water is collected using the methods mentioned above. A person who has never seen a lone date palm at the base of a dune may find this method questionable, but it is nevertheless correct.

### Wells

Wells have been dug by men for thousands of years; they are often carefully concealed, and only the tracks of animals or footsteps indicate where they are. Only in central Asia is their presence marked for caravans by huge mounds of stones or brightly colored pieces of fabric attached to branches. Until recently, in the Arab countries, warring tribes would poison their enemies' wells and conceal their own, so that a person can pass a few yards from a skillfully hidden well and never see it. In the western portion of the Sahara many of the wells are connected to one another, forming a virtual underground labyrinth.

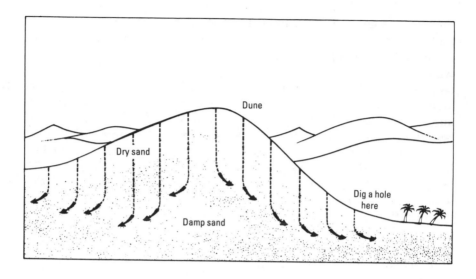

## Brackish Water

Many deserts have large amounts of water at various depths. In the part of the Rubs' al Khali (the "Empty Quarter," at the southeastern extreme of Saudi Arabia) that has been exploited for its oil fields, there are so-called reinjection wells, which are meant to increase the pressure in the oil-bearing layers so that the maximum amount of water can be extracted. Reinjections use water that is pumped from a depth of only a few dozen feet—sometimes less than 66 feet (20 meters). So there is plenty of water beneath the ground of a thirsty person lost in the desert—the only problem is how to get to it. Close to a shore, a simple hole dug below sea level will quickly fill with brackish water. And even in the middle of a continental desert the water found in the ground is often

brackish because of the large number of salts contained in the sand. This water cannot be drunk in its natural state because it contains too many salts (0.14 to 0.18 ounces per quart, or 4 to 5 grams per liter) that are likely to aggravate dehydration and cause diarrhea. The liquid floating on the surface is sometimes less salty than the lower layers and forms

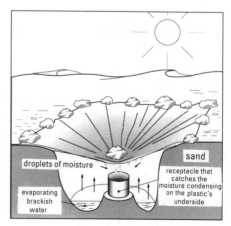

a kind of lens of freshwater. A makeshift distiller can be assembled to desalinize the brackish water, using a plastic sheet and a receptacle, as illustrated below.

In deserts where it gets cold enough, frost can eliminate the brackish portion. Since freshwater freezes before salt water, all you have to do is fill a container and throw out the part that has not frozen (the brine). If it still tastes too salty, the ice should be melted and then allowed to re freeze.

## PLANTS CONTAINING WATER

There is little hope of finding water-bearing plants in the desert. When plants are found, they are always stunted and merely indicate that there is slightly more moisture underground. Some of them may provide a little water if their roots are cut lengthwise. The only exceptions are in those deserts where cacti grow (above all in Central America), especially the barrel cactus, which contains a large quantity of water. Wild gourds also contain water, but they are very rare.

# DIET AND DESERT CONDITIONS

This section is for people planning an expedition to a desert climate who have the logistical means to carry along whatever food they choose. We assume here that the problem of water reserves has been resolved, as a person should eat little solid food or none at all if he has no water.

Since World War II, there have been a succession of many contradictory assertions, unsupported by physiological fact, about diet in hot climates. For instance, we know that a hot climate causes an increase in the catabolism of proteins, the destruction of which is demonstrated by an increased elimination of nitrogen in the urine and in sweat. It is a small step from this observation to suggest an increase in protein intake.

But this suggestion ignores the fact that proteins have an elevated SDA (Specific Dynamic Action), which significantly increases the production of endogenous heat during digestion.

Others have studied the metabolic properties of certain animals that live in hot countries, and on this basis advise an increase in the consumption of lipids. For example, sheep and jerboas have special deposits of fats in their tails. Sisels (susliks) have this fat under their skin, and camels and dromedaries have it in their humps. The special property that all these creatures have is that they produce a significant amount of water through oxidation of the adipose tissues they have in reserve. In this way camels and dromedaries are able to recover 42 quarts (40 liters) of water by burning the fat in their humps. But advice to increase the quantity of lipids in rations to be eaten in hot countries ignores the high caloric content of lipids (9 calories per gram *vs.* 4 for proteins and carbohydrates), a content that will seriously increase the production of endogenous heat. It is also an inappropriate correlation between organisms with very different genetic programming.

Other physiologists have recommended exactly the opposite— that one should decrease the lipid ration in hot countries. It is interesting that most people have a spontaneous aversion to fatty foods when they are in hot countries.

Carbohydrates play a leading role in adaptation to hot climates. They provide more calories than proteins and have a lower SDA, and therefore, in a hot environment, they are still the primary raw materials for exertion. In addition, they have the following advantages:

■ They play an important role in the resynthesis of proteins, as is demonstrated by the decrease in the concentration of amino acids in the blood of those exposed to a temperature of 122°F (50°C) in a thermal chamber.

■ In comparison to a protein diet, a carbohydrate requires less diuresis, which is obviously valuable. The body's work in metabolizing protein increases the amount of urine the body must produce to rid itself of protein-related waste products.

■ Adaptation to a hot climate is much faster with a carbohydrate diet, probably because of the improved muscular efficiency.

Data obtained from soldiers stationed in tropical regions have shown a significant drop in the proportion of ascorbic acid in the blood, because this vitamin is eliminated with sweat. Not only are water-soluble vitamins lost through sweat (vitamin C, $B_1$ and others), but heat also inhibits their normal synthesis. In conclusion, desert rations should include carbohydrates, vitamin C and multivitamins and a minimum of proteins and lipids.

## FINDING FOOD

The order of priorities in a hot region is: secure the water supply first, search for food later. While there are gazelles, antelopes, hares, jerboas, prairie dogs, rats, gophers and lizards in the desert, they are rare and hard to catch. Therefore one should not rely on this source of animal food unless one has a gun or, better yet, a rifle.

If close to a burrow, one can set a trap.

Basically, the only choice is to *gather* food. This, too, is quite limited, unless one is lucky enough to find a palm tree, preferably a date palm. A date contains 70 percent carbohydrates, 2.5 percent lipids, and 2 percent proteins, ideal food for a hot region. But whatever type of palm it is, its heart and sprouts can be used, i.e., the most recent terminal buds. The baobab, which has an enormous trunk, contains water in its roots and fruits. Caper bushes are highly valued by the nomads in Africa and Asia because of their fruits and buds, which are rich in carbohydrates and ascorbic acid (150 mg per 100 grams). Other plants that should be mentioned are wild sorrel (*Rumex vesicarius*), which is widespread in most deserts; eleagnae shrubs (*Eleagnus*), which have oval, sugary fruits; desert gourds; mescal (or peyote); acacia beans; and wild almonds.

In Central and North America there are 1,500 different types of cactus. Thanks to them, survival in American deserts is much easier. Their meat contains up to 95 percent water and their fruits are very edible, particularly after they have been cooked. There is a very simple trick to distinguish between toxic and edible cacti: If a milky sap oozes out of a cut on the cactus, the cactus is not edible. This principle is applicable to all desert plants except for the barrel cactus.

Some shrubs and grasses are adapted to the desert with spines, tough leaves, and long roots or tubers that spread far to find the slightest trace of moisture. Plants that look dead seldom are; they need only a little rain to survive for years. Uncover their tubers or roots to see if they contain water.

## SURVIVING IN THE DESERT

Most preventive measures aim to reduce dehydration.

■ **Avoid physical exertion during the day.** This is the only way to avoid producing endogenous heat from muscular exertion. In addition, and on a par with muscular exertion, the number of calories burned is much greater in a hot environment than in a temperate one. Therefore, all physical activities should be done at night, not only to conserve calories but also to protect the body from the sun's radiation.

■ **Avoid the sun.** Screen yourself against the sun's rays, which are responsible for 70 percent of the exogenous heat supply. Any shelter (the wing of a plane, light-colored clothing) is effective, but it is not ideal because it offers no protection against the indirect radiation from the sand. The best shelter is a hole about 3 to 6 feet (1 to 2 meters) deep, dug into the ground. Remember that at a depth of 12 to 16 inches (30 to 40 centimeters) the sand is considerably cooler and often less dry than at the surface.

At a depth of 5 feet (1.5 meters) the temperature of the sand remains constant between 50 to 62.6°F (10 and 17°C) all year, irrespective of what time of day it is. This fact, which has been verified in most deserts, seems to be the decisive factor for survival and directly determines the type of shelter that should be constructed: a fabric-covered hole at least 3.3 feet (1 meter) deep and large enough for a person to stretch out in. The fabric will prevent direct solar radiation and should be placed high enough to permit the wind to ventilate the surface above the hole. A double thickness, providing an air space of a couple of inches (several centimeters) is best, and, if possible, the fabric should be light-colored.

There is no need to fear burrowing snakes that live in the sand as they are harmless.

■ **If the temperature rises above 104°F (40°C) in the shade, avoid exposure to the wind and remain covered.** At this temperature the wind no longer refreshes the body and, in fact, it causes an increase in exogenous heat through convection. Experiments conducted in a thermal chamber at tempera-

tures over 104°F and a simulated wind speed of 6 miles per hour (10 kilometers per hour) showed that unclothed individuals felt better at first because of the evaporation encouraged by the current of air, but they lost 17.5 ounces (500 grams) of water per hour. On the other hand, once they put on a burnoose or other clothing, their water loss dropped to 12 ounces (340 grams) per hour. There is a good reason why men of a desert are never stripped to the waist. Clothing should be loose and well ventilated so that heat cannot accumulate and inhibit the evaporation of sweat. In order to achieve this, the cuffs and collar should be wide and there should be adjustable openings for varying temperatures. In addition, the clothing should be of as light a color as possible to decrease absorption of the sun's ray.

■ **Water should be drunk in small doses, and not all at once.** Studies have shown that people who drank 1 quart (1 liter) of water all at once lost 6.76 to 16.9 fluid ounces (200 to 500 milliliters) of water in their urine. The same amount of water divided into three doses of 11 fluid ounces (333 milliliters) each caused a urinary loss of only 4.7 to 10 fluid ounces (140 to 300 milliliters); the differences depended on the temperature. Finally, and above all, when the individuals drank 2.8 fluid ounces (83 milliliters) of water every hour for 12 consecutive

## LENGTH OF TIME A HUMAN BEING CAN SURVIVE IN THE DESERT

| MAXIMUM TEMPERATURE IN THE SHADE | WATER RESERVE | APPROXIMATE NUMBER OF DAYS ONE CAN SURVIVE IN THE SHADE AND AT REST | APPROXIMATE NUMBER OF DAYS ONE CAN SURVIVE TRAVELING ONLY AT NIGHT AND STAYING IN THE SHADE DURING THE DAY | DISTANCE THAT CAN BE TRAVELED |
|---|---|---|---|---|
| Over or equal to 100°F (38°C) | No water | 2 to 5 days | 1 to 3 days | 19 mi (30 km) |
| | 4 quarts (4 liters) | 3 to 7 days | 2.5 to 4 days | 31 mi (50 km) |
| 80°F to 100°F (27°C to 38°C) | No water | 5 to 9 days | 3 to 7 days | 19 to 40 mi (30 to 65 km) |
| | 4 quarts (4 liters) | 7 to 13 days | 4 to 9 days | 28 to 59 mi (45 to 95 km) |
| less than 80°F (27°C) | No water | 9 to 10 days | 7 to 8 days | 40 to 59 mi (65 to 95 km) |
| | 4 quarts (4 liters) | 13 to 14 days | 9 to 11 days | 59 to 149 mi (95 to 240 km) |

hours, the urinary loss was, at most, 1.7 to 3.4 fluid ounces (50 to 100 milliliters) at the same temperatures, i.e., four to five times less.

■ Dividing up the doses of liquid in a hot atmosphere enables 90 to 95 percent of the water drunk to be used for thermoregulation, i.e., for sweating. If the water is drunk in one portion, 25 to 50 percent of the water ingested is eliminated as a pure loss in the urine and therefore takes no part in thermoregulation. It is essential to start drinking water *before* you feel thirsty (see the chapter on "Thirst").

■ **Do not take salt nor eat any food unless there is a sufficient amount of water available.** Salt tablets are frequently misused. Using them is even more misguided if you lack water, and you risk superimposing "osmotic thirst" over hypovolemic thirst. In a survival situation in which water is rationed, or even nonexistent, eating even normal food can result in an excessive intake of salt. Avoid eating at all if you do not have water. Remember that a person dies of thirst in the desert, not of hunger. Again, see the chapter on "Thirst."

■ **Travel by day only if circumstances make it impossible to wait until night fall.** Know the direction and distance to the place you are going. The distance should not exceed 9 to 12 miles (15 to 20 kilometers) and should

be covered in three to four hours at most. Carry only a reserve of water and the bare necessities. Wear a wide, light-colored garment, and cover the nape of your neck. Sunglasses are mandatory. If you do not have any, place a piece of cloth with slits over your eyes to cut down on the reflection. Tie your pants below the ankle to prevent sand and sand lice from entering your shoes. If sand gets into your shoes during a long walk it will stick to the damp, sweating skin and will abrade the skin with each step. Each time you stop for a rest, air and dry your feet and remove all sand, especially from the delicate skin between the toes.

In order to conserve energy, walk at the foot of the dunes. The sand is firmest here, and sometimes it is replaced by a stony plateau (called a gatch in Arabic). The location makes it more difficult to get one's bearings, but the amount of energy conserved by walking on a firmer surface is significant. Each step in soft sand causes an energy loss that becomes very significant after a few tens of thousands of steps. Try to stay at the same level as much as possible, avoiding going up and down across the dunes. Distances are deceptive in the desert; estimates tend to fall short.

■ **As a general rule, stay close to the car or the plane,** if for no other reason than to make sure that you have some refuge with water

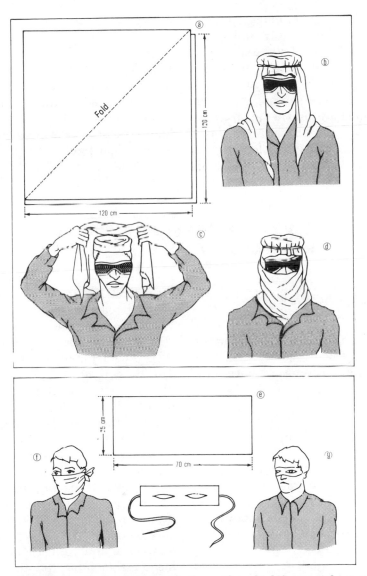

Making a headband and glasses for protection with makeshift materials: A. Pattern for a headband; B. Headband on the head; C. Protection for head and neck against the sun and insects; D. Burnoose; E. Pattern for a face-band; F. Protection of face against the wind; G. Protective glasses made out of a piece of cloth (6 to 8 inches long) with holes for one's eyes.

available. A car or plane is a much larger reference point and source of identification for search parties. Moreover, it offers protective shade, and removable parts can be carried to the summit of a dune to create a fire as a signaling device. All plastic parts will burn, giving off plenty of black smoke, and if you drain the oil and mix it with gasoline it will also give off smoke. If all the gas is gone, oil can be used like candle wax, along with a wick made from upholstery, rags or cardboard. Any material soaked in oil and thrown into an already burning fire will create plenty of black smoke. Sand soaked in gasoline can create a "night light," which lasts a long time.

# THE VITAL IMPORTANCE OF THERMAL LAYERS IN AN ARID REGION

## Isothermal Layers in the Lowest Atmosphere

A friend who was a military officer in Chad recently took temperature readings above the ground in the Faya Largeau region:

■ The surface temperature of the ground was 169°F (76°C);
■ 3 feet (1 meter) above the surface the temperature was only 122°F (50°C);
■ 6½ feet (2 meters) above the ground the temperature dropped to 100°F (38°C).

These dramatic discoveries corroborate my own experience in a part of the Arabian desert and confirm a significant temperature gradient starting with the first 3 feet above the ground. The importance of this information for survival is clear: "If your car breaks down in the desert, lie on the roof. While the temperature there will still be immensely hot, it is nevertheless cooler than on the ground. The Tuaregs and Bedouins probably have an indirect understanding of this, since they live on the backs of their camels during their wanderings. It is noticeably cooler on top of a dromedary than it is at ground level. This is undoubtedly one of the reasons for the particular adaptation of camels and dromedaries: large feet, long legs, and the major part of their bodies between 6 and 10 feet (1.8 and 3 meters) above the ground.

## Isothermal Layers of the Shallow Subsoil

With a surface temperature of 169°F, the subsoil temperature at a depth of 6½ feet (2 meters) is at

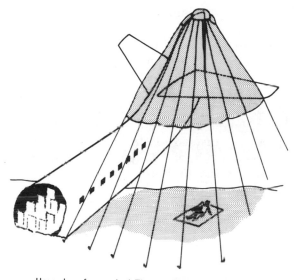

Hazardous for survival: The survivor lies at ground level

Best means of survival:
The survivor lies as high
as possible on the wreck
of the plane

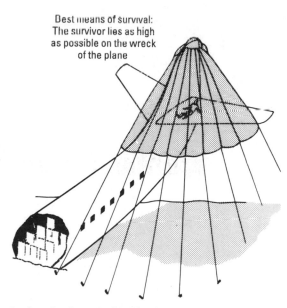

**A simple means of increasing the length of survival in the desert**

most 82°F (28°C). This gradient, which is even greater than in the air, suggests that burrowing into the ground will also provide some protection from extreme heat.

Many desert creatures make use of this principle and dig burrows of varying depths: from the little jerboa through to the huge aardvark (the male can be 198 pounds [90 kilograms]), which digs burrows to a depth of almost 20 feet (6 meters): these burrows are large enough to allow the animals to hide and to keep cool.

The members of the Barrot family, who lost their way in the Sahara, would have had a better change of survival if they had climbed onto the roof of their car instead of staying inside or next to it, or if they had burrowed into the ground.

# THE JUNGLE

- Facts

- Myths

- Weather and Geography

- Water Supply

- Food Sources

- Walking

- Special Dangers

- Physical Stress

# FACTS

⊙ An enormous variety of plant species can be found in the jungle: 30,000 in Burma alone. One single tree may have as many as 30 parasitic plants living off it.

⊙ The climatic conditions are such that some types of bamboo may grow 21.5 inches (55 centimeters) in 24 hours. This applies to many other plants, and for this reason a path cut through the jungle with a machete can be very temporary.

⊙ Only 10 percent of the light and radiation from the sun reach the earth in the jungle.

⊙ The jungle covers 60 percent of Brazil and 40 percent of Vietnam. The best survival school for the jungle is the Brazilian army's Centro de instruçao de guerra na selva (CIGS; "Center for War and Survival Training"), located near Manaus.

# MYTHS

⊙ *The "Traveler's Tree" (Ravenala) always points in the same direction, which enables one to get one's bearings. If you are in doubt, the moss on the tree confirms the direction:* No. The Traveler's Tree gets its name from the water it harbors, not from any other special virtues. Moss can be a sign, as long as you know the dominant winds.

⊙ *The jungle has infinite dangers, the most fearsome being big game.* On the contrary, it is the smallest creatures in the jungle that present the greatest danger.

# WEATHER AND GEOGRAPHY

Great expanses of jungle encircle the globe on both sides of the equators, in equatorial Africa; Madagascar; southeast India; Southeast Asia; the Philippines; the Sunda Islands, including Borneo, in the Malay archipelago; New Guinea; Central and South America; and the Greater Antilles. The jungle shares the climatic features of the tropical regions: it has an average temperature of 75° to 84°F (24° to 29°C) all year. Solar radiation is 100 kcal per square meter (per 1.19 square yards), twice as high as in a temperate zone, but it only affects the upper layer of the forest (the canopy), which rises to 164 feet (50 meters) above the ground. At ground level, only 10 percent of the radiation penetrates. The relative humidity is very high, and the air is often saturated with water. Precipitation is heavy with a minimum of 6½ feet (2 meters) per year and a maximum as high as 39 feet (12 meters) at Sherapundji in India. Several mountain peaks (on Borneo and New Guinea) receive about 32.9 feet (10 meters) per year.

Generally speaking, there are two seasons, and the rains correspond to the equinoxes. Apart from these periods, which last several weeks during which rain pours down in torrents, the weather can be very sunny. The humidity never varies, trapped in the gloomy lower layers of the forests. The permanent humid heat gives rise to an extraordinary flora, and new species are constantly being discovered. Despite a cooler temperature than in the desert (a maximum of 86°F, or 30°C), the conditions can be worse for the human body because the high humidity—often 100 percent—prevents thermal regulation by sweating.

Frequent fogs turn the surroundings into a fantastic landscape of intertwining vegetation where the lianas sometimes grow to 656 feet (200 meters) and have a diameter of 8 inches (20 centimeters), the parasitic plants range from orchids to strangle figs, and mosses and ferns may grow in the soil or tumble down from the trees. This plant world is always green. There are several layers in an equatorial forest: The upper level is made up of giant, solitary old trees that grow to 197 feet (60 meters) and have smooth trunks and no branches. Below them is a stratum of trees, which does not exceed 131 feet (40 meters); the trees form a more uniform, almost continuous layer and have branches. Still lower, there are trees between 33 to 66 feet (10 and 20 meters) high, especially many varieties of palm. Finally, the lowest layer is composed of various shrubs, which are sometimes so dense that they become impenetrable: bamboo, ferns and lycopods, giant grasses, and all kinds of bushes.

There are two types of jungle:

■ primary or virgin tropical forest, untouched by man, strongly tiered, but passable because one can get around the innumerable parasitic lianas and shrubs; and
■ secondary tropical forest, reshaped by volcanic eruptions or man's intervention (fires, leveling of forests, etc.). This forest is less tiered than virgin forest, with scattered giant trees dominating the lower layers of trees and a profusion of undergrowth, which makes it very difficult to penetrate. The roots of the trees are shallow, and the fall of a huge solitary tree often pulls trees from the lower layers down with it, making the entire area into a tan-

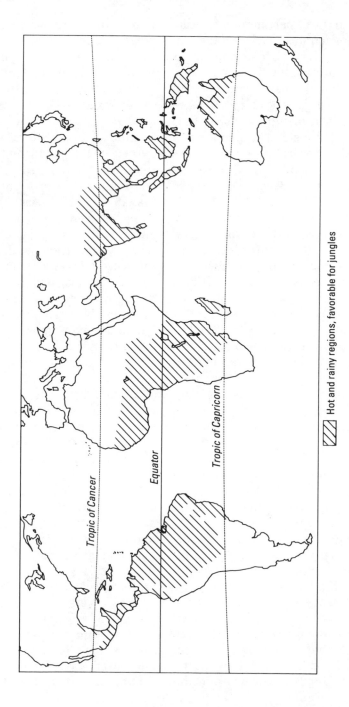

Hot and rainy regions, favorable for jungles

gled mass. These secondary forests are found particularly in Central and South America, Central Africa and some parts of Southeast Asia.

## WATER SUPPLY

Heavy precipitation, and the many forms in which water can be retained in the jungle, make it easy to find something to drink. Water is everywhere: flowing in rivers, springs, streams and ponds; standing in stagnant pools, in swamps and in puddles that remain on the saturated soil; collected in the crevices in rocks or at the base of large leaves; and draining in channels down the trees. It hardly evaporates at all in the saturated atmosphere, and a jungle without water would not be a jungle. The only drawback is that these water reserves, which are open to the sky, can be contaminated by microbes or parasites. Therefore it is best to drink from a water bottle filled from running water and routinely add one permanganate tablet per quart (liter). Wait at least 30 seconds for the tablet to take effect, although better not to drink until the tablet has dissolved completely. **Never trust stagnant water;** it always contains parasites. Animal tracts frequently lead to potable water sources.

Apart from these sources, which are immediately visible to the eye, there are also other very valuable water-bearing plants, with the advantage that they do not contain parasites:

■ The Traveler's Tree: Wide-ranging throughout tropical regions, and also found in the jungle. The large fan-shaped leaves do not point in a specific direction as is sometimes believed, but their stems each contain about one pint (half a liter) of water. They take their names from this life-saving water resource.

■ Bamboo: This species is well known for its thousands of uses, and the water-bearing variety also provides a permanent source of fresh and cool water. Bamboo that contains water can be recognized by its sharp inclination in relation to the ground (about 45°) and by its yellow-green color. It grows in humid regions, and you can hear the water splashing inside if you shake it. Two knots about 3 feet apart contain 2 to 21 ounces (200 to 600 grams) of water. This water is clear and has an agreeable taste; it does not need to be treated in any way and always maintains a temperature of 50° to 54°F (10° to 12°C), even if the temperature of the environment is very high.

This shrub is truly a miracle for a traveler because, in addition to supplying him with pure water, it provides a ready-made "cooler": All the traveler needs to do is to cut a stalk of bamboo above and below two successive knots, and he obtains a "bottle" that maintains its precious water at an ideal temperature.

■ Maloukba: This large water-bearing tree can be found in all the jungles of Southeast Asia through to New Guinea and is a real godsend for those who can recognize it. Make two cuts in the form of a "V" to collect 105 to 158 quarts (100 to 150 liters) of water, depending on the size of the tree. The leaf or bark of a banana tree can be used for a trough. Be patient and wait until the sun sets, since the water does not flow during the day (probably due to a nocturnal inversion of the sap flow).

■ The "life-saving" reed: Well known in Burma, this plant is much more modest in size, and its stem contains about one glass of water for every 6½ feet (2 meters). The water is clear and has a slightly acidic taste.

■ Lianas: These are plentiful, and they are the primary cause of the tangled vegetation characteristic of the jungle. Most of them contain enough water in a cavity in their lower stem close to the ground to quench a hiker's thirst for several hours. It is very difficult to tell them apart, and you should only drink from those that have a clear liquid that is not bitter to the taste. If, when the plant is cut with a machete, a colored or cloudy liquid oozes out, the liana should be discarded. I remember a liana in Borneo that looked like all the others, but the Dayaks prevented me from drinking the fluid because it contained a strong poison with which they smeared the arrows for their blowpipes. The fluid was cloudy and slightly whitish.

Many other plants contain water, among them the baobab, which is found in the African and Australian bush.

Water supply in a jungle is safe and certain, as long as you do not drink stagnant water or plant sap that is bitter and/or cloudy.

---

# FOOD SOURCES

## ANIMALS

The tropical forest shelters many species of large mammals: elephant, hippopotamus, rhinoceros, buffalo, wild boar, all the large cats (lions, tigers, jaguars, pumas, panthers), and numerous species of deer and monkey. It also provides a home for large amphibians: crocodiles and alligators.

A traveler should be neither surprised nor disappointed if he does not come across any of these animals: They are in fact rarely seen, and avoiding them means avoiding their dangers. Since traveling on foot in the jungle is relatively slow, and since visibility is extremely limited because of the vegetation, you are more likely to encounter reptiles, particularly snakes, and insects and larvae that are quite edible once they have been cooked (they can be found in rotting stumps).

Hunting in a jungle is much more difficult than you might think. The Dayaks of Borneo only eat meat when there are major migrations of wild boar and deer. Apart from these periods, they are limited to birds, which they kill with their blowpipes, and fish, which they catch in nets in the streams. Sir Henry Morton Stanley, the famous explorer, was astonished at how little game he killed in the African jungle despite his numerous attempts at hunting.

## FISH

The Dayaks catch large catfish by throwing pebbles into certain spots in a river. The fish come to check out the pebbles and are caught in a casting net, which is thrown out by the fishermen two to three seconds after he has thrown the stones. If the fishermen believe that the catch is too heavy and could escape through the bottom, they jump into the water and catch the fish by hand. On average, 6 to 8 out of every 10 casts they make are successful.

Another equally original way of fishing consists of killing the fish with various plant poisons based on rotenone. Many jungle tribes use this substance, which they extract from certain lianas in South America (*Paulinia pinnata, Lonchocarpus, Magonia pubescens*); from some roots (the roots of *Kro* in Vietnam and Sri Lanka); and from some fruits such as the *Barringtonia*, a small dark green tree with pink flowers, which grows along the banks of rivers. Even if you are not familiar with them, they can be recognized by the disagreeable suffocating odor they exude when their leaves are crushed between the fingers. They are easy to use: The shoots, leaves and roots are crushed with a stone, and a quantity of several pounds are thrown into the water. Within about 15 minutes, the first dead fish float to the surface. This poison causes vasoconstriction of the vessels that irrigate the gills, thus inhibiting the respiration of the fish. About 11 pounds (5 kilograms) are required for stagnant water and 33 to 44 pounds (15 to 20 kilograms) for the bends in water courses. This very effective substance is harmless to man, and some survival kits contain tablets of concentrated rotenone. However, even if such tablets are taken along, do not forget to also take along a large number of fishhooks, for reasons that will become clear below.

## PLANTS

The number of edible plants is so great that an exhaustive listing here is impossible. Plants constitute an essential part of the diet in the jungle, and most can be found along water courses, around swamps and in open areas.

- The coconut palm is very widespread and its 49- to 66-foot (15- to 20-meter)-tall trunk supports nuts that have a thousand uses. Each of them contains half a pint (one-quarter of a liter) of coconut milk, which is always cool because it is protected by a very thick fibrous shell. The white meat is very rich in lipids (44 percent). In order to reach the nuts that grow very high up, you must climb up the trunk like the natives, with a belt around your waist, using the tree trunk as a support for your feet.
- The breadfruit tree, or jacquier, is also a very rich source of food. Its enormous fruits, which weigh more than 66 pounds (30 kilograms), can be eaten both raw and cooked.
- Mango, banana, guava and cashew trees are all well known.
- The yam comes from a liana that can be found in all jungles. There are 700 species, and their enormous tubers are highly valued by people who live in the tropics. They must be cooked, like manioc, because they are poisonous if eaten raw. The natives cut the tubers into small pieces, leave them to soak in water for two to three days, and then take them along on their excursions into the forest. When they want to eat them, they dig a hole into which they pile stones on which they make a fire. When the stones are hot, they place the pieces of yam, wrapped in banana or palm leaves, on the stones. Half an hour later, the tubers, which taste like potatoes, can be eaten.

This very incomplete list includes plants that are used most frequently. However, be aware that most of the 300,000 or more plant species on the planet are edible, and that a guide dealing with them would take up several volumes. We can, however, mention a few elementary principles valid for all environments.

## DETECTING INEDIBLE PLANTS

1. Observe the feeding habits of other mammals. The food they eat is generally also suitable for humans. This principle does not apply to birds as their physiology is totally different.
2. Any questionable plant should be tested by tasting it. If it tastes bitter or disagreeable it should not be eaten, and one should rinse out one's mouth. An acid or bitter taste is always a bad sign.
3. Any plant with a milky sap should be rejected and skin contact with this sap should be avoided. There are four ex-

ceptions to this rule: the barrel cactus, the breadfruit tree, the papaya and the wild fig.

4. Do not eat berries unless you can identify them. Avoid all grasses and cereals whose grain is parasitized by ergot, i.e., a small, black, oblong growth caused by a poisonous fungus (ergot from rye is used in medicine as a powerful vasoconstrictor). If you have the time, let tubers steep in water for two to three days and then cook them before tasting the first small piece. If nothing happens within the first 12 hours, the danger is minimal.

All roots that look like onion or lily bulbs should automatically be rejected.

As far as fruits are concerned, it is advisable to boil them and taste a little before eating a larger amount. If there are poisonous substances in plants, they are primarily concentrated in the grains or the roots. On the whole, large juicy or meaty fruits are not dangerous as long as they have an agreeable taste. However, one should spit out the pips or seeds, because they may have a concentration of toxins.

## WALKING

Traveling through a jungle is often very difficult, especially in a secondary forest where the layer of vegetation on the ground is inextricably tangled. This is made even worse by the hot, humid atmosphere, which is not conducive to physical exertion. The traveler has to circumvent swamps, climb over tree trunks, extricate himself from mosses, avoid slipping on soil that is always moist and cut through lianas and grasses.

Sweating is ineffective in maintaining suitable body temperature, as we have already mentioned, because the relative humidity is very high and the total absence of any wind prevents evaporation. It is normal to lose 1 quart (1 liter) of sweat per hour when walking.

It is possible to thread your way through a primary forest, but you cannot traverse a secondary forest without a machete. If you diverge from a trail by only a few steps, you can get lost. If you are cutting your own trail, you can progress at only one to two miles a day. It is very difficult to find your bearings without a compass because the sun is hidden by the canopy of vegetation and you cannot identify the stars at night. Even with a compass you should check your bearings at least every 300 feet (90 meters).

It is advisable to stop for 10 minutes every hour to rest, get your bearings, remove leeches and refill water bottles. Whenever you set up camp, dry your socks and shoes as much as possible to avoid chilblains, fungal infections and superinfection of small sores.

Set up camp one hour before nightfall, which comes quickly between 5:00 and 6:00 P.M. Choose an elevated location that is as dry as possible, at some distance from stagnant water and the insects that live by it, and away from rotting trees and lianas. The best solution is a hammock covered with mosquito netting, which offers protection against crawling animals and insects. A topical insect repellent is very useful, as is fly paper inside the shelter. If you have the time and the necessary materials (bamboo, large leaves), you can build a more sealed shelter. It is advisable to keep a fire going to dry clothes and keep away mosquitoes, gnats and wild animals.

Although you might assume it would be difficult to start a fire in such a humid environment, the banks of water courses are often littered with pieces of dry wood. Moreover, a large, very damp branch will always have a relatively dry center. Finally, the fibers from the base of palm leaves provide excellent kindling, as does the interior of any dry anthills you may come across.

There is no such thing as a jungle without rivers or streams, and the best thing to do is to follow them. Unless you have a very good reason to cut through the forest, traveling along the water courses has several advantages: You can walk much more quickly, it is easier to take bearings since you can see the stars, there is a much better chance of coming across some of the natives (if that is what you want) and it is the only way of being found. If you want to move unobserved, rivers at night are the only way, even though they can be dangerous in the dark because of obstacles and rapids. Traveling at night through a secondary forest is impossible.

If you need to construct some means of traveling on water, a bamboo raft is best. Ten pieces of bamboo, each 15 feet (5 meters) long, will support two people. The pieces should be joined together with two other cross-pieces of bamboo and tied with ropes or lianas. Poles can be made, several feet in length, for propelling the raft against the river bed, for removing obstacles and for holding onto roots (in order to do this, make a notch in one of the poles, which can then act as a gaff).

The choice and preparation of the bamboo stems is important. Do not use bamboo that has holes in it or that is grayish in color. Holes indicate that there are insects, often dangerous Hymenoptera, inside. Before starting to work on the stems, remove the irritating bristles that are located under the leaves at the joints. Bamboo has many uses, but handle it carefully: It has extremely sharp edges!

# SPECIAL DANGERS

## ANIMALS

Apart from lions, tigers and jaguars, which are dangerous if they are taken by surprise or are wounded, the buffalo is truly dangerous and behaves just as unpredictably and wildly in the jungle as in the grasslands. Crocodiles and alligators will only be found in or close to major water courses, and they seldom attack humans. They can be frightened off easily by making a lot of noise or by beating the water. The greatest danger from animals in the jungle comes from the smallest: snakes, insects, leeches, parasites and bacteria.

## INSECTS

Apart from Hymenoptera and arachnids (see the chapter on "Other Venomous and Poisonous Creatures"), blood-sucking insects are numerous and can make the jungle a living hell all by themselves. The humidity and heat provide ideal conditions for them to breed in great numbers. The Anopheles and Aëdes mosquitoes transmit malaria, yellow fever and filariasis; and the Phlebotomi and Glossinidae flies transmit leishmaniasis and trypanosomiasis (African sleeping sickness), respectively. There are also Reduvioidea, a species of assassin bug that transmits a type of trypanosomiasis specific to South America; Stimulii; Chrysopa; and many more. Detailed descriptions of these tropical diseases are for a more specialized book, and we note here only that there are many of these insects and that their stings can be more than merely disagreeable.

Maximum precautions are in order. Be reassured that quinine will prevent malaria and a vaccination can prevent yellow fever. As far as the other diseases and the sometimes intolerable discomfort of itching are concerned, follow the advice given above in respect to camps. In the middle of a jungle infested with mosquitoes and other flies, and lacking chemical protection or protective clothing, a thick layer of mud will provide a somewhat unappetizing but very effective protection once it has dried. Some tribes mix buffalo dung with ashes. Liquid repellents are important primarily at night, because during the day they will quickly be washed away by sweat. A short haircut provides no protection against insects, and many ethnic groups allow their hair to grow for this reason. Others in New Guinea and New Caledonia rub themselves down with lemon juice. Some cover their bodies with oils extracted from coconuts or from some ordorous rushes (lemongrass). In the Philippines the natives keep flies and bugs away by slipping the fruits of the breadfruit tree into their beds. In New Guinea they get rid of ants by placing bits of molding lemons on the anthills. Ants are formidable because of their numbers, and sometimes because of their size, and they cause a multitude of tiny, unbearable bites.

Ticks are numerous in some regions. Once they have become attached to the skin, they should not be pulled out, because the pincers that remain in the skin will become infected. Instead, burn the tick off. This is one of the very rare instances when a cigarette is beneficial, because its glowing end, with a temperature of 1,292°F (700°C), is appreciated no more by ticks than by leeches.

The activity of insects increases considerably at dusk and lasts all night. Mosquitoes are attracted to carbon dioxide and therefore will find your face, even if it is buried in a sleeping bag. Take along and use as many deterrents as possible: repellents in liquid, spray, and cream form; flypaper with insecticide (particularly in enclosed shelters and close to one's face); and mosquito netting. Phlebotomi are very small and can get through the mesh of normal mosquito netting, so the finest mesh is required. Use the smoke from a campfire to chase insects away.

## WATER PARASITES

A large number of parasitic tropical diseases can be contracted in the water, among them schistosomiasis, strongyloidiasis, and other hookworm diseases. Since this book is not meant to be a discourse on tropical medicine, we will only mention methods of avoiding these parasitic diseases, which, while usually not fatal, can nevertheless be extremely debilitating because they cause bleeding in the digestive tract and vesical mucous membranes.

These parasites live in the water as larvae, and they penetrate through the skin (often of the legs), invading the bloodstream. Avoid bathing in stagnant water, and only choose water with a fast current. Wear high boots and long pants for sufficient coverage. Boil all drinking water and grill all food (this will prevent amebiasis, trichinosis, etc.).

## LEECHES

Leeches are always a scourge, whether it is the rainy season or not, and they get in everywhere, even through elasticized pant cuffs. Some are so thin before they swell up with blood, that they can get through the eyelet holes on shoes. During the rainy season they hide everywhere, not only on the ground but also on leaves and branches, and they can easily get inside the collar of a shirt when they fall from the trees. Because their bite is painless (they probably secrete an anesthetic), you have to search for them systematically. If you are not careful, you can find yourself, after several hours, covered with several dozen leeches, inflated like balloons. It is not necessary to stop every five minutes to remove these pests. Instead, force yourself to ignore them and walk on for an hour. Then stop, pull up your pants, maybe take off your shirt, and calmly remove every leech. They should not be pulled out, because their mouth appendages will remain in the skin and may cause infection. There are several effective means of removing leeches:

■ Burn the leeches with a cigarette (which one has, naturally, lit for this sole purpose).
■ Rub them with salt.
■ Paint them with tincture of iodine or tobacco juice (those who like to chew tobacco are particularly fond of this method).

There are liquid repellents that claim to prevent leeches, but their effectiveness is dubious. Once the leeches have been removed, apply come antiseptic to the wound: tincture of iodine, alcohol, etc. Sometimes these injuries bleed for 20 minutes because the leech secretes an anticogulant. There are 250 species of tropical leeches, and there is no reason to learn how to tell them apart; it is enough to know that you cannot avoid them because they are attracted to the vibrations of footsteps and they move very fast, literally leaping into boots and disappearing under clothing

within seconds. They will not be a problem, however, if you follow the measures described above.

## MISCELLANEOUS ANIMALS

Keep away from the large, hairy, stinging caterpillars, which are often multicolored (black, pink and yellow), and avoid the temptation—evoked by their iridescent colors—to touch them. They can cause very painful allergic reactions on contact.

There are also some tiny frogs that are very dangerous because of the poison concealed in their integuments. Some tribes use them to poison their arrows.

Piranhas are small fish that can be found in freshwater in South America. Their projecting jaws have teeth that are as sharp as razor blades. They live in shoals of several dozen to several hundred and are extremely dangerous if they smell blood. This smell puts them into a frenzy, and an injured mammal can be turned into a skeleton in a matter of minutes. Men have suffered this fate, and experiments made with cows have shown that the stories are not mere myths.

## PLANTS

The potential dangers of eating tropical plants were mentioned above. Here we note the poisonous attributes of some plants and trees whose secretions may be toxic through simple contact with the skin or through a minor injury.

### The Guao

This plant is widespread in Central and South America as well as in the Caribbean, and its white sap, drawn out by dew or raindrops, can drip onto the skin of a man standing below. Contact with the sap causes a severe rash, swollen and oozing, accompanied by intolerable itching, headaches and dizziness. The problems can last up to two weeks, but then disappear, leaving no aftereffects.

### The Manchineel Tree

This tree belongs to the same family as the guao, and its latex is very poisonous. It is very widespread in regions of America and the Caribbean, where it is also called the "poison tree" or the "tree of death." Its shade is considered to be deadly in the Antilles. Never camp under this seemingly harmless tree, particularly if it is raining. Its fruit looks like a small apple. Simply touhing its moist trunk causes headaches, colic and even an allergic swelling in the mouth.

### The Han Plant

This is a large nettle, found in Southeast Asia, that can cause painful burns.

### Poison Sumac (or Toxicodendron)

The poisonous sap is secreted on the underside of the leaves and remains active for several days. A vehicle that brushes against poison sumac bushes will be coated with the sticky sap; its driver can suffer acute itching and his skin can become covered with blisters if he has to change a tire and touches the sap even after it has been on the vehicle for several days. The bark of these bushes looks resinous and oozes a black sap if it is cut.

The best protection against these plants is to wear long sleeves as much as possible, and to wear a hat with a wide brim. This clothing also helps protect against insects, leeches and scratches from sharp-edged grasses or spiny leaves.

### THE DANGER OF INFECTION

Apart from infections caused by the proliferation of microscopic fungi on damp feet, outright boils or carbuncles can develop in several hours or days after a minor sore or scratch. This bacterial proliferation doubles every 10 degrees above a temperature of 59 °F (15 °C). Simple regular disinfection of scratches from plants and superficial sores left by ticks or leeches will be enough to prevent infection in most cases.

In cases of serious wounds, it is best to know how to debride, disinfect, and sew up a wound, placing a drain on it if necessary. Before departure, you can practice on a piece of fresh steak. Ask any doctor to teach you the elementary principles of sewing up a muscle with an absorbable thread and integuments with horsehair or silk.

# PHYSICAL STRESS

Many people abruptly confronted with the humid environment of the forest are literally paralyzed by surroundings they find nightmarish. At first they feel they will not be able to survive—they are frightened by the slightest sound, paralyzed by the tangled appearance of the landscape, the alarming semidarkness, the humid, suffocating heat, the total absence of the wind, and the widespread, hostile presence of all kinds of creatures.

This negative mental attitude toward the forest, which some might call a concrete manifestation of childhood fears, is paradoxical, because the forest is in fact a very propitious environment for survival. Water, food, shelter and tools are all readily available. If you succeed in getting past the first few days, you should be able to survive indefinitely.

With a minimum of knowledge gained from books, and with a developing understanding of the situation, fear disappears. You will know that the suffocating feeling is partly due to the great concentration of carbon dioxide found at ground level in the jungle: 0.4 percent instead of 0.04 percent, a difference accounted for by the rotting of the thick carpet of leaves and other plant debris. You will realize that is will be better to sleep on an overhang or simply in a hammock that is hung high enough. You will know that the background noise of the jungle is due to birds, monkeys, insects, falling trees and streams beneath the mosses—in other words, nothing dangerous. You will be able to tell the exact time, since certain birds and certain insects stop or start their song every day at the same time according to the height of the sun.

And you will rediscover your old instincts as a tropical animal.

# THE MOUNTAINS

- Figures

- Myths

- True Tales of Survival

- Thermal Regulation

- Water

- Diet

- Frostbite

- Altitude Sickness

- Lightning: Countermeasures

- Solar Radiation: Countermeasures

- Shelter

- Snow, Avalanches and Crevasses

# FIGURES

○ 450 million people live in the mountains worldwide, 25 million of them above 9,840 feet (3,000 meters).

# MYTHS

○ If lightning strikes a person, it is always deadly, and the best protection is a fault, a small crevice in the rock, or an overhang: False, in all respects.

○ Lightning has a tendency to strike any kind of metal, irrespective of its shape: No. A pointed rock will be more dangerous than a rounded piece of metal.

○ Do not drink in the mountains because it will reduce your endurance: Bad advice. The dry air at high altitudes makes it essential to drink water, and to drink a lot.

○ Mountain air is always wonderful for one's health: Sometimes true, and sometimes not. This depends on the person's state of health and, above all, on the altitude. No one can stay above 19,680 feet (6,000 meters) for any length of time.

○

# TRUE TALES OF SURVIVAL

**On the Mont Blanc Massif** (adapted from *342 hours in the Grandes Jorasses*, by René Desmaison, 1973.)

February 15, 1971. The two men wake up after spending an agonizing night, each of them suspended from a peg driven into the rock above. Below them stretch 2,952 feet (900 meters) of void, stretching from the peak of Mont Blanc to the Leschaux glacier at the bottom of the sea of ice. They are only 984 feet (300 meters) from the summit, Walker Point (13,802 feet [4,208 meters]), which they are trying to reach in a direct ascent up the north face in winter, a feat that has never before been accomplished.

Walker Point is at the end of a for- midable 1.22-mile (2-kilometer)-long barrier of rock and ice known as the Grandes Jorasses. The name alone is enough to send a cold shiver down the spine of those who remember its long list of victims. The men started the climb four days ago, and the ascent has proved to be very difficult, requiring a high degree of technical skill. The ice covering every fissure is not thick enough for them to hew out any steps. The granite wall has many overhangs and threatens a mountain climber with every conceivable danger. Under these conditions, a pair of woolen gloves lasts only a day—but that is not a problem. The two men still have enough equipment and food

**249**

for the two or, at most, three days that separate them from the peak.

The younger of the two, 23-year-old Serge Gousseault, has the physique of an athlete and was among the top students in the Chamonix School for Guides the previous year. He has been training for months, climbing snow-covered mountains without gloves, to get used to the cold and realize his dream: a winter ascent with René Desmaison.

The two men are in good shape, despite their painful hands, which are swollen from contact with the frozen rock. Desmaison had suggested, before the continuing bad weather, that they rappel down, but Gousseault had refused, asserting that he felt fine.

February 16. The blizzard is still blowing. Desmaison, who has been the leader on the rope from the beginning, explores the different routes they can take, foot by foot, returning to where he started after each exploratory trip. Gousseault belays him from below and climbs up only after Desmaison has laid out the track and put in the pitons. But why is he climbing without gloves?

"Serge, put on your gloves!"

"My hands aren't cold!"

"There's no reason to climb without gloves. Take care of your hands. We're not out of danger yet. Put on your gloves."

Gousseault puts on his gloves, but as soon as he arrives at the next relay stop, 66 feet (20 meters) higher up, he takes them off again, having recovered only some of the pitons.

"Good Lord! Why have you taken your gloves off again?"

"Why do you keep asking me that?"

"Look, Serge, as the second on the rope, there's no reason for you to take them off. I can check you with the rope, it's no problem."

"Okay, I won't take them off again."

"How are you feeling, Serge? Are you okay?"

"Why are you asking?"

"No reason!"

"I'm fine, I really am."

The two men prepare a tiny platform on which to spend the night. Gousseault loses his ice ax, which he had detached from the safety cord. The loss worries him. Desmaison reassures him.

February 17. Gousseault's right hand is a little more swollen, but he still has his sense of touch and can move his fingers easily. He lags behind a little during the preparations for departure. The slow ascent continues all day. Gousseault does not recover all the pitons and does not seem to hear all the instructions given him by his companion, who keeps calling down to him to hurry up. In the evening, once again, they cannot pitch a tent to shelter them from the snow. The two men slip into their sleeping bags suspended in empty space.

"René, look at my hand!"

Desmaison shudders when he sees Gousseault's hand. It is extremely swollen, and the skin is peeling off. He has seen hands injured by the cold before, but never this badly. Despite his own apprehensions, he spends a long time reassuring Gousseault. It is still snowing. Tomorrow they absolutely must get out of this trap.

February 18. Desmaison helps his companion get ready to depart; the nightmare starts all over again. The second cord, which permanently connects the two men, is severed by a falling piece of granite. Gousseault finds it increasingly difficult to pull out the pitons. He no longer has the strength to use the hammer hard and precisely. Desmainson can hardly hear the hammer blows.

"Hey, Serge! You can come up now."

No response.

"Can you hear me? You can come up now!"

Gousseault does not move; he is held by the cord over a 3,280-foot (1,000-meter) abyss, his arms dangling by his sides. Some words, cut off by the wind, float up to Desmaison.

"Can't climb    my hands . . . no feeling any more."

Suddenly Desmaison senses the void beneath him, the imminence of tragedy. Gousseault is giving up, it's over, he won't move another foot. Yes he will. With Desmaison hauling on the rope, Gousseault manages to climb the few feet up to the site they have chosen for the night.

February 19. A miraculous reprieve; Gousseault finds the strength to help Desmaison haul him up another 66 to 98 feet (20 to 30 meters).

February 20. This time it's over; Gousseault will not climb any farther. Desmaison shares his last food with him. He cannot decide whether to leave his companion and climb to the peak that is now so close, or to go to get help.

Finally, in the afternoon, a helicopter engine echoes through the mountains. The helicopter approaches and comes close enough to see the difficulties the roped party are having. Desmaison forgets to give the conventional distress signal, and he misinterprets the signal given him by one of the passengers in the helicopter.

In fact, when they return to the valley, the helicopter crew reassures Si-

mone Desmaison, who is deathly worried: "They're almost there!"

February 21. The rescue team does not come. The two men have no more water, no more food. Gousseault's face is swollen from the cold but he feels no pain. From time to time he falls asleep.

February 22. Gousseault starts to hallucinate, his face is distorted, and he believes he can hear "his" helicopter coming to look for him. No, it is still not coming. Gousseault braces himself one last time as if to reject this mountain he has loved so much, and he dies, his eyes wide, staring at the sky. Desmaison's throat is burning, dried out by thirst. He is hungry. His wrist, swollen by an abscess, is aching.

February 23. Down in the valley they have finally decided to send out a rescue party, but it will undoubtedly arrive too late. The weather makes it impossible to land close to the peak.

February 24. This is the 14th day; both men must be dead. No one has any illusions.

February 25. The Puma from Chamonix abandons the attempt to land—the winds are too strong. An Alouette III takes off from Grenoble and succeeds in landing. Several guides descend toward the camp using a winch, searching for the bodies.

Then they hear Desmaison call. Not only is he still alive, he still has the strength to call out!

The first guide to reach him cannot contain his astonishment, and comments on Desmaison's toughness.

Desmaison certainly was tough because he not only survived the cold, uremia and questions that his leadership caused his partner's death, but two years later, he climbed the last

263 feet (80 meters), and with two other friends, he—once again as the leader on the rope—finally succeeded.

The high mountains are a particularly hazardous environment because in addition to the cold and altitude, climbers deal with storms, the anguish of difficult traverses, the fear of seeing a team member "crack," and apprehensions about their own competence. The mountain claims not only individuals, but teams as well. It does not easily forgive those who undertake a climb without giving it enough consideration, or without knowing each other well enough. It is just as merciless toward a young person who overestimates his abilities as toward an old climber who pushes his limits.

In this chapter we will review the special features of a mountaineer's environment, elaborating more precisely what has already been mentioned in connection with adaptation to cold, frostbite, hypoxia caused by altitude, solar radiation, dietary and water needs, and physical exertion.

## THERMAL REGULATION

Cold increases with altitude: the temperature drops about 1.8 °F (equivalent to 1 °C) every 328 feet (100 meters) in the middle strata. At the same time, the wind increases and causes cooling through convection in proportion to the exposed body surface. A third factor varies depending on the altitude and partly counterbalances the other two: relative humidity. The thermal conductivity of water is 20 times greater than that of air, which explains why a person is less tolerant to damp cold than to dry cold. With altitude, the humidity decreases very quickly: At 6,560 feet (2,000 meters) the relative humidity has decreased by 50 percent in comparison to sea level; and at 13,120 feet (4,000 meters) it has decreased by 75 percent. The drop in humidity makes keeping warm easier; on the other hand, it necessitates drinking more, as we shall see further on. Although cold is expected in the mountains, one can also encounter intense heat. In fact, one can die of cold during the night in the mountains and be in danger of heat stroke during the day. People in mountain cultures seem to have discovered this long ago and for centuries have worn hats with wide brims.

Solar radiation causes a flow of heat to the body that is in proportion to the exposed skin surface and can reach the considerable value of 1,000 watts per square meter (per 1.19 square yards), especially in the rarefied atmosphere of the high mountains. In addition, long-wave infrared rays are reflected from the rocks. To protect oneself, one must always wear a hat in the mountains.

## WATER

We have already mentioned that at 13,120 feet (4,000 meters) the relative humidity decreases by 75 percent. Above 19,680 feet (6,000 meters) the air inhaled is almost completely dry.

Whatever the altitude, the air in the lungs is saturated with water vapor after it passes through the mucous membranes of the upper air passages and goes into the pulmonary alveoli, where some of the oxygen is removed and where it is enriched with carbon dioxide. This means that every exhalation dehydrates the body to some extent. As always, a lack of oxygen is compensated for by hyperventilation, which increases the higher we go and the more effort we exert. All this affects our "hydric balance," resulting in a loss of water through respiration, generally on the order of about 6.6 fluid ounces (200 milliliters) per hour, i.e., 1 quart (1 liter) per five hours of climbing at a high altitude. If we are exposed to solar radiation, which is especially intense at high altitudes, we will have an additional water loss though sweating, leading to a daily loss of 4 to 5 quarts—almost the same as in the desert!

After his tenth day above 13,000 feet, René Desmaison felt "the mucous membranes burning his throat, and his swollen tongue impeded his breathing." Since he had nothing with which to melt the few pieces of ice he had left, he would have died of dehydration rather than of cold had the rescue team not arrived at the last moment.

In any case, "drinking" ice is harmful for two reasons: because of the cooling it causes and because, like the snow, it provides a hypotonic fluid that is devoid of all mineral salts, which is extremely harmful both to hydroelectrolytic equilibrium and to digestion. Moreover, it is impossible to ingest the equivalent of 4 to 5 quarts of water per day by sucking on ice. Mountaineers should carry a small hot plate and food to which the melted ice can be added, such as soups, powdered fruit juices or syrups. Having something with which to make the liquids more palatable in various ways is particularly important for long expeditions because the higher one goes, the less thirsty one feels, even if one's body is dehydrated.

# DIET

Diet has always been a problem for mountain climbers, who typically suffer a steady loss of weight during expeditions. No totally satisfactory explanation has yet been found for this, although a decrease in appetite, which is commonly experienced by climbers, can be considered to be the proximate cause. Hypoxia might also play a role through direct inhibition of the centers of hunger. There could also be a decrease in absorption in the intestines, as one study demonstrated among individuals who were acclimatized to 20,664 feet (6,300 meters).

Whatever the explanation, at higher altitudes there will be an inevitable loss of appetite (anorexia), possibly with an aversion to fatty foods (the opposite of what happens at lower altitudes). The problem becomes greater at an altitude over 13,000 feet and becomes serious for long expeditions; this is less of a problem in the Alps than in the Himalayas or the Andes. At the base camp (13,120–16,400 feet, or 4,000–5,000 meters), anorexia is usually caused by altitude sickness, but it will decrease or disappear once the individual has become acclimatized. The best proof of the effect of acclimatization is that when mountain climbers return from their high-altitude camps, they generally eat 4,000 calories per day in the same base camp in which they had had no desire to eat before the ascent.

In high-altitude camps, especially above 2,000 feet, anorexia is constant. The mountain climber more or less rejects food and can usually eat only 1,000 to 1,500 calories per day, which is clearly insufficient compared to the 4,000 a day needed for an ascent between 20,000 and 23,000 feet. The result is significant weight loss:

- 2.2 pounds per week (1 kilogram per week) between 15,000 and 20,000 feet, or between 4,500 and 6,000 meters;
- 4.4 pounds per week (2 kilograms per week) above 20,000 feet or 6,000 meters.

This weight loss seems to be at the expense first of the body's water, then of the adipose tissues, and finally of the muscles themselves, as the protein ration is almost always insufficient. The loss of muscle mass causes a drop in athletic performance, which is already decreased because of the rarefied air. In the chapter on "Physical Exertion" we have, in fact, already seen that at a normal altitude the more energy the muscles require, the more the metabolism supplies. On the other hand, above 20,000 feet, aerobic energy reactions are overcome by the lack of oxygen, and this aggravates the difficulty of any exertion. This being the case, is it useful to put on weight before leaving on an expedition? There is still dispute about the practice, but I support the idea, if for no other reason than that it can do no harm.

Weight varies according to two factors: the muscular, or lean mass, and the fat reserve, or fatty mass. Increasing weight through muscular mass means training, and there is no question that this is important for all sports activities. Increasing the fat reserves depends on eating a high-calorie diet before departure.

The best approach is a diet that will increase the stock of glycogen (see the chapters on "The Survival Diet" and "Physical Exertion"), using the technique of "depletion-overcompensation," which alternates intense exertion with meals rich in carbohydrates. This is the "Scandinavian dissociated" diet, which is suitable for intense exertion that lasts only for a limited time—for example, a cross-country ski race.

If the primary aim is building fat reserves, keep to a mixed diet, with a large intake of lipids. These regimes will also train the body to mobilize its fatty acids and economize on the carbohydrate reserves whenever this becomes necessary at a high altitude.

## FROSTBITE

We have seen how important a decrease in blood flow is in causing frostbite on hands and feet. At high altitudes hypoxia causes a compensatory increase in the number of red blood cells, which increases the viscosity of the blood. We also know that altitude is often accompanied by dehydration through exertion. Dehydration will also increase the viscosity of the blood. This leaves a mountaineer susceptible to frostbite because this "thicker" blood will have greater difficulty in entering the capillaries of the hands and feet. The risk of thrombosis increases. One cannot affect the increase in red blood cell production—that is obviously physiological and involuntary—but one can drink large quantities of liquids to prevent dehydration and lessen the risk of frostbite.

The following practices may help to prevent frostbite:

■ Whenever you stop, practice static muscular contractions, which will activate circulation.
■ On a traverse, for example, one tends to crouch down while waiting. Avoid this squatting position, because it compresses the large arteries in the legs. Put your hands on your stomach or under your armpits to help keep them warmer.
■ Avoid wearing clothing that is tight around the wrists or ankles.

Socks that leave a mark, cuffs, a watch strap that is too tight, or a ring that is embedded in the finger—all of these can impede circulation. Blood returning through the veins is very close to the surface of the skin and must be permitted to circulate freely.

■ Avoid all contact with metal because it has excellent thermal conductibility and may cause frostbite on contact. Also keep clothing dry, and change it if it gets wet: Dampness increases the effects of cold.

■ Watch for any loss of sensitivity in your extremities. The great danger of frostbite is it insidiousness.

---

# ALTITUDE SICKNESS

Just like the underwater environment, the mountains can induce a pathology found nowhere else; and just as all divers should know about the "rapture of the deep" or excess pulmonary pressure, every mountaineer should be familiar with the general outlines of the syndrome called "altitude sickness." Failure to recognize this sickness can lead to death.

Prevention consists of ascending slowly and descending immediately at the smallest warning sign. Altitude sickness includes the three separate phenomena outlined below.

## ACUTE ALTITUDE SICKNESS: ("AAS")

This affects 50 percent of individuals of both sexes above an altitude of 8,200 feet (2,500 meters) after at least six hours. Mountain climbers and cross-country skiers are also prone to AAS. Even experienced mountain dwellers, who have never suffered from this problem, can suddenly suffer an attack. You cannot know in advance whether you will suffer from it, so take preventive measures. Although these measures will slow progress, they are worth any inconvenience. Doctors who specialize in this problem codify AAS according to a scale of severity based on the number and nature of certain clinical symptoms and prescribe therapeutic treatment accordingly. But in a survival situation, without a doctor, you will have to adopt a much more simplified scheme.

The affected individual will have one or more of the following symptoms:

■ headaches in 95 percent of the cases
■ nausea and loss of appetite in 30 percent of the cases
■ insomnia in 70 percent of the cases—followed by drowsiness during the day. Sleep is often restless and filled with nightmares.

Dizziness and extreme shortness of breath occur more rarely
■ vomiting and a decrease in urinary flow in severe cases

Any one of these symptoms, whether isolated or not, should make one think of AAS. The cause of these symptoms is cerebral edema, which is itself caused by the body's failed response to hypoxia. Hypoxia (a deficiency of oxygen reaching the tissues) causes an increase in cerebral blood flow that results in an increased pressure inside the microcirculation (the very fine channels of the circulatory system), causing a forced filtration through the capillaries, and thus edema.

The more normacapnic (having a normal tension of carbon dioxide in the blood) the breathing is, the more serious the edema will be: In fact, hypocapnia (a deficiency of carbon dioxide in the blood) caused by hyperventilation in turn causes respiratory alkalosis (a condition of increased alkalinity and/or excessive loss of acid) and cerebral vasoconstriction, which counters the increase in flow.

Studies by King and Robinson have demonstrated that AAS occurs more frequently and is more intense among individuals whose adaption to hypoxia involves only a slight increase in breathing. Therefore it is believed that the fact that the cerebral flow returns to normal in five days is due to an increase in the strong vasoconstriction factor that constitutes hypocapnia. In addition to the effect of individual factors, the sensitivity of the respiratory centers to hypoxia can be decreased by sleep and by abuse of sedatives or alcohol.

People who adapt properly to hypoxia are those whose reaction to reduced oxygen is rapid hyperventilation that itself causes greater hypocapnia and thus cerebral vasoconstriction, which diminishes or eliminates the effects of the increased blood flow.

Since the skull is not expandable, the effect of a cerebral edema is to compress the cortex and the various command centers in the brain. This very "mechanical" cause is the reason for the headaches, nausea, dizziness and insomnia.

If you are on an expedition well equipped with a first aid kit and a minimum of proper medicines, you should stop the ascent and take a couple of aspirins for the headache and a diuretic for the cerebral edema. If the symptoms are not alleviated after the rest, go back down several hundred yards and wait for an improvement. If the symptoms are severe—for example, extreme fatigue, behavioral problems or labored breathing even when resting—an additional anti-inflammatory treatment based on cortisone should be administered for the cerebral edema, and you must be taken down immediately without waiting for the treatment to take effect. If you are alone and your condition is sufficiently critical, you can treat yourself, but prevention is the best cure. If you have access to oxygen, this is obviously the best additional treatment. If you have no equipment or medicine, the only answer is to descend as rapidly as possible.

To prevent AAS, do not ascend more than 2,296 feet per day (700 meters per day) between 5,576 and 11,480 feet (1,700 and 3,500 meters) of altitude, and go no more than 1,148 to 1,312 feet per day (350 to 400 meters per day) above that altitude. Acetazolamide (Diamox) is an effective preventive measure for AAS, and 250mg can be taken every 8 hours immediately before, during and after an ascent.

Generally speaking, AAS is benign and transitory and will improve after a day of rest or, in a severe case, if one descends to a slightly lower altitude. It rarely puts a permanent end to the ascent, even though the delay it causes is often annoying.

A Uruguayan rugby team whose plane crashed in the Andes at an altitude of more than 12,000 feet in 1972 began suffering from severe altitude sickness almost immediately. After 5 to 10 hours, several of the survivors manifested headaches and behavioral problems that negatively affected the whole group. During the night following the crash, several of the crash survivors started to get headaches and nausea, became dizzy and had behavioral problems. For example, Carlos Roque, a mechanic, the only member of the crew to survive, believed Eduardo Strauch was an assassin out to kill him, because he stayed astride him for several minutes as he was trying to get out of the wreck. "Show me your papers!" he shouted. "Your name! Your name!" When Strauch did not reply, Roque started to scream that Strauch was trying to kill him and became hysterical. Another man, Pancho Delgado, got up and headed for the door saying "I'm just going to the store to get a Coca-Cola." During the first few days, several of the crash victims walked in their sleep and had nightmares, filling the small cabin with their hallucinations. These problems caused by AAS disappeared after the first week, and the victims became fully aware of their extremely critical survival situation.

## HIGH-ALTITUDE CEREBRAL EDEMA (HACE)

This is a complication due to neglected AAS or to AAS that has developed extremely fast. It can lead to death within a matter of hours unless you immediately do the only correct thing: descend.

Intracranial hypertension quickly leads to coma and death. Typically it happens to a young individual between the first and the fifth day of an expedition at an altitude between 9,840 and 18,040 feet (3,000 and 5,500 meters). It sometimes also happens to a person who is well acclimatized but whose heart decompensates (fails to maintain adequate circulation) following extreme exertion above 26,240 feet.

The headaches caused by HACE are unbearable, and not even morphine can get rid of them; the person becomes delirious and suffers from auditory and visual hallucinations. Mountain climbers who have climbed to very high altitudes have told stories of hallucinating about an imaginary companion with whom they lived, for whom they waited at the relay stations, and with whom they shared their food.

The sense of time, awareness of one's surroundings, and the ability to make sound judgments disappears, making it particularly difficult for a lone mountain climber to realize that he is suffering from the sickness. Going alone above the "death zone" of 26,240 feet (8,000 meters) is taking a grave risk.

Once it has occurred, treating HACE with diuretics is insufficient or totally useless. Corticoids (such as Dexamethasone, 4 to 12 mg every 4 to 6 hours) are useful, but insufficient. Oxygen can be useful but does not work miracles with HACE, and once oxygen is started, it cannot be stopped without causing acute and fatal hypoxia.

The only treatment that is at once preventive and curative for HACE is to descend quickly to an altitude below 9,840 feet (3,000 meters). If you are alone at a very high altitude with no way to descend quickly, you should know that descending a few hundred yards may be enough to stop an edema from getting more serious.

## ACUTE HIGH-ALTITUDE PULMONARY EDEMA (AHAPE)

This is another complication of inadequate adaptation to altitude and it can prove fatal. Even the most hardened "professional" mountaineers can suffer from it. The pulmonary alveoli become flooded with blood serum, due to an excessive increase of the pressure in the capillaries lining the alveolar cells. It is certain that the movement of blood serum into the air space is due to hypertension in the pulmonary artery, but the exact cause of the phenomenon is not yet known. Some important factors for the possible origin of the syndrome are a steady increase in the blood volume, accompanied by a decrease in its fluidity due to increased red cell production; as well as a decrease in the peripheral veins' ability to dilate, which modifies the distribution of the blood volume.

The majority of cases occur between 13,000 and 16,500 feet (4,000 and 5,000 meters), i.e., at the same altitudes as most trekking excursions take place and most base camps are set up. Every year 30 to 60 climbers are stricken with AHAPE in Nepal, both when taking part in climbing expeditions and when trekking. Acclimatization provides no protection: Natives of high plateaus—both Peruvians and Himalayans—are often stricken with AHAPE when they return home after spending several days at a lower altitude. The first symptoms occur between 36 hours and three days after arriving at that altitude.

After 10 days at a high altitude one can assume that one has passed the danger point.

In most cases, AHAPE starts gradually with symptoms of maladjustment: headaches, nausea and fatigue. This means that the moment you notice the warning signs, you should keep to the recommended speed of ascent, be cautious and stop to rest. Later symptoms of AHAPE become more specific: respiration will be fast and shallow, and tachycardia will be so severe that it will be difficult to take a pulse. There will be a significant dry cough and difficulty in breathing normally. The sick person will become uneasy and begin to show signs of cyanosis, and the cough, which was dry before, will start to produce frothy pink sputum. The sputum transfers the passage of blood serum through the alveolar cell membranes; it is frothy and pink because it is a mixture of air and blood. This virtual "drowning from inside" will be accompanied by panic at the feeling of suffocation. If you place your ear at the base of the victim's thorax, you will hear a sputtering sound with every respiratory movement. If nothing is done at this stage, it will progress to torpor, coma and death within one to six hours.

Immediate treatment is imperative: As always, you must descend. The effect of the descent is always spectacular and numerous cases have been described in which quick descents (for instance in a helicopter or a cable car) have led to a complete cure within a matter of minutes. In a life-threatening situation, you must drop everything and descend using the fastest means possible—in many cases a difference of 1640 feet (500 meters) will be enough.

If medicines are available, the following are recommended:

■ A diuretic: Two Lasix administered intravenously and slowly. This powerful diuretic immediately decreases the blood volume and thus excess pulmonary pressure.
■ Morphine: A 15-mg dose administered intramuscularly. This

drug supresses anxiety, pain and the dilation of the veins. The latter action also decreases pulmonary pressure. Normally it should be administered by a doctor because it can cause respiratory depression, but in a survival situation it will have to be administered without a doctor.

Oxygen, if available, is always the best auxiliary treatment.

If it is impossible to descend, the victim must rest in a semisitting position to facilitate spontaneous respiration; and if only one medicine is taken along, it should be a fast-acting diuretic (see "First Aid Survival Kit").

To Prevent AHAPE:

■ Ascend slowly, following the criteria described previously. Trekkers who are dropped at a high altitude from a plane at the foot of Mount Everest, for example, often run a greater risk.

■ Avoid intense exertion during the first few days. This is extremely important.

■ Avoid all potentiators (cold, anxiety, etc.).

■ React to the first warning signs: Stop, observe, and administer treatment or descend immediately at the slightest suspicious sign.

---

○

---

# LIGHTNING: COUNTERMEASURES

## August 21, 1966

René Desmaison is part of the group led by Gary Hemming on a mission to rescue two Germans, stuck on the rock wall of the Dru peak in the Mont Blanc massif. Desmaison tells the story:

"The incredible descent begins. The void is enormous. The ropes and braces are firm. At the 'wedged block' we find the support rope. The last camp, tomorrow, may be Chamonix. It is snowing; I look at my watch: 2:00 in the morning. Three more hours till daylight. In the distance there are flashes of lightning and rumbles of thunder; the storm is approaching at an incredible speed. The spot where I have been sleeping is so narrow that I have had to attach myself to the rock so I would not fall and dangle in empty space. There is a flash of lightning and I feel a violent discharge through my body. In spite of myself I cry out. The smell of sulfur is in the air. We are at the center of the storm. It is impossible to move. A terrible silence weighs down on us. An explosion, like the end of the world, bursts in my head. A second discharge runs through me, from my head to my toes. Fear slowly engulfs me.

"My friends seem to have been hit by less violent discharges. A few seconds .—.—. and I get hit for a third time with unbelievable violence by the lightning. Lying on the snow, I can hardly breathe. Everything hurts. My companion, Vincent, who is lying next to me, is hit by the same discharge. 'Vincent, we've got to get away from here.' But we are surrounded by the void. Suddenly I have the feeling that the next flash of lightning will be the fatal one. I am terribly afraid. A sack of pitons and snap hooks is hanging about two feet from my head. This mass of metal acts like a lightning conductor; I have to get rid of it. I am afraid to touch the pitons, but I quickly make my decision; it is my only chance.

"I throw the pitons farther away in the snow. At that moment a fourth discharge throws me down on the snow. I feel as if I am suffocating. I groan. My powerlessness increases my fear.

"The snowflakes fall thick and fast; calm returns. Right through to daybreak I struggle to breathe normally again, and I realize the severity of the shock I have suffered. At 7:00 in the morning the long descent into the void begins. Rappel after rappel, we slowly approach the Dru glacier."

---

Lightning strikes are rare in the plains but not in the mountains. This phenomenon is logical if one understands the mechanism of lightning.

There can be no lightning without cumulonimbus clouds. Cumulonimbus is the only type of cloud that is accompanied by hail or lightning. These clouds are very deep, reaching all the way up to the boundary of the tropopause. The tropopause is higher as it approaches the equator, and this explains the exceptional violence of storms in tropical latitudes. The interior of the cloud is the center of very strong anabatic (upward-moving) winds and downdraughts (around 66 feet per second [20 meters per second]), giving the water particles an up-and-down cycle until they become ice in the higher strata.

These powerful movements create an ionization of the cloud that turns into a gigantic electric generator within a matter of hours with an energy equivalent to millions of kilowatts per cloud.

Positive charges accumulate in the upper layer and negative ones in the lower layer. The surface of the earth's crust is normally covered with negative charges but the polarity is inverse at the bottom of the cloud, creating differences in the potentials of several hundred million volts between the base of the cloud and the earth. The layer of air between them acts as an insulator. As the day progresses, particularly in summer, the heat of the earth accelerates the convective currents in the center of the cloud, making storms more frequent in the afternoon. Mountains often act as the destablizer that unleashes the storm, partly because the earth and cumulonimbus clouds are closer together in the mountains.

It is easy to imagine the ideal grounding effect provided by a massif like the Dru, bristling with a granite peaks, where cumulonimbus clouds arriving unimpeded from the west can get impaled. The burned forest areas that prevail throughout the Dru bear witness to this. Lightning originates through contact between the lightning tracer coming from the cloud and the returning arc from the earth, each with an opposite polarity. It is attracted by areas of the earth that are rich in positive charges.

A law of physics states that positive charges concentrate in areas with a strong curvature, so lightning is attracted to all pointed objects—lightning conductors, isolated trees in a plain or rocky peaks in the mountains. Assuming an equal height, a massif like the Dru is hit by lightning more often because it has so many huge rocky darts aiming at the sky. This effect depends on the peak's shape, not its material as is so often believed.

How can one protect oneself against lightning in the mountains?

The moment you see the purplish-gray, huge mass of a cumulonimbus cloud approaching, waste no time, particularly if you hear so-called bees (a buzzing sound, caused by the ionization of the air). Avoid the direct impact of the lightning by getting away from all projections and all ridges as quickly as possible. If you are on a ridge, descend at least 66–98 feet (20–30 meters). Find shelter from a potential point of impact: You are much safer at the bottom of a rock than isolated in the middle of a mountain pasture, where you will be the projecting point. Everything depends on knowing a few rules:

■ The rock at which you seek shelter should be at least 16 feet (5 meters) high. If it is 66 feet high, so much the better.

■ Consider that the area sheltered by the rock from direct impact is a circle, centered on the rock, with a radius equal to its height.

■ The best area, in fact, would be in a ring of rock, since it is advisable to sit at a distance of at least 6 feet from the foot of the rock, in order to avoid getting hit by branching currents.

Our instinct may tell us to look for holes, fissures, caves or the shelter of an overhang. But all these "hiding places" are strong points of attraction to lightning, whereas the area described above, which is open to the sky is less likely to be hit.

A person must also protect himself against discharge currents, which instantly follow a lightning hit. These discharge currents are directed toward the earth's crust by the paths of least resistance, such as water, which has excellent electric conductivity; fis-

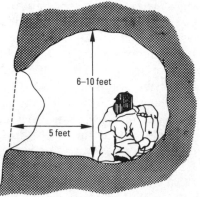

In a cave that is sufficiently large and has no water trickling into it

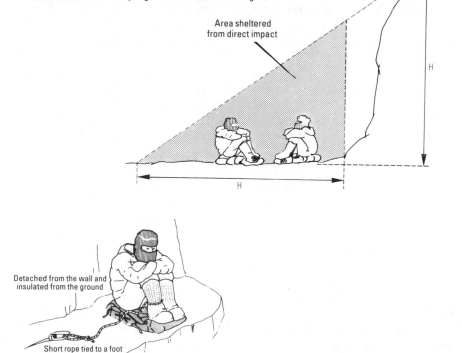

6–10 feet

5 feet

Area sheltered from direct impact

H

H

Detached from the wall and insulated from the ground

Short rope tied to a foot

**Good locations**

sures; troughs; and channels. These tempting hiding places are, in fact, traps that should be avoided at all costs.

If you are climbing a mountain and are taken by surprise by a storm while in the middle of a rock face, you will need to insulate yourself as much as possible to minimize the effect of any cur-

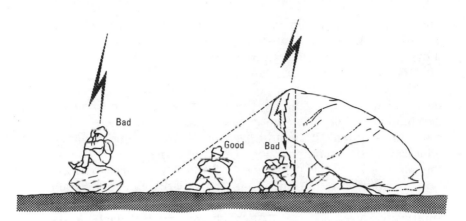

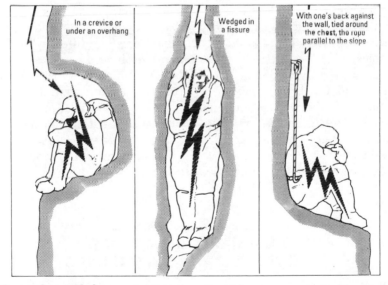

**Locations to be avoided**

rent that might hit. To accomplish this, take the following precautions:

■ Sit on a bag, a coiled rope or a pile of stones. Never forget that the body, particularly if it is wet from rain or sweat, offers less re-

sistance than a rock and therefore will provide the primary path for lightning. "Anti-storm" sacks made of aluminum, which act like a Faraday cage, are available.

■ If you are on a traverse, get as far away from the rock wall as possible, and be sure to be attached by a rope so that you will not be thrown into the void as a result of the violent muscular movements that are often caused by the discharges. The rope should be as horizontal as possible, so that it will not follow the descending trajectory of the current. In addition, it should be attached to your foot, and not to the waist or shoulders. This position prevents the current from passing through the vital organs such as the heart or lungs. (After Desmaison was thrown down on the snow, he had difficulty in getting his breathing back to normal, doubtless because of a transitory "stroke" in his respiratory muscles).

■ Curl up tightly to decrease the distance of the body's points of contact from the wall as much as possible. The difference in the potential created is proportional to this distance.

■ Make sure that the piolet (ice ax) is not sticking out of the rucksack.

If all these measures are taken, the risk of being struck by lightning will be considerably diminished.

Out of 16 people treated for lighting strikes in Chamonix during one year, there were seven deaths and nine survivors. The number of survivors confirms that death and lightning strikes do not necessarily go hand in hand. Desmaison is one of the many witnesses to this fact. A lightning strike has an effect rather like electrocution, with clinical results ranging from instantaneous death to survival with or without aftereffects (neurological, cardiac, skin, or hearing and vision defects). A lightning strike often produces an apparent death—cessation of heartbeat and breathing—which will develop into real death if there is no one present to administer mouth to mouth resuscitiation or heart massage.

# SOLAR RADIATION: COUNTERMEASURES

Of all the electromagnetic types of radiation emitted by the sun, three groups concern the animal world, especially man: infrared rays that supply heat; visible light ranging from red to violet; and ultraviolet (UV) rays, the origin of life on earth (the chlorophyll cycle). All these rays are modified to a greater or lesser degree by the

thickness of the atmosphere. The higher the mountain, the thinner the layer of atmosphere. The solar heat becomes greater, colors become sharper and ultraviolet rays become harsher. The intensified action of ultraviolet rays on a high mountain makes it necessary to take some preventive precautions.

UVC rays, which are incompatible with life, are stopped almost totally 49,200 feet (15,000 meters) from the earth's surface.

On the other hand, UVB rays become more intense the higher the elevation. Their number increases by 4 percent every 984 feet (300 meters); that is, at 9,840 feet, or 3,000 meters, their intensity is doubled.

Two dangers must be protected against: severe sunburn and damage to the eyes.

Apart from the decrease in atmospheric quantity, a second factor—reflection—plays a role in the mountains in facilitating such burns. The albedo is the power of reflection of the rays from a given element. For example, the albedo of snow is 75 to 90 percent, depending on its quality (whether it is dirty spring snow or fresh powder). This power of reflection explains why, even if an individual is sheltered from the direct rays of the sun—under a rock ledge, for instance—he can be burned in the same way as on a snowfield. As a comparison, the albedo of grass on an alpine pasture in summer is only 3 percent.

## SNOW BLINDNESS

Snow blindness, or uveitis, is caused by the burning of the cornea, the transparent surface that covers the eye and protects it from the exterior. This disorder, which is very painful but quickly reversible within 48 hours, is caused by

ultraviolet rays. It can be avoided by wearing sunglasses.

Snow blindness can be very crippling, so it is important to be able to recognize its symptoms. It occurs very abruptly and were it to happen, for example, to a solo pilot preparing to land on a glacier, it would obviously result in a crash.

Even if a person is exposed only intermittently, the lesions can accumulate if the intervals between exposures are less than 24 hours, and, even when the sky is overcast, the UVB in the mountains will penetrate a thin stratus or a high-altitude cirrus layer more or less intact. Above 6,560 feet (2,000 meters), even with cloud cover, 50 percent of the ultraviolet rays will get through.

The signs of ophthalmia (inflammation of the conjunctiva or eyeball) are easy to identify at the end of the day, even if there has been no bright sunshine. The individual manifests the same symptoms as with conjunctivitis: He has the feeling that he has grains of sand under his eyelids, and this quickly becomes painful and is accompanied by photophobia (the slightest source of light causes extreme pain and copious watering of the eyes), blurred vision and reddened and swollen lids. All these symptoms are signs of a dry, roughened cornea, eroded by micro-ulcerations caused by the UV rays. In 48 hours the cornea will be replaced by a new one. The individual should stay in the dark. At high altitude he should wear a tightly sealed blindfold over his eyes. The pain can be moderated with compresses of cold water or of snow on a piece of gauze. Every mountain climber should have in his survival kit an atropine-based eyewash to prevent the painful closing of the pupil. An antiseptic eyewash and a vasoconstrictor are useful adjuvants. On a more general level, painkillers (aspirin, ibuprofen, Tylenol) and sleeping pills could also prove useful (see "First Aid Survival Kit").

After 48 hours the mountain climber can continue on his way without any aftereffects, but he should wear suitable glasses, i.e., ones with protectors on the side that will protect the cornea from lateral UV rays and from the wind, which is an additional irritating factor. The quality of the glasses is important; they should be chosen carefully.

■ The filtering power against light (glare) and UV rays is effectively assured by strongly tinted glasses with a "C" label, i.e., those that absorb 85 percent of the UV rays ("A" and "B" absorb 15 percent and 65 percent). The color itself has no effect on the filtering power, contrary to what some believe. Therefore, yellow glass is as effective as maroon or pink but has the added advantage that the

bright color makes it easier for the wearer to see in a fog.

■ If, for some reason, the individual does not have any glasses, collyrium will provide effective protection only up to 6,560 feet (2,000) meters, and only as long as it is applied every four hours. Above 9,840 feet (3,000 meters), under no circumstances should a person travel between 10:00 A.M. and 2:00 P.M. without protection; this is the time of day when the sun is highest and is very poorly filtered by the rarefied atmosphere.

## SOLAR ERYTHEMA OR SUNSTROKE

In the mountains the "common" sunburn can turn into a painful and serious injury. It starts as a warm sensation and redness of the skin due to the action of the infrared rays. The local heat causes the release of local vasoactive substances (kinins, serotonin, histamine), followed by vasodilation, which produces the red color.

Tanning is the skin's attempt to protect itself against this radiation: Skin adapts to the sun in that it immediately darkens through melanin pigmentation under the action of the UV rays, and then, in subsequent days, new pigment is formed. Another form of self-protection is simultaneous thickening of the skin.

Despite all these protective reactions, the radiation is so strong in the mountains that it often exceeds the protective ability and leads, at its worst, to second-degree burns, possibly accompanied by blisters and general symptoms. After several days the skin peels off, leaving scars.

In the long term, these insults to the skin make it age prematurely because of changes in the elastic fibers in the dermis. As a result, some incorrigible sun worshipers develop a "creased" skin after they turn 50; this condition is irreversible. Professional mountaineers, just like sailors and farmers, develop a skin that is "chiseled," i.e., exceedingly pigmented in patches, furrowed, and dry. Skin cancer is the most serious stage of this chronic overexposure to the sun.

Prevention of burns depends on the use of products for protection against the sun. There are two kinds:

■ sun protection products that permit gradual tanning while reducing the danger of burning; and
■ sunscreen products, which ensure total protection by blocking the ultraviolet and visible rays. A "total screen" can be found in any pharmacy.

Only *sunscreen products* are of use to the mountain climber.

Above 13,000 feet (4,000 meters), the screen should be applied to the whole face, especially to the forehead and nose, which are the most sensitive areas.

Under special circumstances these protective measures should be applied at a much lower altitude: if the person is blond or redheaded with "sensitive skin," and burns but does not tan easily. For greatest effectiveness, the sunscreen should be applied hourly.

Orientation has a determining effect on the intensity of sunlight. Remember that in the northern hemisphere sunlight on the western and eastern slopes in the mountains is almost identical to that on a horizontal surface, while on southern slopes the effect is twice as strong. In the middle of winter the steep northern slopes do not receive any direct sun (nor do steep southern slopes in the southern hemisphere). The steeper the gradient, the more this rule applies, and it is essential in determining the proper orientation of the camp: The camp should be sheltered from the wind at night and in full sunlight during the day (facing south in the northern hemisphere). Orientation also determines the danger of avalanches depending on the type of snow: Wet snow avalanches occur most often on the sunny slopes and dry snow avalanches on the slopes in shadow.

# SHELTER

In order to spend the night on the mountain, a climber must take with him a special tent that enables him to camp attached to the rock wall, or a more comfortable tent for flat terrain. Whenever possible, the tent should be pitched on the leeward side, away from the dominant wind. Therefore it should be pitched behind a natural obstacle, or behind an obstacle created artificially with rocks and snow. This will prevent the tent or its fastenings from being torn away and will reduce loss of heat through convection. The tent, in fact, should become rather like a second, much larger sleeping bag, in which a microclimate will be generated by body temperature. Even if it is lined, the tent will still preserve this "bubble" of heat better if it is not subjected to the dominant winds. Using these methods, one should, where there is no significant wind, be able to attain a temperature inside roughly 36°F (20°C) higher than the exterior.

For a man in an unexpected survival situation—for example, on a glacier—there is no possibility of constructing a permanent igloo, although it is suggested in almost every book of survival. The cold, hypoxia and the enormous amount of energy expended to build such a structure will create not an igloo but a coffin. Furthermore, in order to cut the snow one would need a saw, a machete or a first-class survival knife. An igloo is a method best left to the Alpine Light Infantry when they go on maneuvers (see "The Poles").

About 20 years ago, a mountain pilot landed late in the day on a glacier in the Mont Blanc Massif. Surprised by the uniform whiteness and the sudden loss of reference points on a large expanse of snow that was not lit up by the sun, he flared out before landing blindly and bounced, ending with the plane upside down. Since his radio would not work, he could not send out a distress signal, and he prepared to spend the night on the glacier. He was not particularly worried, as he believed he was clothed well enough and thought the cabin of the airplane, which was still relatively airtight, would provide shelter. He was surprised when he spent the worst night of his life, shivering with cold in the cabin, surviving only because the temperature that night was relatively mild, only -4°F (−20°C) with no wind.

The cabin of an airplane is useless as a shelter except as a wind barrier. Its metal and Plexiglas infrastructure has a significant thermal conductibility and an insulation coefficient that is almost equal to zero, thus making the cockpit as cold as the outside.

The pilot piled error upon error—apart from the mistake he made in flying—by landing in the shadow on a glacier after 3:00 P.M.

and staying inside his plane, despite the fact that he had a shovel and the snow was several yards thick where he landed.

All he would have had to do was dig a shelter, 6 feet below the surface and shaped like a sock, and then block the entrance with a door from the plane that he covered with snow. In this way he could have spent a night at around 32°F (0°C) with no problem. A lighted candle in such a shelter is enough to raise the temperature several degrees above freezing.

## SNOW, AVALANCHES AND CREVASSES

Whether he is a mountain climber or a cross-country skier, the mountaineer will, at some time or other, come across a virgin slope of snow. The dozens of deaths that are due to avalanches every year in the mountains should make even the most experienced people very wary.

Apart from a minimal knowledge of meteorology, some knowledge of snow is useful and important. Too many skiers disappear every year due to ignorance of the terrain across which they are traveling; they are carried away by unexpected avalanches or fall down crevasses covered by an unstable bridge of snow.

Snow is not the exclusive property of the mountains, and since the traps one can fall into are also found in other environments, it has been dealt with more thoroughly in the chapter below called "Snow and Avalanches."

# THE POLES

- Facts

- The Physical Geography of the Arctic

- Fighting Against the Cold

- Walking in the Arctic

- Dangers Unique to the Arctic

- The Antarctic

## FACTS

○ The antarctic continent is crushed beneath 30 million billion tons of ice. The total mass of icebergs that break off every year would be enough to supply two-thirds of the planet with freshwater. The largest iceberg ever seen was 198.7 miles long (320 kilometers).

○ The Antarctic is 1,863 miles (3,000 kilometers) from the Cape of Good Hope, 1,242 miles (2,000 kilometers) from New Zealand, and 683 miles (1,100 kilometers) from Cape Horn.

○ The poles are cold deserts where water is no more abundant than in the Sahara and there is a threefold problem in obtaining it: the need for water increases greatly in the dry air, melting the snow or ice is costly in calories, and it is not always easy to obtain nonsaline water on an ice floe.

## THE PHYSICAL GEOGRAPHY OF THE ARCTIC

The Arctic covers 9,650,000 square miles (25 million square kilometers) of the northern hemisphere, including 15 million square kilometers of marine expanses. It covers the northern regions of Alaska, Canada, and Greenland; Norway's Jan Mayen Island and Spitsbergen; and the northern regions of the former Soviet Union (the frigid Arctic Ocean, the Barents Sea, the East Siberian Sea, etc.).

The polar seas are enormous: 5,018,000 square miles (13,000,000 square kilometers) of the 6,562,000 (17,000,000) that make up the non-Russian Arctic (the polar seas of the Arctic Ocean, the Beaufort Sea, the Greenland Sea, the Chukchi Sea, Baffin Bay, and Hudson Bay). This geography, dominated by seas, has determined the character of the many expeditions to the North Pole over the centuries.

A large part of the Arctic Ocean is covered year-round with ice that reaches a thickness of about 9 feet (3 meters). The ice is not static, and it drifts at the mercy of the winds and currents at a speed that varies from 0.6 to 1.2 miles (1 or 2 kilometers) to 15.5 miles (45 kilometers) per day. The drifting of the ice varies greatly, but generally takes an east-west direction. Some explorers have tried to take advantage of this drift to reach the pole by using the floating ice to get them there. The Norwegian explorer Fridtjof Nansen did this with his ship, the *Fram*, in 1924.

The sometimes chaotic landscape of the Arctic—blocks mov-

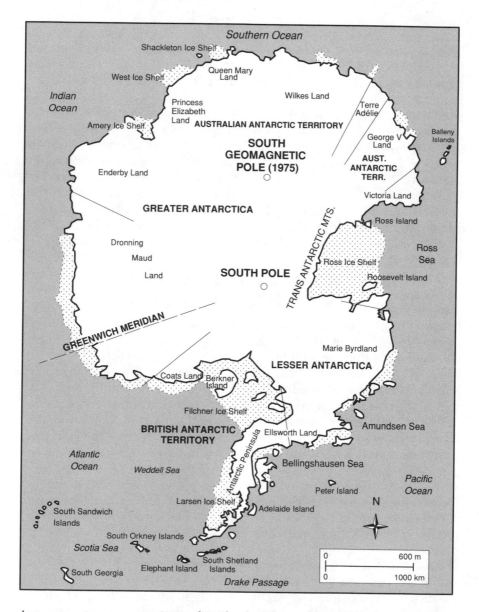

ing apart, uncovering frigid waters, colliding with enormous inertia, causing miles of ice ridges of broken pieces called *torose load casts* to rise to various heights, or small ridges of hills called hummocks that rise 10 to 12 feet in the open seas and up to 30 feet closer to shore—is all caused by the varying speeds with

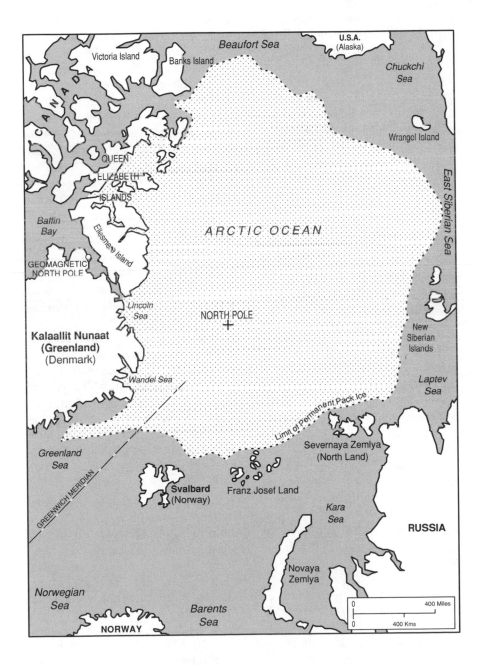

which different parts of the ice move. These zones of chaos are intersected by huge flat expanses. The prospective explorer must know the origin of these obstacles and should not believe that he is entering a universe that is in a constant and total state of change.

The average annual temperature never rises above 32°F (0°C) and the average winter temperature is around −40°F (−40°C), dropping down to −58°F (−50°C). Since these temperatures are almost invariably accompanied by strong winds, they present formidable barriers to keeping warm, as is shown buy the eolian windchill index table below.

The wind significantly increases cooling as soon as it exceeds a speed of 4.35 miles per hour (7 kilometers per hour)— only the speed of a man walking. At the other extreme, a blizzard blowing at 40.37 miles per hour (65 kilometers per hour) at a temperature of −58°F causes windchill equivalent to a temperature of −148°F (−100°C) without wind (such a temperature has never been recorded; the lowest temperature on record is −115.6°F [−82°C]).

Beyond 59 feet per second (18 meters per second) the increased effect of the wind is negligible, and anyway, winds rarely exceed 65.6 feet per second (20 meters per second) at the poles (see explanation in chapter "Weather and Survival"). These strong winds blow only in winter. Fogs and overcast skies are frequent, particularly in summer, which is a great handicap if one needs to get location and bearings from the stars. A compass is almost useless at these latitudes so close to the magnetic pole.

## AN ICE FLOE: WHY? HOW?

Why is it cold at the poles, and why does the seawater freeze? This is caused by a combination of several factors:

- There is no sun at all during the winter months.
- While the sun's rays strike the earth almost perpendicularly at the equator, they come at a very oblique angle at the poles, which results in much lower radiation.
- The reflection power of the ice reaches 90 percent because of its white color. This high albedo prevents solar heating.

Before the ice floe forms, there is an intermediate stage that is called sludge. This is made of isolated microcrystals, similar to snow, that cannot melt in water that is too cold. These crystals slowly join together, weighing down the surface, as oil does, calming the surge. The first pieces of drift ice appear; they have a circumference of several meters and are about 4 to 12 inches (10 to 30 centimeters) thick. These are

# COOLING POWER OF WIND EXPRESSED AS "EQUIVALENT CHILL TEMPERATURE"

| WIND SPEED | | TEMPERATURE (°F) | | | | | | | | | | | | | | | | | | | | |
|---|---|---|---|---|---|---|---|---|---|---|---|---|---|---|---|---|---|---|---|---|---|---|
| KNOTS | MPH | 40 | 35 | 30 | 25 | 20 | 15 | 10 | 5 | 0 | -5 | -10 | -15 | -20 | -25 | -30 | -35 | -40 | -45 | -50 | -55 | -60 |
| CALM | CALM | | | | | | | | EQUIVALENT CHILL TEMPERATURE | | | | | | | | | | | | | |
| 3–6 | 5 | 35 | 30 | 25 | 20 | 15 | 10 | 5 | 0 | -5 | -10 | -15 | -20 | -25 | -30 | -35 | -40 | -45 | -50 | -55 | -65 | -70 |
| 7–10 | 10 | 30 | 20 | 15 | 10 | 5 | 0 | -10 | -15 | -20 | -25 | -35 | -40 | -45 | -50 | -60 | -65 | -70 | -75 | -80 | -90 | -95 |
| 11–15 | 15 | 25 | 15 | 10 | 0 | -5 | -10 | -20 | -25 | -30 | -40 | -45 | -50 | -60 | -65 | -70 | -80 | -85 | -90 | -100 | -105 | -110 |
| 16–19 | 20 | 20 | 10 | 5 | 0 | -10 | -15 | -25 | -30 | -35 | -45 | -50 | -60 | -65 | -75 | -80 | -85 | -95 | -100 | -110 | -115 | -120 |
| 20–23 | 25 | 15 | 10 | 0 | -5 | -15 | -20 | -30 | -35 | -45 | -50 | -60 | -65 | -75 | -80 | -90 | -95 | -105 | -110 | -120 | -125 | -135 |
| 24–28 | 30 | 10 | 5 | 0 | -10 | -20 | -25 | -30 | -40 | -50 | -55 | -65 | -70 | -80 | -85 | -95 | -100 | -110 | -115 | -125 | -130 | -140 |
| 29–32 | 35 | 10 | 5 | -5 | -10 | -20 | -30 | -35 | -40 | -50 | -60 | -65 | -75 | -80 | -85 | -100 | -105 | -115 | -120 | -130 | -135 | -145 |
| 33–36 | 40 | 10 | 0 | -5 | -15 | -20 | -30 | -35 | -45 | -55 | -60 | -70 | -75 | -85 | -95 | -100 | -110 | -115 | -125 | -130 | -140 | -150 |

WINDS ABOVE 40 HAVE LITTLE ADDITIONAL EFFECTS.

LITTLE DANGER    INCREASING DANGER (Flesh may freeze within 1 minute)    GREAT DANGER (Flesh may freeze within 30 seconds)

DANGER OF FREEZING EXPOSED FLESH FOR PROPERLY CLOTHED PERSONS flat and look like paving stones. The surge lessens more and more until it stops altogether, and enormous uniform fields of ice are formed. Thus the whole of the Arctic Ocean is covered with a huge wandering raft that is no thicker than 16.4 feet (5 meters) on the surface of waters that generally reach a depth of 16,400 feet (5,000 meters). This is why a nuclear submarine can move for thousands of miles under this thin film, and even surface in the middle of the ice (the explorer J.-L. Étienne was very surprised one day on his explorations in 1986 when he heard a strange, diffused noise that seemed to come from beneath his feet: It was a submarine passing by). The ice floe is reshaped and jostled by the wind, the currents and the tides, especially when there is a new moon and during a syzygy (conjunction of opposition of the moon and the sun).

The seasonal rhythm of sunshine in the Arctic is the most significant factor in producing its hostile environment. At the 66° parallel there are six months of night followed by six months of polar day. At the North Pole, the polar day lasts for 190 days during the summer and the polar night lasts for 175 days during the winter. The difference in the number is of no interest to a polar explorer; what is important is that a polar explorer caught by the ice at the beginning of winter will have to survive about six months of polar night—and that is impossible without a ship or a prepared shelter.

## FIGHTING AGAINST THE COLD

To understand the physiological mechanisms of the fight against cold, the reader should refer to the chapter on "Cold" in Part I.

Despite great advances in polar equipment, it is impossible to maintain body temperature outside for more than a few hours at best. Two things are necessary for survival in the Arctic:

■ shelter during the hours of sleep; and

■ a diet that provides at least 4,000 calories per day.

Complex equations and curves have been used by various researchers, integrating the ambient temperature and the power of thermal insulation of different types of clothing (expressed as "CLO" units). The table on page 288 summarizes the value of various types of clothing. Involved charts have been drawn up factoring in the number of "clos" of the clothing, the windchill and the amount of physical exertion planned. But they ignore the variation among individuals, which makes the charts somewhat illusory.

## SHELTER

The survivor should cover himself as best he can with whatever he has and he absolutely must construct a shelter against the cold and the wind. He has at his disposal a very good thermal insulator: snow. Snow is composed of 50 to 90 percent air, more than most modern insulating materials. In addition, snow is very easy to mold. This should not be taken, however, as a recommendation to build an igloo. Igloos demand too much physical exertion and should be attempted only if there is a large number of people with plenty of food, and if the group has decided it will not move.

The temperature inside a hole in the snow that has been carefully covered generally exceeds the exterior temperature by a range of 27° to 36°F (15° to 20°C). If a few stearin candles or some cubes of solidified alcohol are available, the temperature can be raised by 38° to 50°F (20° to 28°C) compared to the exterior. Piling up lumps of snow around the tent will serve as a windbreak and will considerably decrease cooling by convection.

Some perfectionists have completely surrounded their tent with about 19.5 inches (50 centimeters) of snow and have thus been able to maintain a temperature that is 27°F (15°C) higher than the temperature outside without using any other means of heating. Once again, the construction of the shelter requires only the minimum of inventiveness that any potential survivor must possess. Those who get lost in the Arctic should remember a few basic principles:

- The thickness of snow is not uniform. In many cases it might be only a foot thick, so it is not always possible to dig as deep as one might want to.
- Look for hollows where the snow has accumulated through the action of the wind.
- On a windward slope the snow can be very compressed but still malleable enough for a man with a knife, a shovel, a saw or a machete to be able to dig a hole or trench large enough to accommodate him.

The ideal shape is that of a burrow, just large enough for a man to sleep in, with an access tunnel. The entry to this tunnel should be lower than the "room," so that it will serve as a "cold trap" where the unheated air and any possible carbon monoxide can accumulate.

- If it is impossible to dig deep enough, a mound of snow should be built on both sides of the trench and covered with some

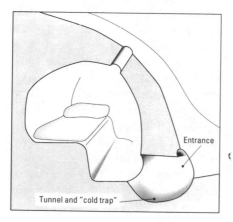

Entrance

Tunnel and "cold trap"

Fabric

cloth, a sled or a piece of wreckage.

The table on p. 281 shows a number of shelters that have proved to be most effective in maintaining a higher temperature inside than the temperature outside, with and without wind.

As the table demonstrates, windbreaks are highly effective, and snow has exceptional insulation qualities, whatever the sophistication of the shelter itself.

Even a tent with a double thickness should be surrounded by a mound of snow to act as a windbreak. This has a double advantage:

■ better insulation because of the decrease in convection; and
■ less risk that the fastenings of the shelter will be torn away by the wind.

While an igloo is of proven efficacy, the simple principles of its construction take at least five to six hours, and a man alone in a survival situation would get as much benefit from a simpler shelter that is less costly in calories. (Digging in snow in the Arctic climate costs 650 to 700 calories per hour—or 1,500 to 4,500 calories to construct an igloo in two to six hours.) In Lapland, the igloos are covered with snow but are basically made with peat, which is also an excellent insulator (telluric elements are generally the best means of protection against all kinds of radiation and variations of temperature).

Whatever shelter you choose, the bed should be insulated with a snow base (to prevent cooling through convection) and should be a little higher than the rest of the ground. Two simple stearin candles can raise the temperature inside the shelter above freezing even if there is an exterior temperature as low as −22°F (−30°C). Solid alcohol cubes or animal oil

| SHELTER | CONDITIONS OUTSIDE | | INCREASE IN REAL TEMPERATURE, TAKING WIND INTO CONSIDERATION |
|---|---|---|---|
| | TEMPERATURE °F | WIND MPH | |
| Snow hut covered by a parachute or any kind of fabric | −13° | 5.5 mph | +45° |
| Arctic tent without any special protection | −44° 10° | 4.1 mph 0 mph | 58° 14° |
| Artic tent surrounded by walls of snow | 40° | 4.1 mph | 72° |
| Burrow in the snow | −22° | 4.8 mph | 81° |
| Cave in the snow | −13° | 0 mph | 36° |
| Igloo | −13° −40° | 4.8 mph 2.7 mph | 63° 63° |

can also be used (such as bear, seal or walrus). An oil lamp is the most suitable way to heat up the shelter: Two or three wicks made of any kind of material (cloth, pharmaceutical gauze, a handkerchief) and placed on the surface of some oil in a can will provide quite enough heat.

### DIET

At the highest latitudes, especially in winter, the Arctic has no vegetation, and animals are the only source of food. At slightly lower latitudes, particularly during the summer, a few plant resources can be found. The Arctic and Antarctic ecosystems have one thing in common: They are based on food chains that originate not from terrestrial plants but from phytoplankton, i.e., algae from the sea (see the chapter on "The Survival Diet").

### ANIMAL RESOURCES

In the tundra there are numerous groups of reindeer, white caribou and wolves, as well as red and Arctic foxes, mink, sables, martens and raccoons. There are many migratory birds that can be hunted: guillemots (which are often cooked by the Eskimos with their feathers), great auks, a large number of little auks (sometimes caught in a net), barnacle geese and partridges. The master of these parts is, without a doubt, the polar bear, which will go all the way to the pole in search of food. The polar bear feeds on seals and therefore can be found close to open water. It will lie in wait next to a hole it has found and will use its paws to club the first seal that pokes its head out. If the polar bear cannot find its favorite prey, it will eat fish (its enormous, slightly webbed paws enable it to swim well), or it will move to another area, sometimes traveling up to 62 miles (100 kilometers). The Arctic traveler must be aware of the bear's habits in order to determine the probability of meeting one.

There are many marine mammals in the sea that sometimes climb up onto the ice floe and therefore can be hunted; among them are seals, walruses and sea calves. Seals are able to survive under ice because they can use their teeth to make holes in the ice through which to breathe. Walruses are unable to do this and so can live only in the open sea. They can weigh up to one ton and are highly valued by the Eskimos

for their skins and for their nourishing meat and internal organs. Among the small animals of the Arctic are lemmings and hares. But, above all, there are many birds: about 150 species, which are especially numerous on the Arctic islands. There are also more than 150 species of fish (cod, haddock, salmon, plaice), which can easily be caught along the shores or through holes in the ice.

There are also masses of insects, and the tundra and taiga are made virtually unlivable by clouds of all kinds of them: mosquitoes, gnats that will get through all normal mosquito netting, Canadian "brûlot" gnats, and black flies, whose bite literally takes out a small chunk of skin. The only creatures that are not found in the Arctic are reptiles: Not a single species of reptile lives there.

Bears and sea calves can be found right up to the North Pole, but only an extreme optimist would depend on hunting them for survival. All the polar experts in the world agree that no one can depend on hunting for survival in the Arctic, less because of the scarcity of local fauna than because of the extreme difficulty in getting close enough to catch them. Nevertheless, the Arctic traveler should always remember that a single seal will enable him to survive for a very long time and that a gun is a mandatory part of the survival equipment.

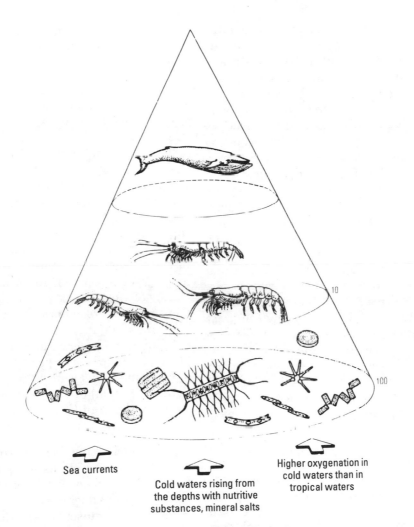

Sea currents

Cold waters rising from
the depths with nutritive
substances, mineral salts

Higher oxygenation in
cold waters than in
tropical waters

## FISHING

Fishing in frigid waters is very productive. The convergence of the ocean currents with the cold upward currents from the depths, which provide nutritive materials, causes a proliferation of plankton in the well-oxygenated cold water. Plankton is the foundation of a food pyramid that continues up to the great whales via various fish and marine mammals—a food chain that has enabled polar tribes to survive for millennia. This proliferation of aquatic fauna in the high latitudes is illustrated by the legendary stories of fishing in Iceland and of hunting polar whales. Eskimos fish in winter through holes in the ice floes. The naturally occurring holes are tiny to begin with and enable seals to breathe through the ice. All a fisherman has to do is find these holes and enlarge them with an ice spear—a wooden pole armed with a cutting edge to cut the ice (called a "toroute" in Greenland). A strong line is then dropped into the depths for about 650 feet (200 meters), with secondary lines set at different levels and armed with large hooks encased in lumps of seal fat or various internal organs. In this way it is possible to catch seals, walruses, narwhals and various types of fish, including the great sleeping shark, which is as omnivorous as its cousins from tropical waters. In Greenland the seal forms the base of the Eskimos' diet, and they even eat its entrails and eyes.

## RATIONS

The survival diet must of course be high in calories, but over the last 30 years or so there have been great changes in what is believed to be the minimum: In the past Soviet explorers lowered the recommendation from 6,200 calories to 5,000, while the Americans retained 6,000 calories in the Antarctic. More recent practice calls for about 4,000 to 4,500 calories, but strives for a better dietary range. Jean-Louis Étienne worked with several civilian and military dietitians in order to determine the best rations for his expedition:

■ The ration did not exceed 2.2 pounds (1 kilogram) per day and was designed for average physical exertion;
■ The distribution was 50 to 55 percent carbohydrates, 30 to 35 percent lipids and 10 to 15 percent proteins. The higher proportion of high-calorie lipids is important.
■ The calorie total was 4,000 per day, divided into three main meals plus snacks en route consisting of almond paste, chocolate and pieces of bread enriched with olive oil and butter.
■ Water rations were 4 to 5 quarts (4 to 5 liters) of water per day.
■ Vitamin rations were 1,000 milligrams (1 gram) of vitamin C and a multivitamin pill.

Jean-Louis Étienne's normal weight was 143 pounds (65 kilograms). For a man weighing 165 pounds (75 kilograms), or for more intense muscular exertion, 500 to 1,000 extra calories should be added.

## PEMMICAN

This mixture of dried meat and fat has always been the base product of all Arctic and Antarctic expeditions. Americans used it as far back as 1853 during an expedition to Greenland. Robert Peary, the first to reach the North Pole in 1909, sustained himself on pemmican seasoned with dried fruits. Roald Amundsen and Admiral Richard Byrd used only pemmican enriched with dried vegetables and oat flour in their Arctic explorations in the 1920s. In 1933, on his second expedition to the Antarctic, Byrd made pemmican that was enriched with 17 ingredients. Pemmican's weight to calories ratio is excellent, and there is no problem in preserving it, whatever the temperature.

## SPECIAL DIETARY FEATURES

The body quickly becomes deficient in ascorbic acid (vitamin C) and thiamin (a group B vitamin) at very low temperatures. Therefore a person should take 1 gram of vitamin C and some multivitamin pills every day.

## PLANT RESOURCES

These are nonexistent in winter on land, and all year round on an ice floe; they exist only on the tundra in summer. There are not many plant varieties, but a large quantity of edible berries can be found: blackberries, cranberries, mountain blueberries, red bilberries, crowberries and bearberries. The traveler can also eat angelica stems and viviparous polygol bulbs, the leaves and stalks of polar spikenard, or lyrate groundsel.

There are also many lichens, especially cladonia or polar lichen, which is very widespread and has roots that are shaped like coral. After soaking for two days, the thallus makes a jelly that is edible after it has been boiled for 20 minutes. Eskimos eat rock lichens, peeling them off the stones that they cover like a loose skin. They are soaked in water, then dried and pounded, and the powder is cooked, producing a soup rich in vegetable proteins. Algae piled up on the Arctic shores are also rich in proteins and carbohydrates.

## WATER

Since the Arctic is the realm of ice and snow, one would think that obtaining water would be the least of one's problems, ranked after cold, hunger and the difficulty of traveling on an ice floe. But water is actually not easy to come by, and water losses are considerable in latitudes where the temperature is below freezing.

The main reason the need for drinking water increases is a significant loss through respiration: The cold, dry air is reheated and humidified through evaporation in the pulmonary system. Additional reasons are sweating, due to physical exertion under well-insulated clothing, and the difficulty in finding enough fresh water. Melting 4 to 5 quarts (4 to 5 liters) of water a day to fulfill a person's needs is no easy task; it is very costly in calories and it is difficult from a practical point of view. The poles are very dry regions, rather like cold deserts. There is very little precipitation: only 5.5 inches (14 centimeters) per year in the Antarctic, no more than in the Sahara. A little more falls in the Arctic but not to the point that it sufficiently increases the humidity of the atmosphere. One must force oneself to drink large quantities in polar latitudes. Exposure to the cold causes an increase in the frequency of urination but no increase in the volume of urine produced, so this is not a factor in dehydration.

closer this layer gets to the ice, the higher the concentration of sodium chloride will be—and this increases to a point at which it becomes undrinkable.

■ In order to economize on fuel, use body heat to melt snow. Eskimos use sacks made of walrus gut, which they fill with snow and slip under their fur clothing. The modern survivor will be more likely to use flexible water bottles with noninsulating walls (plastic), which he will tie around his body. In this way half a quart of water can be obtained in 10 hours from a half-quart water bottle made of flexible polyethylene.

## SNOW

Even when compacted, snow only produces 10 to 15 percent of its volume as water, which means that a person has to "work" a volume of 10.5 quarts (10 liters) of snow to get 1 quart of water. Therefore 42 quarts of snow would have to be melted to obtain 4 quarts of water, and this is very costly in calories. As an example, at −49°F (−45°C), 700 fuel calories would be used to obtain 4 quarts of water. The best method to obtain water from snow is as follows:

■ On an ice floe only snow from the upper layer should be used (4 to 6 inches [10 to 15 centimeters]), since it is the least salty. The

## ICE

The ice from the ice floe is frozen seawater, and thus is undrinkable before it has been transformed by spontaneous desalination. This transformation takes time and only older ice is usable. Younger ice has a large number of cavities full of concentrated saline solution. The proportion of salt in such ice can be as high as 25 percent, making it totally unusable. The spontaneous process of desalination takes many years. When the winter ice partially melts during the summer months, the cavities grow larger, lengthening downward through the force of gravity and sometimes opening up to the air and letting their saline solution run out. Over the years, the salt content gets lower and lower, and the upper crystals of ice become less and less salty.

Therefore on fields of ice that are broken but stable, the upper part of very old ice is almost totally fresh. Old ice is steely blue, glittering and weathered (its color is reminiscent of glaciers in the mountains). Young ice is dark green when cut and looks like a piece of glass.

The frozen sea is flat and more or less grayish and the color gets darker as the layer grows thinner. Seen from an airplane, it is often thought to be open water, although the ice can carry the weight of a man and his sled team.

## MELTED WATER

This can be found on the surface of the fields of ice and makes multitudes of pools everywhere, which sometimes unite into genuine lakes of sweet water. The water is clean, has a very low salt content, and does not need to be treated by boiling or adding a chemical disinfectant. On the other hand, in the tundra, water found in marshes and streams should be boiled to disinfect it.

# WALKING IN THE ARCTIC

Anyone who walks in the Arctic must take specific preventive and remedial measures.

## CLOTHING

There are two very vulnerable areas for the polar walker: the feet and the head. There are various materials to protect the feet against the bite of the cold, ranging from down or felt to the modern Gore-Tex. Whatever the quality of the boots, additional protection is always useful: Place a covering or some fabric over the outside of the boots to collect the moisture, and wear a plastic bag between two pairs of woolen socks. This trick with the plastic bag will increase the insulation space around the foot and help keep it warm, but some people find that it also increases irritation.

Thermal losses through the head, if it is unprotected, can represent 50 percent of the body's total calorie production at 23°F ($-5$°C) and 75 percent at 5°F ($-15$°C). A very thick, tightly sealed, lined hood is therefore essential in a cold atmosphere.

## THE PITFALLS OF THE TERRAIN

When he was walking across a flat area, Jean-Louis Étienne covered about 3 to 3.7 miles per hour

## THERMAL INSULATION VALUES OF SOME CLOTHING (IN CLO)

| | |
|---|---|
| Special clothing for Arctic expedition | 5 |
| Winter clothing | 2 |
| Regular clothing (between seasons) | 1 |
| Light summer clothing | 0,5 |
| Sports clothing | 0,3 |
| Arctic sleeping suit | up to 10 |
| Furs of large Arctic animals | up to 10 |

Richalet Table (from *Médecine de l'Alpinisme*, Masson, 1984)

(5 to 6 kilometers per hour). When he was in an area full of hummocks, he covered at most a couple of hundred yards per hour, or even less if he had to circumvent obstacles. It is very difficult to assess the height of objects from a distance, and it is better to find a way around them within a radius of about 1,000 to 1,600 feet (300 to 500 meters) rather than to try to cross directly over them. Areas of open water can often be discerned from a distance by the darker color of the lower layer of clouds (stratus). The low cloud cover often acts as a mirror and reflects areas of shadow in proportion to the surfaces of open water. The power of reflection is such that, under certain conditions, pieces of the ice floe several dozen miles away are reflected in the clouds. Open waters can also be detected by the mists they produce as they evaporate. These mists above open water have a characteristic dark brown color and look like columns of smoke. The fracture zones in the ice can be linear and straight and easy to cross or, on the other hand, they can be irregular, unstable and wide. Methods of crossing them range from jumping over them to using a canoe, or floating on a piece of the ice floe, a method that should be used only as a last resort.

It is useful to know that an arm of the sea can close quickly under the effect of glaciation. Depending on its degree of salinity and its movement, sea water freezes around 28.4° to 26.6°F (−2° to −3°C). The thickness of the ice that can be expected after 24 hours is:

- 0.3 inches at 23°F (0.8 centimeters at −5°C)
- 0.59 inches at 14°F (1.5 centimeters at −10°C)

- 0.98 inches at 5°F (2.5 centimeters at −15°C)
- 1.25 inches at −4°F (3.2 centimeters at −20°C)
- 1.5 inches at −13°F (3.8 centimeters at −25°C)
- 1.75 inches at −22°F (4.5 centimeters at −30°C)
- 2.15 inches at −31°F (5.5 centimeters at −35°C)
- 2.5 inches at −40°F (6.5 centimeters at −40°C)

The speed of thickening on a preexisting layer decreases by about one-third. Under these conditions, and if one bears in mind that ice is not safe until it is at least 4 inches (10 centimeters) thick, a person would have to wait for two days at a temperature of −40°F and four days at a temperature of −4°F before crossing it. In an emergency, 48 hours at a temperature of 23°F should be enough for it to support the weight of a man. Ice increases from the bottom. The newly formed ice is identifiable by the dark color, through which the darkness of the ocean can still be seen, and sometimes by a layer of even snow, which is fine, homogeneous and unaltered by the wind.

If the ice gives way while you are walking across it, quickly lie down, so as to distribute your weight over the largest possible surface, and hook your knife into the ice. This is the only way to avoid being totally immersed. If you do fall in by accident, you must remove your clothing, whatever the conditions, and however unbearable this may sound. Continuing to walk in soaked clothes will make it impossible for the body to control its temperature.

If you cannot change your clothes, you must wring them out well. The best solution would be to put up a shelter to avoid excessive cooling.

A storm in a polar environment is especially dangerous because of the disorientation it causes, the increased cooling and, above all, the danger of falling into a fault in the ice floe. In a storm the traveler must stop—it is not only unsafe to go on, but ineffective as well. Walking speed will drop from 3–4 miles per hour to a tenth of that speed, while the energy exerted will radically increase to more than 600 calories per hour. The current of icy air can also inhibit respiration, making inhaling and exhaling equally difficult. There are innumerable stories of explorers lost and suffering in a storm just a few yards away from their shelter. At the first ominous signs of an approaching storm (heavy fall of snow, or increasing wind speed), stop and put up a shelter. Then wait until the storm is over before continuing—even if it takes several days.

In the summer, the difficulties in walking are quite different:

Open sea makes it impossible to advance on the ice floe, while enormous mosquito swamps take over the tundra.

# DANGERS UNIQUE TO THE ARCTIC

## OPTICAL ABERRATIONS

Especially in a fog, the ice floe takes on a uniformly white color, making it difficult to distinguish objects and gauge their distance. Hummocks can be invisible until they are tripped over, and it is very difficult to assess their height from a distance. The smallest obstacles sometimes look enormous, and some snowdrifts can look like mountains. If there is no fog, this phenomenon is called a whiteout.

There is considerable refraction caused by the large difference in temperature between the low layers of the atmosphere and the water or ice. The differences in density generate refractions that totally distort objects. The apparent horizon rises or drops, and mirages appear. American teams have found a solution in their permanent bases in the Antarctic: They have surrounded the bases with posts and have attached ropes to the bottom of them. One simply has to find the end of one of these ropes, then walk around the post until one finds another, continuing in this way to the entrance to the shelter.

## ANIMALS

### Polar Bears

Polar bears usually weigh about 1,100 pounds (500 kilograms) and are about 10 feet (3 meters) tall; these are dangerous animals and they often invade camps looking for food.

They have a very good sense of smell and can detect the slightest odor from a distance of more than 6 miles (10 kilometers). Although the bears are slightly short-sighted, a man without a gun does not stand a chance. Before he set off on his expedition, Jean-Louis Étienne decided that he would not burden himself with a rifle, but he regretted not having a hand gun the day he discovered fresh polar bear tracks on the ice floe. A .44 magnum with a few explosive bullets would not have been very bulky, and it could have saved him a few sleepless nights.

Polar bears are not afraid of man, whom they do not consider as prey, and who presents no danger to them. But they are so curious that they want to come into contact, and thus can become dangerous.

## White Wolves

Rare in Greenland but numerous in Alaska, these predators are, despite misinformation to the contrary, very timid. They never attack man.

## The Orca or Killer Whale

These highly intelligent whales with huge jaws often travel and hunt in groups. Orcas, which are 20 to 33 feet long, often circle round the flimsy kayaks of the Eskimo, signaling their menacing presence with a dorsal fin that can be as high as 6½ feet (2 meters). They are the only whales that eat warm-blooded animals, but they do not attack men in the water. They are rare in Greenland but numerous in Alaska and Canada.

## SIGNALING AND LOCATION

People in trouble in the Arctic are extremely difficult to see from an airplane because of the shadows, the crevasses and the open waters. The crevasses look like black lines or spots scattered over the snow cover. Only colors can catch the eye—but not necessarily the colors one would expect. Dark blue, green and dark red cannot be seen. On the other hand, orange can be seen clearly, particularly the shade of orange used on the wing tips of airplanes. Recently, a series of experiments was conducted in this context in the far north of Canada. A pilot

who was searching for hikers wearing red and blue failed to see them until he was right above them, but when one of the men on the ground climbed out of his tent wearing yellow, the pilot saw him immediately. All the other usual methods remain valid: flares, smoke flares, luminous sticks. But a person is seldom found on the first fly-over. As far as radios are concerned (see Appendix: "Technical Equipment"), the occurrences of aurora borealis, which cause magnetic storms, also cause radio interference and sometimes make communication impossible. Snowstorms also cause interference in communication.

## SICKNESSES

The major health problem is hypothermia with all its consequences, and the reader should refer to the chapter on "Cold" for more details. If intense physical effort must be exerted, a person's underclothes could become saturated with sweat even in the coldest temperature. Because of this, the insulating layer of air provided by these clothes will turn into a liquid "shell" that is highly conductive. Once the exertion has ceased, cooling will be extremely rapid. Therefore some of these clothes should be taken off, or at least the collar and cuffs should be unbuttoned, before the exertion starts. This problem has been largely solved by the development of special synthetic fibers that remain weatherproof while still allowing sweat to evaporate. (See Appendix: "Technical Equipment").

Another disorder common to the Arctic is snow blindness. This occurs not only on snowy, sunlit expanses in the mountains but also on ice. The albedo (power of reflection) of the snow is just as high on an ice floe as in the mountains and frequently causes conjunctivitis even when there is only a moderate amount of sunshine. Entire expeditions have had to turn back because all their members were suffering from this blinding sickness (see the description in the chapter on "The Mountains"). The only way to treat it is to eliminate all light for one to two days. A daily application of a 0.25 percent solution of zinc sulfate, or of a 20 percent solution of albucyde, is helpful, and snow blindness can be cured completely with no aftereffects. Cloudy weather is no safeguard; if anything, it is just the opposite because the whole optic field is a homogeneous bright white, which makes people strain their eyes to distinguish obstacles, increasing the eye's exposure to ultraviolet rays. The best prevention is wearing sunglasses with mirror lenses. The Eskimos protect their eyes with thin sections of perforated caribou bones, but any suitable material can be used, ranging from birch bark to photographic film, and from a piece of cardboard to a leather headband with slits in it.

A sickness that is more specific to the Arctic environment, and that often occurs among individuals who use the local resources for their food, is Vitamin A poisoning from eating the liver of a polar animal: seals, whales, walruses, sharks, and above all, polar bears. Since the 16th century, men have suffered from this sickness, which often attacks anyone who eats the liver of a carnivore. Symptoms are strong headaches, nausea, vomiting, diarrhea, fevers and insomnia. These symptoms appear a few hours after eating the liver and disappear after one to three days. A characteristic symptom enables the individual to diagnose the problem in retrospect: His skin literally peels off in strips three to fours days after eating the liver. Considering that man's daily need of vitamin A is 5,000 international units (1.5 mg), and that 1 gram of the liver from a polar bear contains 20,000 units, the degree of poisoning after eating a 7-ounce (200-gram) slice (4 million units in one go—800 times the required amount) will become obvious.

There are many intestinal parasites, which affect 70 percent of the dogs and 50 percent of the polar bears. For example, trichinosis and helminthiasis will be found in the meat of many polar animals, including sea calves, seals and Arctic fish, as well as dogs and bears. There are specific treatments for this (for instance, Vermox), but a man in a survival situation should be more concerned with prevention, which is very simple in this case: A person must never eat raw meat.

## LOCAL ETHNIC GROUPS

The approximately 40,000 Eskimos who have been living a traditional, unchanging life for 9,000 years on the Arctic coasts between the Bering Sea and the east of Greenland are proof that survival in these regions is quite possible—provided one is informed about how to survive. The Eskimos have always lived by hunting the large marine mammals and the caribou and musk oxen of the tundra and have become Russians, Americans, Canadians or Danes without changing their style of life to any great extent (though we should mention the devastation caused by alcohol among certain groups). They do not much like the name "Eskimo," which means "eater of raw flesh," and prefer the name "Inuit," which means "human being." They live according to a seasonal rhythm: They spend the winters in stone houses, half underground and covered with wood and peat. At the end of winter, the population goes off to hunt, and the group disperses for the summer, constructing temporary igloos on the ice or snow. The Eskimos travel in dog sleds and kayaks made of driftwood that is covered with sealskin.

The Western adventurer may also meet the Lapps to the north of Norway. In contrast to the Eskimos, they have domesticated the reindeer and use it as a draft animal to pull a sled made in the characteristic shape of a boat with a central runner. It is believed that they invented skis. It is difficult to get near any of the other ethnic groups that live in the huge former Soviet territories: the Tunguses and the Mongols, who lead a nomadic life both in summer and winter and build cylindrical tents of skins, for example; the Yakuts, who come from the south; and various other paleo-Siberian populations who also live from breeding reindeer.

Of all these populations, it is the northern Eskimos who live at the outer limits of survival, as the only primary materials they have are driftwood, horn, bones and the skin and tendons of animals. They thrive in areas that have horrendous limitations, and they survive the cold, the night, undernourishment and isolation.

# THE ANTARCTIC

The pole "at the bottom of the world" is geographically very different from the North Pole. While the latter is an abstract point above permanently drifting ice, the South Pole is centered on a true continent, half again as large as the United States. Ninety-eight percent of the continent is covered with a huge layer of ice, the polar ice cap, which has an average thickness of 7,216 feet (2,200 meters) and contains 90 percent of all the ice in the world. Several permanent scientific research bases have been established on the continent where the layer of ice conceals all the secrets of the climatic and volcanic evolution of the world for the last 150,000 years. However, survival on this continent differs to some extent from what is encountered at the North Pole, because there are no enormous moving ice floes; instead there are ice mountains sometimes rising to 9,840 feet (3,000 meters), and very strong winds that can exceed 155 miles per hour (250 kilometers per hour). The Antarctic extends, in fact, from the roaring gales of the 40th latitude to the howling winds of the 50th latitude. The only advantage of these winds is that no insect can survive them: There is not a single flying insect in the Antarctic.

This land is so inhospitable that it was uninhabited right through the first scientific explorations at the beginning of the 20th century. Robert Falcon Scott and Roald Amundsen both led parties to the enormous, 9,840-foot-high central icy plateau. (Roald Amundsen and his party were the first to reach the South Pole.) This plateau, called the continental ice sheet, is broken up by seracs and deep crevasses that make traveling extremely difficult, rather like traveling across glaciers in the mountains. The pitfalls that ice floes present can only be found at the edges of this "ice cap," and the transition from the plateau to the sea is often made by impressive cliffs of ice where icebergs are born.

Whiteouts also take place in the Antarctic, with the addition of some of the optical aberrations, found in the mountains, that distort perceptions of distance and topography. Some years ago a group of New Zealanders, whose country is only 1,240 miles (2,000 kilometers) away from the pole, had the idea of organizing some overflights of the American Antarctic base in a DC-10. In December 1979, the pilot was deceived by a whiteout and the plane crashed into an old volcano that was over 9,800 feet high. Two hundred and fifty-seven people lost their lives. There are also mirages that are unique to the Antarctic, called "fata-morgana," in which a person sees huge cliffs and tries to circumvent them even though they do not exist. In addition, there are reflection-related phenomena, in which a person sees a mountain range that is a reverse image of a true range, or sees all the details of a landscape beyond the horizon.

The food chain of the Antarctic is certainly no poorer than that of the Arctic, with hundreds of millions of tons of tiny shrimp—known as krill—forming the base diet of the whales in this region and the beginning of the food chain for all the other animals. Krill follows the movements of plankton, descending by day and coming back up at night. It is so characteristic of this region that some say they can tell they have reached the waters of Antarctica as soon as they find krill. However paradoxical this may seem, microscopic algae multiply rapidly in these frigid waters, while their productivity in tropical waters is very low. This is attributable to the water's capacity to dissolve more gases as the temperature drops: In winter, the polar waters (Arctic as well as Antarctic) are replete with oxygen, which permits the multiplication not only of Diatoma, but also of microalgae, which benefit especially from the ascending nutritive salts. This is why, as soon as the sun appears at the poles, the open sea becomes a veritable grazing ground for krill

and the whales that feed on them.

Krill are so bountiful in the Antarctic that commercial fisheries have been set up to harvest them for animal feed. In a survival situation at the edges of an ice floe, one can catch the krill with a plankton net. It is not only the basic diet of marine mammals with baleens, but also of fish, birds (especially the penguin) and some seals—so why not of a human being in a survival situation? Unlike the Arctic, there are no terrestrial mammals in the Antarctic. Antarctic seals are only found near the coast of the continent and therefore never come closer than 500 miles (800 kilometers) from the South Pole.

Penguins are found only in the Antarctic (while auks and guillemots can only be found in the Arctic). It is one of the few birds that cannot fly, but its atrophied wings enable it to swim remarkably well under water in search of krill. Its white stomach protects it from being seen by the killer whales and leopard seals, while its black back makes it invisible from the surface. If penguins are unable to find food, they economize their fat reserves as much as possible by reducing their movements to a minimum and standing in a way that keeps caloric losses very low.

The petrel and the cormorant should also be mentioned among the diving birds of the Antarctic.

## Geography of inhospitable environments

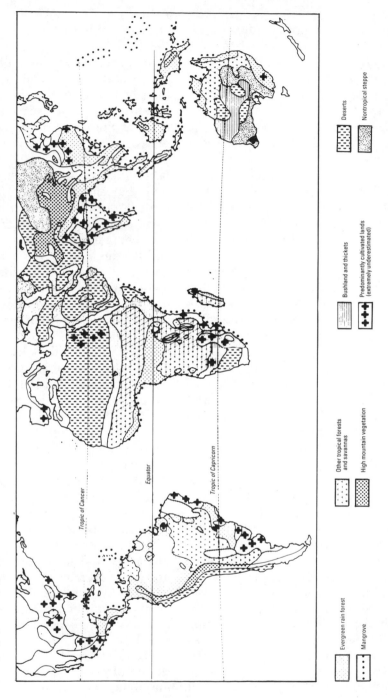

Legend:

- Evergreen rain forest
- Mangrove
- Other tropical forests and savannas
- High mountain vegetation
- Bushland and thickets
- Predominantly cultivated lands (extremely underestimated)
- Deserts
- Nontropical steppe

Tropic of Cancer

Equator

Tropic of Capricorn

The albatross spends very little of its time on the continent and searches for its food up to 800 miles (1,300 kilometers) out to sea. It is not possible to survive by eating Antarctic fauna, so it is absolutely essential to take along all the food that will be needed during an expedition to the southernmost continent.

# PART III

# Science and Survival

# WEATHER AND SURVIVAL

- Propagation of Heat

- Atmospheric Pressure

- Humidity

- Highs, Lows and Fronts

- Important Local Phenomena

- Storms

- Hurricanes

- Water Spouts and Tornadoes

Whatever the environment, weather conditions can be critical for survival. Proper protection against intense cold, torrential rains, violent winds or an implacable sun may make all the difference.

All weather activity takes place in the atmosphere, a very thin gaseous skin about 18 miles (30 kilometers) wide that gradually becomes rarefied until it disappears altogether into interplanetary space. The atmosphere is so thin that if the earth were represented by a sphere 6½ feet (2 meters) in diameter, the part of the atmosphere in which weather takes place would only be .19 inch (5 millimeters) thick. The consequences of so much activity in such a thin layer are significant: There is a preponderance of horizontal movements, and there is an enormous disproportion between the vertical variation and the horizontal variation of the different atmospheric variables. Thus the vertical variation of the pressure is on the order of 1 millibar per 33 feet (10 meters) at sea level, while the horizontal variation is on the order of 1 millibar per 62 miles (100 kilometers). (A drop in

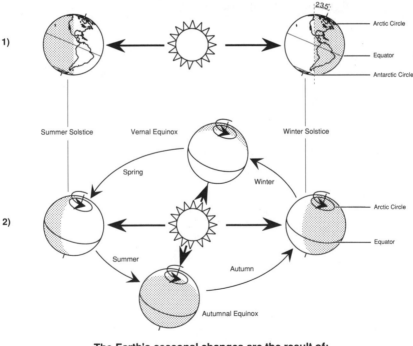

The Earth's seasonal changes are the result of:
1) the angle of the earth's axis, and
2) the earth's yearly orbit around the sun

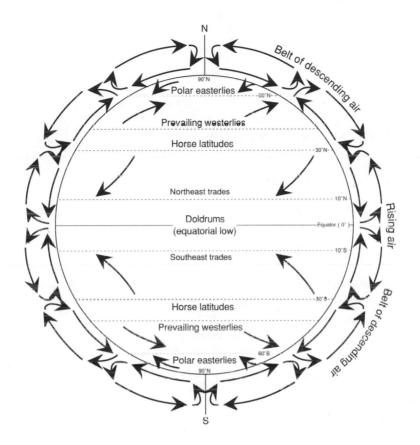

pressure of 5 to 10 millibars per 62 miles is exceptional and is a forerunner of a deep depression or a storm).

The atmosphere is composed of several layers, the most important for our purposes being the troposphere, which is characterized by a regular decrease in temperature as the altitude increases: 10.8 to 12.6°F per 3,300 feet (6 to 7°C per 1,000 meters). Therefore, in a temperate region, there will be a temperature of −68.8°F (−56°C) at the tropopause, the boundary be-

tween the troposphere and the stratosphere. On the other hand the temperature in the stratosphere increases with altitude because solar radiation at that height is no longer absorbed by the ozone.

The atmospheric phenomena discussed below are confined to the troposphere. The difference in the height of the tropopause at different latitudes is significant and determines the intensity of meteorological phenomena, particularly storms.

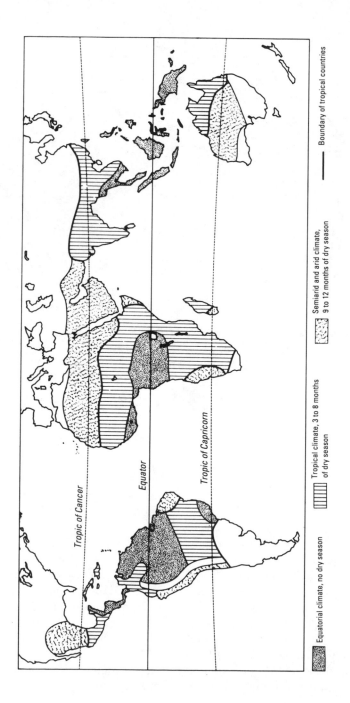

Tropic of Cancer

Equator

Tropic of Capricorn

Equatorial climate, no dry season

Tropical climate, 3 to 8 months of dry season

Semiarid and arid climate, 9 to 12 months of dry season

Boundary of tropical countries

The tropopause is only 5.5 miles (9 kilometers) high at the poles, 10.5 miles (17 kilometers) at the equator, and 6.8 miles (11 kilometers) at temperate latitudes. Decreases in atmospheric pressure therefore occur much more rapidly at the poles than at the equator. This probably explains why some members of one Antarctic expedition became sick at the summit of the Erebus volcano (13,195 feet [4,023 meters]), although they had no problems at 26,240 feet (8,000 meters) in the Himalayas.

# PROPAGATION OF HEAT

## CONDUCTION

Conduction plays a negligible role because the air, the water and the earth's surface are not good conductors of heat.

## CONVECTION

Convection plays a significant role in the atmosphere: Heated air at the earth's surface rises and is replaced by cold air, which heats up in its turn, and so on. This is how cumulus clouds are formed, growing as the day passes and the increasing heat of the ground causes more intense convection.

## RADIATION

Radiation is of primary importance because it provides solar energy. Solar radiation heats the atmosphere indirectly through the intermediary of the ground: The atmosphere is heated from the bottom, an essential point in meteorology. In its turn, the heated ground radiates toward the atmosphere; the less cloudy it is, the more heat radiates back, and this helps explain why nights can be so cold in deserts and icy in high mountain regions.

# ATMOSPHERIC PRESSURE

Atmospheric pressure is determined by the density of the column of air rising above the point of measurement. The column over the poles is much narrower (5.5 miles or 9 kilometers), but as it is denser because of the low temperature, the average pressure at ground level remains on the order of 1,013 millibars (or 29.6 inches [76 centimeters]) of mercury.

■ The lowest pressure is found in tropical cyclones (often less than 900 millibars in the eye of a hurricane).
■ The highest pressure can be found in winter in continental

cold anticyclones (sometimes more than 1,070 millibars in Siberia). These cold and "heavy" anticylcones are very stable and are the reason for the periods of beautiful weather that last for several weeks in winter.

# HUMIDITY

Water contained in the atmosphere plays a regulatory role because of its capacity to absorb infrared rays and its strong caloric inertia. Under a cloudy sky, temperature differences between night and day are minimized.

The high relative humidity is also the reason for the stability of the high temperature in the jungle. The warmer the air, the more humidity it can contain up to the maximum point of saturation. If air is cooled, the humidity that is in a gaseous state will condense into droplets if it is above freezing, and ice crystals if it is below. In this way, in summer, a particle of air that rises by convection into the center of a cumulonimbus cloud, which is beginning to form, will cool at that high altitude, and its water vapor will transform into ice in the upper layers of the cloud before descending. During the descent, the ice melts as the particle warms up, and then it rises again under the action of convection currents: six to eight such cycles can follow one another during the formation of a cumulonimbus cloud.

The process of nocturnal condensation through cooling causes morning fogs. As the daytime heating begins, these fogs generally disappear during the morning when the low cloud cover rises. If the mists and the low strata have not disappeared two hours after the zenith, the fog will probably not lift in the afternoon. This simple rule is important to survival if a person is stuck because of a fog in the mountains or on an ice floe. Navigating close to shore and flying are also dangerous under such conditions.

# HIGHS, LOWS AND FRONTS

## ISOBARS

Isobars at the surface of the earth form curved lines, some of them concentric—centered on either a depression or an anticyclone. A depression is an area of low pressure in relation to the surrounding regions. An anticyclone is an area of high pressure.

In a depression the isobars are inclined toward the center; the opposite is true for an anticyclone, where they slope toward the outer edge. The slope is not sharp, about 3 feet per 6 miles (1 meter per 10 kilometers) close to the ground, but it increases with altitude up to 3 feet per .6 mile (1 meter per 1 kilometer). The intensity of atmospheric phenomena, particularly wind, is proportional to this slope: The closer the isobar lines, the stronger the wind. In the northern hemisphere the wind has the high pressure on the right and the low pressure on the left. The opposite is true for the southern hemisphere. In addition, the wind follows a curved trajectory into a depression and out of an anticyclone. This is the result of three combined forces: the Coriolis force, the centrifugal force and atmospheric pressure.

Using these simple concepts, it is possible to determine whether a depression is approaching or moving away simply by observing the changes in wind direction. This is vital in navigating on the high seas: When a front passes in the northern hemisphere, the wind turns counterclockwise, while in the southern hemisphere the wind changes in a clockwise direction.

## HOW A DISTURBANCE IS FORMED

The earth is capped by two cold and stable polar air masses with a mass of unstable warmer air in between. The two masses of air are separated by the polar front, which moves between the 40th and 60th parallels. To the north of the polar front, the cold air generally has a west to east direction and to the south the hot air generally has an east to west direction.

A disturbance is formed when there is a ripple in the polar front. This ripple is caused by a thrust of cold air into the hot air in a north to east, south to west direction. Since cold air moves faster than hot air, the cold front is trapped and the hot air is driven upward (forming an occlusion).

The occlusion signals the final stage of the disturbance, ending a process that takes about a week, during which the disturbance moves 3,105 to 4,347 miles (5,000 to 7,000 kilometers). Usually a group of three to five disturbances forms and is more or less tiered in latitude. It is this mechanism that maintains the thermal equilibrium of the earth with the polar air descending all the way to the tropical latitudes while the hot air reaches the polar regions. Such a disturbance is accompanied by specific clouds, which make it possible to determine which stage the disturbance has reached: high, wispy cirrus clouds precede a warm front and often announce the arrival of a disturbance on the following day.

The clouds become heavier and lower (cumulus-stratocumulus), and rain begins to fall (nimbostratus). The wind veers from southeast to southwest while the warm front passes and drizzle sets in under low clouds (stratocumulus-stratus). Abruptly the wind veers to the northwest as the cold front passes, while the rain starts again (altostratus-stratocumulus). A clearing sky follows on the next day, with isolated cumulus clouds and the very good visibility typical after a disturbance has passed.

This rather simplified description naturally has many variations, but an all-terrain traveler should not ignore the general outlines.

---

# IMPORTANT LOCAL PHENOMENA

## SEA BREEZE

During the day, the sea is colder than the coast above which convection currents come into being. The breeze usually blows toward the shore between 10 A.M. and 6 P.M. Therefore a shipwrecked person will have a better chance of reaching a coast by day than by night (naturally assuming there are no opposing ocean currents or major atmospheric winds).

## LAND BREEZE

During the night, the coast cools more quickly than the sea (through radiation) and therefore between 9 P.M. and 7 A.M. the wind will blow from the coast out to sea. Therefore it would be better to leave an island during the night rather than by day (as long as there is no danger of running aground).

## DAY BREEZE IN THE MOUNTAINS

Due to the effect of the sun's rays on snowy slopes, two breezes spring up:

■ a breeze that blows from the bottom to the top of the slope,

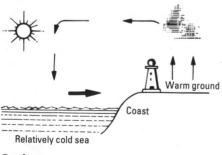

**Sea breeze**

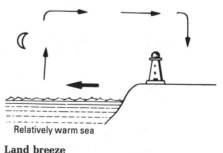

**Land breeze**

**The day wind in the mountains**

particularly on the sunny sides; and

■ a breeze that moves up the valley.

Gliders, in particular, make use of these breezes, but they are equally well known to the amateur mountaineer.

### NIGHT BREEZE IN THE MOUNTAINS

The phenomenon is reversed during the night.

### TOPOGRAPHY'S INFLUENCE ON WEATHER

Remember that all meteorological phenomena are intensified by

**The night wind in the mountains**

topography. The effect of the Foehn wind is well known; it is caused by a strong, hot wind blowing from the south through the Swiss and Austrian Alps and causing many avalanches.

There are many equivalents to this wind throughout the world, and therefore it is worth summarizing its mechanism. When a humid cloud system crosses a mountain, the topography forces it to rise, causing cooling, condensation and rainfall. By the time it arrives at the other side, the cloud system has lost a large part of its water and, in addition, it is forced to move downward by the wind. This causes it to become warmer again through compression, and the warming becomes especially significant because the air no longer contains water vapor. This phenomenon increases in intensity depending on the size of the mountain range and on the strength of the wind. It can cause a simple lull in precipitation, or a totally clear period.

Usually, the following can be observed:

■ on the windward side: a thickening of the cloud masses, stronger and longer-lasting precipitation and the threat or outbreak of storms.

■ on the leeward side: a thinning or total disappearance of clouds, a lull in or a total stop to precipitation and a decrease in storm activity.

# STORMS

Storms are especially dangerous in the mountains and in the equatorial seas, and it is important to understand their mechanism. A storm is synonymous with thunder, lightning and cumulonimbus clouds. There are of course storms without hail, but there is never hail without cumulonimbus clouds. If, during the night, hail falls on a boat, be prepared for a hard fight to come, and take down the sail (if lightning, thunder or the wind itself have not already been warning enough).

Storms are frequent in the tropics and rare in the polar regions (a few during the summer) and in the desert, where they constitute the sole source of precipitation. In the continental regions of the temperate zones, they occur mainly in summer.

Two conditions are necessary for a storm to form:

■ strong humidity in the troposphere; and
■ a tall column of air with a steep temperature gradient, enabling the air particles to rise all the way to the tropopause. The peak of the storm is always at the level of the tropopause, i.e., 5.5 miles at the poles and 10.5 miles at the equator.

This huge vertical development explains both the infrequency and the limited violence of polar storms and the extreme violence of equatorial storms.

All fronts can cause storms. However, cold front storms are more violent, often forming a continuous line of squalls that can be seen from afar. They are especially intense during the day (because thermal convection reinforces frontal convection).

The storm cell forms in 30 to 45 minutes and changes from a large, whitish, thick cumulus cloud into a "calvus" cumulus cloud that is very high and has a threatening gray color. The anvil that tops the cloud indicates that it is in the process of dissipation.

Precipitation accompanies the most violent descending currents that rebound from the ground or the sea and take a horizontal direction, which can turn 180° in a matter of seconds. The ascending currents can reach a speed of 197 feet (60 meters) per second, and commercial planes have special radar so as to avoid these dangerous clouds.

A skydiver was caught in this way in the United States and was found hundreds of miles away: He died of cold and asphyxia having probably been thrown up to more than 32,800 feet (10,000 meters). His body was still frozen when he was found. A glider pilot was luckier: He was drawn into a storm, lost consciousness because of the lack of oxygen and woke up several hours later very close to the ground. The storm in which he had been caught was probably in the process of dissipating, and the glider survived the violent vertical currents.

# HURRICANES

These are very violent storms that occur exclusively on certain expanses of the warm tropical oceans. They are called hurricanes if the wind exceeds 65 knots. It can, in fact, exceed 150 knots (174 miles per hour, or 280 kilometers per hour) and be accompanied by a tidal wave. This type of storm, which develops in four to 10 days, attains a diameter of 370 to 620 miles (600 to 1,000 kilometers) and the pressure at the center is often less than 950 millibars.

There are no hurricanes in the eastern part of the South Pacific, from the east of Polynesia to the American coast, or in the South Atlantic. These two regions are, in fact, cooled by cold currents from the South Pole: the Benguela current (Africa) and the Humboldt current (South America).

The winds are very calm in the eye of the hurricane; the problem is getting out! The sea is wild, with waves exceeding 50 to 66 feet (15 to 20 meters) causing tidal waves along the coasts. A hurricane causes a very long wave surge, which can be felt as far as 620 miles (1,000 kilometers) away and provides the best warning of approaching trouble.

The usual path taken by a hurricane is parabolic, generally starting in a warm equatorial sea (a sea with a temperature above 80.6°F [27°C], then moving in a westerly direction, then northwest, and finally northeast, rejoining the polar circulation.

Specific conditions are necessary for a hurricane to form:

■ very high humidity in the air (they form over the surface of the sea).
■ strong convection currents: latent instability of the air and especially a significant warming of its base. Where the ocean tempera-

**Tornado**

ture is below 80.6°F a hurricane will not form. This temperature is never reached in the South Atlantic or the South Pacific. The Caribbean islanders often talk about "hurricane years," when they notice an exceptionally long period of sunshine. They are correct in the sense that sunshine will raise the temperature of the oceans up to 80.6°F or even higher. The necessity for the temperature to rise

this high explains why most hurricanes occur at the end of summer, in August, September and October.

■ the existence of the Coriolis force, which causes the circular movement of the air. This explains why hurricanes always develop at latitudes above 5°. Therefore, in the dangerous season it is better to navigate along the line of the equator.

# WATER SPOUTS AND TORNADOES

Their mechanism is fundamentally different from that of hurricanes. They are also circular disturbances but are limited in size, with a vertical axis, and are associated with the path of a cumulonimbus cloud.

The air particles undergo a twofold movement, which circulates very rapidly upward and gives them a spiral trajectory. They occur in masses of hot, humid and unstable air.

## WATER SPOUTS

Appendages or "funnels," which do not necessarily reach the water, can be seen under some cumulonimbus clouds. The diameter of the funnel varies from a few to several dozen yards, and its height from 98 to 4,920 feet (30 to 1,500 meters). Its passage is

accompanied by a strong depression that is very localized. The funnel is formed by a circle of ascending droplets, thrown to the outward edge by centrifugal force, and there is a descending column at the center that has no droplets. It would be wise to try to circumnavigate this funnel.

## CONTINENTAL TORNADOES

This is a phenomenon analogous to the water spout, but it originates on land and it is much more dangerous. There are no appendages below the cumulonimbus clouds, but there are very violent circular winds (100 to 150 knots, i.e., 112 to 167 miles per hour [180 to 270 kilometers per hour]) and the diameter is only a few hundred yards. It is extremely destructive and can sweep clean an area a dozen or more miles wide as it travels past. Tornadoes occur frequently in the United States, but actually they can be found in all continental countries where cold fronts separate two very different masses of air.

# SNOW AND AVALANCHES

- Facts and Figures

- Types of Snow

- Temperature and the Stability of Snow

- Natural Avalanches

- What to Do in an Avalanche

- Wind and Snow

# FACTS AND FIGURES

☸ When fully developed, an avalanche can attain a mass of one million tons and a force of impact of 145 tons per square meter (per 1.19 square yards), 48 times the force needed to destroy a house.

☸ The air speed of an avalanche of powdered snow can reach 223.5 miles per hour (360 kilometers per hour), i.e., twice the record speed of a skier.

☸ The deadliest avalanche occurred in Peru in 1970. The town of Yungay was destroyed and its 18,000 residents were killed; the country's estimated death toll climbed to 50,000.

☸

## December 1916

Italian and Austrian troops are fighting for dominance over the Dolomites, which both countries claim as their own. Twenty-two-year-old Erwin Aichinger is a lieutenant in the Austrian ski troops. He recounts what happened: "For three days it had snowed constantly. Very strong winds plastered the snow against the avalanche slopes. When the blizzard stopped, the fighting started again. We watched each other from the two sides, while the cannon fire set off avalanches. Then the artillery had a diabolical idea. They raised their sights to the enormous masses of snow perched on the summits of the mountains, and brought them hurtling down the mountainside.

"Below, the terrified soldiers fled for their shelters but the avalanches wiped them out. The rescue parties were also killed. Within 48 hours, 6,000 Austrian soldiers died, and among the Italians, who knows how many more."

It is estimated that 17,000 soldiers from both sides were killed during these two apocalyptic days. This battle was a sinister foreshadowing of the modern control of avalanches with explosives.

## TYPES OF SNOW

It is useful to know the fundamental principles of the formation of snow in order to survive in the mountains, but also for better adaptation to snowy milieux in general, mountainous or not. Whether one is pitching a tent in a winter fog in northern Canada or in a blizzard on an ice floe, crossing a bridge of snow over a

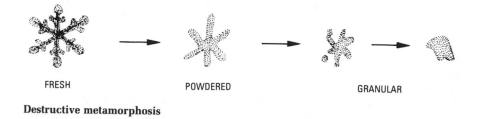

FRESH                POWDERED                GRANULAR

**Destructive metamorphosis**

crevasse or following the line of the ridge on a windward slope, one will have to weigh the risks involved in living with snow.

Depending on time, local meteorology, and increasing water content, snow ranges from magnificent crystals to impressive seracs of bluish ice. This transformation is caused by two main types of metamorphoses, which often happen simultaneously: "destructive" metamorphosis and "constructive" metamorphosis. There are widespread misconceptions about these two types of metamorphoses, encouraged by pedantic explanations in books. Once the mechanisms are understood, all the rest fits logically into sequence, and a little bit of common sense is enough to understand the essence of the matter.

## DESTRUCTIVE METAMORPHOSIS

This kind of evolution starts within the first few hours and acts on the freshly fallen snow. The term "destructive" has nothing to do with the danger of an avalanche, but with the destruction

of the fine branch-like structures of fresh snow to form larger structures. Evaporation occurs at the tips of the crystals and deposits are made in the cavities of the flakes due to differences in the tension of water vapor. The flakes move toward a simplified structure, changing from the star shape, which often has many branch-like structures, to a powdered form, where only the rough outline of a star is discernible, and ultimately to a final spherical shape, called "granular."

It is said that nature abhors a vacuum, and this transition from a sophisticated shape to a rounded shape plays a role in the gradual settling of the snow. This metamorphosis is an irreversible phenomenon, and snow can never return to a powdered form once it has become granular. Frequently people confuse the terms "fresh" snow and "powdered" snow, though the latter is snow that has already been partially transformed.

This metamorphosis takes several days and occurs more rapidly as the temperature climbs closer to 32°F (0°C). However, it has nothing to do with fusion. It is a relatively favorable phenomenon from the point of view of stability because it causes the snow cover to settle.

## CONSTRUCTIVE METAMORPHOSIS

This is due to the temperature difference between the snow surface, where the average temperature over 24 hours is very cold (often 5°F [−15°C]), and the deep layer in contact with the ground (often as high as 30.2°F [−1°C]). The greater the difference in temperature, the faster the change in structure. The particles close to the ground become sublimated (changing directly from a solid state to water vapor), and the water vapor produced in this way moves toward the surface layers, which are still aerated and much colder. Therefore the vapor condenses around the upper cold particles and gives them a characteristic pyramidal or reversed goblet shape. In this way, ice is moved upward, weakening the lower layers and making the whole mass much more unstable.

The formation of the "pyramid-goblets" is the reason for the term "constructive" metamorphosis, though it is a deceptive description because the goblets have no cohesion and can roll like balls, forming "flowing snow." This is a very dangerous phenomenon.

This development will not occur if a new snowfall covers everything: The new layer of fresh snow, in fact, will lower the temperature gradient within the preceding layer and settle it under its own weight, making it less porous and preventing any vertical circulation of the vapor.

From the point of view of constructive metamorphosis, the whole layer will thus be protected by the one above it, as long as the new snow falls in time. If it does not fall until the constructive metamorphosis has already occurred, it will cover what is now a carpet of balls, making the whole area extremely unstable. This is why there is a very great danger of avalanches when winter comes late and thick layers of snow fall in January over a single first layer that had fallen at the beginning of December. Such a pattern makes everything into a veritable "rolling carpet."

## COMPRESSION METAMORPHOSIS

In this kind of metamorphosis, the crystals meld together under the weight of successive layers, consolidating the whole area exactly like cubes in an ice bucket, which have a tendency to meld and settle. This metamorphosis consolidates the snow cover.

## METAMORPHOSIS DUE TO THAWING

Following a long period of sunshine when the temperature rises above 30°F, there is an inverse mechanism to that of constructive metamorphosis: The surface snow melts, and the water runs down into the cover and freezes around the particles lower down, which still have a temperature below freezing point. This time, the ice moves toward the base, which becomes increasingly compact. This is how spring snow forms and, over a longer period, builds up to form the névé, or firn—snow that remains at high altitudes from one year to the next.

## TEMPERATURE AND THE STABILITY OF SNOW

It seems logical to assume that the colder the snow is, the more resistant it will be. This is true as a general rule, but the type of snow will strongly modify this principle:

■ Flowing snow has no mechanical resistance at any temperature (the carpet of goblets mentioned above).
■ Spring snow, which is very wet by definition, is very soft at 28.4°F ($-2$°C) and as solid as concrete at $-22$°F ($-30$°C). This kind of snow loses its resistance when warmed, as its water content increases: It is an enormous mass of water on the point of melting, which explains why old snow crumbles more readily than fresh or powdered snow.
■ Cooling will not improve the mechanical resistance of fresh, powdered or flowing snow to any great extent, as it will with wet snow.
■ In respect to powdered snow, cooling merely causes a negligible increase in resistance by interweaving the star-shaped flakes. Most significantly, this cooling hinders destructive metamorphosis and prevents the crystals from evolving and, as a result, they maintain their unstable equilibrium and seesaw at the slightest impact (wind, pebbles, a skier, a sound wave).

## NATURAL AVALANCHES

### AVALANCHES OF POWDERED SNOW

This is the most dangerous type of avalanche because of its speed, the other types of avalanches it can set off, and its aerosol nature, which can literally drown a skier or hiker who is caught in it.

This avalanche develops through paroxystic branching—that is, it starts at a specific point and spreads widely. Fresh or powdered snow can cling to vertical rock walls, more or less glued there by the wind. In other words, a mountain is as dangerous as it is beautiful. It only takes a few cubic centimeters to break off, and this can cause a chain reaction, resulting in an avalanche hurtling downward at up to 155 miles per hour (250 kilometers per hour).

How can it reach such a speed, if the powdered aerosol only weighs about 33 pounds (15 kilograms) per cubic meter—15 times more than air, but 70 times less than water? Several explanations have been put forward that are indefensible from the perspective of physics. Some people have even gone so far as to claim an avalanche speed of 375 miles per hour preceded by a sonic boom that tore apart the lungs of some victims.

This very fast-moving avalanche, which is made up of light particles, strikes against immobile air, causing an ascending vortex and forming a characteristic cloud. The greater the speed of the compression zone ahead of the avalanche, the greater the damage it causes.

An avalanche need not be especially large to cause a critical survival situation. Even a small avalanche of powdered snow can sweep away, bury and drown an unfortunate or incautious skier or hiker within a matter of minutes. The aerosol penetrates into the respiratory channels like a vaporizer, instantly inundating the pulmonary alveoli and causing a kind of very rapid drowning if the victim is not given emergency treatment immediately or cannot himself escape within the first few seconds.

An avalanche of powdered snow can start even when there is no sun, and primarily occurs in winter following a recent snowfall; at such times the greatest caution is required. A person can be subjected to this type of avalanche in any mountainous region of the world, from Alaska to Tierra del Fuego, from the Appalachians to Mongolia. The mountain climber, the skier, the trekker, the hunter and anyone who is lost in the mountains should all beware.

---

In October 1972, a plane carrying a Uruguayan rugby team crashed at approximately 13,000 feet (4,000 meters) in the Andes. Although 27 of the survivors of the crash had been saved by the plane's fuselage, which had miraculously remained intact, their numbers were later decimated by an avalanche of powdered snow, which engulfed the cabin and suffocated eight of the survivors in a matter of seconds. They had already spent a couple of weeks in their makeshift shelter at the foot of sharp slopes with enormous, threatening layers of snow. On the first day, they had watched one of the survivors who had been thrown some distance from the crash site, and was trying to rejoin them: He had slipped on the mantle of snow and disappeared forever in an avalanche of powder.

None of the survivors was a mountaineer, and none had even thought of the possibility of an avalanche. Had they thought about it, they would have blocked the gaping entrance to the cabin on the side facing the mountain. When the big avalanche of powdered snow started, it silently engulfed the interior of the cabin, drowning all those sleeping inside with an icy aerosol, piling up to the ceiling in some places, burying the unfortunate people, and paralyzing them. All those who were unable to free themselves quickly either drowned or suffocated.

## WET AVALANCHES

Wet avalanches are more often started by the sun and their speed does not exceed 25 to 62 miles per hour (40 to 100 kilometers per hour). They do not cause a cloud; they produce little wind, do not go over major obstacles and are often triggered in the spring when there is a rise in temperature or some rainfall.

If the snow is very wet (due to rain or a warming trend that has melted the ice), it is unable to form globules, and it descends like a torrent, ending in a fan shape on a slope that is less steep. This is called "decomposed snow." The fan settles and takes several months to thaw.

All avalanches have some physical characteristics in common, especially their tendency to become as hard as concrete when they hit a resistant obstacle. All types of snow contain a large amount of air. If this porous material is dragged along at great speed and then abruptly stopped against some obstacle, the air is violently compressed and does not have time to escape. This compression causes heat that quickly transforms the snow into a material that is compact in proportion to how wet it is. In an incident at Val-d'Isère, France in the 1970s, dozens of people who were trapped inside a restaurant had to be dug out with picks. Those who did not have the presence of mind to clear a small space in front of their faces did not stand a chance. In such a situation, the matrix is so dense that it is impossible to move at all, even to breathe.

The two tables below will help to distinguish the different types of avalanches.

## DISTINCTIVE FEATURES ACCORDING TO THE STATE OF THE SNOW

| TYPE | SUBTYPE | SNOW |
|------|---------|------|
| Avalanche of dry snow (in decreasing order of lightness) | avalanche of powdered snow with cloud | powdered |
| | avalanche of powdered snow without cloud | flowing (in goblets or amorphous) |
| | wind sheet avalanche | hard, windblown, dry |
| Avalanche of wet snow (in increasing order of wetness) | sheet avalanche | wet |
| | globular avalanche | springtime (hours of warmth) |
| | fusion avalanche | decomposed |

## DISTINCTIVE FEATURES ACCORDING TO THE BEHAVIOR OF THE SNOW

| | |
|---|---|
| The snow flies | cloud of powdered snow |
| The snow slides | avalanche of powdered snow without a cloud |
| The snow rolls | avalanche of globules |
| The snow descends in a block | sheet and board avalanches |
| The snow flows | fusion avalanche |

(According to P. and B. Caillat, *Connaître et prévenir les avalanches*, Albin Michel)

# WHAT TO DO IN AN AVALANCHE

It is irrelevant whether one is dealing with a "total" avalanche (the whole mass, down to the ground, moves) or a sheet avalanche (a slide involving a thicker or thinner layer of the snow cover), whether the break is in a line or at a specific point, whether the general shape is a panel, or a river, or a pear, whether the snow is wet or dry—all of these determinations are made later, but the actions that must be taken immediately are always the same.

## ESTIMATING THE DANGER

The meteorological conditions for the day should be ascertained, taking into account those of preceding days: What were the daytime temperatures? The nighttime? How deep is the snow? How long has it been on the ground?

These parameters will enable even a layman to estimate the danger. For example, abundant dry, cold, very heavy snowfalls for several days add up to a risk of an avalanche of powdered snow. Assuming the same kind of snowfall, but spread over alternating warm days and cold nights there should be no danger because of the metamorphosis that will have occurred. Zero degrees at 9,800 feet (3,000 meters), or rain at a higher altitude on thick layers of

snow translates into danger of avalanches of wet snow. In summer, heavy avalanches are the rule.

## PREVENTIVE MEASURES

■ Avoid combes (deep narrow valleys) dominated by large snowy stretches on inclines. If you have to pass them, take the line of the greatest slope, and do not cross it; the imprint of a ski can act as a knife, detaching a large sheet of the unstable surface snow.

■ If you have to cross it, do so as high up as possible.

■ If you are in a group, pass one at a time and watch the person exposed: If an avalanche occurs, the search should be restricted to the point where the person disappeared.

■ The shortest route from one point to another may not be the best, as you may have to pass through thalwegs. The best route is making use of the line of the ridge, supporting yourself as much as possible on rocks or against trees. Animal tracks are no guarantee of safety. If you have a map, you should determine the route beforehand according to the contour lines.

■ You should not be roped to each other, the safety bindings on skis should be released and the ski poles should be held over the loops. You should get rid of everything that could inhibit the movements of your limbs.

## DURING AN AVALANCHE

■ Cover your face with a hood or a cap, anything that can prevent the penetration of the powdered aerosol into the lungs.

■ Whatever the type of avalanche, you must "swim," making breaststroke-type movements with your arms and legs, as this is the only way to stay at the surface.

■ You must not try to go against the flow: This would be ludicrous, and would merely guarantee that you will be buried.

■ Before the snow mass stops moving you must use the "rollball" technique, moving your arms and legs in such a way as to retain a space in front of your chest and around your mouth. You must continue to move your legs as much as possible, for as long as possible, because you can only move while the avalanche is moving. Pierre Paquet, a guide who was totally buried far from any possible rescue on the Pilatus glacier in Switzerland, was able to get out all by himself because he was able to dig the snow away with his pocketknife, thanks to the cavity he had formed around his chest. His companion, who was either less fortunate or less athletic, died.

There are various rescue methods ranging from very effective dogs trained to find avalanche victims, through to electronic markers, but listing them would not be appropriate in a book giving advice on survival for a sole person or an isolated group. Suffice it to say that the key to survival is to be dug out quickly.

# WIND AND SNOW

The combined action of these two elements plays a role in forming wind sheets, cornices and bridges of snow, which are potential traps in the mountains, in the Far North, in the Antarctic and on an ice floe. On the other hand, snowdrifts can be potential shelters. Snow will start moving when the wind reaches a speed of 13 feet (4 meters) per second in the case of fresh snow and 33 feet (10 meters) per second in the case of firmer snow.

## WIND SHEETS

The wind causes a thinner layer of snow cover on the windward slope and a thicker layer on the leeward slope because swirls sometimes decrease the thickness on some combes by several yards. As a result, there are two types of wind sheets:

■ The ones on the side toward the dominant winds are plastered down more evenly and adhere more uniformly to the lower layers.

■ Those on the leeward side are subjected to swirling, irregular winds and only adhere to the lower layers in some places, rather like spot-welded sheet metal; they are not very resistant to the shock caused by a falling cornice and break under the weight of a person. Therefore, if one must walk, it is safer to do so on the windward side.

## CORNICES

The wind blowing across an arête (a sharp ridge) transports the snow and forms cornices that sometimes overhang several yards of empty space. If in doubt, follow the line of the arête, moving a few yards below it on the windward side.

## SNOW BRIDGES

These straddle crevasses and are made of snow that has metamorphosed faster because it has been blown by the wind. These bridges are often invisible on glaciers, and the only sign that they are there is a slightly grayer color or a slight difference in the contour. A person is less likely to sink into a snow bridge than into the surrounding snow. This is due to the metamorphosis of the snow on the vertical sides of the hole, a metamorphosis that occurs not only from above, but also from below on the overhanging surface.

On a glacier, members of the group should be attached by a rope. If you are alone, you must probe ahead with an ice ax or another improvised tool. A fall into a crevasse is usually fatal, either from the initial impact or from cold.

The term "snow bridge" is inappropriate, because it conjures up an impression of solidity that is seldom attained. Only arches of ice spanning a crevasses are solid. As the spring advances, more snow bridges form at the crevasses, and the trap they present is extremely dangerous.

# ORIENTATION

- Orientation

- Determining a Position

# ORIENTATION

## FINDING THE SOUTH WITH A WATCH AND THE SUN

This method is accurate within 10°—plus or minus 5°—depending on your aptitude for guesswork. It is applicable in the temperate zones, i.e., between 23.5° and 66.5° latitude south or north.

Between two successive sunrises or sunsets, the sun performs an apparent rotation around the earth of 360° in 24 hours, i.e., 15° per hour (of course, it is the earth that has turned on its axis, but for an observer on earth it makes no difference). In addition, since the sun rises in the east and then sets in the west approximately 12 hours later, it has a series of successive positions above the horizon and it is possible to determine cardinal points, especially the south, in relation to them.

If you have a watch—not a digital watch, but one with hands—first set it to Greenwich Mean Time. This is the same as U.S. Eastern Standard Time plus five hours. In the northern hemisphere if you now point the hour hand at the sun, south is halfway between the hour hand and the 12. In the southern hemisphere the principle is the same: Point the number 12 at the sun, and north is halfway between the 12 and the hour hand.

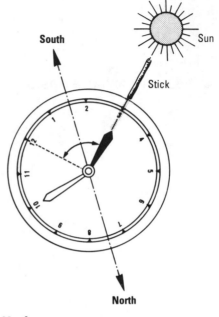

**Northern temperate zone**

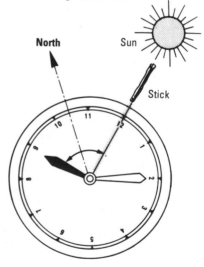

**Southern temperate zone**

326

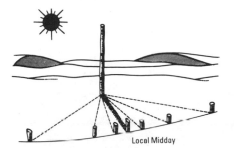

Local Midday

Determination of local midday: The short-est shadow indicates local midday.

## FINDING THE TIME OF DAY WITHOUT A WATCH

The line connecting two succes-sive positions of the tip of the shadow from a pole always moves in an east to west direction. This is the principle of the sundial, il-lustrated left.

| PHASE | EAST | SOUTH | WEST | NORTH |
|---|---|---|---|---|
| NEW MOON | 6 h | 12 h | 18 h | 24 h |
| FIRST QUARTER | 12 h | 18 h | 24 h | 6 h |
| FULL MOON | 18 h | 24 h | 6 h | 12 h |
| LAST QUARTER | 24 h | 6 h | 12 h | 18 h |

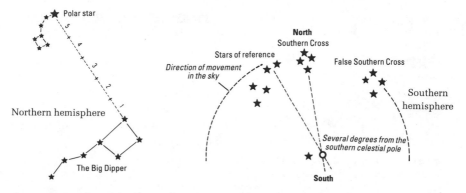

**Approximate determinations of variations in latitude according to the height of the stars above the horizon. (According to Callahan, *À la Dérive*, Laffont)**

## ORIENTATION ACCORDING TO THE PHASES OF THE MOON

At midnight the moon indicates the south when it is full, the west in the first quarter, the east in the last quarter, etc., as illustrated in the table on p. 327.

## ORIENTATION BY NIGHT

Stars are visible all year round if the sky is clear, and they can easily be located. The diagrams below illustrate how to determine direction by the stars in the northern and southern hemispheres.

## TRAJECTORIES OF THE SUN ACCORDING TO THE SEASONS

■ In a given place, south is indicated by the position of the sun at noon, solar time.
■ At the spring and fall equinoxes, April 21 and September 21, the sun rises in the east at 6:00 A.M. and sets in the west at 6:00 P.M. solar time.
■ At the summer solstice, June 21, the sun rises in the northeast at 4:15 A.M. and sets in the northwest at 7:45 A.M. solar time.
■ At the winter solstice, December 21, the sun rises in the southeast at 7:40 A.M. and sets in the southwest at 4:20 P.M. solar time.

# DETERMINING A POSITION

## LONGITUDE

Determining longitude is very easy using the sun and a watch, by comparing the difference in time between the local midday and Greenwich Mean Time at that moment. Local midday is determined

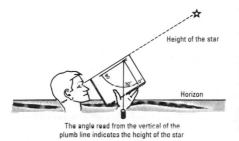

The angle read from the vertical of the plumb line indicates the height of the star

be plus or minus 4°. In a survival situation—a shipwrecked person drifting, a hiker making daily progress on foot—it is often more important to determine the daily difference in longitude, rather than to determine the precise position.

by means of the shadow thrown by a pole, as described above. The sun is vertically over the local meridian at the moment when the shadow is the shortest.

Assume that the difference in time is 6 hours and 52 minutes. To determine longitude, multiply the hours by 15° and the minutes by .25°, and then add these totals together. Thus, in our example $(6 \times 15°) + (52 \times 0.25°) = 103°$ longitude.

For greater accuracy, you will need a time equation table, which would enable you to correct variations in the angular speed of the sun's movement according to the seasons. Even without this table, though, the maximum error will

## LATITUDE

In the northern hemisphere, one of the easiest methods is to measure the height of the polar star above the horizon in degrees. The sextant is the scientific instrument designed to do this, and it is very accurate. Unfortunately, it is seldom available in a survival situation and you will often have to make do with some kind of protractor. The height of the polar star corresponds approximately to the latitude at which the observation is made.

Steven Callahan used an even more archaic means to calculate his position during his 72-day odyssey in the middle of the Atlantic, by simply using pencils:

---

### Basic Navigation

"I estimated my east-west position by guessing the approximate speed and direction of the current, and then adding to it the speed of my drift. To estimate latitude, I fashioned a sextant out of pencils.

"Above to the left: the North Star, or the Polar Star, is directly above the North Pole (the magnetic north is a totally different problem). You can

see that the man, above left, is looking straight at the Polar Star, an angle of 90° from the horizontal plane, i.e. his horizon. The man at the equator sees the Polar Star on his horizontal plane. The man, on page 330, on the raft, is looking straight at the Polar Star on the horizon, and therefore he must be at the equator—the man standing on the globe between the equator and the pole is looking at a point at ×° above the horizontal to

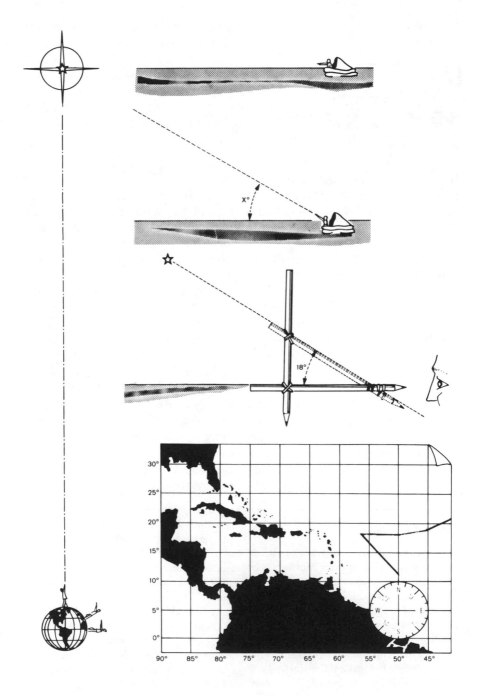

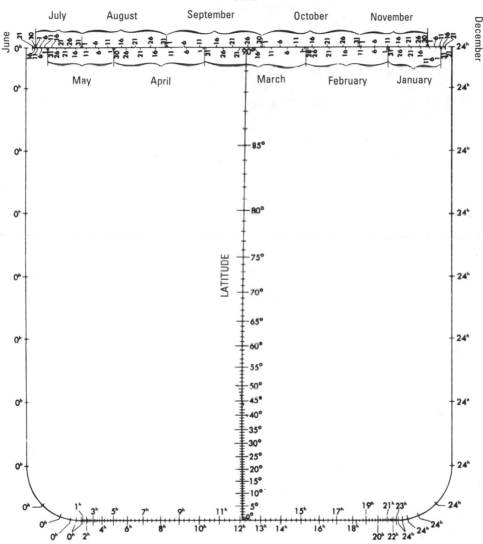

DATE

**Diagram to determine latitude according to the length of the day**

see the Polar Star. Therefore he is at ×° latitude, exactly like the man, a little lower, on the raft.

"I joined three pencils together, and angled two of the arms at 18°, which is my estimated latitude. I use the compass dial on the map as a protractor, as it is divided into 360°. First I must align the horizontal pencil with the horizon. Then, trying not to move the instrument, I lower my eye so as to be able to see Polaris along the raised pencil. If Polaris is not aligned, I adjust the pencils until it is, and then measure my latitude using the compass dial."

---

Another method of determining latitude can be used if the stars are not visible at night. It makes use of the exact length of the day, between the beginning of sunrise and the end of sunset. This length of time for a given day in the year differs depending on the latitude. All you need is a watch, a straightedge and a double-entry table like the one below to be able to determine latitude precisely.

For example: On August 20, a person determines that the day is 13 hours and 54 minutes. Lay the straightedge on the diagonal between the date and the amount of time, and the line it forms crosses the central scale of latitude at 45° 30'.

# THE SURVIVAL DIET

- Hunger

- The Dietary Needs of an Adult in a Normal Situation

- Elementary Principles

- Carbohydrates

- Proteins

- Lipids

- Vitamins

- Mineral Salts

- Diet and Special Situations

- Drugs

Some situations make increased muscular activity necessary (for example, forced marching on rugged terrain), others involve rapid use of the involuntary muscle system, and still others demand specific increased tolerances, to cold, to heat, to lack of oxygen, to seasickness. Finally, some survival situations require an improvement of specific physiological functions: better eyesight (traveling underground, traveling across blinding snow), or easier digestion (diving, underwater hunting).

There are appropriate dietary measures for all of these cases. In both types of survival situations— those that are planned for and those that require improvisation—availability and portability of food must also be considered. Therefore we will cover here both the general principles of diet and the minimal needs for specific survival situations.

## HUNGER

Hunger can occur in many "individual vs. environment" conflicts, but it is seldom a cause of death in itself. It can become the cause if a different type of stress is added to it, especially cold, which consumes a great number of calories. In other words, a person can "die of hunger" at the same time as he dies of cold, since adaptation to cold requires calories that an undernourished body cannot supply.

Hunger and appetite are not synonymous. Hunger is a biological process that occurs in the stomach. Appetite is the desire to eat, which is in the mind and depends largely on willpower. Therefore one must use common sense and not use up reserves of food at the first sign of stress.

In fact, many people have a tendency to try to forget their present problems by overeating. This natural inclination is well known in naval forces, where meals are often the only true recreation, enabling the men to forget their isolation and the absence of a social life. Many sailors and submariners return from their missions having put on considerable weight. In a survival situation such behavior is particularly detrimental, as it prematurely exhausts reserves and causes serious group conflicts. When the people on the raft from the French frigate *La Méduse*, which was shipwrecked in 1816, indulged in acts of cannibalism after drifting for only two days, their actions must have been the result not of hunger but of a sudden collective behavioral aberration, a fear of being deprived. In fact, it could be said that a person who has always eaten whenever he was hungry— at whatever time he wanted and in unlimited quantities—has in some sense a food addiction. If he suddenly finds himself in a survival situation, he could easily act in self-destructive ways, giving priority to the quest for food instead of the search for water or other vital emergency measures. A person incapable of sustaining a long fast should be identified before the expedition starts. The only way to identify such a person is by means of a simulated situation, such as a trip to the mountains that lasts several days, or a cruise at sea. With the exception of cold regions, death is due to thirst rather than hunger when neither food nor water is available.

During the first few days, the feeling of hunger can cause cramping stomach pains that radiate toward the anterior and toward the shoulders. These cramps should not force a person to use his reserves: They are not serious and they usually disappear on the third or fourth day of the fast.

The body cannot be trusted to select the food it needs instinctively. It is true that at a high altitude one spontaneously has an aversion to meat and that on an ice floe one will be inclined to eat fats, but in a survival situation, even more than in a normal situation, one must learn to control those impulses and distrust them.

## THE DIETARY NEEDS OF AN ADULT IN A NORMAL SITUATION

■ The needs of the basc metabolism decrease with age, physical training and sleep. A woman's metabolism is lower and, as a result, she needs fewer calories.

■ The metabolism is increased by stress (up to 50 percent), a cigarette (up to 20 percent, which may explain why some smokers are so thin), caffeine, and other stimulants (up to 50 percent).

■ The calorie need for muscular activity varies greatly, depending on the activity: for a 150-pound person, 600 calories per hour for a cross-country ski course at 10 miles per hour or a long-distance walking race; 660 for long-distance cycling at 13 miles per hour; 500 for kayaking, rugby football, or boxing; 420 for singles tennis; and 350 for doubles tennis. An expedition to the Far North will require about 3,000 calories per day.

■ SDA, or specific dynamic action, describes the efficiency with which the body extracts calories from various foods. For example, the digestive tract uses 30 calories to extract 100 calories from protein, giving an SDA of 30%. The SDA is 12 percent for lipids, 6 percent for carbohydrates. The lower the SDA, the more efficiently the food is metabolized.

The body's primary source of energy is glucose, which is a carbohydrate. Fats, on the other hand, produce more energy for each gram consumed. For these reasons, carbohydrates and fats are the best sources of energy. Protein is least effective because it has to be extensively metabolized by the body to make glucose.

A body that weighs 154 pounds (70 kilograms) is composed of 88 pounds (40 kilograms) oxygen, 33 pounds (15 kilograms) carbon, and several pounds of hydrogen and nitrogen. In addition, it includes some amounts of minerals, metals, metalloids and vitamins in very small quantities.

# ELEMENTARY PRINCIPLES

These principles can be followed even in a survival situation with very limited rations because they concern methods, not quantities.

## DIVISION OF CALORIES

Carbohydrates = 55 percent of the total calorie intake.
Lipids = 30 percent of the total calorie intake.
Proteins = 15 percent of the total calorie intake.

## THE IMPORTANCE OF BREAKFAST

Breakfast should provide 25 percent of the daily calorie ration. The English and American habits in this area are better than the Continental. The French, for example, eat almost no breakfast, continuing to fast between dinner the previous evening at 8:00 P.M. and lunch at 1:00 P.M.—17 hours with hardly any food except the 50 to 100 calories of a Continental breakfast. Between 1:00 P.M. and 8:00 P.M. they usually have two big meals, absorbing 3,000 calories within seven hours, versus a couple of dozen during the subsequent 17 hours. Feelings of exhaustion at the end of the morning, and the host of work accidents and of circulatory problems that accompany it, are the consequence of these eating habits.

## OPTIMUM MEAL PLANE

Eating four or five times a day is more efficient than one or two large meals. Having this number of meals avoids the tiredness that often follows meals and secondary hypoglycemia that follows meals that are too rich. Irrespective of what reserves are available in a survival situation, they should be divided up in the same way.

# CARBOHYDRATES

Carbohydrates are sugars in the broadest sense. Their primary function is to supply energy and they should provide 55 percent of the overall calorie ration. Glucose is the final form of utilization of all carbohydrates, the basic energy molecule. Glycogen is the form in which the sugars are stored. There are no more than 400 grams at one time in the body, which is very little compared to the pounds of fats that an individual can store. The 400 grams are distributed in such a way that 50 grams are in the liver and 350 grams in the extracellular fluids and, above all, in the muscles. During physical exertion, a person consumes 3 grams of glycogen a minute and therefore has great difficulty in continuing this activity much beyond two hours without additional intake of sugar. If there is no intake of sugar, the fats will take up the slack but they are much less efficient.

■ **Monosaccharides** are the simplest carbohydrates and are directly assimilated during digestion.

■ **Disaccharides,** on the other hand, must undergo digestive hydrolysis to be transformed into monosaccharides, and therefore they are "slower": During intense exertion, a glucose tablet is better than a lump of sugar for providing quick available energy.

■ **Polysaccharides** provide more than 10 molecules of monosaccharides through hydrolysis. Starch is the most important and contains a large amount of glucose. Cellulose can be found in the bran of cereals, in vegetables and in fruits. It is not broken down by man's digestive juices, and it acts as roughage while moving through the intestines. It sometimes has a troubling laxative effect. While fruits and vegetables, particularly in dried form, have distinct benefits (see below), food rich in cellulose should be avoided as a source of carbohydrates in a survival situation.

■ **Sugar and candy** should not make up more than 10 percent of the total calorie intake because they contain only sucrose and no vitamins or mineral salts.

■ **Honey** is made up of 50 percent fructose and 50 percent glucose, which makes it a good energy-providing carbohydrate that can be used very quickly. Therefore it is a backup ration for an athlete, and it is obviously valuable on an expedition.

■ **Chocolate** has many beneficial properties: It has a high caloric value (due to its high content of lipids), considerable quantities of group B vitamins, and tonic and diuretic properties. It contains magnesium, which is important when performing sports. In other words, it is a food that is very important for survival. (There are dark chocolates on the market that do not melt even in hot latitudes.)

■ **Vegetables** contain plenty of carbohydrates, a few proteins and no lipids, but their primary content is 80 to 90 percent water and therefore they should not be taken along for a survival situation unless they are dehydrated. On the other hand, dry vegetables are very important, especially when enriched with meat or fish. They can also be dehydrated in order to make up dried soup packages. These packages are very useful because they are light, can be preserved for a long time, and take up little space, and their diversity can provide a varied diet.

■ **Fruits** also contain 80 to 90 percent water and only carbohydrates. Their acidic taste is due to organic acids, which make them into great appetite stimulants. Only dried fruits should be taken along in a survival situation. Their significant content of vitamin C is important, but it is obvious that a compressed package is more practical than several pounds of fresh fruit. Dehydrated fruits can be bought, and there are also naturally dry fruits that are very nourishing, such as dates and figs. They are easy to digest and provide an excellent boost of carbohydrates and minerals, which is very useful in a survival situation.

## CARBOHYDRATES AND STRESS

In a survival situation carbohydrates should make up 55 percent of calorie intake. Carbohydrates are the essential energy source for a heavy laborer, an athlete or a person who is under stress in general. More than 55 to 60 percent would be excessive because sugars curb the appetite, and such an excessively high carbohydrate diet could also mean that the individual is not obtaining sufficient quantities of proteins and lipids. If, on the other hand, the diet contains less than 50 percent carbohydrates, physical performance decreases considerably. Experiments have also shown that during exertion the muscles' consumption of carbohydrates increases by a factor of 20—the same increase as that of oxygen.

Environment considerably modifies the body's need for carbohydrates: cold, heat, high altitude, or a stay under water or under ground cause additional stress that makes demands on carbohydrates in the same way as physical exertion. Rats subjected to a temperature of 33.8°F (1°C) for 45 days had extremely diminished reserves of carbohydrates despite a food intake that was much higher than that of a control group. This suggests that, in very cold environments, the body uses its sugar reserves before any of the others. In man, increased hyper-

# FOOD SOURCES OF CARBOHYDRATES

| FOODS | COMMENTS | CALORIC VALUE (calories per 100 grams) |
|---|---|---|
| FLOUR (bran) and SEMOLINA (wheat) | Difficult to utilize without preparation | 350 |
| BREAD, RUSKS | Easier to digest toasted or stale | 250 |
| COOKIES, PASTRIES | Provide more calories than bread | 400 |
| GINGERBREAD | Easily digestible | 320 |
| RICE | Easily digestible | 110 |
| PASTAS | Contain exclusively starch | 375 |
| POTATOES | Contain potassium and vitamin C | 80 |
| CEREALS | Corn flakes, tapioca | |
| DRY VEGETABLES (split peas, lentils, beans) | Contain 23 percent proteins, vitamin B and trace elements | 330 |
| SUGAR (beet, cane) | Only sucrose. Nothing else that is quickly utilizable | 400 |
| HONEY | Composed of fructose and glucose. Quickly utilizable | 320 |
| CANDIES, CONFECTIONERY | Same as sugar | |
| CHOCOLATE | Cocoa plus cinnamon sugar, vanilla, hazelnuts, powdered milk . . . vitamins, magnesium | 500 |
| JAMS, JELLIES | Few vitamins | 275 |
| PULSES | 70 percent carbohydrate (fructose). Trace elements (potassium, magnesium, iron, copper) | 335 |
| DRIED FRUITS | 70 percent carbohydrate (fructose). Vitamin C (potassium, iron, copper) | 275 |

glycemia has also been observed when the internal temperature drops. Man cannot tolerate cold for long without this increase in blood sugar. This is why hot drinks enhanced with honey or sweetened concentrated milk and snacks based on dried fruits are so important in cold regions.

In a hot region, the calorie needs are lower (3,000 calories), but any increase should be primarily in carbohydrates and the percentage may go as high as 60 percent.

At an altitude above 16,500 feet (5,000 meters), water intake is of primary importance and the daily food ration should contain over 4,000 calories while maintaining the proportion of 55 percent carbohydrates. Above 19,700 feet (6,000 meters) the ration decreases because the body is merely in a state of "suspended animation" and never accepts more than 2,500 to 3,000 calories. In this case, too, carbohydrates should make up at least 55 percent of the ration.

# PROTEINS

Only proteins can provide the nitrogen and amino acids necessary to maintain homeostasis. The amino acids are to proteins what glucose is to carbohydrates: the simplest base chemical element.

Proteins are large molecules that are the principle factor in very diverse functions, ranging from the creation of the contractile material of the muscles to the composition of hormones, enzymes and antibodies—all of them molecules that are necessary for adaptation to different types of stress, infection and allergies. Dietary proteins supply about 30 amino acids, including eight that are indispensable because the body cannot synthesize them. A total lack of intake of these eight acids will lead to death just as inevitably as lack of water or food. The only difference is the length

of time of survival: only a matter of days without water but several weeks without proteins, i.e., the time it takes the body to exhaust its own protein reserves. Where protein intake is limited, there will be a rapid loss of muscles and an attendant decrease in physical strength.

Thus, in a survival situation, obtaining the minimum vital amount of these proteins is essential: The shipwrecked person should fish or filter plankton, and the person who is lost should eat any living materials he can find, however repugnant.

In a "dynamic survival" situation, i.e., one that consumes energy (physical exertion, tolerance to cold or heat, etc.) carbohydrates take precedence; in a "static survival" situation (for example, imprisonment) proteins will be the determining factors to maintain vital functions in the long run.

The complex catabolism of proteins leads to nitrogen residues that are found in the urine: urea, uric acid, ammonia and creatinine. These nitrogen residues can be evidence either of the metabolism of normal dietary rations, or of the gradual self-destruction of the tissues in a body whose protein needs are not being fulfilled.

## FOOD SOURCES OF PROTEINS

The best proteins are animal proteins, but some plants do contain small quantities of some of the important ones (dry vegetables, cereals, bread). Contrary to widespread beliefs, all meats supply the same nutritive value, whether they are red or white, well cooked or rare. Their primary importance is that they supply 15 to 20 percent proteins, and this is the only parameter that one should take into account. Having said this, if there is a choice between several types of meat or parts of meat, it would be useful to remember the following in a survival situation:

■ In a questionable region, cooking is the only guarantee against the dangers of parasitosis, pork worm, or taenia. Contrary to what was believed for a long time, meat does not necessarily have to be eaten raw to retain its nutritious qualities.

■ Corned beef, badmouthed by generations of soldiers, is still an excellent means of providing proteins, but it is a little bulky to carry along.

■ Pemmican, which goes back to the 19th century, is prepared from concentrated dried meat and continues to be an excellent means of survival in all environments (see the chapter on "The Poles").

■ Liver contains 20 to 22 percent proteins, as well as numerous trace elements and vitamins: group B vitamins ($B_1$, $B_2$, $B_6$, nicotinic acid, $B_{12}$), vitamin A, and vitamin C (30 mg per 3.5 ounces [100 grams]). Any kind of liver is valuable, except that of carnivorous animals, which can be poisonous. The organ is a virtual biochemical factory, synthesizing, catabolizing, transforming and storing all kinds of molecules. Because of its functions, all nutritional elements can be found in it in significant quantities, and therefore the liver can be a primary source of protein.

■ Gamebirds usually provide meat that contains few lipids, but ducks and geese are rich in lipids (up to 33 percent) because of their thick protective layer of fat.

■ Fish is as nutritious as other meats. Trout, eel and salmon can be smoked and preserved for long periods of time. Herring, cod and haddock can be salted or smoked to preserve them.

■ In a survival situation it is useful to know the fat content of specific fish. In the rivers, salmon and eels contain five times as many lipids as trout: 25 percent vs. 5 percent. In the sea, tuna fish contains five times as many lipids as rays, dolphin fish or the spotted dog-fish. During the 76 days when he was drifting in the Atlantic, Steven Callahan was only able to catch dolphin fish, and a school of them constantly harassed his rubber boat. This single source of protein enabled him to survive and retain the muscles he was using (especially his arms and chest), but he did not have an ounce of fat on him when he was rescued. Molluscs and crustaceans are of course edible, but remember: they are very poor in lipids; they may cause an allergic reaction; they can be toxic and, above all, they can contain viruses because of their large filtration capacity (several dozen quarts of seawater per day).

■ Eggs: The yolk is very rich in proteins and lipids and is the most nutritious part. The white contains most of the sodium but is poor in lipids. The proteins cannot be utilized by the body unless the white is cooked. Eating raw eggs may be practical under certain circumstances, but doing so deprives one of the proteins contained in the white: A raw egg is less nutritious than a boiled egg.

■ Milk has a high value as a source of protein (the proportion of amino acids is very good) and is man's primary source of calcium. It has a perfect balance of the necessary amount of phosphorus, and a small quantity of vitamin D. Therefore, it plays an important role in a survival situation if one can find it locally, and it can be taken along on an expedition, though not in its natural form, which is impractically heavy. Two forms should be considered in a survival situation: sweetened concentrated milk, which provides an excellent source of energy due to its enrichment with sugar; and whole milk in powdered form, which contains less water (less than 6 percent) and has a very good calorie/weight ratio: 500 calories per 100 grams.

■ As far as milk products are concerned, only cheeses with a low water content should be considered: especially Gruyère, which keeps for a long time and contains only 35 percent water. It is rich in lipids, protein and calcium. It contains almost no carbohydrates.

## COMPARISON OF PROTEIN SOURCES

In a survival situation it is not a disaster if the individual cannot find meat as long as he has fish, eggs or milk; 100 grams of meat can easily be replaced by:

■ 100 grams of fish
■ 2 eggs
■ 250 grams of sweetened concentrated milk

## FOOD SOURCES OF PROTEINS

| FOODS | COMMENTS (Composition, method of consumption) | CALORIC VALUE (per 100 grams) |
|---|---|---|
| BUTCHER'S MEAT | 15–20 percent proteins + phosphate, iron and vitamin B₁, | 170 |
| LIVER | The most important. 20–22 percent proteins + iron + trace elements + phosphorus + B vitamins + vitamin A + vitamin C. | 115 |
| OFFAL FEET, CHEEKS SNOUT, SWEETBREADS KIDNEYS TRIPE BRAINS | To be eaten quickly. Not very abundant in muscles, to be eaten if there is nothing else. | |
| CORNED BEEF | | 235 |
| PEMMICAN | Mixture of meat and dried fats. Easy to preserve. | 590 |
| GAME | To be eaten before it is gamy, and should be roasted (lean meat). | |
| POULTRY | Comparable to butcher's meat. Chickens, geese and ducks are rich in lipids (33 percent). | |
| FISH | 15–20 percent proteins + phosphorus, sulfur, iron, copper, iodine, group B vitamins, vitamin A + vitamin D. | 80–200 depending on whether they are lean or fatty |
| MOLLUSCS AND CRUSTACEANS | 10 percent proteins, very few lipids (1 percent) Rich in trace elements (manganese, copper, iodine and zinc), phosphorus, vitamins B₁, A and D. | |

## FOOD SOURCES OF PROTEINS (*continued*)

| FOODS | COMMENTS (Composition, method of consumption) | CALORIC VALUE (per 100 grams) |
|---|---|---|
| WHITE<br><br>EGGS<br><br>YOLK | 13 percent proteins, no lipids, sodium.<br><br>13 percent proteins + 12 percent lipids + iron + potassium + calcium + vitamins $B_1$, $B_2$, A and D. | 160 |
| SWEETENED CONCENTRATED MILK | | 350 |
| POWDERED WHOLE MILK | Very important for survival. | 500 |
| DRY CHEESES | Contain up to 30 percent animal proteins, clearly more than meat itself, and there are no problems with preservation. | 400 |

- 60 grams of powdered milk
- 30 grams of a solid cheese such as Gruyère

### MINIMUM DAILY PROTEIN INTAKE

Generally speaking, 1 gram per 2.2 pounds (1 kilogram) of weight per day is enough for average physical exertion, but not necessarily for intense activity. Physical activity is accompanied by an excretion of nitrogen (through the urine), which is evidence of the utilization of proteins. If the intake is adequate, these proteins will be dietary proteins; otherwise they will be the body's own proteins. If there is no protein intake, death will occur once 25 to 30 percent of the body proteins have been used up, and this will occur faster if the body is deprived of carbohydrates and lipids. The minimum in a survival situation is approximately 30 grams of protein per day for an average adult.

### THE QUALITY OF DIFFERENT PROTEINS AND THEIR APPLICATION IN A SURVIVAL SITUATION

One protein can be replaced by another as long as there is a sufficient intake of amino acids. Amino acid intake is more efficient when the composition of the proteins is similar to that of the human body:

■ Animal proteins contain essential amino acids in amounts that more closely meet human amino acid requirements than do plant proteins. Therefore priority should be given to animal proteins. However, mixtures of different plant proteins can be nutritionally equivalent to animal proteins.
■ The perfect situation is to provide the body with proteins that have similar proportions of amino acids to its own.

Naturally, no voluntary scientific experiment has ever been done, but numerous examples of forced cannibalism argue for this means of survival, which is very efficient though barbaric. After spending two months at 13,000 feet (4,000 meters) in severe cold and extremely stressful conditions, the Uruguayan rugby players lost in the Andes after their plane crashed (1972) were able to perform sustained, intense physical exertion due to their unique source of food: the corpses of their companions who had died at the beginning of their ordeal. Two of the survivors were medical students and directed the selection of the starving people to the most nutritious parts: first the muscles

and, to the extent that they got used to their macabre work, the liver and other nutritious internal organs. This food not only enabled them to survive—they also launched several exploratory excursions into the mountains, one of which finally led them back to civilization.

## STEROIDS AND SURVIVAL

It is appropriate to mention steroids in relation to proteins, because all the hormone drugs given to athletes aim to encourage muscular hypertrophy, which can only be done through protein intake.

Some high-protein diets have been used to increase the muscle weight of athletes (javelin or hammer throwers, weight lifters, and body builders). The American weightlifter Paul Anderson was the strongest man in the world in 1955 and drank a bottle of milk between each series of muscular exercises. This practice was based more on folklore than science, but today's anabolic steroids certainly increase muscle bulk, though with various unpleasant side effects.

They should certainly not be included in a survival kit, especially as stress causes the secretion of testosterone, a male hormone that has an anabolic effect similar to steroids and induces the optimum use of the proteins at the body's disposal. The only justified action preceding an expedition is to gain weight in a balanced manner, that includes all areas:

■ the provision of an energy reserve through a significant intake of carbohydrates, which will increase the muscle and hepatic reserves of glycogen

■ an increase in the muscle mass through a balanced intake of proteins

■ an increase in the adipose tissue through the provision of a reserve in fats (lipids)

## LIPIDS

The cells of the brain and kidneys depend exclusively on glucose to function normally. All other tissues, especially the muscles, are able to use not only carbohydrates but also, if necessary, fatty acids. The fatty acids are the final unit of the decomposition of lipids, just as glucose is the base unit of carbohydrates and amino acids are that of proteins. Lipids are very important both for survival and as a potential energy reserve.

A man weighing 154 pounds (70 kg kilograms) has about 22 pounds (10 kilograms) of reserve fats, deposited mainly under the skin in the so-called adipose layer and around some internal organs. Based on a caloric value of 9.3 calories per gram, this reserve therefore represents approximately 95,000 calories for a normal individual. This number explains why it is possible to survive for several weeks without eating anything at all if the person is at rest in an environment of normal temperature. It should also be compared to the 50,000 calories stored in proteins, but only 3,000 in glycogen. If there is a need for energy, proteins and lipids convert into glycogen.

There is a close link between lipids and carbohydrates, as the metabolism of fatty acids directly depends on that of glucose:

■ If the dietary intake of carbohydrates is sufficient for the physical exertion, the lipids will be placed in reserve in the fat tissue.
■ If there is no food intake, the lipids in reserve will be used to help create glycogen. This is also what happens if there is stress through the action of secreted hormones — adrenocorticotrophic hormone (ACTH), catecholamines, thyroid stimulating hormone (TSH). One of many adaptations will occur to help the body use all possible channels of defense when nourishment is lacking. The loss in weight, due to the decrease in fat reserves, will occur more rapidly if the fast is accompanied by significant physi-

cal exertion, or by a cold atmosphere.

## FOOD SOURCES OF LIPIDS

Fats can come from animals or plants, and they are more beneficial if they are easy to digest. The metabolism of lipids depends on several factors:

■ Liquidity: the more liquid they are, the more the fatty substances can be broken down by the digestive juices. Therefore oils are easier to assimilate than animal fat.
■ The fusion point: if the fusion point is below 98.6°F (37°C)—body temperature the sub stances will be digested more easily.
■ Preparation: fatty substances decompose above a specific critical temperature and produce indigestible, or even toxic, byproducts.

In a survival situation it is very difficult to take along foods such as butter and cream—fats that melt easily and contain a lot of water. A useful source is lard, which is obtained through the fusion of the fats that surround the muscles and internal organs of animals. The product is very rich in lipids: 95 percent, compared to 85 percent for butter. It provides 900 calories per 100 grams compared to 750 for butter. Its only disadvantage is lack of vitamins.

Oily fruits, such as olives, and nuts, such as hazelnuts, almonds and peanuts, are also rich in lipids (50 to 60 percent on average with a caloric value of 600 calories per 100 grams) and in vitamins. Many foods also contain "composition" lipids: cheese and milk, as well as fatty meats (mutton, pork), fatty fish (tuna, salmon), and fatty game (goose, duck).

## LIPID NEEDS

The ideal proportion of calories provided by lipids should be 30 percent, i.e., 120 grams per day in a daily ration of 3,500 calories. Ideally, half of the lipid intake should be through fats in dressings (50 to 60 grams of oil, butter or margarine). In a survival situation, it is difficult to keep to this proportion and it would be better to proceed according to availability: for example, 100 grams of olive oil provide 900 necessary calories and contain carotene, vitamin E and essential fatty acids.

Although the energy they supply is useful, it is not the only reason why a minimum daily dose of fats is indispensable. Fats play an important role in supporting fat-soluble vitamins (A, D and E). Recently it was discovered that these vitamins are significant to the functioning of muscle cells.

The body is able to put significant amounts of fat in reserve, while proteins and sugars can only be stored in limited amounts. Though these fat reserves may have been increased before leaving on an expedition, they should always be kept within reasonable limits so that the excess weight will not be detrimental. Recent experiments have demonstrated the very rapid utilization of non-esterified fatty acids (NEFA) by active muscles. The concentration of the NEFA in the blood is 10 times less than that of glucose but its turnover is 40 times faster, and a single molecule of NEFA provides three times more energy (through the Krebs cycle) than a molecule of glucose. Should one therefore conclude that the fats should be substituted for sugars? No, the superiority of high-carbohydrate diets over high-lipid diets during continued exertion is unquestionable, but the NEFA are a form of complementary energy that is instantly utilizable by the muscles in the same way as glucose. The heart, in particular, draws the greater part of its energy from the NEFA.

Canadian researchers have verified that muscular and psychomotor output is better if fatty substances are ingested every two hours. In a survival situation, it should be remembered that, although sugars are easy to use and are sufficient, they can be replaced by fats for intense exertion if necessary. Lipids are especially highly recommended in one area of survival: adaptation to cold.

## LIPIDS AND ADAPTATION TO COLD

Exposure to cold means an increased need for calories, and it is logical to believe that lipids, which have more than double the calorie value of sugars and proteins, could play a decisive role. This theory has, in fact, been verified by experiment.

Johnson and Kark studied two groups of soldiers performing the same activities, one group working in a temperature of 91.4°F (33°C) and the other in a temperature of −27.4°F (−33°C). The former needed 3,000 calories per day, the latter needed 5,000.

Not all people subjected to cold have a "hunger for fats," as used to be alleged, but rather just plain hunger—for proteins and carbohydrates as well as for lipids.

There are three determining factors in the struggle against cold:

■ The overall calorie ration must be increased (to 4,000 calories).
■ Proteins are of no use in the struggle against cold, and they may even be an aggravating factor.
■ In addition to carbohydrate intake, the intake of lipids should be increased because of their high caloric value on the one hand, and because they increase the adipose layer on the other. This layer plays a role in thermogenesis by increasing the thickness of the

"shell" that protects the nucleus and, in addition, it forms a significant calorie reserve that is utilizable on demand.

# VITAMINS

When preparing for a survival situation, one should understand the necessity of vitamins. There are multivitamin preparations on the market that contain all the necessary vitamins. They can be taken along on an expedition in addition to vitamin C.

When caught unexpectedly in a survival situation, remember that the liver of all mammals and fishes is rich in vitamins, both in variety and in quantity, and therefore it is the first part of the anatomy that should be eaten—always avoiding the livers of carnivores, which are toxic. Cod liver oil is as rich in vitamins as it is objectionable in taste.

## VITAMIN C (ASCORBIC ACID)

Man can neither synthesize vitamin C nor keep it in reserve, so it has to be supplied on a daily basis through green vegetables or fresh fruit. These foods are too heavy to carry along (85 percent water) and are often difficult to find during an expedition. In addition, the needs in a situation where exertion is necessary are 200 to 300 mg per day, i.e., twice that of a person not engaged in physical exercise. This amount would mean eating 1.5 pounds (700 grams) of tomatoes, 6.6 pounds (3 kilograms) of green vegetables, pears, apples, or carrots, or 13.2 pounds (6 kilograms) of grapes! Looking at the positive side, a person would only need to eat 14 ounces (400 grams) of citrus fruits. In addition to this, cooking destroys 50 percent of the vitamin C (and 20 percent of vitamin B₁). Vitamin C is extremely sensitive and simply storing or transporting it also means a considerable loss. For all these reasons, 500-mg vitamin C tablets should be taken along.

In contrast to some other vitamins, it is impossible to overdose on vitamin C, as the body only takes what it needs and eliminates the rest very quickly. The high doses of 2 to 3 grams advocated by some trainers to prevent fatigue are useless.

The vitamin has a positive effect on physical condition, resistance to fatigue and acclimatization to cold. It seems that it also increases the body's resistance to histaminic shock (venomous bites, insect stings) and may play a role in fighting infection, combining with microbial toxins in order to neutralize them (thus preventing infections that could be facilitated under stressful conditions).

On the biochemical level, vitamin C serves as the transfer element between vitamins and hormones (which are important in adaptation to stress); it increases the storage of glycogen in the liver and muscles, and it encourages hematopoiesis (an increase in the number of red blood cells, necessary for adaptation to high altitudes).

Vitamin C deficiency causes scurvy, a disease that results in the demineralization of the bone, skin degeneration and loosening of the teeth. This must be avoided.

## OTHER VITAMINS

We will only consider those vitamins that are most useful within the framework of survival, and we will disregard those that could have a "doping" effect in some sports activities (especially vitamins $B_6$ and $B_{12}$).

### Vitamin B₁ (Thiamine)

This is present in liver, as well as in the husks of cereals and in yeast. It especially encourages the storage of glycogen in the liver and the transmission of nerve impulses (and thus reflexes). On the physiological level, it improves performance and it decreases fatigue and the time necessary for recuperation. It also helps control muscle cramps. Lack of this vitamin causes beriberi, which killed thousands of sailors right through to the 19th century before it was discovered that the disease was caused by the ingestion of white rice without the husk. The latter carbohydrate was the only one found on board most ocean-going ships. The disease is still widespread in Asia where "polished rice" is eaten.

### Vitamin A (Retinol)

An adequate supply of this vitamin is important for actions that necessitate good night vision: speleology, night flying, deep-sea diving, nighttime competitions. Deficiency of this vitamin causes a loss of twilight vision. During World War II, pilots who flew at night "stuffed" themselves with carrots, rich in carotene, which is the antecedent of the vitamin. Vitamin A also possesses anti-glare properties, which makes it very useful in some very bright environments. Therefore it can be recommended for Nordic ski trips. Vitamin A can be found in milk, butter, egg yolks, liver, kidneys, carrots, papayas and mangoes.

### Vitamin D

Deficiency of this vitamin causes rickets. Provitamin D is transformed into vitamin D by ultraviolet rays. This vitamin enables the fixation of calcium and phosphorus to the bones and teeth. In addition, it plays a role in muscle tension, as the latter's stimulation depends on calcium.

# MINERAL SALTS

About 20 of these are indispensable for life and are an integral part of the skeleton (calcium, phosphorus) and of some enzyme systems (iron for hemoglobin, which is necessary to transport oxygen in the blood); others regulate the functions of the cells, especially in respect to neurological and muscular stimulation (sodium, calcium, magnesium). Still others are necessary in trace amounts: fluorine for bones and teeth, zinc for insulin, cobalt for vitamin $B_{12}$; and there are many others whose role has not yet been determined (such as copper, manganese, arsenic and lithium).

There is no need to become obsessed with these trace elements in a survival situation that lasts for several weeks or months for two reasons: the time is not long enough to cause a dangerous imbalance, and the smallest intake of food—either animal or plant— even if it is irregular, will supplement the requirement of these trace elements, as they are quantitatively very minor. The minerals that must be taken into consideration in a survival situation are as follows:

■ Potassium (K): necessary for muscle efficiency. It is found in large quantities in milk and in a large number of plant foods, especially fruits and dried vegetables. In a survival situation, a person should not burden himself with fresh fruits, but he should have dried fruits and/or vegetables. The daily requirement is 0.50 gram and this is usually supplied even by a restricted diet.

■ Sodium (Na): its concentration in sweat can be quintupled during physical exertion in a hot climate, and an intake of 5 to 15 grams per day is enough. Most of this amount is provided through a normal diet, and salt tablets must not be taken if there is no intake of water. Deficiency in salt causes painful muscle cramps, feelings of malaise, insomnia and sometimes fever.

■ Phosphorus (P): necessary for catabolism; it can be found in fish, meat, liver, eggs, milk and cereals.

■ Magnesium (M): Some believe that its deficiency, together with that of calcium, leads to a tendency to have convulsive seizures. Without following this rather reductive medical theory, it can be said that some athletes lack magnesium, as do malnourished individuals. The deficiency causes fatigue and muscle contractions (both of striated and smooth muscles). Magnesium can be found in starches, oily fruits and chocolate.

■ Calcium (Ca): necessary for normal neuromuscular and heart activity, for the formation of bones and teeth, for coagulation, and for some enzyme systems; there is often an insufficient intake in a survival situation. In practice, it is impossible to eat enough calcium unless one has milk or cheese, and therefore calcium tablets should be taken along.

■ Iron (Fe): necessary to transport oxygen. Iron is found in liver, meat, dried vegetables, dried fruits, cereals, eggs and chocolate. A person can become deficient in iron in a survival situation, as well as in conjunction with muscular activities in the mountains (increase in ventilation and polycythemia).

In summary, the problem of mineral intake can be ranked after that of carbohydrates, lipids and proteins, since they are often found in the same food source.

# DIET AND SPECIAL SITUATIONS

We have already discussed the creation of a diet with the foods available in various environments. In this section we will merely define more precisely some of the major principles, without dwelling on rules based on a normal diet in a normal environment.

## DIET TO COUNTER EMOTIONAL STRESS

Anxiety, even more than muscular activity, can empty the glycogen reserves through the discharge of adrenaline that it causes. Therefore, in a situation involving mental stress, the ration of carbohydrates should be increased, especially if one must also face physical stress.

This rule also applies if the physical stress has nothing to do with muscles, but, for example, with the climate: An anxious person will be much less tolerant to cold. It is significant to see the extent to which death is "contagious" in a group of mountain climbers stuck because of bad weather: The first victim makes the others doubt their own tolerance and, due to the apprehension, all the other members of the group become more sensitive.

## DIET AND INTENSE EXERTION

In a survival situation, it can happen that survival itself depends on the ability to perform a specific physical act at a predetermined time (escape, crossing an arm of icy water, holding one's breath for a long time). To the extent that a person can decide on the particular moment himself, he should wait three hours after eating before engaging in vigorous physical activity. In fact, the digestive system will be activated for three hours, moving blood circulation away from the brain and muscles and toward the digestive tract.

## DIET AND ENDURANCE RECORDS IN A CONFINED SPACE

Such situations (an endurance record in windsurfing, for example, or circumnavigating the world in the *Voyager*) require that the individual be artificially constipated in order to avoid the problems of relieving the intestines, especially in small flying machines. During the three to four days before departure, all foods that aid digestion or increase the gastric contents must be avoided, especially milk and vegetable fibers. A mixture of carob bean and cocoa should also be added for their constipating effect.

## DIET AND MOUNTAIN CLIMBING

Above 9,800 feet (3,000 meters) food must compensate for physical exertion, cold and altitude. One must economize on oxygen and therefore avoid proteins, which need oxygen to transform their nitrogenous radicals into urea. Above 19,700 feet (6,000 meters), this should present no problem, since most mountain climbers have an aversion to meat. Two thousand calories are enough in the high mountains,

not only because of a loss of appetite, but also because of a general slowing of the entire metabolism. In practice, the recommendation is 50 grams of proteins, 50 grams of lipids and 300 grams of carbohydrates (total: 1,850 calories).

Depending on the nature of the route, choose from the following foods:

- whole milk in powdered form
- dried fruits (raisins, figs, prunes, apricots
- oily foods (hazelnuts, almonds, peanuts)
- chocolate, candies, honey
- wholemeal bread
- tea or coffee
- cheese

And if there is still some room: sweetened concentrated milk and dried sausage.

## DIET AND DIVING

Diving is soon accompanied by cooling, and the 400 grams of glycogen in reserve in the liver and in the muscles can be burned up within an hour. If the exertion is to continue beyond this length of time, the lipids will be utilized but they have a much lower output. This means that there should be an intake of "quick sugars" before the exertion begins, especially in relation to underwater activity, where the protective role of sugar in cerebral hypoxia must be remembered. This intake can be supplied by, among other foods, sweetened concentrated milk.

## DIET ON THE HIGH SEAS

On board a sailboat, meals can provide recreation but they can also be a dreaded duty. Everything depends on the weather and on organization. Once again, more than in any other situation, four meals are necessary, and one must avoid taking the easy way out by repeatedly preparing the same foods. If this happens, a person's appetite quickly disappears. The meals should be normal in quantity and quality whenever the condition of the sea makes it possible to prepare a varied cuisine. Before departure, one should provide things other than rice, pasta and tuna fish. In bad weather, exhaustion and the inability to prepare proper meals quickly lead to snacking on unnourishing food. This is one more reason to be sure to pack and use vitamin supplements.

The record holder for solo navigation around the world, Philippe Monnet, supplied his trimaran with 150 food rations which were varied and high in energy supply: 3,600 to 4,000 calories per day. The carefully selected ingredients of these rations enabled the young skipper to arrive in top physical condition after 129 days at sea.

## DIET AND HIKING

Around the hiker's 15.5 miles (25 kilometer) mark the glycemia curve decreases appreciably and drops below the fateful point of 0.80 grams, after which one feels drained and exhausted. Therefore one should take sugar: either a tablet of sugar that can be swallowed if chewing a lump of sugar leads to thirst, or sugared water (for example, 20 grams of honey in one-half cup of water). Do not wait until the problems start: The best method is to take some sugar every 5 miles (8 kilometers).

# DRUGS

It is obvious that the use of hard drugs is deleterious in any survival situation. But legal drugs—tobacco and alcohol—present significant problems as well and a word on these is in order.

## TOBACCO

A person who smokes more than 20 cigarettes a day creates an artificial hypoxia in his pulmonary alveoli, equivalent to what is found at an altitude of 8,200 feet (2,500 meters). Carbon monoxide from the burning of the tobacco replaces the oxygen in specific receptors in the red corpuscles, depriving the body of essential fuel. As a result, two mountain climbers on the same peak can be at totally different physiological alti-

### RELATION    NICOTINISM-HYPOXIA    ALTITUDE
#### (according to Evrard)

| REAL ALTITUDE OF A NONSMOKER | PHYSIOLOGICAL ALTITUDE OF AN INDIVIDUAL WHO SMOKES 20 CIGARETTES PER DAY |
|---|---|
| 0 feet (0 meters) | 8,200 feet (2,500 meters) |
| 9,840 feet (3,000 meters) | 14,800 feet (4,500 meters) |
| 19,700 feet (6,000 meters) | 23,000 feet (7,000 meters) |

tudes: the nonsmoker is at 9,840 feet (3,000 meters) while the man who smokes 20 cigarettes a day experiences the stress of 14,800 feet (4,500 meters). If it becomes necessary to descend quickly due to the weather, and stress is added to hypoxia, the whole situation can turn into a tragedy for the smoker. It is not too much to say quite bluntly that smokers should not be mountain climbers.

A skydiver who jumps from 14,800 feet (4,500 meters) after smoking 20 cigarettes during the past 24 hours can have a stroke when he leaves the plane because he is, in fact, at a physiological altitude of 19,700 feet (6,000 meters)! Therefore he can easily lose consciousness, in addition to suffering from hypoxia, the low temperature (about 14°F at 13,000 feet is equivalent to −45.6°F at 155 miles per hour), and psychological stress due to the usual anxiety that precedes a jump into empty space.

Apart from the harmful effect on the transport of oxygen from the lungs, tobacco decomposes vitamin C and thus increases the tendency to get tired. It also encourages hypoglycemia when fasting (an initial hyperglycemic effect due to the secretion of adrenaline when the smoke is inhaled, followed by a secretion of insulin causing secondary hypoglycemia). It is clear that tobacco is truly an "anti-exertion drug," because of its effect on both respiration and the metabolism. Its regular consumption is totally incompatible with physical endurance, which is often required in a survival situation.

### ALCOHOL

During an expedition it is more difficult to take or obtain alcohol than tobacco, and it is important to mention the abuse of this drug only because of the innumerable therapeutic values erroneously ascribed to it.

We have all seen films in which a dying person overcomes his pain with a large gulp of alcohol, gives himself courage with a shot of whiskey, gets through a blizzard with a brimming glass of "rotgut," recovers from a snakebite by getting roaring drunk. What is the message? Not an accurate one. Ethyl alcohol has two virtues: it is an effective antiseptic at solutions over 40 percent or 80 proof, and therefore can be used to disinfect wounds if nothing else is available. And it is a partial anesthetic to the extent that it affects the central nervous system and numbs the senses in proportion to the amount drunk. In this way it can help in minor surgery in emergencies where no morphine or valium is available. But it cannot keep a person warm enough to survive a blizzard or serve as an antidote to snakebite.

Alcohol does supply calories, apart from all the harmful effects that inevitably accompany its ingestion. Though the idea is rather farfetched, this means that if a person is stuck in the snow with a barrel of whiskey and nothing to eat, he could drink a specific amount of whiskey each day to provide the minimum necessary calories for survival. Some people feel a bracing "rush" immediately after imbibing alcohol. This effect cannot be denied but, unfortunately, it is always followed by a phase of tiredness and a decrease in muscle output.

# FOOD GATHERING

- Mushrooms

- Algae, Lichens and Mosses

- Other Edible Plants

# MUSHROOMS

Mushrooms are condiments rather than food staples, and they are of interest in a survival situation only to enhance the taste of food rations that are often bland.

## DIETARY VALUE

The best edible mushrooms contain 72 percent water and most of the other species contain 80 to 92 percent water. As a result, in order to have a nutritional value equivalent to 2.2 pounds (1 kilogram) of medium-quality meat, one would need to eat 33 pounds (15 kilograms) of morels, 44 pounds (20 kilograms) of Lactarius and 88 pounds (40 kilograms) of chanterelles!

Together with Portuguese men-of-war and other medusa jellyfish, mushrooms are the species of animal or vegetable that contain the largest quantity of water: Under the best circumstances, one will get 200 grams of dried food per 2.2 pounds of fresh mushrooms, i.e., about 600 calories, approximately the same amount expended by the muscles in order to gather them! As far as nutrition is concerned, mushrooms contain 3 percent albumins, which cannot all be assimilated by the human body; very few lecithins (phospholipids); very few sugars and mineral salts; and 10 to 20 percent of indigestible substances such as chitin and cellulose. They are not a valuable source of vitamins, because any kind of fish oil will provide 7 to 10 times more per pound. In other words, they offer almost nothing that can be used by an undernourished body.

## RICH BIOTOPE

Mushrooms cannot be found everywhere. Apart from a few species that have adapted to the desert, they need high humidity, so the argument that they should be looked for and gathered because of their high water content is gratuitous. Nevertheless, wherever edible mushrooms grow there is also water: in the crevices among rocks, in hollows in the trees.

Mushrooms usually grow in rich humus that is also conducive to the growth of many other plants that may not taste as good but may be much richer in nutritional value.

## SOME SIMPLE AND USEFUL GUIDELINES

It is important to avoid the 20 or so species of mushroom that are toxic.

■ Do not expect to find any mushrooms after a mistral wind or following 48 hours of high wind. These eliminate fungal growths. On the other hand, dew and fog are very conducive to growth. Snow protects the mycelia (microscopic roots, which are abundant

| STEM | | To be rejected |
|---|---|---|
| | With ring | |
| | With covered cup at the base | ☠ |
| | With ring and cup | (All *Amanita*) |

| CAP | ACTIONS TO BE TAKEN | MAIN TYPES |
|---|---|---|
| with gills (Fig. A) | Throw them all away | *Amanita* (phalloides, destroying angel, fly agaric) Entoloma Cortina fungus and false chanterelle with cortina Psilocybe |
| with pores (Fig. B) | The meat turns blue when cut: throw them away | Satan toadstool, or Devil's boletus |
| | The meat does not change color: keep them | |
| with pinprick-like pores (Fig. C) | Edible | *Hydnum repandum* |
| with folds (Fig. D) | Edible | Chanterelles *Cantharellus* Honey agaric |
| with alveoli (sponge-like appearance) (Fig. E) | Edible | Morels |

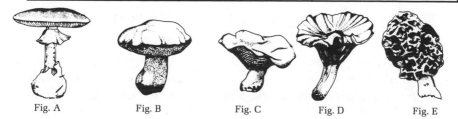

Fig. A          Fig. B          Fig. C          Fig. D          Fig. E

in the soil and give rise to mushrooms) from freezing. This means that one can find cryptogams (plants that reproduce without seeds) up to an altitude of 6,560 to 10,500 feet (2,000 to 3,200 meters) at European latitudes, depending on the species (if you come across them in the mountains, you can be sure that you are below 10,500 feet). Saline soils are definitely hostile to fungal flora, so do not even try to look for them near the seashore.

■ When you find mushrooms whose edibility is in question, they must be sorted rigorously, according to the criteria summarized in the table below. They can be sorted quite simply according to the hymenium, i.e., the lower part of the cap, the part that produces the spores. Even though, naturally, some edible mushrooms will also be discarded if this criterion is used, you will at least be certain to discard all poisonous ones.

■ The presence of an annulus (ring) and a volva (cup) means that they should be discarded and, once again, you will be throwing away some good mushrooms along with the poisonous.

However, the absence of a ring or cup does not necessarily mean that the mushroom is edible, and you should refer to the table. These very simple principles are sufficient in survival situations for those who are not experienced mycologists.

■ Once picked, all mushrooms considered to be edible should be cut lengthwise, to make sure they do not contain the larvae of insects (often wrongly called "worms").

■ They should be eaten as quickly as possible and should not be kept for more than 24 hours in warm weather. If they cannot be eaten quickly they should be dried, because almost all species are very suitable for desiccation, which can be achieved by laying them on the rocks in the sun or stringing them up in the wind. Mushrooms are nitrogenous foods and therefore can become dangerous when spoiled, like meat, eggs, and fish. The degradation of their albumins produces ptomaines, which are poisonous. This biochemical degradation means that fresh mushrooms must be eaten quickly.

## ALGAE, LICHENS AND MOSSES

In many environments these are the only plants that survive—in seashores, steppes and the taiga, for example. Algae, lichens and mosses are all edible, but one must keep in mind that, though they are harmless from the perspective of toxins, their taste is either bland or offensive.

All algae—including sea lettuce with large, dark-green leaves; tapered laminaria with saw-teeth; fucus (brown algae); or red algae—are edible after they have been washed in fresh water and, if possible, boiled. They form a jelly, which is rich in proteins and can be mixed into all kinds of food (rice, powdered milk, etc.). Lichens can be eaten after they have been cooked for a long time to eliminate their strong bitter taste. None of the lichens are toxic.

## OTHER EDIBLE PLANTS

More than 300,000 different plants flourish on earth and in European and North American latitudes alone there are 100 families, including 18 that contain one or several toxic species. It is obviously impossible to provide an exhaustive list, and describing a few dozen plants would be totally arbitrary, although many survival manuals do so.

The traveler should consult specialized books and memorize several plants that are known to be common in the relevant area. Unfortunately there are no universal rules that would enable the safe elimination of all toxic plants, as there are with mushrooms, algae, lichens or mosses. The feeding habits of other mammals can give an indication, even if it is not absolute. On the other hand, watching what birds eat is useless, because they have a fundamentally different susceptibility to plant toxins than humans do.

The edible parts of plants differ according to the season. Generally speaking, one finds the following:

■ in the spring: leaves, stems, young shoots and some fruits
■ in the summer: primarily fruits
■ in the fall: fruits, roots or tubers
■ in the winter: small quantities of overripe fruits

In terms of nutrition, be aware that:

■ Fruits, berries and grains contain sugars and therefore provide the largest amounts of calories. The fruits of some plants that are generally not considered in a daily diet are nevertheless edible: arbutus, hawthorn, prickly pear, elderberry tree, oak, pine, sallowhorn, dogwood and juniper, for example.
■ Roots and tubers, the plant's storage organs, are especially nourishing in the fall.

For specialized information, refer to the bibliography and suggested reading at the end of the book.

# MOTION SICKNESS AND SENSORY ABERRATIONS

- Seasickness

- Airsickness

- Sensory aberrations

# SEASICKNESS

This disagreeable condition can affect experienced sailors and landlubbers alike. It is caused by the real movements of the individual and the apparent movement of his surroundings. Its origin is attributable to several factors, especially a disparity between the sensations registered by the inner ear and those registered by the eyes. Other senses—auditory, olfactory, gastric, musculotendinous and cortical—signal the portion of the brain that controls nausea and vomiting. The multiplicity of the stimuli explains the numerous ways in which seasickness can occur and accounts for the varied nature of the remedies and preventives.

Though it sometimes occurs very quickly, it is less abrupt than airsickness and usually is preceded by warning signs: a decrease in liveliness and talkativeness, a feeling of unease and anxiety, drowsiness followed by yawning, dizziness, muscular clumsiness and finally nausea. There is also an undeniable psychological element, often in the form of an association with similar situations in the past that had caused nausea. As a result, the person in question is afraid that the preliminary signs will occur again, and this invariably causes them. Seasickness is always made worse by fatigue, cold, hunger and lack of sleep.

Many tricks are effective, at least through their placebo effect, for this malady, which is at least partially psychosomatic. Among other things, one could try dry crackers, stale bread, chewing gum, a glass of seawater; I myself have had some success with neophyte divers, who got sick even before they reached the diving location, by giving them a large glass of iced Coca Cola. Whether the drink had real physiological effects, or whether they were simply convinced that I was giving them a miracle remedy, is irrelevant. The fact is that most of them felt better for it.

Seasickness has very different degrees of severity, ranging from simple discomfort to total and utter prostration that does not stop until the individual is back on firm ground. If the individual is susceptible and is subjected to this condition for a long time, the consequences can be very serious, even to the point of collapse. No one can know beforehand how he will react to seasickness. Some people can steer in a storm while constantly throwing up, but others are totally incapable of functioning at all.

Rolling, pitching, the action of swells, and the changes in direction, which can be very abrupt, all play a role in the origin of seasickness. They cause acceleration and deceleration both in a linear and angular direction, and involve complementary Coriolis acceleration, where the movements of the individual himself play a role. The intensity of the movement is less important than the rocking motion. A repeated gentle movement is more harmful than an abrupt, irregular movement.

## PREVENTION

■ The best position is lying down. Sitting up with one's head bobbing around is very bad.
■ Some environmental factors should be avoided as they encourage the occurrence of seasickness: limited air supply; heat; cold and humidity; vibrations; noises; the smell of fuel oil, old cigars, cooking or hot oil. Of course, many of these are unavoidable on board a ship or boat.
■ Sight also plays a role: On the bridge at sea it is better to watch the horizon than the bow, waves or the receding wake. Try to avoid reading when the sea is rough. There is nothing worse at the end of a night watch in a stormy sea than having to go down to the chart table to read and write before going to bed.
■ On the psychological level, the assumption that nausea is inevitable may be the best way to cause it. People who are apprehensive generally suffer from motion sickness more frequently than others.
■ Ninety percent of sailors even-

tually find their "sea legs," or adapt to the sea environment. The body's adaptation takes several days and becomes increasingly stable as the time passes. It disappears after a long stay on solid earth.
■ The location in the vessel is very important. Stay as close as possible to the axes of rotation, because the linear speed of movement becomes greater as one moves away from these axes. Therefore in a sailing vessel one should be as close to the stern as possible to suffer less from the pitching; it is not merely a matter of tradition that the skipper's cabin is always closer to the stern than to the bow, and that the crewmen never fight over the forward cabin! As far as the rolling is concerned, you will suffer less if you stay lower in the hull of the ship, a little below the Plimsoll line and perpendicular to the bottom of the hull. The rolling is much stronger on the bridge. The only thing that never changes, no matter where you position yourself, is the vertical movement.
■ Life on board should be well regulated and should include sufficient and regular times for sleeping. Frequent light, low-fat meals are best. Sleeping between watches is a good way to allay seasickness. It has been shown that relaxation and immobilization of the joints decreases the occurrence of seasickness (dogs and monkeys were put into casts

to immobilize their joints, and they were less sick). Apart from that, physical motion in general is harmful, and lying down is often the best treatment.

## MEDICINES

There are many medicines of varying effectiveness for sea-sickness.

■ Many drugs are available for use as prophylaxis when taken one hour before departure. These include dimenhydrinate (Dramamine) 50 mg; diphenhydramine (Benedryl) 50 mg; meclizine (Antivert) 50 mg and diazepam (Valium) 5 to 10 mg. Promethazine is the most frequently used antihistamine. The combination of ephedrine sulfate (50 mg) and promethazine hydrochlorate (25 mg) was used for the Skylab IV astronauts.

■ Scopolamine is more effective than antihistamines for preventing motion sickness. Its strong anticholinergic action is useful for severe cases when administered by intramuscular injection once a day. Its effect is reinforced if it is combined with a sympathomimetic such as dextro-amphetamine. The most effective medication is through oral ingestion of 0.4 mg scopolamine with 5 mg dextro-amphetamine. NASA uses this for its astronauts. Scopolamine is also available in a skin patch that can be placed behind the ear, and from which 0.5 mg is released slowly over three days. (This patch cannot be used if you have glaucoma.)

All of these products can make you sleepy to a greater or lesser extent and cannot be given to pilots. They also may cause a dry mouth. Vitamin $B_6$ is the only prescription that can be given to a navigator, since it has no side effects.

## AIRSICKNESS

The symptoms, causes and treatments are very similar to those of seasickness. The angular movements and acceleration are faster and more abrupt, and the nausea can come on much more quickly. In contrast to sea-sickness, airsickness happens very suddenly, the passenger going straight from a feeling of slight discomfort to vomiting. Being passive and not knowing the next movement of the plane in advance is also very detrimental.

Airsickness is not likely to affect an individual in a survival situation, but some other kinds of vertigo and some visual aberrations can occur at a high altitude or in the depths.

# SENSORY ABERRATIONS

## UNDER WATER

The chapter "Under the Water" deals with the rapture of the deep, the disorientation caused by nitrogen under pressure in the blood. Another type of disorientation can arise under water when the diver can see neither the surface nor the seabed. This disorientation typically happens when visibility is bad above a deep seabed, especially if there is no sun. The diver finds himself in a three-dimensional space with no specific visual reference. At zero buoyancy, there is no feeling of gravity to allow him to distinguish up from down. He is in the same situation as a pilot entering a homogeneous layer of clouds without any navigational instruments. For a pilot, this can be fatal. For a diver, a long exhalation will be enough to re-create the vertical dimension by watching the column of bubbles.

## AT A HIGH ALTITUDE

The vertigo many people suffer at high altitudes is not biochemical, as it may be under water. It is caused instead by an anomaly of the inner ear. Some people are genetically predisposed to this condition, and it is not necessarily possible to become accustomed to it as many mountain climbers claim.

Any expedition leader who includes crossings at significant heights in his plans should make sure that the team members are suited for it. One method of selection in this area is totally useless: jumping with a parachute. A person may be paralyzed by vertigo on top of a 325-foot (100-meter) cliff yet feel quite at ease on the footboard of a plane with 9,800 feet (3,000 meters) of void beneath him.

## WHITE OUT

Many airmen, as well as survivors on mountains, have suffered from whiteout. Accidents are often caused by the difficulty of estimating distances when the topography is covered with snow. The uniformity of the snow covering prevents the eye from adjusting to the proper distance. It is therefore very difficult, if not impossible, to land on a glacier that is covered with fresh snow and is not lit up by the sun. If there are no crevasses, rocks or some other form of reference, one may easily crash into the glacier at full speed without seeing it, or alternatively start to flare out a few hundred feet above it, believing that one is merely a few yards up. It is one of the major difficulties in flying in the Far North.

Another cause of accidents due to faulty visual reference is the similarity that often exists between a snow-covered slope and the white cloud right behind it. As a result, a pilot can crash into the mountain believing it to be a nimbostratus cloud. Several planes crash into mountain peaks every year in this way, because the pilots sees them too late.

An isolated survivor can experience a whiteout caused by fog. Some years ago, a pilot crashed into a snow-covered slope in Vercors, France. Miraculously, the angle of the crash was such that he and one passenger survived. Enveloped in a layer of fog, the pilot decided to descend to find help in the valley. While he was still close to the wreck, he stepped across a small snow drift and fell several hundred yards to the bottom of a huge cliff, which he had not realized was there.

This is also the reason why people walking in the Arctic have great difficulty in estimating the distance and the presence of obstacles. It also applies to the desert, where a person is faced with dunes whose monotonous curves stretch for several dozen miles into the distance, making it very difficult to estimate distances; multiplying the estimated distance by three often gives a result closer to the truth.

In some circumstances optical adaptation makes it necessary to readapt before returning to normal life. Members of long speleological expeditions require readaptation, as do submarine crews, who lose the ability to accommodate their vision to distance after spending several months under water. After months of seeing objects only up close, the muscles that act on the crystalline curve lose their ability to adapt to distance. Gradual retraining is necessary.

# MISCELLANEOUS TECHNIQUES

- Practical Seamanship

- Wild Animal Tracks

- Trapping

- Wilderness Techniques

# PRACTICAL SEAMANSHIP

There are thousands of different knots, many of which are best suited to very specific activities. The reader should consult a specialized book on knots for complete information. A few of the most useful knots are described below.

## TWO HALF HITCHES

This knot is quick and easy to make and is a good substitute for the clove hitch. It is just as solid and has the advantage that it does not tighten itself like the clove hitch. Therefore it is easy to untie.

## THE BOWLINE KNOT AND ITS MULTIPLE USES

This is the ultimate survival knot and the one knot to know.

■ Purpose: to form a loop that will not slip and will be of the desired size at the end of any kind of rope.
■ Disadvantages: almost none.
■ Advantages: The more one pulls, the more solid the knot becomes without being difficult to untie. This knot does not slip. It can be untied easily even if the rope is wet. It can be made with any rope or string.
■ Execution: It can be made in various ways. There is the eye method, the "pulling" method, the two-finger method, the one-

hand method. Preferable is a mnemonic device that is well known among some commandos; this consists in comparing the free end (called the "running part") to the head of a rabbit and the "standing part" to a tree over a hole indicated by the overhand loop (the "bight") that forms the first stage of the knot.
■ "The rabbit pokes its head out of the hole, rises, goes around the tree, and descends into the hole." This very simple method will enable you to make the bowline even in the dark.
■ Applications: These are infinite and can replace numerous other more complicated knots.

### Bowline Bend

This knot is used to join two towlines, to extend a rappel rope, etc. It is simply made of two bowlines, and is sometimes called, simply, two bowlines, or a hawser bend. It is a good substitute for the square (or reef) knot, which can slip, particularly if the two ends have different diameters or textures.

### Running Bowline

This is very useful to catch game and has all the advantages already mentioned. It can be used to join and hang objects to ropes of different diameters. The weight

TWO HALF HITCHES          RUNNING BOWLINE

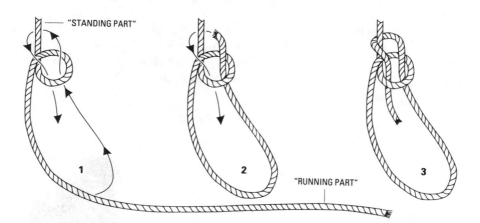

"STANDING PART"

"RUNNING PART"

BOWLINE

BOWLINE BEND

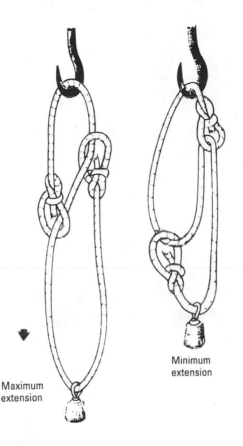

Maximum
extension

Minimum
extension

The Poldo Hoist

of the object will ensure the necessary tension for the knot to grasp.

## The Poldo Hoist

The concept of this hoist is brilliant, because it allows one to lift a tree trunk, or any other load, alone using a simple rope without a pulley. It can be used on board a sailboat to hold a rope tight, in the mountains during a rescue mission, or in any situation where it is necessary to move heavy loads for short distances (a vehicle that is stuck, a boat that has run aground, etc.).

It is easy to make, following the diagram below, and all one has to do is pull the section indicated by the arrow. The range is limited by the length of the hoist.

## Bowline

The bowline is known as "the king of knots." The simple bowline can be used to hoist up a mast or a tree, to rescue a man who has fallen overboard, to hoist the sails, etc.

Roe-deer

Reindeer

Antelope

Red deer

Canidae

Felines

Bear

Forepaw    Hind paw

Wild boar

---

# WILD ANIMAL TRACKS

Although identifying the species can be useful in hunting, usually identification of the family to which the animal belongs is sufficient.

## Cervidae

These can be found everywhere except in Australia.

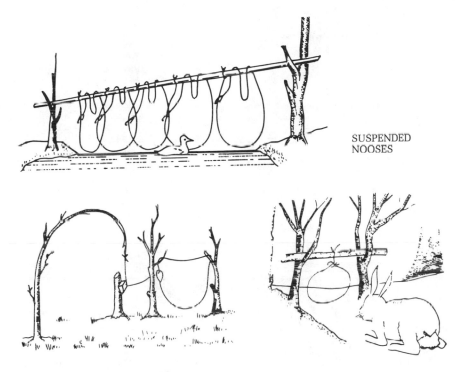

SUSPENDED
NOOSES

SPRUNG TRAPS

## Canidae

These are found everywhere except on a few islands including Madagascar and New Zealand. Foxes, wolves and dogs have similar prints with four pads, prolonged by the claws.

## Felines

From the domestic cat to the tiger, all felines also make a print with four pads, without the claw marks because the claws are retracted when a cat walks. Like the Canidae, the feline's fifth pad at the back is much longer.

## Bears

The prints are easy to recognize: They have five closely set pads with very clear traces of the claws. The elongated print at the back is reminiscent of a human footprint. The size of these prints may be as long as 11.7 inches (30 centimeters).

## Wild Boars

The prints left by the wild boar's hooves resemble those of the Cervidae. But they differ in that the wild boar leaves the im-

**BRANCH PROVIDED WITH TRAPS**
(nooses of one-half to 1 inch)

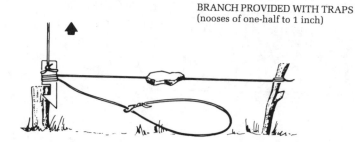

BAITED NOOSE UNDER TENSION

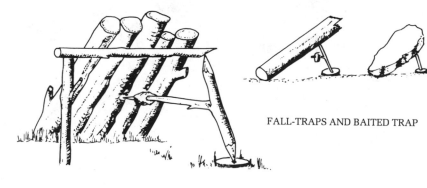

FALL-TRAPS AND BAITED TRAP

FALL-TRAP WITHOUT BAIT

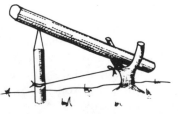

print of the lateral phalanxes, particularly on loose ground.

Many other animals may leave characteristic prints on dusty or muddy ground, but their light weight makes detection difficult, and other signs will identify their presence with more certainty: burrows and droppings for rabbits, hares, and other rodents; gnawed trees around a water source for beavers; characteristic nests for squirrels; well-beaten paths for badgers; holes under river banks for otters.

## TRAPPING

There are hundreds of ways of trapping game and infinite varieties of traps, ranging from the simplest noose snare or running knot, through to a spear or spiked trap, with or without bait. In a survival situation, the ability to make do with what is at hand plays a major role.

Preprepared snares can easily be purchased and stowed away at the bottom of one's rucksack. Brass wire is an extremely useful material for trapping. And finally, a fishing rod can be used to catch various birds.

# WILDERNESS TECHNIQUES

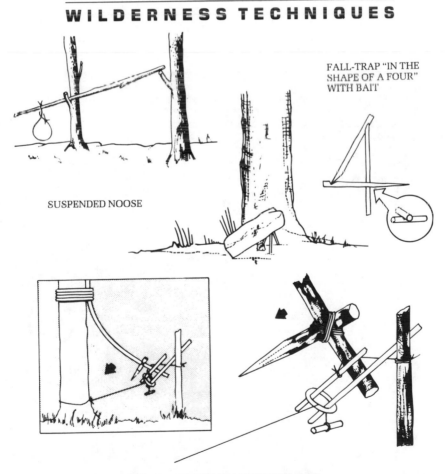

FALL-TRAP "IN THE SHAPE OF A FOUR" WITH BAIT

SUSPENDED NOOSE

SPEAR OR SPIKED TRAPS WITH PLATES
(designed to kill wild boars, deer, etc.)

By rubbing (rope and shavings)

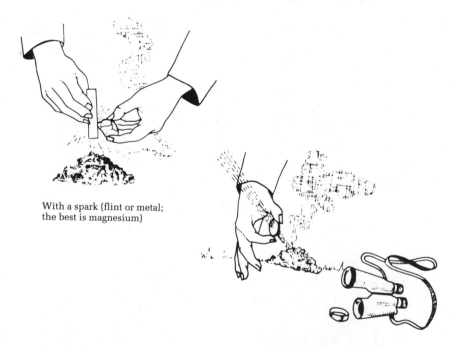

With a spark (flint or metal;
the best is magnesium)

By concentrating solar energy
(a makeshift magnifying glass)

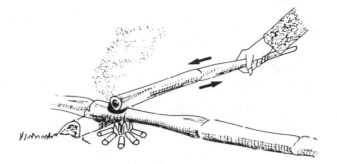

By rubbing wood against wood

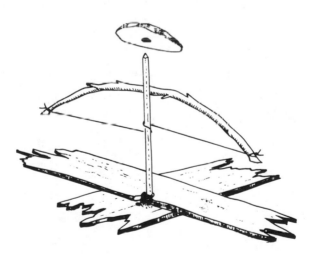

By rotational friction

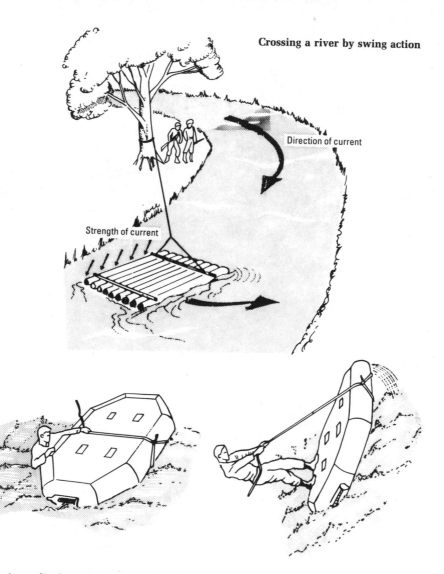

Crossing a river by swing action

Direction of current

Strength of current

Turning a dinghy right side up, using the
wind and the waves

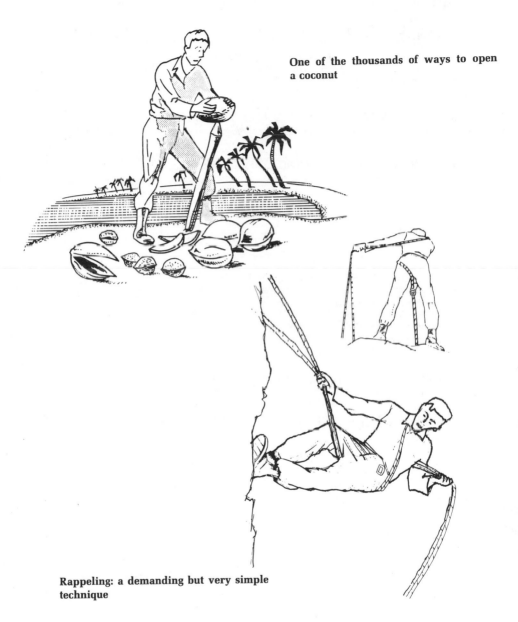

One of the thousands of ways to open a coconut

Rappeling: a demanding but very simple technique

# MEDICINE WITHOUT A DOCTOR

- Vaccinations Before the Expedition

- Prevention of Some Exotic Diseases

- Common Symptoms Among Travelers and Measures to Be Taken

- A Word About First Aid

- Wounds and Sores

- Additional Materials

- First Aid Survival Kit

The advice given in this chapter is that of a responsible doctor addressing healthy people who may find themselves alone in an unfavorable survival situation. It should be clearly understood that this advice is not a substitute for proper medical care. It will serve, however, to facilitate a discussion with your doctor about your plans for survival situations.

Please refer to the list of medicines in the section "First Aid Survival Kit."

## VACCINATIONS BEFORE THE EXPEDITION

The choice of vaccinations for a person who may find himself in a survival situation has nothing at all to do with the normal schedule followed in industrialized countries. It depends on several factors:

■ The individual's age: Most adults will already have become immune in childhood to illnesses such as whopping cough, measles, diphtheria and toxoplasmosis (for women) through either vaccination or natural immunization. Repetition of these vaccines is unnecessary.
■ Evaluating the risk: The risks to be faced in any region depend in part on the individual's physical condition. It should not be necessary to give a healthy younger traveler the influenza vaccination, which is generally reserved for older people, or the anticholera vaccination, which is limited to undernourished populations in regions where there are epidemics.
■ The method of administration:

If the traveler is pressed for time, all the vaccinations may be given within two weeks, although it is best to start getting them two to three months ahead of time. For example, the yellow fever vaccination and booster shots for tetanus and polio can be given on the same day.

The region you are visiting must always be considered: It would be pointless to have a yellow fever vaccination if you are headed for the North Pole or for Asia. It would be extremely useful for anyone leaving for the Brazilian Amazon or for Mongolia to have a vaccination against cerebrospinal meningitis (see Table).

The U.S. Public Health Service issues a pamphlet annually containing immunization requirements and recommendations for foreign travel. You can consult your doctor or purchase the latest edition of this document from the Superintendant of Documents, U.S. Government Printing Office, Washington, D.C. 20402.

# TABLE OF USEFUL OR INDISPENSABLE VACCINATIONS DEPENDING ON DESTINATION AND IN DECREASING ORDER OF NECESSITY ACCORDING TO STATISTICS

| VACCINE | MANNER | EFFECTIVENESS AND TIME IT REMAINS ACTIVE | START OF IMMUNITY | COUNTRY OR REGION |
|---|---|---|---|---|
| Tetanus | 3 subcutaneous injections at 3-week intervals | 100 percent immunity. Booster after 1 year and then every 5 years. | Starting with the second subcutaneous injection. | The only vaccination that is indispensable throughout the world. |
| Yellow fever | 1 subcutaneous injection in a USPHS-authorized Yellow Fever Vaccination Center | Very effective immunity for 6 months. | 10 days after injection. | Latin America from Guatemala to Bolivia. Intertropical Africa |
| Hepatitis B | 3 subcutaneous injections at one-month intervals | Effective immunity. Booster after 1 year and then every 5 years. | Starting with the second injection. | Above all, Africa and Southeast Asia, but epidemics are possible anywhere in the world. |

| Disease | Vaccination | Immunity | Protection | Regions |
|---|---|---|---|---|
| Meningitis (A+C) | 1 0.5-ml subcutaneous injection | Effective immunity. Booster after 3 years. | After several days | Brazil, Uruguay, Mongolia, Morocco. The belt that includes all of Africa between the equator and the Tropic of Cancer. |
| Poliomyelitis | Oral: 3 doses of 0.5 ml at one-month intervals | Booster after 1 year and then every 5 years. | Starting with the second dose | Latin America, all of Africa, all of Southeast Asia (but not Australia) |
| Tuberculosis | BCG if tests are negative | Very variable. | Only if the test becomes positive (uncertain) | A large number of countries, especially India, Africa, Hong Kong, Singapore, Thailand, Guatemala and Colombia. |
| Typhoid-Paratyphoid A and B | 3 subcutaneous injections at 2-week intervals | Booster after 1 year and then every 5 years. | Starting with the second injection | Africa, Far East |
| Cholera | No vaccination necessary unless there is a local epidemic (sulfa drugs or tetracycline are more effective) | | | |
| Smallpox | The vaccination should be refused (the disease has now been eradicated) | | | |

## TETANUS

This is the only vaccination that is as indispensable as it is effective and safe: 100 percent immunity and rarely any complications. During World War I, 600,000 deaths were due to tetanus on the French front. During World War II, among American soldiers, who were all vaccinated, there was not a single death from tetanus on any front. These numbers speak for themselves. The tetanus bacillus, *Clostridium tetani*, is a telluric bacillus (it is found in the soil) that is ubiquitous and very resistant. It enters the bloodstream through the smallest scratch and can cause death.

## YELLOW FEVER

This is very effective and absolutely necessary for Latin America and tropical Africa.

## MENINGITIS

This is useful in the regions indicated in the table above, and the knowledge that this additional danger has been eliminated provides ease of mind for those who travel.

## HEPATITIS B

This is the first vaccine obtained through genetic engineering. It is recommended for those visiting Africa and the Far East.

## OTHER VACCINATIONS

It is advisable to have other vaccinations according to the country to be visited. The TAB vaccine against typhoid and paratyphoid is useful for Africa and the Far East. The well-known D.T.-TAB vaccine combines vaccines against diphtheria, tetanus, typhoid and paratyphoid in the same vial. It seems particularly well suited to people who travel often and widely.

The BCG (bacile Calmette-Guérin) vaccine against tuberculosis is useful in exceptional cases if one's test results were negative and one is going to visit affected tribes. There are head-hunting tribes in Borneo that have been decimated by tuberculosis, and if you visit them you should take stringent precautions—in particular, you should have lung X-rays after your return.

## CHOLERA

Although cholera vaccination is still required by some countries, it has some drawbacks:

■ it only provides immunity in 50 percent of the cases, which means that it is not reliable;
■ the immunity—assuming it takes—lasts only for six months;
■ if there is any danger, preventive measures should be taken

with tetracycline or sulfa drugs: for example, long-acting sulfonamides taken as 2 to 3 tablets of 500 mg at one time, possibly repeated 15 days later, or tetracycline 500 mg every 6 hours for 8 doses. This medicine can be taken along to questionable regions (India, Pakistan, Asia and Africa), especially as it is also effective in treating various other exotic diseases.

## SMALLPOX

Since 1985, the World Health Organization (WHO) has recommended that this vaccination not be given, as the disease is thought to be eradicated. Some countries still require it, however, so check with your doctor or write to the World Health Organization in Washington, D.C. for information.

# PREVENTION OF SOME EXOTIC DISEASES

It is impossible to give a detailed list of tropical diseases, which are very numerous and often very complex; instead, we will suggest fundamental symptomatic medicines, plus preventive and curative measures, which will enable you to deal with most tropical diseases even if you are not a doctor.

## MALARIA

Since 1630 people have talked about "swamp fever," without knowing that it is carried by an inhabitant of those areas: the female anopheles mosquito. Even then, the Peruvian Indians already knew of the curative power of quinine bark, but it took until 1940 before Western attention focused on chloroquine. This disease is present in all tropical countries, with rare exceptions.

Therefore, in all these regions, oral prophylaxis is essential.

■ Chloroquine: 1 100-mg tablet per day for six days out of 7, or
■ Flavoquine: 3 200-mg tablets once a week.

In regions where the malaria strain is resistant to chloroquine the best protection is Lariam (mefloquine hydrochloride) by Roche Laboratories. Dosage is one tablet per week. The first dose should be taken a week before departure, and the last should be taken three weeks after one's return (no more because of the delayed action of the medicine). This medicine is very important in a survival situation, as it covers all the strains, and a few tablets are sufficient for a stay of several months. It seldom has side effects, and if it does, they are benign, usually occurring between four and eight hours after ingestion of the tablet (nausea, itching); lying down for a few hours solves the problem. A woman must avoid getting pregnant if she is taking Lariam.

Chloraquine is suitable for the following regions: West Africa, Central America, the West Indies and the Middle East.

In the following regions, Lariam is necessary: Southeast Asia, South India, Pakistan, the Amazon basin, Guyana, Tanzania, Kenya and Central and South-West Africa. If in doubt, take Lariam.

## AMEBIASIS

According to the WHO, 10 percent of the world's population is infested with amebiasis, which does not mean that they are sick. The disease is caused by a unicellular protozoan, which can become encysted, primarily in the liver, and can be reactivated many years later if it is not properly treated to begin with. There is no prevention through medicines or through vaccines. Therefore, all one can do is keep to the rules of hygiene and administer adequate treatment.

Required hygiene consists of avoiding raw fruit and vegetables, ice, water that has not been boiled—everything that in one way or another could have come into contact with contaminated water. This is easy to say on paper

and much more difficult to do in practice. It is advisable to take along a good amebicide in order to nip this disease in the bud, as it can become chronic if it is not treated at the very beginning.

### Medicines

In an isolated situation, and if in doubt, treat the disease for the maximum length of time to ensure total elimination of the parasite.

Flagyl (metronidazole) is an easy to obtain amebicide. The dose is 6 to 8 250 mg tablets, taken one or two at a time throughout the day for 7 to 10 consecutive days.

Metronidazole is the simplest and least toxic regimen, and it will cure about 90 percent of patients. Combination therapy raises the cure rate close to 100 percent. If the liver becomes infected, additional treatment may be necessary.

Other effective drugs are iodoquinol, 650 mg three times a day for 20 days, and diloxanide furoate, 500 mg three times a day for 10 days. Either of these drugs can be combined with metronidazole when intestinal symptoms are moderate or severe.

### CHOLERA

This is a disease that has been known for centuries and continues to spread according to the flow of modern life. It attacked the African continent for the first time in 1970, where it was a new disease and there was no protection. It is endemic in the large deltas of the Ganges and Bangladesh. During the last 25 years there have been a series of epidemics from the Celebes to South Africa, via China, Nepal, the Middle East, and even spilling over into Eastern Europe. It reached the periphery of the Mediterranean, sparing France but taking over all of Africa.

It is a disease found in countries that lack proper hygiene, and, in order to become infected, a person must have direct contact with an infected person or a corpse, or must ingest food or water contaminated by human excretions. A Westerner in an unfavorable situation could become infected.

Cholera vaccine gives only partial protection. Prompt prophylaxis with tetracycline, 500 mg every six hours for 8 doses, is useful after exposure. This same regimen, along with fluid and salt replacement, is used for treatment of infection.

There are many other exotic diseases (trypanosomiasis, or sleeping sickness; bilharziosis, which is very widespread in Egypt; filariasis; leishmaniasis; kala-azar), but they are less widespread, and you can consult a specialist on tropical diseases to find out the precise risks for your destination. Remember that the risk of contracting these diseases is very much lower if you are in good condition. It is useful, however, for a man alone to treat specific symptoms, even if he cannot link them to the characteristic syndrome of a specific disease.

# COMMON SYMPTOMS AMONG TRAVELERS AND MEASURES TO BE TAKEN

### "TRAVELERS' " DIARRHEA

This affects close to 50 percent of all travelers in tropical regions. This "acclimatization diarrhea" is caused by many things: food, water, climate, infections (*coli* bacillus, shigella, Salmonella, virus, etc.). Whatever the origin, it is relieved by drinking water, eating rice and starches, and administering treatment for the symptoms: imodium (2 2-mg capsules after each bowel movement). One should avoid all spicy foods. If the case is severe, all stimulants should be avoided: tea, coffee, spices, and, if possible, physical exercise.

### FEVERS

Most of the major exotic diseases can cause fever. If one takes the recommended preventive measures, malaria, yellow fever and hepatitis can be eliminated.

■ If the fever is accompanied by diarrhea, it may be amebiasis or salmonella, an intestinal parasitosis, which can be treated with an antibiotic and by drinking water.
■ If there is no diarrhea, but there are pains in the joints and headaches—in other words, flu-like symptoms—consider that it may be dengue, a virus transmitted by mosquitoes, and use a symptomatic treatment (aspirin).
■ If you have no idea at all what it could be, take a broad-spectrum antibiotic such as tetracycline or a sulfa drug (Bactrim).

This therapeutic regime is not what a doctor would recommend, but for a person alone in a precarious situation it will provide relief in most cases.

### ALLERGIES TO FOOD

These typically occur in a situation of shortage, when people are tempted by anything that comes along, and the treatment is symptomatic: Imodium for diarrhea, chlorpheniramine tablets or dexamethasone to be injected depending on the severity of the allergic reaction (itching, nettle rash, swelling, general feeling of being unwell).

### ATHLETE'S FOOT

Fungal infections are very widespread in hot countries, but they also occur in cold countries if sweating results in skin irritation—especially on the feet. Prevention is based on hygiene: do not use undergarments and socks made of synthetic materials, such as nylon. Apart from special materials such as Gore-Tex, synthetic cloth prevents perspiration from escaping. Therefore undergarments should be made of cotton. Try to wash once a day (not more) and carefully dry your skin as often as possible.

The area between the toes is most often affected. There are many good over-the-counter products to treat athlete's foot fungus. Selenium sulfide, known throughout the world under the brand name Selsun, is extremely effective against versicolored pityriasis (patches on the skin), and it is recommended as a preventive measure, especially if used as a soap or a shampoo. Washing twice a week with this liquid and allowing it to work for 20 minutes before rinsing it off is sufficient to significantly decrease the risk of mycoses.

Another place where fungal infections frequently occur among hikers is the crotch, and the infection spreads to the bursa and the thighs on contact. This is not the same fungus as athlete's foot, but anti-fungal medicines are equally effective.

In the case of superficial fungal infections that can hinder walking but are not serious, the interdigital cracks may not totally heal until you return to a temperate climate. They may recur in summer because the spores are very resistant; and it may be necessary to discard the hiking boots, which can retain the infection.

## SEXUALLY TRANSMITTED DISEASES

As important as it is to be wary of these diseases in Western countries, the warnings are all the more important in developing countries. In Africa in particular, and also in Asia, there has been a veritable explosion of sexually transmitted diseases, including AIDS. Without further advances in the epidemiology of these diseases, the only approach is prevention. For a man this means wearing a latex contraceptive (a condom), and for a woman it means insisting that her partner do so. Prevention for both sexes is both easy and mandatory: In the age of AIDS, neglecting this kind of protection anywhere in the world is totally unconscionable.

# A WORD ABOUT FIRST AID

In this book, we will not duplicate the information available in the many good books devoted to first aid. It is obvious that fracturing a limb will cause major stress and that it must be immobilized in some manner before one continues on one's way, and that a wound must be closed up and protected.

Of course, many survival situations are faced alone, but the following points concern group survival situations.

## MOUTH-TO-MOUTH RESUSCITATION

As far as methods of respiratory resuscitation in survival situations are concerned, the one and only method is mouth-to-mouth. Remember that the air breathed by the "rescuer" into the upper air passages of the individual in trouble still contains 16 of the 21 percent oxygen inhaled. This 16 percent is enough to provide normal oxygenation. Try to maintain the normal rhythm of breathing, i.e., 12 to 15 breaths per minute. Gently pinch the nostrils of the nose closed before beginning respirations.

### Placing the Head in an Extended Position

One very simple action is frequently forgotten in an emergency: the victim's head should be placed in an extended position if he is unconscious. This will prevent the person from "swallowing his tongue"—that is, having the tongue block the upper air

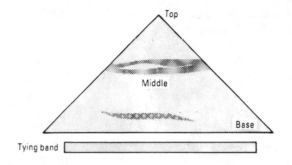

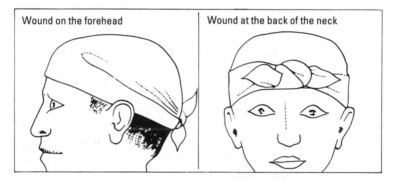

**A triangular piece of fabric: ideal for all bandages and to immobilize a limb**

passages. Tip the head backward and maintain this position with the help of some object placed under the victim's shoulders. If the person is breathing spontaneously, this simple gesture may save his life. If he is not breathing spontaneously, apply mouth-to-mouth resuscitation in the same extended position.

If the lungs do not expand with mouth-to-mouth breathing, try repositioning the head. If this still does not work, the airway may be blocked by a foreign object. Careful finger sweeps (so as not to push a foreign object further into the airway) and manual abdominal thrusts (the Heimlich maneuver), repeated as necessary, can be used to reopen the blocked airway.

## TRACHEOTOMY

It is impossible to perform a tracheotomy on oneself, but, within limits, anyone can perform it on

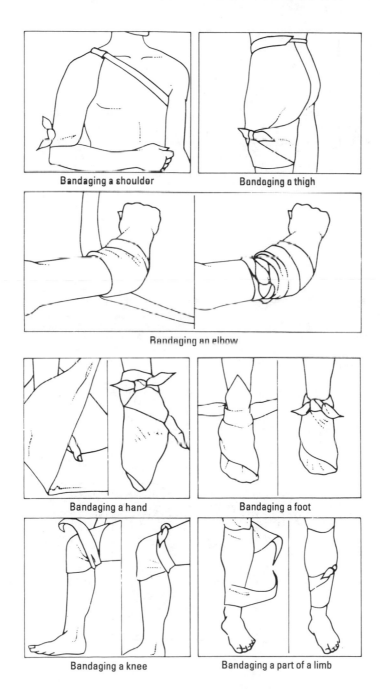

Bandaging a shoulder

Bandaging a thigh

Bandaging an elbow

Bandaging a hand

Bandaging a foot

Bandaging a knee

Bandaging a part of a limb

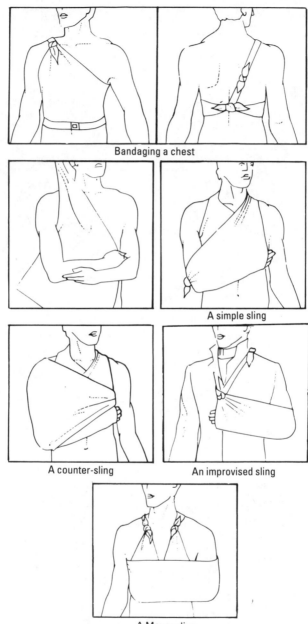

Bandaging a chest

A simple sling

A counter-sling

An improvised sling

A Mayor sling

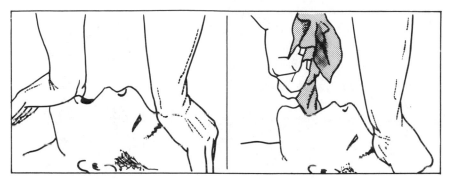

Opening the mouth                    Cleaning out the mouth

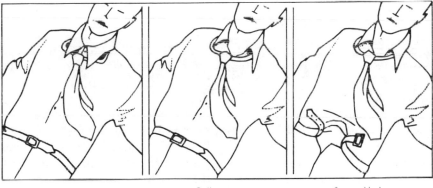

Tie ...                Collar ...                Opened belt

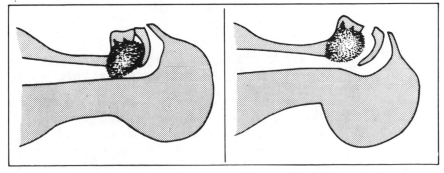

Obstructed air passages              Freed air passages

**Danger of asphyxia if an individual's neck is bent: The simple act of placing the head in an extended position prevents the tongue from obstructing the air passages**

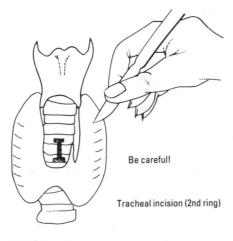

Be careful!

Tracheal incision (2nd ring)

**Tracheotomy**

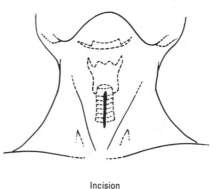

Incision

another person. This act short-circuits the upper air passages that are occluded by a foreign object, or by an edema of the pharynx as sometimes happens in relation to a snakebite, a sting by Hymenoptera on the neck, or allergic shocks after any kind of envenomation. The act involves making an incision into the trachea between the bottom of the thyroid cartilage (Adam's apple) along a strictly median line about one inch (3 to 4 centimeters) long. The act is more sensational for the one who performs it than for the victim, as the latter is unconscious due to the start of asphyxia. The individual's head should be placed in a forced extended position so as to free the neck and expose the trachea as much as possible. Seize the Adam's apple between the fingers of the left hand, and make the incision downward from the level of your fingers.

Do not hesitate to cut hard and deep, since the median portion of this area is devoid of all important vessels. As soon as you see the cartilaginous rings of the trachea, perforate them with a scalpel or a knife blade and insert something rigid into the wound: The best thing is a special probe, but the tube from a ball-point pen will do the job well, and will save the life of the victim.

## CARDIOPULMONARY RESUSCITATION

This may be necessary after a lightning strike, drowning or other shock to the heart. It is very easy to do. It absolutely must be done on a hard surface, and must be alternated with mouth-to-mouth resuscitation. Push firmly with both hands on the sternum while positioning oneself directly

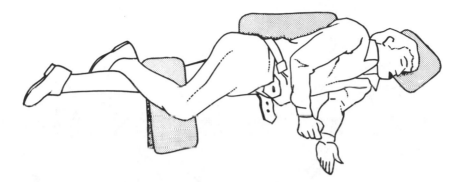

above the victim in order to compress the heart between the sternum and the vertebral column. A single rescuer should alternate two breaths with 15 cardiac compressions delivered at a rate of 80 to 100 per minute. With two rescuers, give one breath after every five compressions. Perform heart massage if you cannot feel a pulse (carotid or femur) or if the victim's pupils are dilated (a sign that the brain is not receiving oxygen).

## PLACING THE INDIVIDUAL ON HIS SIDE FOR SAFETY

This is the safest position for an unconscious person since it allows him to breathe normally, allows the spontaneous discharge of any fluids from his mouth (water, vomit, blood) and provides a stable position for his body.

## WOUNDS AND SORES

Knowing how to sew up a wound is a necessary part of first aid because a gaping wound will become infected and will need a lot of time to close up. Any doctor can show you how to do it using a piece of raw meat as a model. If you have nothing else, a sewing needle will do the job well, the important thing being to close up the wound as quickly as possible and to disinfect it regularly.

## ADDITIONAL MATERIALS

**Tincture of Iodine or Iodized Alcohol**

To disinfect all wounds, especially bites by leeches, ticks and other insects and snakes.

**Adhesive Bandages**

To immobilize a fracture.

**Hydroclonazone Micropure Capsule**

To disinfect questionable water.

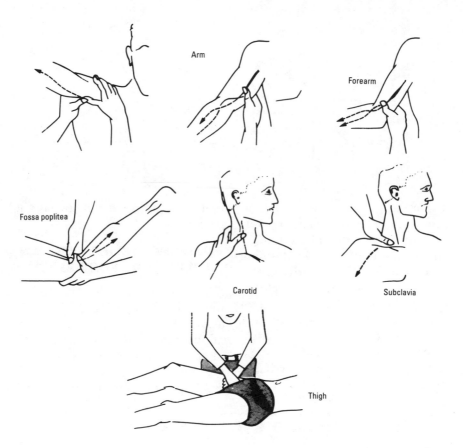

Arm

Forearm

Fossa poplitea

Carotid

Subclavia

Thigh

### Biogauze

This special gauze is very practical for use on burns or any other wound that should not be open to the air.

### Cigarettes

These are useful for removing ticks and leeches. They also can be used to destroy the heat-sensitive venom of Hymenoptera, sting fish, scorpion fish and sting rays: Hold the glowing end close to the wound without burning it. This method has proven very effective in preventing pain and inflammation if it is used soon after the injury is inflicted.

# FIRST AID SURVIVAL KIT
## INDISPENSABLE AND VERY USEFUL MEDICINES

Medications available, and their generic names, vary from country to country. In addition, countries have different regulations about which drugs can be bought without a prescription. The United States tends to have stricter regulations than other industrialized countries. It is important to establish with a local pharmacist which locally available drugs are equivalent to the ones recommended here.

| PRODUCTS (Commercial and chemical names) | DESIRED PHARMACO- LOGICAL ACTION | REACTION OF THE IN- JECTABLE FORM TO TEMPERA- TURE | INDICA- TIONS | DOSAGE AND METHOD | ENVIRONMENTS | | | | | COMMENTS |
|---|---|---|---|---|---|---|---|---|---|---|
| | | | | | Jungle | Sea | Mountains | Desert | Miscellaneous | |
| Dexametha- sone | Corticoid | Freezes at −40°F (−40°C), stable at 122°F (50°), protect from light | Allergies, asthma, ven- omous stings, edema, the beginnings of drowning, acute altitude sickness | Comes in 5-ml vials. A single dose is 0.25 to 1 ml IM. | x | x | x | x | x | Use in low- est effective dose for shortest pos- sible time. |
| LEVSIN | Antispas- modic | | Renal, biliary and intestinal colics | 0.5 ml 1 to 4 times a day administered per IV or IM | x | x | | x | | Can't be used if glau- coma pre- sent. |

397

| PRODUCTS (Commercial and chemical names) | DESIRED PHARMACOLOGICAL ACTION | REACTION OF THE INJECTABLE FORM TO TEMPERATURE | INDICATIONS | DOSAGE AND METHOD | ENVIRONMENTS | | | | | COMMENTS |
|---|---|---|---|---|---|---|---|---|---|---|
| | | | | | Jungle | Sea | Mountains | Desert | Miscellaneous | |
| VALIUM 10, injectable | Sedative, minor tranquilizer, antiepileptic, muscle relaxant | | Pains, any type of agitation, and anesthetic | 4 to 8 IM or IV per day | x | x | x | x | x | Diminished vigilance |
| ADRENALIN 1 per 1000 vial | Sympathomimetic | Shake well after reheating. Is destroyed at 122°F (50°C). | Venomous stings with heart problems | 1 IV, maximum of 5 per 24 hours | x | x | | x | | Dangerous medicine. Not to be used except for very serious problems |

398

| Drug | Type | Climate note | Indications | Dosage | | | | | Comments |
|---|---|---|---|---|---|---|---|---|---|
| Chlorphenira-mine | Antihistaminic | | Food allergies, insect bites | One capsule in the morning and in the evening | x | | x | x | Causes drowsiness (can be used as a sleeping pill, especially in the jungle) |
| LASIX vial (Furosemide) | Fast-acting diuretic | No problem in cold or heat. | Heat stroke, sun stroke, "HACE" (high-altitude cerebral edema), "AHAPE" (high-altitude pulmonary edema) | 1 vial administered slowly per IM or IV, or 1 to 4 tablets per 24 hours | | | x | x | Dangerous medicine |
| MORPHINE vial | Strong pain-killer | | Any kind of intestinal pain, fractures, etc. | 1 vial IM | x | x | x | x | |
| DIAMOX tablets (Acetazol-amide) | Diuretic | | Prevention of acute altitude sickness | 2 250-mg tablets | | | x | | Decreases vigilance |

| PRODUCTS (Commercial and chemical names) | DESIRED PHARMACO-LOGICAL ACTION | REACTION OF THE IN-JECTABLE FORM TO TEMPERA-TURE | INDICA-TIONS | DOSAGE AND METHOD | ENVIRONMENTS | | | | | COMMENTS |
|---|---|---|---|---|---|---|---|---|---|---|
| | | | | | Jungle | Sea | Mountains | Desert | Miscellaneous | |
| XYLOCAINE 2 percent (20-ml bottle) (Lidocaine) | Local anesthetic | | Local or re-gional anes-thesia | 5 to 10 ml, depending on the size of the area to be anesthetized | x | x | x | x | x | Allergies are very rare. In an emer-gency, can do an ap-pendectomy under Xylo-caine |
| CALCIUM CHLORIDE 10-ml vial | | Freezes at 21.2°F (−6°C). No problem over 122°F (50°C). | Acute allergic manifesta-tions (venom-ous creatures, especially spiders) | 1 slow IV, maximum of 2 per day | x | x | | x | | Calcium glu-conate: less concen-trated, but can be ad-ministered per IM |

| | | | | | | | | |
|---|---|---|---|---|---|---|---|---|
| CELESTONE SOLUSPAN injectable (Betamethasone) | Corticoid | Solidifies within 1 hour at 68°F (20°C). No chemical changes. No problem at 122°F (50°C). Protect from light. | Acute altitude sickness, allergies like hives or nettle rash | Comes in 5-ml vials. Give IM 0.5–9 mg a day. | | x | x | Use in lowest effective dose for shortest possible time |
| CALCIPAR-INE vial | Anticoagulant | | Snakebites | 0.1 ml per 22 pounds (10 kilograms) of weight, administered subcutaneously | | | | Should be administered subcutaneously in the abdomen |

# USEFUL MEDICINE FOR LESSER EMERGENCIES

| PRODUCTS (Commercial and chemical names) | DESIRED PHARMACO-LOGICAL ACTION | INDICATIONS | DOSAGE AND METHOD | ENVIRONMENTS | | | | | COMMENTS |
| --- | --- | --- | --- | --- | --- | --- | --- | --- | --- |
| | | | | Jungle | Sea | Mountains | Desert | Miscellaneous | |
| Diphenhydra-mine (benadryl) | Antihistamine | Allergies, in-somnia | 25 or 50 mg half an hour before ex-pected bed-time | x | x | x | | | |
| Valium, 5 mg | Minor tran-quilizer | Discourage-ment, anxiety | 5-mg tablets once or twice a day | x | x | x | x | x | May de-crease vigi-lance at the beginning of the treat-ment |
| Lariam | Antimalarial (mefloquine) | In regions where malaria is resistant to chloroquine | 1 tablet per 8 days | x | | | | x | Start 1 week before ar-rival; stop 3 weeks after return |

| | Type | Indication | Dosage | | | | | | Notes |
|---|---|---|---|---|---|---|---|---|---|
| Aralen | Antimalarial (chloroquine) | Regions susceptible to malaria | 1 tablet 6 days out of 7 | X | | | | X | Start first day in the country; stop 45 days after return |
| Vitamin C, 1,000 mg | | Various envenomations, fatigue, stressful situations | 500 mg per day, divided into several doses | X | X | X | X | X | Buy tablets that contain both vitamin C and calcium |
| Vitamin B₁, 250 mg | | Bites by Elapidae | Large dose as required | X | X | | | | |
| Imodium | Parasympatholytic | Diarrhea if one does not know its origin | 2 2-mg capsules after each liquid bowel movement. Maximum 6 per day | X | X | X | X | X | |
| Flagyl | Tissue amebicide | Acute amebiasis | 6 to 8 0.250-g tablets, taken in 2 to 4 doses for 7 to 10 days | X | | | | X | Can be used by women infected with Trichomonas vaginalis |

| PRODUCTS (Commercial and chemical names) | DESIRED PHARMACOLOGICAL ACTION | INDICATIONS | DOSAGE AND METHOD | ENVIRONMENTS | | | | | COMMENTS |
|---|---|---|---|---|---|---|---|---|---|
| | | | | Jungle | Sea | Mountains | Desert | Miscellaneous | |
| Metronidazole | Amebicide | Amebiasis, trichomoniasis, giardia | 6 to 8 tablets per day, each 250 mg, for 7 to 10 days | x | | | | x | |
| Bactrim | Anti-infective | Respiratory, urinary, and digestive infections (typhoid) | 2 tablets in the morning and evening | x | x | x | x | x | Discontinue immediately if rash or other side effects occur |
| Ampicillin | Acid-resistant penicillin; antibiotic | Respiratory, urinary, digestive infections, ENT (ear, nose and throat) | 4 250-mg tablets per day for 8 days | x | x | x | x | x | Contraindicated if there is an allergy to penicillin |

| | | | | | | | | | |
|---|---|---|---|---|---|---|---|---|---|
| Cloxacillin | Penicillinase-resistant penicillin | Respiratory and skin infections | 1 250-mg capsule 4 times a day for 8 days | X | X | X | X | X | This antibiotic should be chosen against furuncles (boils) |
| Doxycycline | Tetracycline antibiotic | Respiratory infections, ENT, etc. | 1 or 2 50-mg tablets 2 times a day for 8 days | X | X | X | X | X | Its antiparasitic action against malaria is very important. Should not be used in last half of pregnancy. |
| Vermox, tablet | | Intestinal parasitoses | 2 per day for 3 days, to be repeated 8 days later | X | | | | X | Intestinal parasitoses, which occur very frequently when traveling |

# USEFUL MEDICINE FOR LESSER EMERGENCIES (continued)

| PRODUCTS (Commercial and chemical names) | DESIRED PHARMACO-LOGICAL ACTION | INDICATIONS | DOSAGE AND METHOD | ENVIRONMENTS | | | | | COMMENTS |
|---|---|---|---|---|---|---|---|---|---|
| | | | | Jungle | Sea | Mountains | Desert | Miscellaneous | |
| Marezine, tablets | Anti-seasick-ness | Seasickness, airsickness | | | x | | | x | Causes drowsiness |
| Selsun, bottle | Selenium sul-fide | All mycoses | Every day as a curative treat-ment, twice a week as pre-ventive treat-ment | x | x | | | | Indispens-able product in all hot countries |

* All these products are better in their injectable form, when one exists, but this form is more sensitive to variations in temperature. The indications described are those that may be important in a survival situation. We have not mentioned indications in the pathology of "urban," everyday living.

IV = intravenous, which is an emergency measure and should, in principle, be administered slowly to an individual who is lying down.

IM = intramuscular, to be used in less urgent situations.

Miscellaneous = islands, poles, temperate forests, the bush, etc.

# APPENDIX: TECHNICAL EQUIPMENT

- Weapons

- Signaling

- Diving Equipment

- Equipment at Sea

- Polar Equipment

- Miscellaneous Equipment

When Robert Falcon Scott was stranded close to the South Pole at the beginning of this century, it was with hundreds of pounds of materials, a large number of dogs and several teammates. Jean-Louis Étienne traveled to the pole alone in 1986 without any dogs, dragging a 110-pound (50 kilogram) sled.

The diving suits at the end of World War I weighed 264 pounds (120 kilograms) on a harness. The modern frogman works down to a depth of 328 feet (100 meters) thanks to super-light, self-contained equipment.

Just 50 years ago, climbing to the top of Mont Blanc required enormous logistics. "Empty-handed climbers," climbing alone, have now scaled several peaks 13,000 feet (4,000 meters) in less than 24 hours.

These feats are due not only to a constant improvement in technique, but to the increasing miniaturization of equipment. In this chapter we will briefly describe the minimum amount of equipment we believe to be indispensable, covering equipment that has not already been specifically recommended for each environment.

# WEAPONS

Weapons have served as an extension of the arm since the origin of man. Weapons allowed man to hunt and to survive among wild animals and rival peoples. Modern man in an extreme situation is almost always confronted by the same kind of problems that confronted his primitive ancestors. Weapons are a necessity in a survival situation, both for hunting and for self-defense.

## FIREARMS

It is often difficult, if not impossible, to take a firearm along on an expedition, since many countries forbid the import of guns. In the Far North of Canada, for example, it is advisable to obtain the gun of one's choice on the spot. Choose a large-caliber gun capable of shooting a bear and containing as few moving parts as possible. This eliminates guns with complex mechanisms, as there is a greater danger that they will jam in the intense cold. Because of the cold, choose guns that develop as little pressure as possible. Stay away from handguns.

### A .44 Revolver

It is one of the very accurate weapons (especially the 8-inch barrel), but it has a strong recoil and therefore requires some arm strength. In addition, the ammunition is very heavy. The model 29, which is 6 inches long, is best. This caliber exists in stainless corrosion-resistant metal, a feature that is important in a survival situation and indispensable at sea.

## A .45 Automatic

Many specialists consider this to be the best, and it has proved itself on all fronts from the Argonne trenches to the jungles of Vietnam. Even though it is a bit light for shooting a bear, it does have good stopping power. It works equally well in the sands of the desert as in the Far North, or in the highest humidity. It is very accurate and bullets are widely available (choose the .45 ACP round-nosed bullet weighing 230 grains).

Aboard a boat, two weapons are indispensable:

■ A large-caliber hunting rifle can shoot through a hull at a distance of several hundred yards and therefore acts as a deterrent from afar. It should be of sufficient caliber to deal with any size of animal. One should use a round-nosed bullet for small animals.
■ The riot gun is a 12-gauge shotgun with a magazine for four cartridges and a barrel that is no longer than 17.5 inches (45 centimeters). Such a weapon, provided with buckshot, fires the equivalent of 12 .22 longs in a pattern 2 yards in diameter at a distance of 27 yards (25 meters).

Apart from its "spraying" ability, it is a very rugged weapon that is recocked manually, never

jams and enables firing without putting it up to the shoulder. It needs a minimum of maintenance and will remain operational even if maintenance is neglected at sea. The "Remington 870," or the "Winchester" 1200 "defender" model in stainless steel are ideal on a boat. These are the only riot guns that have a double rod for recocking, which eliminates twisting and therefore cannot jam. If necessary, you can remove the magazine capacity reducer, which limits its contents to three cartridges instead of five. All 12-gauge shells can be used in this rugged and very reliable weapon, as well as cartridges ranging from 9-grain 00 buckshot to a Brenneke slug. It is also very useful to have a reserve of signal shells, which are sold six to a box in blue, green or red.

## PROJECTILE WEAPONS

### Hunting Bows

This is the ideal backup weapon if one has no firearms. It can be made from certain branches, and the American Indians have been doing this for centuries: They primarily use black spruce branches that grow along the banks of rivers. This location makes the shrub curve, and the growth rings are close together. Tensing the bow in the opposite direction to the growth rings doubles its power. Modern bows are made from many different types of wood, and their resistance comes from epoxy resin that coats several layers of glued laminated wood. The recommended power of a hunting bow is 30 pounds for a woman and 50 pounds for a man (a hunting bow is always smaller and more powerful than a sporting bow). Some "compound" bows develop even greater force by means of pullies, but they are not very sturdy and should not be taken along. The power of 50 pounds is enough to get any kind of game, including a young wild boar. The ideal distance from which to shoot is relatively short, about 50 feet (15 meters).

Two-piece arrows are available; they are not as solid but are just as accurate. There are several types of hunting arrowheads, the best being the notched arrowhead, which penetrates well and does not slip. Another very specific advantage of the bow is that it can be used for fishing. Many tribes use it for this purpose in the forest. The speed of an arrow is on the order of 262 feet per second (80 meters per second), i.e., a little less that 186 miles per hour (300 kilometers per hour). At this speed, it penetrates water better than a bullet that moves at more than 559 miles per hour (900 kilometers per hour). The arrow is tied to the bow with a string so as to be able to haul back the catch. The bowstring should be made of several strands of Dacron.

## Blowpipes and Spears

The Iroquois make blowpipes from large cut rushes that are about 47 inches (120 centimeters) long and 0.7 inch (1.8 centimeters) in diameter. The arrow is made of cedar, armed on one end with a bone arrowhead and at the other with a wad of bulrush cotton.

The Dayaks carve their spears from ironwood, and also use it to make blowpipes of exceptional quality. Their arrows can kill small animals by piercing them, and large ones with the help of poison. The caliber is always the same, but the dose of poison depends on the size of the animal. The fact that a spearhead can kill a large wild boar makes it into a multipurpose weapon.

In a survival situation, ski poles can be used as a blowpipe to get small game.

## KNIVES

### Survival Knives

Since the "Rambo" legend engulfed the Western world, most arms manufacturers have more or less become cutlers, and there is an infinite variety of so-called survival knives. Some, frankly, are infantile, others are too heavy for no valid reason; yet others are worth considering as they give priority to effectiveness instead of useless gadgets.

A proper survival knife should

be reasonably long, resistant to shearing and to bending; the blade should be a part of the handle with no break or gap. Since the handle must have a minimum size, it should be hollow and waterproof, providing a place for small, useful utensils. The choice of what to put inside is left to the imagination of each individual according to his purpose; items such as surgical blades, pills, tweezers, safety pins, hooks or pencil leads can be kept inside.

The metal alloy must obviously be totally air- and water-resistant, and one must be able to sharpen it. An ideal choice is a model with a second small blade specially designed to debone and cut up game, and which can very easily be transformed into a harpoon. The main blade has deep, double

saw teeth on the back, and they are slanted in such a way that one can saw very effectively in a forward direction.

**The Swiss Army Knife**

This famous little red knife with the white cross has no equal and has constantly been improved so that it now has about 50 uses. Whether in a survival situation or not, this utensil, which is smaller and lighter than an electric razor, should automatically be included in a travel kit. This tool is not sufficient for all environments: it is sufficient for a lifeboat, for example, but it is insufficient, by itself, for the jungle, where cutting bamboo and hacking away at vegetation are necessary. But it is useful everywhere, and sometimes indispensable.

# SIGNALING

Survival often depends on others, and therefore you must be able to signal your location. There are many methods of signaling, depending on the environment.

## SUN REFLECTOR

Also called a heliograph, this is a double-sided mirror with a hole in its center. Point the mirror toward the sun and get sight of the objective (for example, a plane) through the hole. A spot of light will appear on your face. Then

turn the mirror until this spot disappears through the hole, while constantly keeping the plane in sight. In this way the latter will be hit directly by the reflected ray of light (see figure p. 412). This method seems a little ridiculous until you remember that the light of the sun, reflected at 90° from such a mirror, attains an intensity of seven million candles, which is enormous and inevitably must catch the eye of a pilot or navigator passing overhead. When the dirigible "Italia" crashed in the

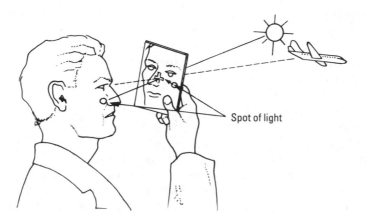

Spot of light

**The heliograph: a simple instrument that, if used correctly, will prove effective**

Arctic in 1928, the survivors were found by the pilots of the rescue plane thanks to a bar of chocolate. A man named Cecioni, the mechanic on the dirigible, made a makeshift mirror by placing the foil from the bar of chocolate around a small, flat piece of wood. The flash of light reflected from this improvised mirror was the only thing that caught the pilots' attention. At an altitude of 3,280 feet (1,000 meters), such a signal can be seen for 15.5 miles (25 kilometers), much farther than any other traditional visual signal. It is a signal that can obviously only be used if the sun is shining, but one that rarely fails.

## SMOKE BOMBS AND OTHER PYROTECHNIC METHODS

There are many types, some used by day, others by night. Some work with a firing pistol.

"Cyalumes" are luminous sticks that are held in the hand; they are made in different colors and do not emit smoke—they should be waved around and are primarily visible at night. Each person should choose which to buy according to his plans. Sailors, for example, should avoid getting magnesium flares, which can make holes in lifeboats. A very practical model is the new "launching pen" to which a flare of the chosen color can be attached. It takes up very little space and each flare rises to an approximate height of 1,320 feet (400 meters), far exceeding the height of average jungle vegetation.

There are signaling flares that can be shot from a 12-caliber gun (a riot gun, or others), and that replaces normal bullets with tracer bullets. Tracer bullets were originally made to correct the aiming of automatic or semiautomatic weapons—they allow you to see the trajectory of the bullet. Tracer bullets can be seen especially well at night—and not only by the person shooting. However sophisticated pyrotechnic methods may be, one should always remember that they can seldom be seen beyond a few miles, and then only if they come into the field of vision of a rescue team or a person on watch.

## WHISTLE

A whistle should be made of plastic without a ball inside, and should be as light as possible. The sharp sound is the only sound that can travel over long distances and penetrate forests, where the human voice is muffled quickly.

## RADIO

The radio is the best modern locator instrument. Although the human contact it affords interferes somewhat with the charm of total isolation, it provides considerable peace of mind at the touch of the hand. The electronics in a radio are less resistant to low temperatures than to desert tem-

peratures, so take along the most reliable models for extreme cold.

## RADIO DISTRESS BEACONS

This is more than a means of being located; it is a means to let the entire world know that you are in trouble. (One day, on his trip to the North Pole in 1986, J.-L. Étienne released his beacon by mistake, causing a state of alert via satellite in a dozen different places, including Borneo.) On the psychological level, the peace of mind that such a safeguard can bring is obviously considerable.

Étienne used an Argos-Sarsat beacon, 3.75 pounds (1.7 kilograms) with lithium SAFT batteries, which made it possible to follow his progress via satellite, or to put out a state of alert on another frequency. The Kannad 406 is a new type of satellite location beacon, used for survival at sea. This system covers all the seas on earth and makes it possible to locate a navigator in distress within two hours with an accuracy within one mile. This beacon is portable and waterproof and emits its own unique signal, which makes it possible to identify the ship or boat in distress. About the size of a milk carton, it starts emitting its signal as soon as it is placed in the water.

# DIVING EQUIPMENT

## THE DIVING SUIT AND ITS ACCESSORIES

A diving suit with a hood is indispensable in cold seas, and the colder the water, the thicker the suit should be. It is also useful in warm seas, not so much for thermal insulation as for protection against injuries caused by corals, stinging by Portuguese men-of-war floating just below the surface, bites or stings by venomous fish or snakes, etc. Gloves and diving shoes are useful, too.

---

G.M. is 44 years old and has made many dives under all possible conditions in the course of his work. What he has been asked to do today is routine: He is to dive to retrieve a stuntman's motorbike after the latter has jumped from a springboard into the Seine River for a scene in an adventure movie. G.M. is a stuntman himself and is not the least bit worried about the driver of the motorbike. The driver starts the bike, picks up speed and launches himself into the air for about 65 feet (20 meters) before falling into the water as planned several feet away from G.M. The driver swims away without any difficulties and makes the sign that everything is okay.

G.M. dives in with a grapnel hook to fish out the motorbike a few feet below the surface. The minutes tick by, but G.M. does not resurface. Perhaps the motorbike is stuck among the numerous metallic hulks that litter the riverbed in this part of the Seine? But no bubbles appear on the surface, and the others begin to worry. After searching for an hour and a half, they find G.M.'s body. He died in water that was only a few feet deep because he lost consciousness the moment he entered it—the victim of what was doubtless the only oversight in his career: He forgot that if one is not wearing a hood, one should never jump into cold water but should enter it gradually.

---

Had he been wearing a simple hood, this accident would certainly never have happened. The head and neck require the extra insulation the hood provides. Diving shoes are also extremely useful, not to avoid unconsciousness, but to slow down cooling. The soles of one's feet play a significant role in venous drainage when walking. With every step, the body's weight compresses the blood in the soles of the feet, driving it back toward the heart. In cold water, this sponge effect plays a role in significantly cooling down the whole body.

## A MASK

The diver's mask should be simple and provide easy access to the nostrils for the Valsalva maneuver. Sophisticated panoramic masks are useless because there is a limit to the visual field under water.

## A BUOY OR A LIFE JACKET?

Whenever possible, have some inflation system around your thorax or against your chest. This does not impede your buoyancy at any depth until it is inflated, at which point it allows you to propel yourself rapidly to the surface if there is an accident on the seabed. There are two systems:

### The Life Jacket

An American invention, this is actually worn like a jacket with a cradle in which an air cylinder sits. It has pockets, and its entire surface inflates from a very small bottle of carbon dioxide, or through a "direct system" that diverts air from the tank on your back. Advocates of this system claim that it has the advantage of providing better stability in all positions because the air moves inside, thus stabilizing a head-first as well as a feet-first position. However, the whole design is cumbersome. Also, the carbon dioxide microcylinders need special refills and, above all, it cannot bring a diver back to the surface from a depth of more than 98 to 130 feet (30 to 40 meters).

Advocates will probably respond that the "direct system" is there to inflate the life jacket directly from the aqualung in an emergency. The problem is that the emergency in question very frequently is that you have run out of air! Survival equipment should be as compact as possible, so I would choose the buoy.

### The Buoy

The best-known type of buoy is the Fenzy, which is light and relatively small, is placed around the neck and attached against the thorax with two straps. The bladder inside is made of very resistant polyurethane and has a covering that is usually orange and is provided with a ventral pocket. Under this pocket is an air cylinder containing 400 ml, inflated at 200 bars, and the valve is easily accessible. Thus the cylinder contains 84 quarts (80 liters) of air, which is guaranteed to inflate the buoy at any depth, and even enables one to breathe via the Fenzy if the bottle on one's back is empty or the pressure reducer is stuck. There is no problem in regulating buoyancy, and the diver is not transformed into an "inflated doll." This buoy can also be provided with a direct system or with a microcylinder of carbon dioxide (which, however, is useless with a 400-ml cylinder of air). Naturally both systems are provided with a safety valve, a blow-off valve, and a whistle so you can be located when you surface.

## THE "AIR BABY-BOTTLE"

This is my own term for a recent American invention, which is sufficiently serious for the U.S. Navy to have ordered more than 8,000 units; its official name is the Heed II (Helicopter Emergency Egress Device, type two).

The bottle is about 11.7 inches (30 centimeters) long and has the approximate diameter of a baby's bottle; it is inflated with enough air to enable an individual to take about 30 breaths while surfacing and, above all, prevents him from drowning at a depth of 98 to 130 feet (30 to 40 meters) if he runs out of air in the main bottles or if the pressure reducer breaks down. This "pocket reserve" is provided with a valve, a mini-pressure reducer, and a fast-acting mouthpiece. It is as useful for helicopter crews who crash into the sea as for divers.

## A DIVING KNIFE

This is indispensable when diving, both as a safety device and a tool. It enables you to disentangle yourself from obstacles (ropes, nets, giant algae) and is also very useful for exploring the seabed. In contrast to normal knives, it should be heavy (its apparent weight decreases considerably in the water). The opposite end of the handle to the blade should be made of metal so that it can be used as a hammer. All small knives should be rejected. Remember that, among other things, it can be used to hit the air bottle, which is one of the best methods of communicating with a team member who is out of sight.

# EQUIPMENT AT SEA

It is absolutely necessary to supplement the equipment that is mandatory on board a lifeboat (see chapter "The Sea and Shipwrecks"). Remember that at least two distillers are necessary.

## SURVIVAL SUITS

These suits are obligatory on merchant vessels and fishing boats. They ensure extraordinary buoyancy and thermal insulation. In 1986 an ultramodern fishing boat sank within a matter of seconds when its stern was engulfed by a swell in the North Sea. Eighteen men were lost and there were nine survivors—the nine who had had time to put on their survival suits. A fisherman cannot work wearing such a suit, so the problem is having enough time to put one on.

The Norwegian Helly Hansen suit, type 303, is a dry suit that includes a hood, gloves and integrated boots. The fabric is multilayered and includes a layer of polyvinyl chloride (PVC), metallic foil, a layer of polyamide taffeta, and reinforcement at critical points. The suit floats spontaneously, with enough buoyancy to hold an adult's head above water, and, in addition, it has an external 30-quart (30-liter) bladder that can be automatically or orally inflated to hoist the shipwrecked person above the water. Automatic inflation is guaranteed within 5 seconds by means of a salt-cap hammer and a $CO_2$ sparklet. The length of time one can survive at a water temperature of 32°F (0°C) in such a suit is 18 hours, and is the equivalent of a drop in internal temperature of 3.6°F (2°C) per six hours. In a best-case scenario, the length of time a clothed person can survive without the suit is about 20 minutes. Each suit includes a plastic whistle, a 4-foot (1.3-meter) connecting rope, an incorporated harness with a hoisting ring, a packet of fluorescein and a luminous cyalume stick (as a marker at night). This suit was tested by the Brétigny Test Flight Center in France and, apart from everything else, ensures extraordinary protection against fire (five seconds exposed to a 3270°F [1800°C] flame; one minute at a distance of 5.75 feet [1.75 meters] from a 1472°F [800°C] heat source).

## THE "SEA-GOLD" PUMP

Costing about $1,400, this is the revolutionary instrument everyone's talking about. It's a manual filtration system that can purify up to 200 l (52 gallons)—enough for several weeks.

# POLAR EQUIPMENT

## THE STOVE

At −40°F (−40°C) some stoves need 45 minutes of preheating before they will get going; such stoves are of course useless. This includes the Coleman Peak 1 that runs on mineral oil. On the other hand, the Mountain Safety Research (MSR) gasoline stove is very flexible and consumes one-third liter to boil 4 to 5 liters of water from ice. The MSR model will burn anything put into it: fuel oil, gasoline, kerosene.

## THE TENT

This should be rounded and oblong to offer the least resistance to the wind. Étienne opted for a Kanuk (a very good Canadian brand for all survival equipment for cold regions); the tunnel

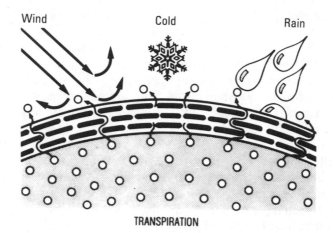

TRANSPIRATION

model can be set up quickly with three carbon-fiber arches and is resistant to gusts of 62 miles per hour (100 kilometers per hour).

## A THERMOS FLASK

The Camping Gaz line, made in the United States, includes a stainless steel flask, which is unbreakable and truly isothermal (this is not always the case with other thermoses), and can keep 1.5 liters of water very hot for 12 hours at a temperature of $-40°F$ ($-40°C$).

## SKI POLES

Superlight Boron ski poles, "Swix" type, have hand grips made of cork and thus ensure good insulation. As the interior of these poles is very smooth and rectilinear, one can make them into very effective blowpipes. Bo-

ron is very solid, and glass fiber is too flexible (remember that metals become brittle in extreme cold!)

## BOOTS

Leather is the best material for boots, but it must be treated to retain its properties (with "snow seal" paste, for example). After several days, it will no longer be impermeable, and you will need to change your boots or put plastic sacks around your feet that stick out at the top of the boots to form a "vapor barrier."

## MISCELLANEOUS CLOTHING

Thermal protection can be successfully ensured through specific modern materials that combine effective thermal insulation with a weight that is much lighter than natural furs. Outer garments are made of Quallofil and windbreakers of Gore-Tex. Gore-Tex is unique; it is impermeable from the outside inward but at the same time permeable to inside moisture, allowing sweat to escape outward during physical exertion. It eliminates freezing due to subsequent cooling. This dual capability is made possible by a microporous texture that stops molecules of water, which are 20,000 times larger than the Gore-Tex pores, from getting in while it allows sweat particles, which are 700 times smaller, to pass.

This Teflon-based material is very thin and light and can be applied to any other kind of fabric. in addition, gore-tex has the advantage of being an excellent windbreaker. unfortunately, its equivalent in the fight against heat still needs to be found.

Sleeping bags of Quallofil or Gore-Tex should be placed on one or two sheets of closed-cell polyurethane.

For gloves, wool still remains the best material, and it can be covered with leather.

# MISCELLANEOUS EQUIPMENT

## GAITERS

Gaiters of ballistic nylon are good substitute for leather boots in the bush or the jungle. They are effective against snakes and take up very little space when stowed away.

## CAMERA

A camera is not particularly appropriate for a survival situation, but if you take one along, it might as well be a good one. All major brands now make high-quality pocket cameras with automatic focus, which are just 9.4 × 14 inches (24 × 36 centimeters); but many of them are not resistant to extreme cold, which jams their mechanism. At this time, the one that works at all latitudes is the Fuji Barouder.

## WATCH

A watch must be waterproof and must have a chronometer that shows the day and the month (one quickly loses one's sense of time in a survival situation), and it should have a new battery to ensure that the watch will go on working for at least two years. Some models are divided into 24 instead of 12 hours (Breitling, Rolex Explorer), which makes it easier to retain one's orientation, but that feature is not indispensable. A model with hands rather than a digital model is best.

## COMPASS

Many survival knives contain a small, round compass at the end of the handle, but one should consider this compass to be a last resort. It is too small to be very accurate. Moreover, its proximity to the other metals in the knife causes additional errors. The only suitable compass is the military type with a protective case and a luminescent dial. Some survival guides offer countless ways to improvise a compass, but I prefer to orientate myself by the sun if I do not have a compass.

The only places where a compass is useless are the polar regions because of the enormous variation between the geographic North and the true magnetic North. Even planes do not trust a compass in these regions (above 60° latitude) and navigate by inertial means and radio communications.

# GLOSSARY

**aerobic** This describes organisms (microbes) or chains of biochemical reactions that need the presence of free oxygen to be viable.

**albedo** The fraction of the energy of radiation (especially luminous) reflected or diffused by a given object: A black object has zero albedo. Snow has a very high albedo (over 80), as does the desert.

**apnea** The longer or shorter interruption of respiration. Such an interruption can be voluntary, as in "free diving."

**anoxia** The decrease in the quantity of oxygen distributed to the tissues by the blood. Can be encountered in diving, at high altitudes in the mountains, or during very intense exertion. If the decrease is small, it is called hypoxia.

**blood volume** This is the total blood volume including the corpuscles and plasma: One part of this volume circulates while the other remains immobile in the reservoirs. The volume changes depending on demand and under commands from the sympathetic or parasympathetic nervous systems.

**catabolic** Contributing to the transformation of various materials assimilated by the tissues into energy. Example: When there is stress, adrenalin causes the catabolism of the reserves of glycogen.

**collapse** A rapid decrease in strength, accompanied by difficulty in moving, almost inaudible speech, depressed pulse, and, frequently, heart failure. It is the final stage preceding death.

**convection** The movement of a fluid due to a variation in temperature. For example, in the afternoon in summer, the ground, heated by the sun, sets off ascending thermal currents that form the base for cumulus and cumulonimbus clouds.

**diuresis** This describes the whole picture of urine output, from renal filtration right through to the excretion of the urine. The volume and concentration vary according to types of stress: heat, cold, thirst, lack of food, etc.

**endorphins** (internal morphine) Hormones secreted in minute quantities in the brain that act directly on specific centers and have a pain-killing, tranquilizing or stimulating effect.

**hemoneurothorax**  A collapsed lung that also involves a discharge of blood into the pleura.

**homothermal**  This describes animals that maintain a constant temperature in whatever environment they are in, due to thermoregulatory mechanisms (example: mammals and birds).

**homeostasis**  The living organism's preservation of various physiological constants: temperature, pH, glycemia, arterial pressure, oxygenation of the tissues, etc.

**hypercapnia** or **hypercarbia**  The excess concentration of carbon dioxide dissolved in the blood plasma due to a decrease of pulmonary ventilation. It can be encountered in diving, during sustained exertion, or due to thoracic compression.

**hyperoxemia/hypoxia**  The increase or decrease in the amount of oxygen distributed to the tissues by the blood. The increase is found in frogmen who breathe pure oxygen in a closed-circuit device for too long a time or at too great a depth. Hypoxia is encountered in many situations: high altitudes, enclosed environ-

ment, bad ventilation, poisoning, etc.

**hypertonic/hypotonic**  Plasma is hyper- or hypotonic in relation to the norm depending on whether it has a greater or lesser amount of electrolytes, i.e., salts. For example, the act of drinking very little and eating a lot will cause "osmotic thirst" through the hypertonia of the plasma.

**hypothalamus**  This small organ is the true center of all homeostatic regulation. Therefore it is a determining factor in all survival situations (thirst, hunger, heat, cold, etc.) in a very direct neurological and hormonal relationship to the pituitary gland (hypophysis).

**hypovolemia**  See **blood volume.** This is the decrease in blood volume. In a case of intense stress, for example, there is hypovolemia in the nonvital organs (digestive system, skin, sexual organs, etc.).

**masseters**  The muscles that raise the lower jaw. In venomous snakes this muscle also contains the venom glands.

**mitochondria**  Small, ovoid structures distributed in the protoplasm of the cells, which free energy and enable cellular respiration.

**mydriasis** The unusual or abnormal dilation of the pupil. It can be observed in darkness, as a result of stress or a sexual act, or in terminal coma preceding death.

**myoglobinuria** The presence of muscle myoglobin in the urine. It can be observed after a person is severely injured, after sustaining burns, and after intense muscular exertion, poisoning, and some envenomations.

**myotoxic** Toxic to the muscle fibers.

**osmoreceptors** Nerve endings that detect an increase in osmotic pressure in the blood and thus set off a secretion of an antidiuretic hormone (the urinary loss that is avoided in this way tends to reestablish normal osmotic pressure).

**osmotic** Osmotic pressure alone determines the exchange of water between the cells and the blood. This pressure is proportional to the concentration of electrolytes. The osmotic pressure of seawater, for example, is much higher than that of freshwater.

**parasympathetic** The part of the nervous system that intervenes in the involuntary functions of nutri-

tion and metabolism. Its hormone is acetylcholine.

**perspiration** The exhalation of water vapor and gas through the skin or the respiratory mucous membranes.

**pH** This symbol expresses the acidity of a liquid according to its concentration in H+ (hydrogen) ions. A neutral solution has a pH of 7, an alkaline solution has a pH over 7 and an acid under 7. The pH of arterial blood is 7.

**pneumothorax** The discharge of air into the pleural cavity between the lung and the thoracic wall, accompanied by a retraction of the lung concerned. A collapsed lung.

**poikilotherms** Cold-blooded animals, whose temperature varies (reptiles, snakes, fish, etc.).

**polypnea** Rapid, superficial respiration that leads to asphyxia at some point.

**sympathetic** The part of the nervous system that enables the body to adapt to action and emergency situations. It is the ultimate system of stress; its hormone is adrenalin.

**tachycardia** This is the acceleration of the rhythm of the heartbeat. It can be caused by exertion or by mental or physical stress.

**thermogenesis** The production of heat in living beings. It increases with physical exertion, during digestion, during intellectual exertion, etc.

**thermolysis** The elimination of body heat (exposure to cold, wind, sweating, etc.)

**thoracocentesis** The puncture of the thoracic wall in order to evac-uate a discharge into the pleura (for example, a hemothorax).

**vasoconstriction / vasodilation** The decrease or the increase in the diameter of a vessel through the action of the muscle fibers.

**vasomotricity** The ability of the blood vessels to dilate or constrict. In my opinion, good vasomotricity is a necessary prerequisite for surviving various types of stress.

# SELECTED
# BIBLIOGRAPHY

## GENERAL

Barril, Paul. *Missions très spéciales.* Presses de la cité, 1984.

Delamare, Gil. *Le Risque est mon métier.* Flammarion, 1967.

Department of the Army. *Survival.* Washington, D.C.: 1970.

Duval, Colette. *S'en fout la mort.* Fanval, 1986.

Julienne, Rémy. *Silence .–.–. on casse!* Flammarion, 1970.

Ministère de la Défense. *Survie au Combat.* Paris, 1985.

Read, Piers Paul. *Les Survivants.* Grasset, 1974. Published in English as *Alive,* Lippincott, 1974.

Troebst, Lord Christian. *L'Art de survivre.* Calmann-Lévy, 1967.

## PHYSICAL EXERTION

Astrand, P. O., and K. Rodahl. *Précis de physiologie de l'exercice musculaire.* Masson, 1980.

Karpovich and Sinming. *Physiologie de l'activité musculaire.* Vigot, 1979.

Collins, Sandra. *Choisissez votre technique de relaxation.* Editions France-Empire, 1983.

Most, P. *Psychologie sportive.* Masson, 1982.

## SHARKS

Bagnis, R., and E. Christian. *Guide sous-marin de Tahiti.* Les Éditions du Pacifique, 1976.

Cousteau, Jacques-Yves. *Les Requins.* Flammarion, 1970.

Johnson, R. H. *Requins de Polynésie.* Les Éditions du Pacifique, 1978.

Pope, Patricia E. *Sharks.* Great Outdoors Publishing Co., 1977.

## SNAKES

### Venomous and Poisonous Animals

Boquet, Meaure, and Vachon. *Morsures et piqûres d'animaux venimeux terrestres.* Sandoz, 1968.

Heuzé, A. *Les Serpents du Tchad et des pays limitrophes.* "M.A.M.", Djaména, Tchad, 1987.

Rivolier, J., and C. Rivolier. *Accidents par les animaux venimeux et vénéneux marins.* Sandoz, 1969.

Villiers, A. *Les Serpents de l'Ouest africain.* Les Nouvelles Éditions Africaines, Dakar, 1975.

Viloteau, Nicole. *La Femme aux serpents.* Arthaud, 1985.

## THE SEA AND SHIPWRECKS

### Diving

Bombard, Alain. *Naufragé volontaire.* Arthaud, 1970.

Callahan, Steven. *A la dérive*. R. Laffont, 1986.

Department of the Navy. *U.S. Navy Diving Manual*. Washington, D.C., 1973.

Dupont, P. *Pirates aujourd'hui*. Ramsay, 1986.

Fructus, X., and R. Sciarli. *La Plongée, santé sécurité*. Éditions maritimes et d'outre mer, 1980.

Robertson, Dougal. *Survivre!* Albin Michel, 1973.

Robin, Bernard. *Survivre à la dérive*. Éditions Chaix, 1977.

## THE MOUNTAINS

Desmaison, René. *342 heures dans les Grandes Jorasses*. Flammarion, 1973.

## THE POLES

Étienne, J.-L. *Le Marcheur du Pôle*. R. Laffont, 1986.

Skrotzky, Nicolas. *Terres extrêmes*. Denoël, 1986.

## METEOROLOGY

Rivolier, C., and J. Rivolier. *Météoropathologie humaine*. Sandoz, 1972.

## NIVOLOGY AND AVALANCHES

Caillat, P., and B. Caillat. *Connaître et prévenir les avalanches*. Albin Michel, 1972.

Direction de la météorologie. *La Neige, ses métamorphoses, les avalanches*. Centre d'étude de la neige, 1982.

Salm, Bruno. *Guide pratique sur les avalanches*. Club Alpin Suisse, 1983.

## DIET

Creff, A., and L. Bérard. *Diététique sportive*. Masson, 1982.

*Place de l'alimentation dans la préparation biologique à la compétition*, Université St.-Etienne, colloque de St.-Etienne, 1979.

## FOOD GATHERING

Couplan, F. *Guide de la survie douce*. Bordas.

## MISCELLANEOUS TECHNIQUES

Bigon, M., and G. Regazzoni. *Noeuds et amarrages*. Éditions maritimes et d'outre-mer, 1981.

## MEDICINE WITHOUT A DOCTOR

Étienne, J.-L. *Médecine et sports de montagne*. Agla, 1983.

Richalet, J.-P. *Médecine de l'alpinisme*. Masson, 1984.

## EQUIPMENT

*Guillaume Tell—Annuaire des armes*. Crepin Leblond, 1986.

Venner, D. *Dagues et couteaux*. Edited by J. Grancher. 1983.

# SUGGESTED FURTHER READING

## GENERAL

American Outdoor Safety League. *Emergency Survival Handbook.* Los Angeles: American Red Cross, 1985.

Canadian Government Staff. *Never Say Die: The Canadian Air Force Survival Manual.* Boulder: Paladin Press, 1979.

Churchill, James E. *The Basic Essentials of Survival.* Basic Essentials Series. Merrillville, Ind.: ICS Books, 1989.

Craighead, Frank C., Jr., and Craighead, John J. *How to Survive on Land and Sea.* 4th ed. Ed. Ray E. Smith and Shiras Jarvis. Annapolis, Md.: Naval Institute Press, 1984.

Department of the Army. *Survival.* Washington, D.C.: U. S. Government Printing Office, 1986.

Henderson, Martha. *The Great Survival Resource Book.* Boulder: Paladin Press, c. 1980.

Olsen, Larry Dean. *Outdoor Survival Skills,* 5th ed. Chicago: Chicago Review Press, 1990.

Read, Piers Paul. *Alive: The Story of the Andes Survivors.* New York: Avon, 1979.

## PHYSICAL EXERTION

Jones, Norman L., et al., eds. *Human Muscle Power.* Champaign, Ill: Human Kinetics Publishers, 1986.

Keynes, R. D., and D. J. Aidles. *Nerve and Muscle.* Cambridge: Cambridge University Press, 1991.

Schneck, Daniel J. *Mechanics of Muscle.* New York: New York University Press, 1992.

Tyldesley, Barbara. *Muscles, Nerves and Movements: Kinesiology in Daily Living.* Boston: Blackwell Scientific Publications, 1989.

## SHARKS

Berger, Gilda. *Sharks.* Garden City, N.Y.: Doubleday, 1987.

Cousteau, Jacques-Yves. *The Shark: Splendid Savage of the Sea.* Translated from the French by Francis Price. Garden City, N.Y.: Doubleday, 1970.

Ellis, Richard, and John E. McCosker. *Great White Shark.* New York: Harper Collins in collaboration with Stanford University Press, 1991.

Pope, Patricia E. *A Dictionary of Sharks.* St. Petersburg, Fla.: Great Outdoors Publishing Co., 1973. Out of print, but widely held by libraries.

Sprinter, Victor Gruschka, and Joy P. Gold. *Sharks in Question: The Smithsonian Answer Book.*

Washington, D.C.: Smithsonian Institution Press, 1989.

Stevens, John D. *Sharks*. New York: Facts On File Publications, Inc., 1987.

## SNAKES

### Venomous and Poisonous Animals

Anderson, Robert. *Guide to Florida Poisonous Snakes*. Altamonte Springs, Fla.: Winner Enter, 1984.

Freedman, Russel. *Killer Snakes*. New York: Holiday House, 1982.

Glass, Thomas G. *Snakebite First Aid*. San Antonio: Glass Publishing Co., 1981.

McCarthy, Colin. *First Sight: Poisonous Snakes*. New York: Watts, 1990.

Phelps, Tony. *Poisonous Snakes*. New York: Sterling, 1989.

Tu, Anthony T., ed. *Rattlesnake Venoms: Their Action and Treatment*. New York: M. Dekker, c. 1982.

## THE SEA AND SHIPWRECKS

Bachrach, Arthur J., and Glen H. Egstrom. *Stress and Performance in Diving*. San Pedro, Calif.: Best Publishing Co., 1987.

Bombard, Alain. *The Voyage of the Heretique*. Translated by Brian Connell. New York: Simon and Schuster, 1954.

Dueker, C. W. *Scuba Diving*

*Safety*. Mountain View, Calif.: Anderson World Books, 1983.

Harrigan, Stephen. *Water and Light: A Diver's Journey to a Coral Reef*. Boston: Houghton Mifflin Co., 1992.

Malatich, John M. *Tricks of the Trade for Divers*. Centreville, Md.: Cornell Maritime Press, 1986.

U.S. Navy Diving Manual, Revision 2. Washington, D.C.: Naval Sea Systems Command, U.S.G.P.O., 1989– (looseleaf). United States Diving, Inc. *U.S. Diving Safety Manual*. Indianapolis, Ind: U.S. Diving Publications, 1990.

## THE MOUNTAINS

Alford, Monty. *Wilderness Survival Guide*. Edmonds, Wash.: Alaska Northwest Publishing Co., 1987.

Angier, Bradford. *How to Stay Alive in the Woods*. New York: Collier Books, c. 1962.

Fry, Alan. *Wilderness Survival Handbook*. New York: St. Martin's Press, 1981.

Petzoldt, Paul. *The New Wilderness Handbook*. New York: Norton, 1984.

## THE POLES

Berton, Pierre. *The Arctic Grail: The Quest for the North West Passage and the North Pole, 1818–1909*. New York: Viking, 1988.

Byles, Monica. *Life in the Polar Lands.* New York: Franklin Watts, 1990.

Flegg, Jim. *Poles Apart: The Natural Worlds of the Arctic and Antarctic.* Lexington, Mass.: Pelham Books/Stephen Greene Press, 1990.

## METEOROLOGY

Nicodemus, M. Lawrence. *Human Biometeorology.* Asheville, N.C.: National Oceanic and Atmospheric Administration, National Environmental Satellite, Data and Information Service, National Climatic Center, 1985.

Sargent, Frederick. *Hippocratic Heritage: A History of Ideas About Weather and Human Health.* New York: Pergamon Press, 1982.

Selvamurthy, W., ed. *Contributions to Human Biometeorology.* The Hague, Netherlands: SPB Academic, 1987.

## NIVOLOGY AND AVALANCHES

Armstrong, Betsy R. *The Avalanche Book.* Golden, Colo.: Fulcrum, 1986.

LaChapelle, Edward R. *The ABC of Avalanche Safety.* Seattle: The Mountaineers, 1985.

National Research Council (U.S.). Panel on Snow Avalanches. *Snow Avalanche Hazards and Mitigation in the United States.* Washington, D.C.: National Academy Press, 1990.

## DIET

Altschule, Mark D. *Nutritional Factors in General Medicine: Effects of Stress and Distorted Diets.* Springfield, Ill.: Thomas, c. 1978.

Brownell, Kelly D., et al. *Eating, Body Weight, and Performance in Athletes.* Philadelphia: Lea & Febiger, 1992.

Coleman, Ellen. *Eating for Endurance.* Palo Alto, Calif.: Bull Publishing Co., 1992.

## FOOD GATHERING

Duke, James A. *Handbook of Edible Weeds.* Boca Raton: CRC Press, 1992.

Elias, Thomas S. *Edible Wild Plants: A North American Field Guide.* New York: Sterling Publishing Co., 1990.

Kindscher, Kelly. *Edible Wild Plants of the Prairie: An Ethnobotanical Guide.* Lawrence, Kans.: University Press of Kansas, c. 1987.

## MEDICINE WITHOUT A DOCTOR

Ferrey, J. Matheson. *The Complete Guide to Home Remedies.* Harbor City, Calif.: AFCOM Publishing, 1986.

Forgey, William W. *Travelers' Self Care Manual: A Self-Help Guide to Emergency Medical Treatment.* Merrillville, Ind.: ICS Books, 1990.

Humphreys, Marylil K. *Staying

*Alive: The Complete Guide to Energy Renewal.* Wilmington, N.C.: Avocet Publishing, 1990.

The Wellness Encyclopedia: *The Comprehensive Family Resource for Safeguarding Health and Preventing Illness.* Boston: Houghton Mifflin, 1991.

## EQUIPMENT

Geary, Don. *The Compleat Outdoorsman.* Blue Ridge Summit, Pa.: Tab Books, 1981.

Montgomery, David R. *Mountainman Crafts and Skills: An Illustrated Guide to Clothing, Shelter, Equipment and Wilderness Living.* Bountiful, Utah: Horizon Publishers, 1980.

Schuh, Dwight R. *Modern Outdoor Survival: Outdoor Gear and Savvy to Bring You Back Alive.* Birmingham: Menasha Ridge Press, 1989.

# INDEX

Main topics appear in **boldface** type.
Illustrations are indicated by *italic* page numbers.
Tables are indicated by *"t"* and the glossary by *"g"*.

## A

AAS (acute altitude sickness) 256–258, 397t, 399t, 401t
abdominal cramps *See* cramps
Aborigines (Australia) 11
acacia beans 225
acetates 71–72
acetazolamide 258, 399t
acidosis 38
acquired immune deficiency syndrome (AIDS) *See* AIDS
acute altitude sickness *See* AAS
adenosine triphosphate (ATP) *See* ATP
adhesive bandages *See* bandages
adipose layer 348–349
adipose pannicle 15
adrenal glands 15
adrenaline 10, 21, 103, 109t, 352, 355, 398t
aerobic activity 20, 50, 51t, 421g
age
    and cold sensitivity 21
    and heat sensitivity 32
    and metabolism 335
    and vaccination requirements 381
AHAPE (acute high-altitude pulmonary edema) 259–261, 399t
Aichinger, Erwin 315
AIDS (acquired immune deficiency syndrome) 389
air mattresses 165, 169t, 192
airplanes
    diving to be avoided after flight 205

hypothermal coma induced during flight 5–8
interior unsuitable for shelter 270
skydiving from 355
air pumps 168t
airsickness 365, 406t
*Albatross* (ship) 160
albatrosses 158, 297
albedo 267, 292, 421g
albucyde 292
alcohol 355–356 *See also* substance abuse
    cold exposure and 4, 20–21, 26
    cubes for heating 280
    diving incompatible with 194
    heat exposure and 35, 39, 47
    snakebite victims urged to avoid 85, 103
alcoholic coma, revival from 11, 17
algae 47, 121, 145, 147, 157, 285, 295, 360–361
Algeria 113
alkalosis 192, 257
allergic reactions
    to caterpillars 245
    ciguatera aftereffects 121
    to food 388
    to Hymenoptera stings 116, 394
    to manchineel trees 246
    to molluscs and crustaceans 342
    to snakebite serum 100–110
    to xylocaine 400t
allergies, treatment of 397t, 399–402t
Alps 254
altitude sickness 256–261, 305
amas (Japanese pearl divers) 11